D0003470

P9-DXG-042 V2

Date Due

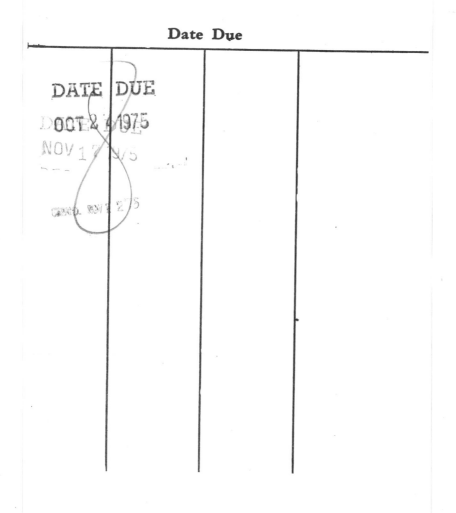

DATE DUE

OCT 2 1975

NOV 1 1975

NOV 2 5

Museum of Fine Arts, Boston

A Centennial History

Museum of Fine Arts
Boston
A Centennial History

Walter Muir Whitehill

VOLUME TWO

Quamquam ridentem dicere verum
Quid vetat?

HOR. *Sat.* i. 24

THE BELKNAP PRESS OF HARVARD UNIVERSITY PRESS
CAMBRIDGE, MASSACHUSETTS 1970

© COPYRIGHT 1970 BY THE PRESIDENT AND FELLOWS OF
HARVARD COLLEGE

ALL RIGHTS RESERVED

DISTRIBUTED IN GREAT BRITAIN BY
OXFORD UNIVERSITY PRESS, LONDON

LIBRARY OF CONGRESS CATALOG CARD NUMBER 70–102674

SBN 674–58875–4

MANUFACTURED IN THE UNITED STATES OF AMERICA

TYPESET BY THE HARVARD UNIVERSITY PRINTING OFFICE

PRINTED BY OFFSET LITHOGRAPHY BY
THE MERIDEN GRAVURE COMPANY

BOUND BY THE STANHOPE BINDERY

Contents

Museum of Fine Arts, Boston

A Centennial History

CHAPTER XIII

The Seventh Decade and World War II

The appointment of T. Jefferson Coolidge as Undersecretary of the United States Treasury caused him to resign the presidency of the Museum of Fine Arts on 25 October 1934. A game of musical chairs ensued, for on the same day Edward Jackson Holmes, the Museum's Director, resigned to become its President, while George Harold Edgell, Curator of Paintings since the previous April, was appointed to succeed Holmes in his former capacity. Edgell retained his curatorship, assisted by Charles C. Cunningham (Harvard A.B. 1932), who had been doing graduate work at Harvard and at the recently founded Courtauld Institute of Art of the University of London. At the end of the year Charles H. Hawes resigned as Associate Director.

Harold Edgell's experience was quite different from that of his predecessors, for he was a combination of undergraduate teacher and academic administrator, rather than a collector like Holmes or a scholar like Fairbanks and Robinson. As a sophomore at Harvard in 1906 he had been one of the presentable undergraduates used as guinea pigs in A. Lawrence Lowell's successful attempt to persuade the faculty to accept the history and literature of a given country or period as a field of concentration. This forerunner of what are today solemnly called "interdisciplinary studies" was devised to attract able undergraduates who had no intention of entering scholarship as a profession. It caught Edgell, who in 1909 received his A.B. *magna cum laude* in History and Literature, especially of the Renaissance; went on to a Ph.D. in 1913 in Fine Arts, and settled down as an Instructor in that department. Although he had a special interest in Sienese painting, his chief forte had been as an elegant and popular lecturer in the introductory survey course in art history known as Fine Arts 1d until 1921 when President Lowell asked him to take over the deanship of the School of Architecture. When Edgell remonstrated that he could not have passed any course given in that school except the one in history, and remarked that the President would hardly make a man who was not a doctor Dean of the Medical School, Lawrence Lowell brushed aside his objections with the characteristic remark that he saw no reason why the Director of the Metropolitan Opera Company should sing. So in 1922, as an Associate Professor of Fine Arts, Edgell became Dean of the Faculty of Architecture. He continued in that post for thirteen years, being promoted to Professor of Fine Arts in 1925.

When James Bryant Conant became President of Harvard in 1933, the wind began to blow from a different direction. As the influence of the Bauhaus was already making itself felt on this side of the Atlantic, the Museum of Fine Arts seemed a more congenial scene for an art historian interested in Sienese primitives than a deanship of architecture in a university that now had a chemist at its head. Thus in April 1934, Edgell accepted appointment as Curator of Paintings at the Museum of Fine Arts, effective in August, with the intention of dividing his time between Boston and Cambridge. A. Lawrence Lowell in the meantime, having leisure to devote to other interests, became chairman of a committee to study the administration of the Museum of Fine Arts, whose activities resulted in major changes in the by-laws, and, incidentally, in the elevation of Edward J. Holmes to the presidency and the appointment of Harold Edgell as Director. Thus at the end of the academic year 1934–35 Edgell severed his ties with Harvard to devote his entire time to the museum.

The form of published annual reports is always a subtle barometer of internal administration. In the first ten issued by the Museum of Fine Arts the Executive Committee, the Committee on the Museum, and the Treasurer had done all the talking, with simple lists of gifts and loans following. In the eleventh, for 1886, Edward Robinson wrote six pages concerning the Department of Classical Archaeology. The next year a report of the Curator of the Print Department was added. Only in 1898, 1900, and 1901 was the Japanese Department heard from. So matters continued until 1902 when Edward Robinson became Director. Then the typography of the report suddenly became presentable. Although the President reported for the Executive Committee, the Committee on the Musum referred simply to the reports of the Director and those in charge of the various collections that followed. The several curators, keepers, and assistants all described informatively and at tolerable length what had occurred with the collections of the museum during the year. Beginning in 1904 Samuel D. Warren reported as President, and the Executive Committee was heard from no more. When Arthur Fairbanks became Director in 1907 the form of individual accountability continued, although the typographic design degenerated. In the consulship of Morris Gray, the President's reports usually contained several paragraphs or pages of reflections on abstract and elevated themes, although from 1920 on the accounts of departmental activity were no longer presented separately but summarized in the Director's report. As President, T. Jefferson Coolidge dispensed with reflections and stuck to brief facts. In 1935 the President's report disappeared for good. G. H. Edgell as Director presented the broad outlines of the year and the individual curators once again reported directly for their own departments.

As the activities of art museums usually reflect the special fields of interest of their directors, it should be noted that Harold Edgell was the first to hold that office who was concerned with Western paintings. General Loring's great love was Egypt; his successors, Robinson and Fairbanks, were classical archaeologists. Edward J. Holmes had a particular affinity for the art of the Far and Near East. In all these areas the Museum of Fine Arts was in a stronger position, in terms of international comparison, than in paintings. There would have been logic in accepting this fact, and concentrating upon existing strengths, for no matter how many and how excellent European paintings an American museum may acquire, there is little likelihood of its rivaling the ancient royal and national picture galleries of Europe. Yet as most men in the street and as some perceptive collectors appraise an art museum chiefly by its paintings, the Museum of Fine Arts had always endeavored to improve the quality and enlarge the constituency of its picture galleries. Even in its earliest and most penniless days, the museum had been fortunate in the gifts that it received from Boston friends whose tastes were in advance of their neighbors. It acquired in 1880, for example, by gift of Mrs. Peter Chardon Brooks, a Chardin *Still Life* of 1733, nine years before that painter was represented in the National Gallery in London. And in 1883 Martin Brimmer gave a second Chardin painted in 1764. The great Roger van der Weyden, given in 1893 by Mr. and Mrs. Henry Lee Higginson, is another case in point. (The pictures are reproduced on pages 77, 78, 87.) The gifts, bequests, and purchases of paintings over the previous sixty years, noted in earlier chapters, had brought together a collection that it was tempting to enlarge and make more representative.

Upon his appointment as Director in the autumn of 1934, Edgell continued as Curator of Paintings, with the assistance of Charles C. Cunningham. Mrs. Haven Parker, who had been Philip Hendy's assistant, continued in the department, preparing a scholarly catalogue of American paintings of the Colonial and early Republican periods. In 1935 James Sachs Plaut (Harvard A.B. 1933), who had done graduate work with Professor Paul J. Sachs, came to work on a catalogue of European paintings. In that year the department purchased the *Kneeling Monk* of Manet and a Degas pastel of a Danseuse.

The most dramatic purchase of 1936 was Gauguin's great *D'où venons-nous? Que sommes nous? Où allons nous?*; the most considerable gift was Vincent van Gogh's portrait of the *Postman Roulin*, received from Robert Treat Paine, 2nd. A year earlier the museum had had no Gauguin and no Van Gogh; now it had Gauguin's masterpiece and one of the most famous of Van Gogh's portraits. The following year a great Renoir, *Le Bal à Bougival*, was purchased with the help of subscriptions from a few friends, while from the income of the Charles Potter Kling Fund was acquired a great Renaissance panel, *The Presentation of the Virgin at the Temple*, attributed to the Umbrian painter-architect, Fra Carnevale. This picture, like its

THE POSTMAN ROULIN. Vincent van Gogh. *Gift of Robert Treat Paine, 2nd. 35.1982*

companion, *The Birth of the Virgin*, which was purchased by the Metropolitan Museum the previous year, came to the United States from the collection of Prince Corsini, who had acquired it at the division of the Barberini estate in Rome.

Another important Italian purchase, announced at the same time, had a less distinguished but peculiarly Bostonian pedigree. A Boston lady cleaning out an attic came upon various oil paintings which she assumed to be nineteenth-century copies of the sort that so many New Englanders had brought home from Italy. To lighten her burdens, she gave them to the Morgan Memorial. (For the benefit of non-Bostonians, it should be explained that, while the Morgan Memorial in Hartford, Connecticut, is a dignified part of an art museum, in

Boston it is the charitable body that collects old clothes, mattresses, broken chairs, and other domestic flotsam and jetsam for repair and [hopeful] resale.) The Morgan Memorial intelligently brought the paintings to the Museum of Fine Arts, where, after careful examination in the Painting Department and in William J. Young's Research Laboratory, one proved to be an original portrait of a Doge of Venice by Gentile Bellini. This discovery, as Harold Edgell described it in his 1937 report,

> brought about a very pretty problem in the Museum since, of course, the Museum had to tell the Morgan Memorial what they had received and at the same time wanted to purchase the painting at a price as reasonable as possible. The situation was further complicated by the fact that the Morgan Memorial had no means of tracing the donor, and if the story of its coming to the Museum in this way were broadcast, it would be possible for many spurious donors to come to the Museum and assert that it was their painting and had been thrown in the Morgan Memorial bag by mistake. Happily the Museum was able to come to an accord with the Morgan Memorial for a price for the painting satisfactory to both, and after the painting was exhibited it was recognized by the donor, who had received it in a large collection of copies and had no reason to think it anything else, and who generously said that she only regretted that the picture might not have come to the Museum from her as a gift.

This comedy of errors, which resolved itself to all the cast's satisfaction in the final act, points the moral that one should never underestimate what traveling nineteenth-century Bostonians might have brought home with them.

When an institution is as complex and departmentalized as the Museum of Fine Arts had become in the nineteen thirties, a director can rarely cope with additional curatorial functions without developing at least a mild case of schizophrenia. Thus in 1937 when the distinguished British connoisseur and art-historian William George Constable resigned as Director of the Courtauld Institute, the Museum of Fine Arts immediately invited him to come to Boston as Curator of Paintings. "W.G.," as he is laconically and invariably

THE BACINO DI SAN MARCO, VENICE. Antonio Canale (Canaletto). *Abbott Lawrence, Seth K. Sweetser, and Charles Edward French Funds. 39.290*

known, accepted, although he was unable to come before March 1938, as he had received a Leverhulme Research Fellowship which would permit him to work in Venice completing his study of Canaletto. He agreed to come to Boston for a term of not less than three years, but, unlike Jean Guiffrey and Philip Hendy, he became a permanent inhabitant and a valued part of the local scene, for he remained until his retirement, after more than nineteen years of service, on 1 October 1957. He will be remembered for his scholarly works on Richard Wilson and Canaletto and *The Painter's Workshop*, as well as for such noble acquisitions as the Rubens *Queen Tomyris with the Head of Cyrus*, Canaletto's *Bacino di San Marco*, Titian's *St. Catherine Adoring the Crucifix* — as handsome as ever today even though the Vatican in 1969 demoted its subject — and Poussin's *Mars and Venus* (fortunately there has been no Olympian Council to downgrade those ancient deities to make room for more recent and "relevant" substitutes).

This enchanting Poussin came from the collection of Lord Harcourt, at whose family seat, Nuneham Park near Oxford, it had hung since 1758. When it arrived in Boston in the spring of 1940, Edward

MARS AND VENUS. Nicolas Poussin. *Augustus Hemenway and Arthur Wheelwright funds. 40.89*

M. Pickman, a trustee annually appointed by the Boston Athenæum from 1933 to 1955, proposed that a suitable welcome be provided. The painting was shown on 28 May 1940 in a corner of the Curator's office, with handsome fabrics behind it. When a toast had been drunk in champagne by the entire staff of the Painting Department and a select group of guests, the picture, to the amazement of its admirers, began to recite the following verses in acknowledgment.

Mes amis, me voilà, et laissez-moi vous dire
Que d'être parmi vous est pour moi un plaisir,
Car je n'ai, jusqu'ici pu trouver l'occasion
De visiter moi-même le musée de Boston.
La presence de tant d'autres artistes chez vous,
Me rendait, je l'admets, un tantinet jaloux!
Le mal est réparé. Votre accueil chaleureux
Me touche au fond du coeur, et me rend très heureux.
J'accepte votre hommage avec reconnaissance,
Et vous quitte en disant avec vous: Vive la France.

Only W. G. Constable and his assistants knew that William Royall Tyler, then a graduate student in Fine Arts at Harvard, later Assistant Secretary of State for Europe, and United States Ambassador to the Netherlands, now Director of the Dumbarton Oaks Research Library and Collections in Washington, was concealed behind the picture to recite the poem that he had composed. Late May of 1940 was a moment when many Bostonians, anxiously thinking of the fate of France, were especially grateful to have this painting safely installed in Boston. Mr. Tyler soon left his medieval studies to broadcast over short-wave station WRUL to occupied Europe.

The death of Miss Grace Edwards in 1938 brought into use a bequest made in 1925 by her brother, Robert J. Edwards, in memory of their mother, Juliana Cheney Edwards. Under this will the museum received a fund of $250,000, whose income was restricted to the purchase of paintings, as well as a magnificent group of pictures that included works of Monet, Sisley, Pissarro, Renoir, and Gainsborough. The Edwards bequest made the museum's holdings of the Impressionist painters, especially Monet, admirably large. It greatly strengthened the general representation of ninteenth-century French painting, which by this time only lacked examples of Cézanne, Seurat, and Toulouse-Lautrec, and further representation of Van Gogh. In 1938 was also received by bequest of Emily L. Ainsley a $57,750 fund restricted to the purchase of paintings, and an unrestricted fund of $115,000. The following year President Holmes added a fine *Nymphéas* to the Monet collection, while in 1941 he gave a number of paintings, including a *Madonna and Child* by the Sienese master Francesco di Giorgio.

During the winter of 1935–36 the Museum of Fine Arts came within an ace of purchasing the greater part of the fabulous Graphische Sammlung Albertina in Vienna. Begun in 1795 by Duke Albert of Saxe-Teschen, and extended by later owners, this collection of prints and drawings in 1919 had been confiscated, with other property of the Imperial Hapsburg family, by the Austrian Government. Some of these properties having been restored to their former owners in 1935, the Archduke Albrecht, living in Hungary, entered into negotiation with Gustav Mayer, a partner in the London firm of P. and D. Colnaghi and Company about possible sale of the Albertina drawings. As Henry P. Rossiter was an old friend, who had often stayed and played tennis at his house, Wistlers Wood in the Surrey hills south of London, Mayer offered the Albertina Collection to the Museum of Fine Arts. At the Archduke Albrecht's insistence, the art dealer had first offered the refusal of these drawings and prints to Andrew W. Mellon, who he found was then interested in paintings only; thereafter he was free to turn to his close friend in Boston. So far as Gus Mayer was concerned, it was then the M.F.A. all the way, but somehow the museum had to find a million dollars very fast.

Rossiter was never dismayed by the size of big game or the difficulties of the chase. Several years earlier he had made a brave but unsuccessful attempt to raise money to buy masterpieces from the Hermitage. When the five-year plan was not coming up to scratch and the Soviet Government needed a considerable amount of foreign money to keep it going, the sale of paintings from the great gallery in Petrograd seemed an obvious solution. Certain pictures were therefore set aside to be sold each month through the intermediary of Colnaghi and Knoedler. Andrew Mellon had the first choice of the first three offered; by accepting it he secured some of the masterpieces that he later placed in the National Gallery of Art in Washington. When word reached the Museum of Fine Arts of the possible availability of Rubens' huge portrait of *Helena Fourment* (subsequently bought by C. S. Gulbenkian), a Rembrandt portrait, and a fifteenth-century Netherlands triptych, Edward J. Holmes, then director, was in Italy getting copies of chairs made for use in galleries. A telegram caught up with Holmes in Florence; he cabled back, suggesting that Henry Rossiter do what he could. The Curator of Prints first approached Robert T. Paine, 2nd, whose recent gift of the great tapestry from Knole had indicated a generous willingness to help the museum. Unfortunately, as Paine had just acquired a remarkable new engine for his boat, he could talk of nothing else that afternoon; disappointed in that quarter, Rossiter turned to Denman Ross, who stated ex cathedra that as one could not get a clear title to pictures bought under such circumstances, he was unwilling to help. So a promising opportunity came to naught for lack of funds.

Harold Edgell responded to the Albertina challenge with greater alacrity. So did the museum staff for, when told by Edgell what was in the wind, they voted unanimously not to present for possible purchase during the next four or five years any objects for their own departments if the Albertina Collection were acquired. Few groups of curators anywhere would have done that. As the museum's funds were still inadequate even after such self-abnegating concentration on a single great goal, Edgell turned to friends in Newport, New York, and Washington. In the early days of June 1935, while Rossiter stayed at Carlton House in New York to keep Gus Mayer amused, the director bestirred himself to considerable purpose in scaring up financial guarantees that would permit an adequate offer. As he was nearing his goal, he wrote Rossiter that he would take the Merchants' Limited to New York on Wednesday and come to Carlton House on Thursday morning. "My doing this will mean your doing business on the Fourth of July, but Mayer is English — naturalized, is he not? — and you are Canadian and will not resent it if we do not celebrate our late disagreeableness with Great Britain." The result of the Fourth of July conference was that Mayer returned to Europe with the promise of a definite proposal from Boston.

A good deal of cloak and dagger work ensued. In subsequent cables references to the Archduke Albrecht were disguised under the unlikely code name of HOLMES, while only the principals knew that a proposed offer of £160 meant £160,000. One of the conditions was that the material must be checked in Vienna by Rossiter, and by Paul J. Sachs (Harvard A.B. 1900, Professor of Fine Arts and Associate Director of the Fogg Art Museum), who had become a trustee of the Museum of Fine Arts on 21 January 1932. Paul Sachs was already in Paris; Henry Rossiter sailed on short notice in the *Ile de France*, in the company of W. G. Russell Allen (Harvard A.B. 1903), a generous collector who had been a member of the Visiting Committee of the Department of Prints since 1922. They proceeded to Vienna where, in the company of Paul Sachs's assistant, Miss Agnes Mongan (since 1969 Director of the Fogg Art Museum), and the lawyer W. A. Roseborough from the Paris office of Sullivan and Cromwell, they joined Gustav Mayer and continued negotia-

THE CONSPIRATORS LUNCHING AT THE HOTEL BRISTOL, VIENNA. Left to right: Henry P. Rossiter, Agnes Mongan, Gustav Mayer, Paul J. Sachs, W. G. Russell Allen, W. A. Roseborough.

tions. Late in the autumn of 1935 it appeared that everything was signed and sealed; Colnaghi's chief mounter was standing by in London to fly to Vienna at a moment's notice to remove all prints and drawings from their mounts and pack them for shipment to England. At this point Mayer and his allies celebrated the beginning of the end of their task with a luncheon at the Hotel Bristol, fortunately recorded by the camera.

It had been a lengthy business. Paul Sachs eventually returned to Harvard in mid-December 1935, excessively late for the opening of the fall term and totally unable, through bonds of secrecy, to explain to his colleagues where he had been or why. Henry Rossiter had, after all, a "blackmail photograph" of him, taken at the Bristol luncheon, a bottle in each hand, seated behind the empty glasses of the entire company. Although Russell Allen and Agnes Mongan returned home before the end of December, Rossiter remained in London to keep a close eye on the situation. On 10 January 1936 Harold Edgell wrote him, saying how much the Committee on the Museum appreciated all that he had done, adding, "All I can say is hang on, keep your teeth in the Albertina, and your tail up." The trustees at their annual meeting on 16 January 1936 voted formal thanks to Allen, Rossiter, and Agnes Mongan "for their devoted assistance in the interest of the Museum in Europe during the past months," and elected Russell Allen a trustee.

By late winter the negotiations, instead of reaching a conclusion, seemed to become increasingly complicated, for press rumors of the sale impeded the owner's negotiations with the Austrian Government. Unfortunately a brief but startlingly accurate statement that, "although not officially confirmed from sources on either side," the Museum of Fine Arts was negotiating for the purchase of the Albertina collection, had appeared in the *Boston Evening Transcript* of 23 November 1935. The *Art News* of 21 December 1935 published a more extended account. However the leak occurred, and it seems incredible that anyone connected with the museum could have been so foolish as to inspire it, the fat was in the fire. By 26 March 1936 the *Basler Nachrichten* published an article, "Die 'Albertina' und der Mister X," while on 10 May the Viennese *Deutscher Telegraf*

PAUL J. SACHS CONTEMPLATING EMPTY GLASSES AFTER LUNCH.

was fulminating about *die ausländischen Kunstjuden*. Publicity from whatever source gave the Archduke Albrecht an excuse for delay; by the summer of 1936 negotiations were broken off, at considerable personal loss to the excellent Gustav Mayer, who had expended large sums of money during the previous year. At the time it seemed a tragedy to those who had worked so hard to achieve the purchase. More than thirty years later, I can be glad that the Albertina is still in Vienna, but it was a magnificently good try.

Notwithstanding this disappointment, the Department of Prints in 1937 commemorated its fiftieth anniversary by opening the year with a carefully chosen exhibition of more than five hundred prints, drawings, and books that illustrated its growth and resources. It closed the year with a comprehensive exhibition of lithographs from 1799 to 1937, to which W. G. Russell Allen lent scores of rare examples, both early and late. In the same year the department received by bequest of William A. Sargent its first great gift of illustrated books, as well as a fund of $100,000, the income of which was to be used for the purchase of prints or illustrated books. Although the Sargent collection was particularly rich in illustrated French books of the eighteenth century, its more than two thousand volumes extended from the Pigouchet-Vostre Book of Hours of 1498 on vellum to examples of English and American private presses of the late nineteenth and twentieth centuries. Russell Allen in 1938 gave 472 early lithographs, which included the rarities and masterpieces that had formed the framework of the 1937 exhibition, while he and Paul J. Sachs gave jointly a collection of more than 1600 prints and drawings. George Peabody Gardner, long a valued friend of the Department of Prints, died in 1939. The following year his widow gave the museum some 200 prints and 9 drawings from his collection that were of considerable importance, and his son of the same name (Harvard A.B. 1910) was elected a trustee.

Although textiles and tapestries have been mentioned in nearly all of the preceding chapters, a Department of Textiles, of which Miss Gertrude Townsend was the first curator, was only formally established on 1 January 1930. The richness and variety of its resources have only been appreciated by the scholars and friends who have frequented its study rooms, for, save for the impressive

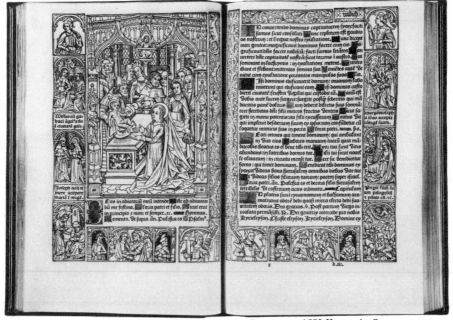

PIGOUCHET-VOSTRE BOOK OF HOURS, 1498. *Bequest of William A. Sargent, 1937.*

Tapestry Gallery, it has had only corridors and odd corners for exhibition space. Moreover its materials are often so fragile that they must be "rested" by removal from exhibition to storage to prevent fading and deterioration from constant light and hanging. Its collections have been achieved through the thoughtful interaction of generous collectors and two scholarly curators. One aspect of these can be readily appreciated by an examination of the two-volume catalogue *Tapestries of Europe and of Colonial Peru in the Museum of Fine Arts, Boston,* by Adolph S. Cavallo, published by the museum in 1967. In this work Mr. Cavallo, who became curator in 1959 upon Miss Townsend's retirement, studied intensively sixty-six of the one hundred European and Peruvian Colonial tapestries owned by the museum at the end of 1967. He points out that, in the earliest years when it was necessary to depend upon the generosity of collectors for the acquisition of original works of art, Boston

harbored so few collectors in the grand manner that the Museum had no occasion to seek, accept and enshrine a few large sets of tapestries and then call it a day, as so many museums in this country did in their formative years. From the very beginning, the administration and staff looked upon tapestries as individual works of art worthy of concentrated study. They were never regarded primarily as prestigious decoration for monumental halls. These circumstances formed a policy which has remained in effect to this day. Because of it, there are no complete sets of tapestries in the collection, and this is certainly a loss. On the other hand, it has given the Trustees and staff a free hand to acquire tapestries on individual merit and in free competition with other works of art.

Thus, as noted in earlier chapters, the museum's first medieval tapestry, the great Flemish *Destruction of the Egyptians in the Red Sea* was bought in 1895 from the Otis Norcross Fund when the first important purchases were being made, while *Two Miracles of the Eucharist* was acquired in 1904 through the James Fund. In 1908 Mrs. John Harvey Wright gave, in memory of her son, Eben Wright, and her father, Lyman Nichols, the fifteenth-century Flemish tapestry *The First Four Articles of the Creed*, which is said to have come from a Spanish cathedral. The eight French, or Franco-Flemish, fragments representing the story of Penelope and of the Cimbri women, which bear the arms of Ferry de Clugny, Bishop of Tournai, who became a Cardinal in 1480 and died in 1483, were purchased from the Maria Antoinette Evans Fund in 1926. These enchanting Gothic pieces, which are closely related to the *Lady with the Unicorn* series in the Musée de Cluny, were recommended for purchase by Miss Townsend, with the enthusiastic support of Denman W. Ross. Three years later, in 1929, the princely gift by Robert Treat Paine, 2nd, of the late fifteenth-century *Christ before Pilate and Herod* that had hung in the chapel at Knole for more than four centuries, set a new standard for the Boston collection.

In quite another direction, Peruvian tapestries of the Colonial period had come to the Museum of Fine Arts as early as 1897 from Denman W. Ross, who, as Daniel V. Thompson recalls, could see beauty wherever it exists, but particularly in the shadow of a lemon. By 1922 he had placed eight complete tapestries of this type, and five fragments, in the museum, through his foresight creating one of the most extensive collections of them in Europe or in either of the American continents.

THE FIRST FOUR ARTICLES OF THE CREED. Tapestry, Flemish, 15th century. *Gift of Mrs. John Harvey Wright in memory of her son, Eben Wright, and her father, Lyman Nichols. 08.441*

ULYSSES HOMEWARD BOUND and PENELOPE AT HER LOOM. Tapestries, French or Franco-Flemish, about 1480–1483. *Maria Antoinette Evans Fund.* 26.53 and 26.54

In 1930, its first year of independent life, the Department of Textiles received 154 accessions, of which 9 were bequeathed, 88 were given, and 57 were purchased. The diversity of these will indicate the ecumenical nature of Miss Townsend's collecting. Three tapestries were received by the bequest of Mrs. Harriet T. Bradbury, the most remarkable of which was the early sixteenth-century *Two Miracles of Saint Claude*, which her brother, George Robert White, had acquired from the estate of J. Pierpont Morgan, who had purchased it from Knole. There were also two seventeenth-century Brussels tapestries, *Thetis and Achilles before the Oracle*, designed by Jacob Jordaens, and *The Anger of Achilles against Agamemnon*, woven after a cartoon by Peter Paul Rubens. The many gifts of Denman Ross that year included a piece of Syrian or Egyptian silk with a design of horsemen, dating from the fourth or fifth century, a particularly fine example of fourteenth-century Spanish-Arabic

brocade, and a seventeenth- or eighteenth-century Indian gold brocade sari with two dupattas. Edward J. Holmes gave 27 pieces of
Peruvian pre-Inca textiles, illustrating types not hitherto represented
in the museum's collection, which the archaeologist Philip Ainsworth
Means was then engaged in cataloguing. Among the purchases were
27 examples of tapestry weaving in silk on linen from Egypt, dating
from the tenth to eleventh century, many of which had Arabic
inscriptions; 2 important examples of late fourteenth-century Italian
brocade; and 2 pieces of Spanish-Arabic weaving of the thirteenth
or early fourteenth centuries. Among the loans were examples of
embroidery from the Greek islands, lent by Mrs. Lacey D. Caskey
for a special exhibition of Mediterranean embroideries that opened
in November. During the summer of 1930 a loan exhibition of
Indonesian textiles was held, from which a number of examples
were subsequently purchased.

The following year the 250 accessions included a number of very
fine Peruvian embroideries of the early Nazca period, which were
purchased through the Woodman, Sweetser, and Cruft funds, and
the gift of Mr. and Mrs. Samuel Cabot. He had been elected a trustee
in 1931, while his wife, appointed to the Visiting Committee in
1927, was for more than forty years a good friend and close
collaborator of the department. Philip Ainsworth Means's *A Study
of Peruvian Textiles in the Museum of Fine Arts, Boston*, was published in 1932, and six years later there appeared a second volume

EMBROIDERED MANTLE. Polychrome woolen threads, on woolen cloth. Peruvian,
Paracas culture, about 300 B.C.–100 A.D. *Ross Collection.* 16.34

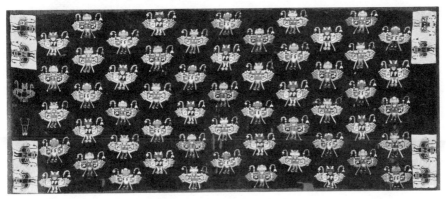

CHASUBLE. Sicilian silk, with woven ophreys and embroidered inscription. Salzburg, from the Church of St. Peter, 12th century. *Ellen Frances Mason Fund.* 33.676

in this series, *A Study of Some Early Islamic Textiles in the Museum of Fine Arts, Boston,* by Mrs. Nancy Pence Britton, who had worked in the department until 1937.

Some remarkable examples of medieval European liturgical vestments fell into Miss Townsend's capacious net. Thus there was purchased in 1933 a bell-shaped chasuble from the Abbey Church of St. Peter in Salzburg of the period 1167–1188, while in 1938 a thirteenth-century miter from the same Benedictine abbey was acquired. The receipt in 1934 and 1935 of the substantial bequest of Charles Potter Kling, the income of which was restricted to the purchase of tapestries or early Italian paintings, greatly enlarged the collecting horizons of the Department of Textiles. Through this fund it became possible in 1936 to buy a superb French late fifteenth- or early sixteenth-century tapestry bearing the arms and devices of Louise de Savoie and Charles d'Angoulême, while in 1938 the Francis Bartlett Fund provided the fifteenth-century tapestry of *The Martyrdom of St. Paul* that had hung in the cathedral of Beauvais until the French Revolution. The first large eighteenth-century French tapestry to enter the collection was the Beauvais *The Luncheon* of 1756, designed by François Boucher, which was purchased in 1940 through the Bartlett Fund.

The systematic collecting of the Department of Textiles and the learning of its curator attracted collectors and students to the department and inspired gifts from outside Boston. Thus in 1938 Philip Lehman gave, in memory of his wife, Carrie L. Lehman, a collection of 363 pieces of embroidery, lace, and weaving, which included many fine examples of types hitherto unrepresented, which there had seemed little hope of ever acquiring. Liturgical and secular gloves from the late fifteenth through the middle of the nineteenth centuries, children's garments of the seventeenth and eighteenth centuries, English embroidered bags of the seventeenth century, Italian and Spanish embroidery and drawn-work in colored silk on linen of the sixteenth and seventeenth centuries were among the rarities that were received in the Lehman Collection. Not long after the receipt of this gift, Miss Elizabeth Day McCormick of Chicago began to lend the Museum of Fine Arts English embroideries of the Elizabethan and Stuart periods. In October 1943 she gave the department her great collection of embroideries, costumes, and costume accessories, which included not only English material of the greatest rarity, but regional costumes of France, Syria, and Persia, as well as Italian, Sicilian, Sardinian, Greek, Macedonian, and Turkish embroideries. At this time the donor's brother, Robert H. McCormick, was elected Honorary Curator of the Elizabeth Day McCormick Collection. Similarly in 1940 William de Krafft of New York City gave a Flanders tapestry of the first half of the eighteenth century, *The Fish Market*, which was probably based on compositions by David Teniers, II.

As the war reduced the ease of contacts with Europe, the Department of Textiles devoted its attention to unfamiliar American material. In May 1941 Miss Townsend arranged an exhibition of New England embroidery before 1800, for which 144 pieces were lent to supplement those already in the museum's collection. These included 59 charming pictures, worked in tent stitch, oriental stitch, or satin stitch. In consequence a needlepoint picture, *The Reclining Shepherdess*, worked about 1776 by Susanna Heath of Brookline, who married John Goddard, was given by Mrs. Anna Goddard Pierce. This activity was particularly appropriate in view of simultaneous developments in the Department of Decorative Arts, which was about to be enriched by the gift of the Karolik Collection.

Mrs. John Chipman Gray once remarked that the Russian Revolution of 1917 had inadvertently benefited Boston by providing husbands for local spinsters. A remarkable case in point was the concert tenor Maxim Karolik (1893–1963) who, having arrived in the United States in 1922, married Miss Martha C. Codman in 1928. In spite of considerable disparity in their ages, backgrounds, and earlier lives, the Karoliks shared a common enthusiasm for the American arts of the eighteenth century. Mrs. Karolik, who had inherited numerous fine pieces from her Codman, Amory, Derby, and Pickman ancestors, had before her marriage helped the Museum of Fine Arts with the acquisition of the woodwork and furniture from "Oak Hill" in Peabody that occupy a conspicuous place in the Decorative Arts Wing. This marriage, like Edward S. Morse's visit to Japan in search of brachiopods, had serendipitous consequences for the Museum of Fine Arts, for in the twinkling of an eye the musical bridegroom became as entranced by the decorative arts of his wife's New England as the Maine-born zoologist had been with Japanese pottery. Maxim Karolik was an exotic bird to have come to roost in Boston and Newport. Although quiet reticence never characterized him, he understood and appreciated the understated arts of the Colonial and Federal periods of his adopted homeland, and devoted his ebullient and intuitive energies to the study and collecting of the most beautiful possible pieces of American furniture of the second half of the eighteenth century and early years of the nineteenth century, together with supporting paintings, prints, drawings, textiles, glass, and silver. In 1939 he and his wife gave outright the fruit of this decade of activity to the Museum of Fine Arts as The M. and M. Karolik Collection of Eighteenth Century American Arts.

Although a number of Mrs. Karolik's inherited heirlooms were included, the collection was singularly free of filio-pietistic overtones. Maxim Karolik would tease his neighbors for buying eighteenth-century chairs, not on account of their beauty but because of who had sat in them, and would then do his best to assemble, with the help and advice of the museum staff, objects that were beautiful in themselves and that would illuminate the period in which they were made. As the collection was destined for the Museum of Fine Arts, before making a purchase, the collectors at every turn sought the advice and counsel of Edwin J. Hipkiss, Curator of Decorative Arts, and his colleagues in other departments. On 7 December 1938 Maxim Karolik wrote Harold Edgell making the formal offer of the gift, with this explanation of its purpose:

> Our dream is becoming a reality!
>
> As you know, Mr. Hipkiss ardently assisted me in completing our collection, which he calls "a display of beauty of 18th century America." With him for the past few years I have often talked, planned, and as they say, "Dreamt dreams" about our Museum plan.
>
> No doubt, Mr. Hipkiss has already told you about the variety of conclusions we arrived at. The final conclusion will be reached in your office, when we talk over thoroughly the whole matter, including some details which are important to me but may seem unimportant to you.
>
> At present, I can only tell you that my wife and I are ready to offer our collection *to the people* through the Museum of Fine Arts.
>
> But before we sit down to discuss the material aspect of our plan, I would like to talk to you about the spiritual aspect, in which, I hope, you and the Trustees will understand the motive that lies behind that plan.
>
> Observing your activities in the Museum, I picture you as a man, who is able not only to understand (that often is not enough) but also to feel and be inspired by an idea . . . . Having such a picture of you, I can freely talk to you, the man and director, and remain assured that my "foreign" ideas will not shock you.

You and Mr. Hipkiss know that our aim was to collect the very best that America created in the Fine Arts in the 18th and early 19th centuries. We have succeeded, I believe. You also know that our approach to the Museum plan is entirely from the artistic point of view.

This collection, in our opinion, represents the *Artist*, whose creative work reflects the taste of an epoch.

Although many items in the collection belonged to my wife's ancestors (the Amory, Codman, Derby, and Pickman families) and, naturally, have family associations and sentiment, also historic value, we look upon them purely from the standpoint of their artistic beauty.

Remembering that the Museum represents the Fine Arts, it is natural for us to think that family sentiment, historic and anti-quarian values are of secondary importance to your institution.

In full sobriety, without false modesty or bombastic pride, I say to you: My wife and I realize the importance of our collection, the value of which lies in the Social, Aesthetic, Cultural, and Educational meaning of it. We know it consists of exceptional examples, among which are many unique specimens.

By the way, Mr. Hipkiss firmly believes that the collection is of *National* importance. I agree with him.

My wife and I want you to know that all our things of true Museum value ought to go to the Museum of Fine Arts. Why? — Because of the great mass of people, we believe *unconsciously* long for beautiful things.

Having the desire to see beautiful things, and not being able to possess them, the average man — not only the student of Art and the intellectual aesthete — will realize that private feeling of pos-session is, after all, of very little importance. He will understand the purpose of this collection: to give him the opportunity to enjoy works of Art in his leisure time for all time. That, we think, will make him feel *finer*, if not better.

To feel better we may only need a good steak; to feel finer we need something more than that. That "something" we want to give, as I have already said, to the people through the Museum of Fine Arts.

And there is another reason why we think our collection should be in the Museum: We firmly believe that in the Fine Arts, as in Music, lie the *permanent* human values — values which cannot be changed by any brown, black, or red shirt, — Fascism, Communism, Nazism, and any other ism. These human values can *never* be changed, because they are above earthly symbols.

Thinking over our Museum plan from many angles, my wife and I came to the conclusion that the only thing we actually lose is the feeling of possession. Yes. I admit, it is a very strong feeling. But when we think of the thousands of people (Mr. and Mrs. Karolik among them) who will enjoy our treasures in the Museum, the reward is enormous, and very comforting.

We are anxious to realize our plan very soon, while we are alive and in good health. We believe in the ancient Hebrew saying: "What we give in health has the value of gold; what we give in sickness has the value of silver; what we give after death has the value of lead." We prefer the value of gold, even though we are off the gold standard.

I would like to impress you, the Trustees, and the People of Boston with the feeling that the gift is coming to the Museum not as a generous gesture of rich persons, who can afford to be generous, or as a noble act of a standardized "Patron of Art" — NO! — but as a feeling, which comes from within.

This letter is quoted in full, in spite of its length and the innocent egoism of its literary style, because the *confessio fidei* that it ramblingly sets forth is a tribute to the motives that had actuated the founders of the museum sixty-eight years before.

It is, moreover, remarkable for a collection to be formed so completely with its usefulness to an institution in mind. Harold Edgell wrote in his 1941 report:

> From the beginning, the collectors had in mind the donation of the collection to the Museum of Fine Arts. Usually when a great collection is made and presented to a museum, it must accept the collection *in toto* without having a say in its assembling. Exactly the reverse was true in the case of the M. and M. Karolik Collection. For eight years, Mr. Karolik collected, never acquiring a piece without consulting the Staff of the Museum. The lion's share of the work fell upon the shoulders of Mr. Hipkiss, but Mr. Constable, Mr. Rossiter, Miss Townsend, Mr. Cunningham, Mrs. Haven Parker, and the Director were all called in on frequent occasions.

Mr. and Mrs. Karolik were extraordinarily successful in acquiring pieces that one would have thought never could have been bought. Important examples owned by well-to-do Bostonians of ancient families who had no need to sell their things were, nevertheless, obtained. The donors were able to point out that the pieces were not being acquired for Mr. and Mrs. Karolik but for the Museum of Fine Arts, and that they could find no more fitting end than inclusion in a collection of this aesthetic importance with a permanent home in the Boston Museum.

The Karolik Collection contained eight portraits by John Singleton Copley, two by Gilbert Stuart, two attributed to Winthrop Chandler, four miniatures, and a Chinese oil of the foreign factories at Canton, as well as a fine selection of contemporary drawings and prints. It was most extensive in its representation of the arts of joinery, for here were secretary-bookcases, desks, chests of drawers, sideboards, tables, stands, and knife boxes, chairs, sofas, clocks, looking-glasses in abundance, largely from New England, but with some fine examples from New York and Philadelphia. Silver, glass, Chinese export porcelain, needlework panels, Argand lamps, wall sconces, candlesticks, and fans were admirably represented.

The extent of the Karolik Collection made impossible its adequate housing by any rearrangement of existing galleries; new space had to be added. Thus, soon after its receipt, work was begun on a small addition to the Decorative Arts Wing, which was completed in the nick of time. On 2 December 1941, only five days before Pearl Harbor, the M. and M. Karolik Collection was formally opened by Governor Leverett Saltonstall. Some 2,500 guests attended the private view at which brief addresses were made by the Governor, and by Messrs. Holmes, Edgell, and Hipkiss. Moreover a detailed folio catalogue entitled *Eighteenth Century American Arts: The M. and M. Karolik Collection* by Edwin J. Hipkiss, with notes on the drawings and prints by Henry P. Rossiter, and with comments on the collection by Maxim Karolik, was published by the Harvard University Press in time for the opening.

A few days later there arrived at the museum as a loan from the children of the late Mrs. Charles McCann of Syosset, New York, a part of the great collection of Chinese export porcelain that she had

M. AND M. KAROLIK COLLECTION, GREEN GALLERY, 1941.

M. AND M. KAROLIK COLLECTION, BLUE GALLERY, 1941.

assembled. The heirs, Mr. Frasier W. McCann, Mrs. Constance McC. Betts, and Mrs. Helena W. Guest, considered the possibility of giving the collection to some institution as a memorial to their mother. As there were more pieces than any museum would have been easily able to exhibit, they divided the collection, sending part to Boston and part to the Metropolitan Museum. The porcelain came to the Museum of Fine Arts as a loan for five years, subject to a five-year renewal, after which the decision would be made as to whether it should become the permanent property of the museum. The heirs, however, retained the right to withdraw the loan at any time, or the museum to return it. With the loan came the woodwork of a polygonal Louis XV room in which Mrs. McCann had displayed the collection at Syosset. In spite of wartime problems, the Tudor room was dismantled from the site where it had been originally installed and moved to the second floor of the Karolik addition. The Louis XV woodwork was installed in its place, and early in 1943 the

HELENA WOOLWORTH MCCANN COLLECTION OF CHINESE EXPORT PORCELAIN.

Helena Woolworth McCann Collection of Chinese Export Porcelain was opened to visitors. In 1951 an outright gift of the collection was made.

The Department of Decorative Arts continued to attract important gifts of silver, both English and American. On various occasions in the thirties and early forties fine examples of English silver were received as additions to the collection of 230 pieces given anonymously in 1933 in memory of Charlotte Beebe Wilbour (1833–1914). The same anonymous donor gave, in 1935, 286 gold coins in memory of Zoë Wilbour (1864–1885), and added other rare gold pieces in 1937 and 1938. By bequest of Frank Brewer Bemis, 92 examples of English silver, ranging from the year 1577 to the middle of the eighteenth century, were received in 1935. The appointment in 1930 as Assistant in Early American Silver of Miss Kathryn Clark, who soon became Mrs. Yves Henry Buhler, brought a very able scholar in that field to the staff of the department. In 1938 Philip Leffingwell Spalding (Harvard A.B. 1892, A.M. 1893, S.B. 1894), sometime president of the New England Telephone and Telegraph Company and later a partner in the banking firm of Estabrook and Company, and a distinguished collector of Boston colonial silver, was appointed Honorary Curator of Early American Silver. Although he unfortunately died on 4 December 1938, his widow and sons, Philip, Oakes Ames, and Hobart Ames Spalding in 1942 gave the museum his splendid collection of some 50 early pieces. A catalogue of the Spalding silver, prepared by Edwin J. Hipkiss, was published in 1943.

The Leslie Lindsey Mason Collection of Musical Instruments became the subject of intensive study in 1935 when Nicholas Bessaraboff temporarily joined the staff of the Department of Decorative Arts to prepare a catalogue. An American citizen, born at Voronezh, Russia, he had been actively interested in music since boyhood, playing various wind instruments. Trained as a mechanical engineer at the Polytechnical Institute at St. Petersburg, he began in 1920 at Rochester, New York, seriously to study the history, construction, and acoustical properties of musical instruments. What began as a small but adequate catalogue, turned into a scholarly and fully illustrated folio of more than five hundred pages, completed in 1939 and published in 1941 by Harvard University Press under the title *Ancient European Musical Instruments: An Organological Study of the Musical Instruments in the Leslie Lindsey Mason Collection at the Museum of Fine Arts, Boston.* Nicholas Bessaraboff's monumental work is an admirable example of the scholarly conscience shown by the Museum of Fine Arts in regard to the collections committed to its charge. The foreword by the Reverend Francis W. Galpin, Canon Emeritus of Chelmsford Cathedral, and author of *Old English Instruments of Music*, from whom William Lindsey had purchased the collection to give to the museum in memory of his daughter, states:

Through the kindly interest of the Trustees of the Museum of Fine Arts and the expert assistance of Mr. Nicholas Bessaraboff the great desire of my life is being realized. For the object of this collection, gathered during a period of forty years, was mainly and engrossingly educational. Neither purse nor inclination led me to pay fancy prices for mere *objets d'art*, though many beautiful, historic, and decorative examples came across my path and have been incorporated in the general scheme. To me a musical instrument is a thing of life, something that will speak to us and reveal the hidden secrets of its sound. Therefore I made every effort to secure specimens that were playable or could be rendered so. To restore the ravages of time and replace the *tale* of years provided for me the greatest joy in their possession. It is with supreme pleasure, then, that, before I pass on, I am assured for my lifelong treasures all the care and consideration to which, by the genius of their makers and the skill of their old-world players, they are entitled. I trust that, whereas we have somewhat failed in England in displaying the stages of evolution through which instruments have passed, the Museum of Fine Arts in Boston may use many of these objects for the practical purposes to which they have been accustomed, that is, for lectures, demonstrations, and concerts of the music of their day. In this way the collection will not only retain its primary value, but will best reflect the charming personality of the lady whose memory is enshrined in its present title and whose whole life was music.

As a native of Dorchester, our old country-town in Dorset, from which, in the days of long ago, so many crossed the water to find

LESLIE LINDSEY MASON.
Photographed in costume during
a visit to the Holy Land.

safe refuge in Boston and its district, which I also know, I accept
with true appreciation the desire of my friend, the late Mr. William
Lindsey, and of the Museum authorities to provide once more in
their famous city a fine and lasting abode for these later pilgrims
from the homeland.

The wholly admirable uses that have been made of these instruments,
which will be noted in succeeding chapters, would have gladdened
the heart of Canon Galpin had he lived to know of them.

The Department of Decorative Arts benefited not only from the
Russian Revolution but from Herr Hitler's ill-judged purges of
German universities, for in 1939 the distinguished German medie-
valist, Dr. Georg Swarzenski, long the brilliant director of the Städel
Institut in Frankfurt, came to Boston as Fellow for Research in
Sculpture and Medieval Art. Thus, for the first time the Museum
of Fine Arts curatorial staff was augmented by a medieval scholar
of international distinction who had, moreover, long museum ex-

LOAN EXHIBITION OF ARTS OF THE MIDDLE AGES, 1940.

perience behind him. The first fruit of Dr. Swarzenski's presence in Boston was a loan exhibition, *Arts of the Middle Ages, 1000–1400*, which was held from 17 February to 24 March 1940, which was a logical sequel to the exhibition *The Dark Ages, Pagan and Christian Art in the Latin West and the Byzantine East* that Francis Henry Taylor had assembled at the Worcester Art Museum in 1937. Although the war prevented any borrowing from Europe, an admirable representation was assembled from private and public collections in the United States. A fine illustrated catalogue was produced, with an introduction by Georg Swarzenski and an essay by Ananda K. Coomaraswamy on the nature of medieval art.

The advantage of Dr. Swarzenski's presence on the staff soon became apparent from the number of distinguished medieval and renaissance objects that he was able to discover and purchase with the limited funds of the department. Soon after the close of the 1940 exhibition several objects included in it were bought for the permanent collection, such as the thirteenth-century bronze aquamanile representing Samson killing the lion, a twelfth-century Lombard Romanesque stone lion, and a Tuscan marble bust of a woman of

AQUAMANILE: SAMSON AND THE LION. Bronze, engraved,
Lorraine or Upper Rhine. *Benjamin Shelton Fund. 40.233*

STONE LION. Italian, late Romanesque, 13th century. *Gift of Mrs. Charles
Gaston Smith's Class. 40.784*

BAPTISMAL FONT. German bronze, by Goteke Klinghe of Bremen, signed and dated 1483. *Alice H. Goddard and Sarah F. Gorham funds.* 41.561

about 1300. Among 1941 acquisitions were a twelfth-century Saxon enamel plaque, and a magnificent bronze baptismal font by Goteke Klinghe of Bremen, signed and dated 1483. In 1942 three purchases were made, of which the first two were a small figure of an angel in limestone from Autun of about 1280 and a Sienese majolica jar of Siena from around 1500, picked up at auction in New York. Of the third, Ned Hipkiss wrote:

> We learned that a local dealer in odds and ends had for sale some objects from the estate of a collector well known to us and whose medieval objects, we believed, were all well placed. Dr. Swarzenki went to see what the dealer had to offer and as a result the Museum purchased an English figure of St. John in alabaster of the Nottingham School, *ca.* 1400. Because of a break now repaired, the price asked was reduced by half and this can be counted as one of the Museum's interesting bargains.

Georg Swarzenski's penetrating eyes and vast learning benefited other departments than his own, as one notes from the Director's report of 1944.

One of the most interesting paintings purchased in 1944 was a small German *Coronation of the Virgin* of about 1400, first noted by Mrs. Swarzenski in an auction room, and bearing the misleading title on a tablet, "Scuola di Avignone." Dr. Swarzenski saw it, and studied it as did Mr. Constable, and it was finally purchased at auction for a very moderate price. It was extremely dirty and much repainted, and its purchase was a gamble, but after cleaning, it was discovered to be in extraordinarily good condition, and an important example of a German art very rare and difficult to come by.

His flair for renaissance sculpture can be seen by the bronze fountain with nymphs from the atelier of Germain Pilon, acquired in 1941 from the Clarence Mackay collection; and by the sixteenth-century kneeling Spanish knight, attributed to Pompeo Leoni, that was purchased in 1944. Such acquisitions show what is possible, even with limited funds, when a learned curator with a keen eye is on the prowl, just as the Dossena fiasco of 1924 illustrates the chaos that can ensue when a committee, with money suddenly to spend,

FOUNTAIN WITH NYMPHS. French bronze, style of Germain Pilon, 16th century. *Alice H. Goddard and Sarah F. Gorham funds. 41.562*

KNEELING KNIGHT. Marble, attributed to Pompeo Leoni (born
Milan 1533, died Madrid 1608),
from a Spanish tomb monument.
1939 Purchase Fund. 44.813

ventures into a field where no scholarly specialist is present on the
staff.

As early as 1934 plans were being laid for the great loan exhibition
of art treasures from Japan that was held in September and October
1936 in conjunction with the Tercentenary of Harvard College.
Because of the reputation of the Japanese collection in Boston, objects
registered as national treasures, which under ordinary circumstances
could not have left the country, were generously lent, producing the
most distinguished exhibition of Japanese art ever held outside the
Orient. His Imperial Majesty the Emperor lent objects from his
own Imperial Household. His Imperial Highness Prince Takamatsu
similarly lent from his private collection, while paintings and sculpture came from the Imperial Museum, the Imperial Art School of

CHINESE SCULPTURE GALLERY IN 1930S.

CHINESE PAINTING GALLERY IN 1930S.

Tokyo, the Imperial University of Kyoto, as well as from many generous private owners. An illustrated catalogue of the hundred and one masterpieces sent was printed in Japan for the museum. Usually a great international loan exhibition brings with it the thrill of novelty, of objects of high quality never before seen on the spot. The 1936 Japanese exhibition, however, gave Bostonians the opportunity to appreciate all the more keenly the range and quality of the collections that they could repeatedly enjoy through the perceptive collecting of Morse, Bigelow, Fenollosa, Weld, and Okakura a generation or two earlier. The presence of the masterpieces from Japan was none the less appreciated, even though they proved to be relatives of old and familiar friends rather than startlingly new acquaintances.

Although the Department of Asiatic Art had long benefited by princely gifts of objects in great number, it entirely lacked restricted funds by which its staff might acquire pieces that appeared on the market that would valuably supplement existing collections. Thus, after the death of Professor Edward S. Morse in 1925, Francis Stewart Kershaw, keeper in the department, undertook to raise a fund in Morse's memory. Within the year $13,731 had been contributed by eighty-nine friends. Although this fund was useful, the department still had to exercise its ingenuity to add works of high quality. Thus in 1932, a year after he became Curator, Kojiro Tomita obtained the great twelfth-century painting of *Kibi's Adventures in China* — the one early and typical Yamato scroll owned outside Japan — only by an exchange of duplicate and near-duplicate objects from the Bigelow collection. The next step came in 1941 when a totally unanticipated bequest of $21,447.26 by John Ware Willard of New York created a fund, the income to be used for the purchase of Chinese and Japanese works of art. In the same year, Kojiro Tomita proposed the creation of a Curator's Fund for similar purposes, the first contribution to which came from Charles B. Hoyt, a member of the Visiting Committee, of whom considerably more will be heard later.

In 1941 the magnificent William S. and John T. Spaulding Collection of Japanese Prints, given some years earlier, was transferred to the museum and installed in the department's Study Room.

KIBI'S ADVENTURES IN CHINA. Japanese scroll. full color on paper, early Kamakura period, late 12th century. *Bigelow Collection (by exchange)*. 32.131

Immediately after the attack on Pearl Harbor, the Japanese galleries were closed to visitors and the most valuable objects removed to a place of safety elsewhere, lest wartime hysteria should lead fanatics to damage works of art. Kojiro Tomita continued as Curator, as deeply loved and respected as always by his colleagues. He had, after all, become a Bostonian a third of a century before. As his assistants Robert Treat Paine, Jr. (Harvard A.B. 1922, A.M. 1928) and David Britton Little (Harvard S.B. 1935), soon disappeared into naval uniform, the work of the department proceeded on a necessarily reduced scale during the war.

The Department of Classical Art, under the direction of Lacey D. Caskey, who had become its Curator in 1912, continued quietly on its scholarly rounds of acquisition, study, and publication. The fiftieth year of the department's life, 1935, was marked by a number of important acquisitions, among them a Cycladic marble statuette of a woman, between 2500 and 2000 B.C., purchased from the William Amory Gardner Fund. The number and quality of coins acquired made 1935 the most important year in this aspect of the

collection since 1904, when the Greenwell-Warren coins were purchased. The greatest of these was a magnificent specimen of the
famous Syracusan decadrachm known as the *Demareteion*, struck in
commemoration of the Greek victory over Carthage at the Battle of
Himera in 480 B.C. which Caskey described as "of unique historical
interest and universally regarded as the supreme gem among Greek
coins as a work of art." A collection of 119 Greek coins, chiefly silver
and gold, and 152 Roman coins, bronze and gold, given anonymously in memory of Zoë Wilbour not only had numismatic interest,
but contained admirable portraits of Hellenistic rulers and Roman
emperors. Problems of installation were becoming acute, for the
Department of Classical Art was the only one that had received no
additional exhibition space since the building was opened in 1909.
Some 900 objects acquired since that time had somehow been placed
on view, 400 of them on the main floor. These included 19 pieces
of sculpture, 32 of the finest vases in the collection, and six cases
containing 350 select Greek coins. Caskey therefore proposed flooring
over the gallery of the classical court, thus achieving a new room 67

NEW CLASSICAL GALLERY, 1938. Achieved by flooring over the Classical Court
at the gallery level.

feet long and 40 feet wide, in which the Greco-Roman sculptures, the Roman portraits, and the Pompeian wall paintings could be impressively displayed. This change, which provided a thousand square feet of badly needed new space at an estimated cost of $6,082, was completed in 1937.

Lacey Caskey continued work on the second volume of *Attic Vase Paintings in the Museum of Fine Arts*. This proceeded slowly, for it was necessary to have many of the vases repaired and cleaned by William J. Young in the Research Laboratory before satisfactory photographs of them could be made. It was providentially discovered that Miss Suzanne E. Chapman, who had been appointed primarily as a library assistant in the Classical and Egyptian departments, had remarkable skill as an artist and could make extremely fine drawings of vases for such publication. Consequently, from 1937 onward she steadily added to the number of plates that were completed for the second volume. Mrs. Agnes Baldwin Brett, Associate Curator of the American Numismatic Society, who had been working on a catalogue of the museum's collection of Greek coins since 1927, was appointed Honorary Curator of Classical Coins in 1937. Her *Catalogue of Greek Coins in the Museum of Fine Arts*, which described and illustrated 2,352 coins, more than 900 of which were previously unpublished, was completed in 1940, although unfortunately not published until 1955, the year of her death.

Caskey himself died in 1944. Although still in his sixties he was the dean of curators for he had served the Museum of Fine Arts faithfully and brilliantly for thirty-six years. The year following his death one of his last acquisitions — a sixth-century finial of an Attic grave-monument surmounted by a sphinx, which is the finest piece of Archaic Greek sculpture in the collection — was put in place, after restoration. It is a vivid reminder of a devoted and scholarly curator. As wartime was no moment to seek a permanent replacement, Dean George H. Chase, a trustee appointed by Harvard since 1918, became Acting Curator of Classical Antiquities in 1945, and continued until his death in 1952. Sir John Beazley, who had collaborated with Caskey on the first volume of *Attic Vase Paintings*, assumed responsibility for the second volume, published by the museum in 1954.

The curatorial work of the Classical and Egyptian departments in

SPHINX. Archaic Greek marble, from an Attic
grave monument, 6th century B.C. *1931 and
1939 Purchase Funds. 40.576*

the nineteen thirties was often greatly assisted by the technical and
scientific dexterity of William J. Young, who came to the Museum
of Fine Arts from England in 1929 to establish a Research Laboratory
for the conservation and study of works of art. Although only twenty-
three at the time, he knew more than most people about this uncom-
mon and exacting discipline, for he was the third generation of his
family to work in it. From his father, who was in charge of conservation at the Ashmolean Museum at Oxford, William J. Young learned
much. During a school vacation, he worked at the museum with C.
Leonard Woolley putting together a large bronze gorgon-headed
shield. After that experience, he went during another vacation to
Lewes House to do similar work with Edward Perry Warren and

Frank Gearing. From this acquaintance sprang the idea that he should go to Boston. Thus the Museum of Fine Arts owes to Warren not only the greatest objects in its classical collection but the genesis of its Research Laboratory, which, during the next forty years, Young made one of the greatest in the world.

The beginnings of the Research Laboratory were modest as to space and equipment, but rich in ingenuity, knowledge, and imagination. Young had been imbued by his father with the notion that if you cannot make a scientific laboratory out of a piece of string and a couple of toothpicks, there is something wrong with you. His cleaning and restoration of an Egyptian bronze *Aegis* of the Twenty-second Dynasty, acquired in 1931 in lamentable condition, soon demonstrated irrefutably that there was nothing wrong with him. This piece, which had so suffered from the ravages of "bronze disease" that its quality could little more than be guessed at, became handsome and exhibitable through electrolysis with a homemade apparatus that cost some fifteen dollars. William J. Young was soon enhancing the usefulness of the Egyptian Department's collections

BRONZE AEGIS. Egyptian, 22nd Dynasty, before and after cleaning in the Research Laboratory. *Adelia Cotton Williams Fund. 31.195*

MYCERINUS, BUILDER OF THE GREAT PYRAMID AT GIZA. Egyptian, 4th Dynasty, colossal alabaster statue. *Harvard-Boston Expedition. 09.204*   The central view shows the statue as partially restored by Joseph Lindon Smith; the left and right views as restored in 1934 by William J. Young and Charles Muskavitch. See also illustrations on pages 261 and 284.

by cleaning silver, mending pottery, restoring a magnificent alabaster vase from Kerma, and treating a series of gold and electrum cylinder sheaths from Nuri. In 1934 he tackled the fragments of the great seated alabaster statue of King Mycerinus, of which the head and one shoulder, the seat, hands, knees, and part of the calves had been found in 1907 by Reisner in front of the east face of the Third Pyramid at Giza. These fragments had been installed in Boston in 1909 in the fragmentary form shown in the early view of gallery E–3 that is reproduced in Chapter VIII. Although in 1911 and again in 1925 Joseph Lindon Smith undertook to model in plaster some of the missing parts, "the majestic dignity of the statue," as Dows Dunham put it, "was marred by unsightly gaps which tended to falsify its proportions and to distract the attention of visitors." So, in 1934 William J. Young cleaned the alabaster statue and throne, restoring the original beauty of the material, while Charles Muskavitch, a former student at the Museum School, modeled replacements of the missing arms and legs, under the direction of Dunham and Smith. Although a clear and unmistakable differentiation was made in the color and texture of the restored parts, this huge Old Kingdom statue, when returned to exhibition in 1935, could for the first time adequately be appreciated as a work of art. Similarly an alabaster statuette of Prince Khnum-baf of the early Fifth Dynasty was reassembled in 1939 from fragments, thanks to collaboration between the Egyptian Department, the Research Laboratory, and David Dennis, who modeled the missing parts in hard wax. Many other such ventures, in which the manual dexterity of William J. Young played a decisive role, converted shattered and unimpressive archaeological fragments into exhibition material of very fine quality.

For the Department of Classical Art he cleaned and mended Greek vases, on occasion even refiring them successfully. When the gold and ivory Minoan *Snake Goddess*, which, it will be remembered,

PRINCE KHNUM-BAF. Egyptian, 5th Dynasty, alabaster statuette, before and after assembly in the Research Laboratory. *Harvard-Boston Expedition.* 24.603

had come to the museum in 1914 as a mass of fragments in a cigar box, showed signs of coming unstuck from its initial reassembly, Young painstakingly took it apart and reconstructed it in permanent and durable form. As the equipment of the Research Laboratory grew from toothpicks and string to spectroscopes and related equipment, he continually conducted minute and extraordinarily accurate chemical analyses of materials, which were of the greatest help to all branches of the museum in the identification of forgeries or the restored parts of original sculptures and ceramics. In 1941, for example, in the course of a spectrographic examination of marbles, he studied specimens of every one of the unusually complete collections of marbles in the University of Michigan.

From the nineteen thirties an increasing amount of work in scientific conservation was going on behind the scenes in various corners of the museum. Alfred Lowe and John Finlayson, restorers attached to the Department of Paintings, were constantly at work cleaning pictures to such purpose that Harold Edgell in his 1941 report remarked that they "again have doubled and tripled the value of many paintings committed to their skilled hands." He mentioned in particular the "perfect cleaning" that they had just completed of Rubens' *The Head of Cyrus brought to Queen Tomyris*, formerly in the collections of Queen Cristina of Sweden, the Duc d'Orléans, the Earl of Darnley, and the Earl of Harewood, from whom it had recently been purchased through the Robert J. Edwards Fund. In the Department of Prints, Francis W. Dolloff was carrying on equally skillful operations in the cleaning and remounting of prints and drawings, employing for the first time in this region techniques developed at the British Museum. With great museums, as with icebergs, there is always considerably more below the surface than is visible to the casual observer. As the Museum of Fine Arts entered its seventh decade, it had reached the stage where it might by any standard be considered a great museum, not only for the richness and variety of its collection but for the indispensable (though often invisible) support furnished those collections by a staff of learned curators and highly skilled scientists and craftsmen, whose constant research and investigation breathed life into the institution. Therein lies the difference between a great museum and a warehouse.

Until the retirement of Benjamin Ives Gilman, in January 1925, the Secretary of the Museum had been in charge of what was called the Department of Publication and Instruction, with an assistant in each of those fields. On Gilman's departure the Librarian, Ashton Sanborn, became Secretary and took charge of Publications, while continuing his former responsibility for the Library, and Henry Hunt Clark, Director of the Department of Design in the Museum School, was appointed Supervisor of Instruction at the museum. Clark continued the same extended pattern of docent service, lectures, conferences, extension courses, loaning of lantern slides, drawing classes for children, visits of school classes brought by bus, talks and evening openings for businessmen and women that had evolved under Gilman. The summer Story Hours for children brought from playgrounds and settlement houses were continued through the Caroline Sumner Freeman Fund of $75,000, established in 1922 by an anonymous donor for this express purpose. In 1928 Teachers' Conferences, presenting the Egyptian and Classical collections in a manner designed to make them of value as source material in teaching, were instituted. Through agreement with the Board of Supervisers of the Boston Public Schools, teachers participating received one point of credit for successful completion of the work. In the same year craft study classes for boys and girls were introduced.

When Henry Hunt Clark resigned in April 1931 to become Director of the Cleveland School of Art, Miss Marion Evans Doane was appointed Supervisor of Instruction. The same pattern of activity continued, although in 1933 Professor Henry Latimer Seaver retired from his voluntary post as Sunday lecturer, after twenty-five years of continuous and devoted service. I suspect that no other volunteer in the history of the museum has ever given such consistent help over so long a period, and to such useful purpose. For a Professor of History at M.I.T. to sacrifice his Sundays to the Museum of Fine Arts over a quarter of a century is a performance above and beyond the call of duty, although entirely in keeping with the character of this charming and learned scholar. When Miss Doane resigned because of illness in 1934, Ashton Sanborn characteristically volunteered to add her work to all his other duties. Thus a supposedly temporary arrangement slid into permanence, for he served as Supervisor of

Instruction from 1934 to 1942. In 1935, however, some of the responsibilities of the department were transferred to Mrs. Anne Webb Karnaghan, who had been Publicity Secretary since 1927, and who was then given the new title of Supervisor of Museum Extension.

While Mrs. Webb (as she was known after resuming her maiden name) continued her old rounds of press conferences, radio talks, and insinuating cards advertising the museum into Boston Elevated and Boston and Maine trains, she soon undertook a new program of cooperation with the high schools of Boston and vicinity. This involved assembling large photographs of works of art in permanent sets, grouped around specific ideas emphasized in school courses in the history, literature, and languages of earlier civilizations; providing a simple but authoritative article with a brief bibliography for use as reference material by the teacher; and having the material in easily transportable form that could be requested by number. With the aid of a grant of $2,500 from the Carnegie Corporation of New York and summer scholarships given by Radcliffe College to a few of its graduate students to help in this effort, forty different illustrative sets, closely related to the school curriculum, were assembled by the end of 1936. Such subjects as *An Introductory Survey of Egypt, Agriculture in Ancient Egypt, The Life of an Egyptian Noble, The Life on a Mediaeval Manor, The Development of the Monastic Ideal, The Mediaeval Hierarchy*, and *Louis XIV and His Circle* were prepared, while members of the department staff lectured at various schools to introduce the sets not only to the pupils but to the teachers. In recognition of their value to the Boston school system, the School Committee bore the expense of printing a catalogue of the illustrative sets for distribution to teachers.

The project attracted the friendly interest of scholars in other institutions. Professor Roger Sherman Loomis of Columbia University, for example, prepared a set of pictures on *The Arthurian Legend*, while Harold Ogden White of Boston University edited one on *The Canterbury Tales in Chaucer's England*. In 1938 the division made 341 loans of sets to a monthly average of 18 different institutions, and the trustees authorized the publication in portfolio format (12 inches by 16 ½ inches) of two sets, *Elizabethan England* and *Athletics and Festivals of Greece in the Fifth Century*, with illustrations reproduced in collotype and the text printed in letterpress. These were printed the following year in an edition of 2,000 copies, while a third set, *The French Renaissance*, was published in 1940. In that year thirty-three unpublished master sets were lent 481 times to 118 different institutions, of which 77 were secondary schools and colleges, while 354 lectures based on the illustrative sets were given to a total of 20,468 students, mostly in their own classrooms. Although the project had started as a high school venture, the quality of the material made the sets attractive to colleges, which is not surprising when one notes that members of the Harvard faculty cheerfully pitched in to help. Dr. George M. A. Hanfmann undertook three sets on the political and social history of Rome, while Professor Crane Brinton edited a *French Revolution.*

The radio program of the Division of Museum Extension was discontinued in 1938 because of Mrs. Webb's expressed belief "that the radio requires a particular technique which has not yet been satisfactorily worked out for the Division and because some small budget for this purpose must be appropriated before the necessary study can be made." In that year, as an appropriation was for the first time made for free concerts, six oratorios were presented by Federal Music Projects, and the choir of St. James Armenian Apostolic Church of Watertown gave a concert that was followed by a lecture on Armenian church architecture by Professor Kenneth J. Conant of Harvard. In the winter and spring of 1938–39 instruments of the Leslie Lindsey Mason Collection — which were then being studied by Nicholas Bessaraboff — were played by the Boston Schola Cantorum in a carefully planned series of concerts of early music.

When Anne Holliday Webb resigned in 1941 as Supervisor of Museum Extension, to the great regret of many people, she was succeeded by William Germain Dooley, widely known as the Art Editor of the recently deceased *Boston Evening Transcript*. The following year he became head of a new Division of Education. The genesis of this was thus explained by Harold Edgell in his 1942 report:

> During the summer the important decision was made to merge the Division of Instruction and the Division of Extension. By doing so, one of the burdens could be lifted from the shoulders of Mr.

Sanborn when he returned [from absence due to illness]. He, on the request of a previous Director, had volunteered to assume the position of Supervisor of Instruction temporarily until a new Supervisor had been obtained, and thenceforth continued to hold it year by year. There seemed to be no logical reason to keep separate the two Divisions. Education is education whether it is conducted by classes, lectures, and docent service in the Museum, or by extension work with visits from lecturers, armed with Museum material, to the schools in Greater Boston. The logical thing seemed, therefore, to create a Division of Education combining the activities of both Instruction and Extension, and this was done, and Mr. Dooley made the Head of it. The staffs are the same, and working in cheerful collaboration, but under the direction of one head. The experiment seems to be working well.

When Dr. Catherine E. Boyd, the Research Associate who had been constantly involved with the illustrative sets, left in 1942 to become a professor at Wells College, the pace of this project slackened, although lecturers in both divisions kept it alive on their own initiative. Claude Jean Chiasson, who had assisted Mrs. Webb with the arrangement of the free biweekly Sunday concerts in the Tapestry Gallery, and had taken over the direction of the series when she left, disappeared into the armed forces. Although budget cuts of more than 25 percent further reduced the staff, music was continued through a series of Victory Concerts for service men and women, sponsored by the USO Greater Boston Soldiers and Sailors Committee, for which able musicians gave their services. (Parenthetically one might note that the Department of Buildings and Grounds established early in 1943 a Victory Garden on a two-acre plot at the end of the Evans Wing, in which some forty museum employees and twenty friendly neighbors, many of whom had never before used garden tools, energetically grew their own vegetables. The museum plowed, harrowed, and fertilized the land, as well as building a 3-foot-high chain link fence of used materials around the area.)

The Division of Education kept a nucleus of the illustrative sets in circulation during the war, and initiated a scheme of assembling sets of twenty-five to thirty lantern slides, with accompanying notes and suggestions, that might be loaned for three-day periods to primary and secondary schools. A Children's Gallery, with picture and story books accessible, and with paintings and color reproductions on the walls, was experimentally arranged in 1943 in a large room in the basement that would accommodate groups of from twenty to seventy boys and girls. This space, however, soon had to be abandoned when the Museum School moved temporarily into odd corners of the museum.

During the thirties the Museum School, when it figured in the Director's report, was normally referred to in terms of change or crisis, while the Treasurer's reports all too often showed a deficit in receipts for operating expenses that had to be made good by the museum. The appointment of Alexandre Iacovleff as head of the Painting Department in 1934 had seemed to provide a solution, for he was a very likeable person with considerable ability as a draftsman. His attractive personality and exotic background — having grown up in St. Petersburg, he had escaped the Revolution by way of China in 1917 — captivated many people. In 1935 Harold Edgell reported:

> The School of the Museum has made conspicuous progress in the last year. Mr. Alexandre E. Iacovleff proved himself a brilliant teacher as soon as he arrived and has worked with increasing success ever since. Not only is he an able artist himself, but he has the ability to inspire students to enthusiastic emulation and the most energetic activity . . . . The School seems to be in a far healthier condition than it was a few years ago, and the Trustees owe this chiefly to the untiring and unpaid efforts of Mr. William James and Mr. William T. Aldrich. Mr. James has volunteered to do work which is really that of the Director of the School. Mr. Aldrich has taken charge as official head of the Design Department and has even given a regular course in the School . . . The enrollment in December 1935 was one hundred and sixty-nine as against one hundred and fifty-two at the same time last year, an increase of seventeen.

Such optimism was short-lived. Iacovleff, who had originally promised to teach for two years, agreed to continue for a third. In 1937, however, he asked for a year's leave in order to devote him-

self entirely to his own work. That autumn his place was filled by
Karl Zerbe, a refugee from Germany whom he had encountered in
Capri. As Iacovleff during his travels died suddenly in the Middle
East, Karl Zerbe's appointment became permanent. Edgell in his
report for 1937 remarked that it is "unfortunate that the School
should have such frequent changes in the teaching staff, especially
in drawing and painting"; he considered that there was not a proper
definition of the relation of one department to the other; that "in
short, the School seems to lack a definite policy." In view of this, he
proposed that the School be studied by a committee of trustees that
would bring in a report with recommendations.

The committee consisted of Dean William Emerson of M.I.T.,
Edward W. Forbes, Director of the Fogg Art Museum, and his
colleague the Associate Director, Professor Paul J. Sachs, with Edgell
as chairman *ex officio*. This group ground to a slow start, for Dean
Emerson was ill and Professor Sachs took off for Europe. By October
1938, however, it was meeting weekly. In 1939, on its recommendation, a Committee on the Museum School, consisting entirely of trustees, was formed, analogous to the Committee on the Museum. This
consisted of the Director, chairman, and the President and Treasurer
ex officiis, with William T. Aldrich, T. Jefferson Coolidge (now
back from the Treasury Department), William Emerson, and
Edward W. Forbes as appointed members. The old semiautonomous
Council of the Museum School, which William James had headed,
was transformed into Visitors to the Museum School, with William
Emerson as a Trustee Visitor. Thus, although its finances were still
treated separately, the school moved closer to a status similar to a department of the museum, with its affairs ultimately determined by the
trustees, and with its external friends organized as a Visiting Committee.

In the autumn of 1940 Russell Train Smith (Harvard A.B. 1927,
M. Arch. 1930), who had practiced architecture, engaged in archaeological work in Guatemala and Virginia, and had organized a department of Fine Arts at the University of North Carolina at Chapel
Hill, became head of the school. Karl Zerbe continued in charge of
painting, Ture Bengtz of drawing, Frederick W. Allen of sculpture;
instruction was also available in commercial design and in jewelry

and silversmithing. The faculty of the school joined in a cooperative effort to examine its curriculum and propose changes that would lead to a broader education for students of all departments. In 1941 the entire school was put on a four-year plan, with certain general requirements in each year, divided into two parts: the first a two-year general course for all regular students, and the second a comprehensive program of specialization in any one of the departments. In 1941 the graphic arts were introduced into the curriculum, and a studio in the basement converted into a printing shop with three etching presses, two wood-block presses, a lithographic press, and a press for use with type. Three of the presses were lent by the Department of Prints through the interest of Henry P. Rossiter. The following year a pottery workshop was installed, and a fifth year added to the curriculum for advanced students who were permitted to submit special projects for study and to select faculty supervisors.

The reorganization came at an unavoidably unfortunate time, for at the outbreak of war many of the older students and some of the staff were called away, with corresponding disruption of the curriculum and loss of tuition fees. For the year ending 30 June 1942 the Museum of Fine Arts was obliged to provide $16,264 toward the year's expenses of $41,272. The following year, when expenses were reduced to $33,357, the deficit was still $10,319. In 1943 it was concluded that the school building might appropriately be offered to the Army or Navy, and the classes somehow be temporarily housed in the museum. On 29 April 1943 Harold Edgell and Russell Smith made such a proposal to Rear Admiral R. A. Theobald, Commandant of the First Naval District. A rental was suggested that would not make money but would permit the school to move without adding a financial burden to the museum. Although the Navy was interested, negotiations proceeded with majestic deliberation. Finally on 1 March 1944 the building was turned over for use as a naval dispensary.

The Museum School thus returned under the roof of the Museum of Fine Arts, where it had not been since the departure from Copley Square. As the Japanese galleries had been closed for the duration of the war, these were assigned to school use, as were three of the ground floor galleries in the Evans Wing. By improvisation space was obtained elsewhere. The Children's Gallery and adjoining space was cleared for classes in ceramics; a basement rest room in the Evans Wing was transformed for classes in jewelry, while adequate, if not wholly desirable, space for a sculpture studio was rigged above the second-floor painting galleries, where the skylights provided good top lighting. These transformations were obtained at a cost of some $27,000. The results were surprisingly happy, for students came into close contact with the museum's collections. Although in the school year 1944–45 enrollment reached a five-year peak of 230 everyone cheerfully fitted in somehow. The next year there were 9 more students, and an operating cash surplus of $14.80 rather than a deficit; in the autumn of 1946, with returning veterans, the enrollment almost doubled to 441. When the school moved back to 230 The Fenway at the end of naval tenancy, certain classes were deliberately retained in the museum building to foster the closer relation between students and the collections that had developed during the years of makeshift. As Edgell remarked in his 1946 report:

> When the School is housed in a separate building, even though a short distance away, the temptation is for the students to go directly there, do their work there, and go directly home at the end of the day. When their program forces them to come into the Museum, their attention is called to what is on view and their work is increasingly inspired. If there is a reason for having a Museum School connected with the Museum, it is in the hope and expectation that the work of the students will be improved by the study of the works of art which the Museum contains. Anything which can further that study should be encouraged in all possible ways.

Looking back across a quarter of a century, it is diverting to note that the Museum School was taken over by the Navy in the same year when it was considered safe and prudent to bring back to the museum major works of art that had earlier been evacuated for reasons of safety. In June 1941, foreseeing the possibility of having to find safe storage for especially important objects in the event of war, the Director had communicated with Williams College, whose President, James Phinney Baxter, offered space in three fireproof buildings. Shortly after Pearl Harbor various van loads of objects moved quietly off to Williamstown, where air-conditioned and humidity-controlled hideouts had been prepared. The press cooperatively maintained a scrupulous silence about these transfers. Shelter space was also prepared in the museum basement to which objects left on display in Boston might be quickly moved if the threat of an air raid became imminent. To make room for these shelters a considerable amount of housecleaning was done. This emergency provided a convenient excuse for writing the owners of some three thousand objects that had been lent, asking that the museum be absolved from responsibility in case of damage in any way connected with the war. Thus some Bostonians suddenly became aware of paintings bought by their parents decades ago, which they had forgotten about. Although some objects were removed, many more were turned over to the museum as outright gifts. Among other things the superb Copley portrait of Mrs. James Russell (Katherine Graves) was given by Miss Elizabeth L. Dalton and Henry R. Dalton; Mrs. Harold Murdock gave an important celadon bowl that had long been on loan from her brother-in-law, the late Admiral Murdock, and Mrs. George R. Agassiz made a gift of some very beautiful Chinese pottery bowls in memory of her brother, C. R. Simpkins.

When objects were evacuated to Williamstown, various subterfuges were devised to fill the gaps in the collections. William J. Young and his assistants in the Research Laboratory made casts of such objects as the slate statue of Mycerinus and his Queen, and other Egyptian and classical sculptures, and colored them so skillfully that, had the labels not honestly described them as reproductions, ninety-nine out of a hundred visitors would not have realized that the originals had been removed. By 1944 it seemed safe to bring the evacuated objects back from Williamstown. This was done unobtrusively, although public announcement had to be made because of a friendly gesture made to Williams College in partial repayment of its helpful assistance. Professor Karl Weston, Director of the Williams College Museum, was permitted to exhibit in Williamstown some twenty-one of the most distinguished paintings that had been secreted there. Thus he had some small satisfaction for the agony of previous years of "lecturing on the art of France in the nineteenth century, with Renoir's Le Bal à Bougival in the next room, and not mentioning it," as Harold Edgell put it, "or lecturing on Flemish art in the seventeenth century, with Rubens' *Queen Tomyris with the Head of Cyrus* in the next room, and not mentioning it." The day after the last load of other objects had arrived in Boston, Professor Weston announced his exhibition, which attracted such interest that Williams College was tactful enough to suggest that it "now regarded itself in debt to the Museum rather than vice versa."

With one of William J. Young's skillful fascimiles, Dows Dunham carried out an experiment that he described in the February 1943 *Bulletin*. To settle the much disputed problem as to whether Egyptian sculpture provided specific likenesses of actual men and women, or generalizations with slight claim to individual portraiture, he dressed a cast of the Fourth-Dynasty limestone bust of Prince Ankh-haf in his own shirt, necktie, coat, and soft felt hat. The result so startlingly resembled a twentieth-century man who might be seen entering a Boston Oriental grocery near Washington Street and Broadway that it added "weight to the conviction that the best works of portraiture were real physical likenesses of actual people who lived and thought and had individuality during a great civilization of the remote past." Moreover, it should be noted that the coat and hat of Dows Dunham, who is six feet tall and weighs 160 pounds, fitted the ancient Egyptian perfectly.

During the museum's seventh decade, with the availability of the new temporary galleries that had been created out of the Renaissance Court, greater emphasis began to be placed upon temporary loan exhibitions. Inspired by the enthusiasm aroused by the Japanese exhibition of Italian art held at Burlington House in 1930. Edgell began in 1938 to try to arrange a similar great showing of Italian painting, which had always been his particular interest. W. G. Constable, the recently arrived Curator of Paintings, was an old hand at this kind of thing, having been closely involved in the great loan exhibition of Italian art held at Burlington House in 1930. Edgell went to Rome, hoping for an interview with Mussolini, but, as he arrived at the moment of the Austrian *Anschluss*, that did not materialize. Although some interest was shown by Italian authorities, nothing could be arranged before 1940. Before that year came, the war began and such international extravaganzas were out of the

question. However the special exhibition galleries were put to excellent use with material nearer at hand. Early in 1938, for example, the
three hundredth anniversary of the birth of John Singleton Copley
was commemorated by an exhibition of his paintings and drawings,
and by the museum's publication of Barbara Neville Parker and
Anne Bolling Wheeler's *John Singleton Copley: American Portraits
in Oil, Pastel, and Miniature with Biographical Sketches*. At the end
of the year the galleries were used for an exhibition of two Boston
painters, intimately associated with the Museum School, Edmund C.
Tarbell (who had died in mid-summer 1938) and Frank W. Ben-
son. In 1939 an exhibition of *Paintings, Drawings, and Prints from
Private Collections in New England*, arranged by Messrs. Constable,
Rossiter, and Cunningham, was installed as part of a cooperative
attempt by seven New England art museums to show strangers, attracted by the New York World's Fair, works of art that would
normally be difficult to see.

The 1940 medieval exhibition, arranged by Georg Swarzenski,
attracted serious visitors from many parts of the United States, but it
produced no pandemonium comparable to the two-month display of
the *Miniature European Period Rooms* designed by Mrs. James Ward
Thorne, which had previously been shown in Chicago and at the
World's Fair in San Francisco and New York. On the first Sunday
of the Thorne exhibition, 6,559 people swarmed in in four hours;
the queue ran half the length of the Tapestry Gallery, and closing
had to be delayed so that those who had stood in line might see what
they had waited for. Altogether this exhibition drew 154,831 visitors.
Such success brought its problems, for Edgell in his 1941 report,
anticipating a showing of Mrs. Thorne's American rooms in 1942,
suggested:

> The Trustees might consider the possibility of having pay days
> which would thin the crowd, and make it easier for friends of the
> Museum to get in with less delay on payment of a small fee. The
> Captain of the Watch, Mr. McLaughlin, has also devised schemes
> for a more efficient handling of the crowd when it arrives. Perhaps
> the Superintendent may even evolve some scheme to protect the
> floor of the galleries which reminded one a little after the close of
> the Exhibition of the tan bark of a circus ring after the show is over.

More sober efforts of 1941 were *Portraits through Forty-five Centuries*, a collaborative effort between departments of material drawn from within the museum, of which Lacey D. Caskey was in charge; Miss Gertrude Townsend's *New England Embroidery before 1800*, in which Mrs. Samuel Cabot and other visitors to the Textile Department collaborated; and a memorial exhibition of the work of William McGregor Paxton. When Mrs. Thorne's *American Miniature Rooms* were shown for three months in 1942, twenty-five cents admission was charged on all mornings except Saturdays from nine until one; thus in the mornings the crowds were bearable and enough money was collected to pay most of the expense of the exhibition.

In Chapter XI it was noted that attendance figures were steadily rising during the nineteen twenties and had reached 406,427 in 1924. The following year the number reached 496,883 — the highest ever — probably because of the completion of the Sargent murals and the memorial exhibition following his death. In 1926 it dropped to 417,098; in 1927 to 351,775, in 1928 to 335,808. Widespread interest in the new Decorative Arts Wing raised 1929 attendance to 394,091. For the next four years the figure fluctuated between 347,520 and 389,105. Although in 1934 a new record of 526,378 was set, the half million mark was not again attained for seven years. Between 1935 and 1950 the low point was 405,521 (1937) and the high 498,974 (1936). Very clearly Mrs. Thorne's Miniature Rooms were responsible for the 512,854 visitors who came in 1941 and the 546,564 of 1942. In 1943 there were 448,986 visitors; in 1944 435,345; and in 1945 463,768.

It was noted in the previous chapter that the Museum of Fine Arts weathered the depression following the 1929 crash remarkably well because of the foresightedness of its Treasurer and of the constant receipt of new gifts and bequests. Although Mrs. Robert Dawson Evans had died in 1917, her estate still produced gratifying surprises close to two decades later. Among the securities that the museum had received from it were 352,365 shares of Yuba Consolidated Gold Fields stock, which were for some years carried on the books at zero. Nevertheless, between 1931 and 1937 dividends aggregating $636,019 were received from the Yuba stock and were credited to the principal of the Evans Fund. By May 1937 this once problematical inheritance had improved to such an extent that, by vote of the Finance Committee, a value of two dollars per share was placed upon the museum's holdings. Thus the principal of the Evans Fund was further increased by $704,730 and the stock was restored to respectability among the museum's investments. Subsequently the major part of the Yuba stock was sold at four dollars per share or more, thus further increasing the museum's indebtedness to Mrs. Evans. Over the past forty years a considerable part of the general expense of operation, as well as the purchase of numerous works of art, were made possible by the Maria Antoinette Evans Fund and the other great bequest of Mrs. Frederick T. Bradbury. For a number of years under Mrs. Bradbury's will the Museum of Fine Arts received very respectable dividends from the Potter Drug and Chemical Corporation, the makers of Cuticura soap, which her brother, George Robert White, had operated. At least once a year trustees of the museum would find at their places, when they arrived for a meeting, a box containing samples of Cuticura soap and shampoo. I always enjoyed the spectacle of various Bostonians frugally carrying home their free samples from trustees meetings, and wondered what they did with them. I certainly never used mine, although I was always grateful to Cuticura and to a once-dubious gold stock for their ensuing role in sustaining the high purposes of the museum.

Thanks to these and other bequests the income of the museum steadily grew, but the increase in operating expenses always grew a little more rapidly. The annual subscriptions, which had tumbled from $94,487 in 1929 down into the thirty thousands in the early thirties, never got more than a few hundred dollars above the $40,031 that was received in 1945. Annual deficits were usual. In 1935, with operating income of $392,342, there was a deficit of $62,357; although the following year, when income had mounted to $586,619, the red figure was only $14,175. Then suddenly for four years there was instead a surplus, a state of affairs unfamiliar since 1899, when the millennial equilibrium achieved by generous gifts was soon unbalanced by the purchase of Fenway land for the present building. I attribute this not only to improving times, but to the election on 21 January 1937 as a trustee and Treasurer of William Henry Claflin (Harvard A.B. 1915, LL.D. 1949), following the death of William Crowninshield Endicott. Bill Claflin has never tolerated deficits, even of the relatively safe kind that some Boston institutional treasurers encourage in the hope of inspiring further gifts. His election as Treasurer of Harvard College two years later made it necessary for him to give up the treasurership of the museum, even though he continued as a trustee and member of the Finance Committee. He was succeeded by a close friend, Robert Baldwin (Harvard A.B. 1917), an officer of the State Street Trust Company, who was elected a trustee and Treasurer on 19 January 1939. Under his direction there were surpluses in 1939 and 1940, and in 1943 and 1944.

Although incidental references to changes in the board of trustees have been made, it is now time to review systematically what has occurred since the account in Chapter XI. The balance of the board remained much as it had been since 1870, for normally when a trustee died or resigned he was succeeded by another who brought similar qualities to the scene. Thus, with businessmen, T. Jefferson Coolidge was elected in 1921 to the vacancy created by the death of Theodore Nelson Vail, while Edwin Farnham Greene, a textile man, was elected in 1923 to George Robert White's place. The architect William Truman Aldrich in 1925 took the place of the painter Thomas Allen. When President Eliot, the last of the 1870 incorporators, died in 1926, he was succeeded the following January by another Harvard administrator, George Harold Edgell. Professor Charles Sprague Sargent was followed by Robert Treat Paine, 2nd, whose magnificent gifts of paintings and the Knole tapestry made him a benefactor of the museum. On the resignation of Edwin Farnham Greene in 1928, Alvan Tufts Fuller, then Governor of Massachusetts, who was both a motor car dealer and a collector of paintings, was elected. The architect Henry Forbes Bigelow was succeeded by the architect Charles Donagh Maginnis in 1930; Holker Abbott by Samuel Cabot in 1931; Augustus Hemenway by Richard Cushing Paine (son of Robert Treat Paine, 2nd) in 1932; Morris Gray by Professor Paul Joseph Sachs, in 1932. When William Endicott resigned in 1935, Edward Jackson Holmes, who had just relinquished the directorship, returned to the board. Collector succeeded collector when William Goodwin Russell Allen took the place of

Denman W. Ross in 1936, and again in 1944 when Philip Hofer (Harvard A.B. 1921) followed Robert Treat Paine, 2nd. It has already been noted how William Crowninshield Endicott was succeeded by William H. Claflin, and how George Peabody Gardner filled the place of his father in 1940.

The annual institutional appointments often followed a similar pattern, for in 1927, when the architect J. Randolph Coolidge retired to Center Sandwich, New Hampshire, the Boston Athenæum designated the architect Charles Kimball Cummings in his stead. Similarly presidents of the Massachusetts Institute of Technology usually filled one of the Institute's appointments. M.I.T. designated the engineer Edwin Sibley Webster in 1926 to succeed the engineer Desmond Fitzgerald. The patterns were not always completely parallel, for among the Harvard designees Dr. William Sturgis Bigelow was succeeded in 1927 by the lawyer Richard Cary Curtis; the artist and collector John Templeman Coolidge in 1945 by the publisher and anthropologist Donald Scott; the classical archaeologist George H. Chase in 1945 by the lawyer Charles Allerton Coolidge. When Charles Knowles Bolton, Librarian of the Boston Athenæum, retired in 1933, Edward Motley Pickman, historian, was appointed in his place. Although the real estate broker George Edward Cabot was designated by the Boston Athenæum in 1934, following the death of the architect Alexander Wadsworth Longfellow, on Cabot's death in 1946 his successor was another architect, Robert Peabody Bellows, a nephew of President Eliot.

Although Governor Fuller was seldom, if ever, seen at a trustees meeting, the museum rejoices in some of the pictures from his collection, as gifts or loans from his heirs. A number of the trustees who were active collectors have repeatedly wandered in and out of these pages as donors of great works of art and active friends and collaborators of the curators. Although there was always a decent quota of businessmen, bankers, and manufacturers, they never predominated, because of the considerable number of men in the learned professions and of officers of universities. In this respect the board of the Museum of Fine Arts has differed from the standard table of organization of institutions in many American cities. It has been different also in the character of many of its principal benefactors.

Frequently great American collectors are men who, having prospered by their own efforts, have later in life acquired works of art from the principal dealers to reinforce the position they have made for themselves. Robert Dawson Evans, George Robert White, and Governor Fuller were men of this type, and the museum has benefited from their collections. But mostly the great Boston collectors were men and women of inherited property, who were free to devote the greater part of their lives to the study and collecting of works of art. We have already seen the multifarious activities of Denman W. Ross, of Edward P. Warren, of Edward Jackson Holmes and his wife and mother, of the Bullards and Spauldings, of William Sturgis Bigelow, and Charles Goddard Weld, and of the Karoliks. Collecting in this manner produces more personal and unified results than even the best equipped safaris into the international art market. The friendship of such collectors for the Museum of Fine Arts has given the institution a special quality rarely found in the United States. Fortunately, such collectors are not an extinct race. Still others will appear in later chapters.

CHAPTER XIV

The Spaulding and Karolik Collections of Paintings

In the autumn of 1945 the Asiatic, Painting, and Print departments collaborated in a temporary exhibition, drawn entirely from their own holdings, entitled *A Thousand Years of Landscape East and West,* in which paintings, prints, and drawings of many countries and periods — having no other unity than subject matter — were juxtaposed. The hanging of this heterogeneous variety of works of art, which in less skillful hands might have resulted in chaos, was left to Kojiro Tomita and his assistants, Robert P. Dart and Robert Treat Paine, Jr., who had returned only a few weeks earlier from three and a half years in the Navy. The result was an exhibition of extraordinary unity and beauty, of which Harold Edgell wrote:

Before the doors were opened we had feared that the delicate landscapes of China and Japan might be overwhelmed by the paintings of the Renaissance and modern times in Western Europe with their vivid color and heavy frames. This danger did not materialize. Indeed, if anything, the Asiatic paintings called more attention to themselves than the Western. It was found that one could place a Christian painting of the Italian Renaissance between a Taoist painting on the right and a Buddhist painting on the left and have the group not inharmonious.

TRIPTYCH OF CRUCIFIXION, ST. NICHOLAS AND ST. GREGORY. Tempera on panel.
Duccio di Buoninsegna, Sienese, 1255–1319. *Grant Walker and Charles Potter
Kling funds. 45.880*

Some of the charm of this exhibition is perpetuated in W. G. Constable's "Random Reflections from a Landscape Exhibition," published in the February 1946 *Bulletin*.

To the Department of Paintings the year 1945 was, however, most notable for the purchase of a triptych of the *Crucifixion* by Duccio di Buoninsegna (ca. 1255–1319), the first great master of the Sienese school. The painting was known to have been in the Ottley Collection in England at the end of the eighteenth century. Early in this century it was bought by J. P. Morgan who kept it in his country house in England; after his death it was purchased at auction by a dealer from whom the museum acquired it. Before buying it, tests made with infra-red, ultraviolet, and X-rays proved that the condition of the painting was almost perfect; subsequent cleaning indicated that the panel was in an even more extraordinary state of preservation than the tests had indicated.

W. G. Constable's annual reports as Curator of Paintings not only record such notable purchases as the Duccio, but contain frequent references to contemporary paintings, given to or bought for the Provisional Acquisitions Gallery established in 1941. This device was developed to open the way to experimental acquisition of modern work, especially of young and comparatively unknown painters, in the hope that the museum might "present a cross section of contemporary activity, while guarding against the danger of being permanently saddled with acquisitions whose interest is only temporary." That the Museum of Fine Arts has never suffered from stultifying unanimity among its learned curators will be seen from a passage in Ananda K. Coomaraswamy's essay, "Why exhibit works of art?" delivered before the American Association of Museums in May 1941.

> It is unnecessary for Museums to exhibit the work of living artists, which are not in imminent danger of destruction; or at least, if such works are exhibited, it should be clearly understood that the Museum is really advertising the artist and acting on behalf of the art dealer or middleman whose business it is to find a market for the artist; the only difference being that while the Museum does the same kind of work as the dealer, it makes no profit. On the other hand, that a living artist should wish to be "hung" or "shown" in a Museum can only be due to his need or his vanity. For things are made normally for certain purposes and certain places to which they are appropriate, and not simply "for exhibition"; and because whatever is thus custom-made, i.e., made by an artist for a consumer, is controlled by certain requirements and kept in order. Whereas, as Mr. Steinfels has recently remarked, "Art which is only intended to be hung on the walls of a Museum is one kind of art that need not consider its relationship to its ultimate surroundings. The artist can paint anything he wishes, and if the Curators and Trustees like it well enough they will line it up on the wall with all the other curiosities."

So, notwithstanding the sharp tongue of their learned and reflective colleague, the Curator of Paintings and the trustees of the Museum of Fine Arts in 1941 began a continuing process of acquiring and provisionally exhibiting contemporary pictures.

ACHILLES ON SKYROS. Nicolas Poussin. *Robert J. Edwards Fund.* 46.463

Dr. Coomaraswamy defined what should be admitted to a museum as "ancient or unique works of art which are no longer in their original place or no longer used as was originally intended, and are therefore in danger of destruction by neglect or otherwise." From 1945 to 1955 so many paintings that met this exacting standard reached the museum by gift or purchase that only a few can be mentioned here. In 1946, for example, a second Poussin, *Achilles on the Island of Skyros*, purchased through the Edwards Fund, came to keep *Mars and Venus* company. As William R. Tyler was by then at the Department of State, this picture was unable to express its pleasure at being in Boston as gracefully as the first Poussin had in 1940. In the same year Richard C. Paine gave, in memory of his father Robert Treat Paine, 2nd, Manet's first painting of his favorite model, Victorine Meurend, while Robert Hall McCormick of Chicago gave an immense Spanish retablo with scenes from the life of Saint Peter by the fifteenth-century Valencian painter Martín de Soria.

Titian's *St. Catherine of Alexandria*, purchased in 1948, provided, with his portrait of 1540–1545 entitled *A Gentleman with a Book* (bought in 1943) and with Mrs. Gardner's *The Rape of Europa* at Fenway Court, an opportunity for Bostonians to see masterpieces in three phases of this great artist's style: in religious art, in portraiture, and in mythology. The *Combat between Carnival and Lent* of Peter Breughel the Elder, bought in 1949, brought lively Flemish secular satire to the galleries, while two imposing French twelfth-century frescoes of the *Flight into Egypt* and the *Visitation*, acquired the same year, provided a harmonious counterpart to the great Catalonian apse paintings from Santa Maria de Mur. Thomas Gainsborough's *The Mushroom Girl*, bought in 1953, and Lucas van Leyden's *Moses after Striking the Rock in the Wilderness*, acquired in 1954, deserve particular mention.

ST. CATHERINE OF ALEXANDRIA. Titian. *1948 Purchase Fund and Otis Norcross Fund. 48.499*

Purchases were by no means confined to masterpieces by great names. Often pictures were bought that represented some special knowledge or enthusiasm of the department staff. W. G. Constable's wide knowledge of Italian painting was a constant resource, while the scholarly studies of Mrs. Haven Parker, who was given the title of Assistant in American Painting in 1946, brought to the department many people particularly interested in that field. In reporting the purchase in 1949 of a small altarpiece of the early sixteenth-century Danube School and an Austrian painting of the same period by Rueland Frueauf the Elder of the *Education of Jesus*, "a work of lyrical sentiment and of rare delicacy in handling," W. G. Constable noted: "Both these discoveries (for they are nothing less) are due to Dr. Hanns Swarzenski."

THE EDUCATION OF JESUS. Rueland Frueauf the Elder, Austrian, 15th century. *Ernest W. Longfellow Fund. 49.1076*

At the end of the war, upon returning from naval service, the Assistant Curator of Paintings, Charles C. Cunningham, had resigned to become Director of the Wadsworth Atheneum in Hartford. For two years Richard B. K. McLanathan (Harvard A.B. 1938, Ph.D. 1951), a junior fellow in the Harvard Society of Fellows from 1943 to 1946, served as an Assistant in the department. When he resigned in 1948 to accept a fellowship in Rome, Dr. Hanns Swarzenski, son of Georg, was appointed Fellow for Research. This able medievalist, who took after his father in many ways, including the ability to discover late medieval and renaissance objects in unlikely places and know what they were, had come from Germany to Princeton when his post with the Prussian Administration of Castles and Gardens at Schloss Monbijou became untenable because of Nazi machinations. During the war he had temporarily been in charge of sculpture at the National Gallery in Washington. Although he often spent half the year lecturing at the Warburg Institute at the University of London, where his knowledge of medieval art history was highly esteemed, Hanns Swarzenski continued in the Department of Paintings until November 1953. The purchase in 1950 of a fourteenth-century Bohemian painting of the *Death of the Virgin* has the sound of a Swarzenski "find."

So far as the Department of Paintings was concerned, the most dramatic event of the years immediately following the war became known only after the death on 23 January 1948 of John Taylor Spaulding, whose will provided one of the greatest bequests ever received by the museum. In Chapter XI the 1921 gift has been noted of the superb collection of Japanese prints that he and his older brother, William Stuart Spaulding, had assembled as a result of a trip to Japan in 1909. As these brothers, who are ranked as Great Benefactors of the Museum of Fine Arts, exemplify so completely the Boston type of collector, their personal history is worth noting. They were the sons of Mahlon Day Spaulding, who lived at 99 Beacon Street and, through the firm of Nash, Spaulding and Co., owned and operated the Revere Sugar Refinery. William Stuart Spaulding, born on 17 February 1865, after being graduated from Harvard College in 1888, worked for the Revere Sugar Refinery. After 1905, when the refinery was bought by the United Fruit Company and Nash,

Spaulding and Co. was dissolved, his business activities were confined to the care of family trusts. John Taylor Spaulding, born on 24 April 1870, attended Harvard College in 1888–1890 and the Harvard Law School in 1890–1891; although he received no Harvard degree, he was considered as a member of the class of 1892. He too worked for the Revere Sugar Refinery until the 1905 takeover, after which, like his older brother, he concerned himself only with family trusts and collecting. As both brothers married late — William in 1909 and John in 1927 — they lived at 99 Beacon Street in the winter, with their widowed mother, until her death, and in the summer at a great house in Prides Crossing, called "Sunset Rock," that they had built for her.

The brothers owned jointly for some years a 200-foot twin-screw steam yacht, *Isis*, of 277 tons gross. They traveled extensively, and through their travels became collectors. Just as they were leaving Japan in 1909, a friend gave them a print by Hiroshige that fired their imagination. Although they had no time to search for more before leaving Yokohama, on their return to Boston they started to look for Japanese prints. The architect Frank Lloyd Wright went to Japan in 1913 as an emissary of the Spaulding brothers, with a considerable sum of money at his disposal for the purchase of prints. In a few years their collection numbered some six thousand prints, among which were many supreme examples. It also included the remarkable group of ninety-six drawings by Hokusai (1760–1849) representing the street life and customs of Edo (Tokyo) in 1819, as seen by the artist. A number of these have been reproduced in *Day and Night in Four Seasons by Hokusai*, a Museum of Fine Arts Picture Book prepared in 1957 by Kojiro Tomita.

After William S. Spaulding married Katrina Fairlee in 1909, they lived at 99 Beacon Street, with John occupying bachelor quarters on an upper floor. Although the brothers officially gave their print collection to the museum in 1921, it remained for some years in Beacon Street, as they had retained a life interest in it. In 1927 John T. Spaulding, then fifty-six, married Marion A. Coleman. They then took over 99 Beacon Street while the William Spauldings wintered for a time in Santa Barbara, California, and summered near Upper St. Regis Lake, New York. In 1934 they settled at 45 Beacon Street, the house Bulfinch had built in 1806 for Harrison Gray Otis.

Long before William S. Spaulding's death on 15 August 1937, his brother John, finding that the law of diminishing returns had set in so far as superior additions to the Japanese print collection were concerned, had turned his attention to paintings. In 1941 the prints were physically transferred to the museum. His lifelong friend, Charles Hovey Pepper, who was chairman of the Art Committee of the Boston Art Club, induced John to join the club and go on the committee with him. As the other members left the arranging of exhibitions to these two, Spaulding and Pepper frequently went to New York, Philadelphia, and Washington to choose pictures for shows they were arranging for the gallery in the handsome Back Bay clubhouse at the corner of Newbury and Dartmouth streets that the architect W. Ralph Emerson had designed in 1881–82 for this now defunct organization. In this way they met many American painters — among them George Bellows, Rockwell Kent, Eugene Speicher, George Luks, Leon Kroll, Robert Henri, Jonas Lie, and Gari Melchers — and John Spaulding bought some of their works for his own collection. From the Guild of Boston Artists he bought one of the Vermont oils of Aldro T. Hibbard, who had been Paige Scholar of the Museum School in 1913. He greatly admired and bought pictures by Arthur Goodwin, which represented Boston in rain, fog, and snow, as well as water colors by Winslow Homer, Dodge Macknight, and Edward Hopper. As the Boston Art Club shows sometimes had modern French paintings, lent by dealers, John Spaulding, whose chief specialized knowledge was in Japanese prints, was instinctively attracted to Degas, Monet, Renoir, Van Gogh, Matisse, and Gauguin who had been considerably influenced by this art. Pepper recalled, of his friend's collecting habits:

> He was a satisfactory client for when he had decided that a painting was one which he wanted, he bought it. Having bought it, he kept it. He rarely exchanged a painting which he owned for another. He believed the time to buy an item he required was when the opportunity occurred. If the price was right he bought. He did not haggle. Dealers often made him a special price because they knew his habit and because they wished the work in his collection.

Thus when he became enchanted with one of a pair of Chardin still-lifes in an exhibition at Wildenstein's, the firm gladly broke the pair

BRONZE GOBLET AND FRUIT. Jean Baptiste Simeon Chardin. *Bequest of John T. Spaulding.* 48.527

to let him have the *Bronze Goblet and Fruit* that he particularly fancied. To continue with Pepper's reminiscences:

The first modern French painting which Mr. Spaulding bought was a sketch by Degas. It was of a red-headed ballet dancer against a vermilion background. It was in a collection brought to Boston by Durand-Ruel. Each year this firm brought paintings to the Brooks Reed Gallery on Arlington Street, next to the Arlington Street Church. With this beginning, room was made on the walls of Mr. Spaulding's home at 99 Beacon Street for more and more French Impressionist pictures. Other Degas' were added, none more satisfactory than his *Degas' Father Listening to Pagans* . . .

Mr. Spaulding bought when the picture he felt he needed came up, as we have said. His handsome flower-piece by Courbet he bought in Geneva. A magazine showed a black and white reproduction of Sisley's *Early Snow at Louveciennes* as a dealer's adver-

tisement. Mr. Spaulding wrote to the dealer in London to know if
the painting was likely to be seen in America. The dealer wrote
that he was so sure that Mr. Spaulding would like it that he would
send it to Boston at his own expense and if Mr. Spaulding did not
like it he could send it back costs paid. Mr. Spaulding bought the
picture — a very choice Sisley. He had another Sisley: a still-life
of *Grapes and Nuts* on a white cloth, one of two known still-lifes
by this artist. His Toulouse-Lautrec, *Woman in a Studio*, is much
more finished than most of this artist's work, painted on a fine
canvas and including not only the timid model but small sketches
on the studio wall and, in the right hand corner, a study of the
artist himself. Mrs. Coburn of Chicago [the larger part of whose
collection is at the Art Institute] bought the picture but returned

WOMAN IN A STUDIO. Henri de Toulouse-Lautrec. *Bequest of
John T. Spaulding. 48.605*

it because of the criticism of a friend. She regretted this soon after and told Mr. Stransky [of Wildenstein's] that she had decided to take it. When he said he had just sold it to Mr. Spaulding, she was greatly disappointed.

John Spaulding bought small still-lifes by Cézanne and Manet, and hung them with his Chardin where he could see them from his reading chair. He built up a group of six superb Renoirs. By Gauguin he had a still-life, a French landscape once owned by Pissarro, and a Tahitian landscape that was one of the artist's last pictures. His

CHILDREN ON THE SEASHORE. Pierre Auguste Renoir.
Bequest of John T. Spaulding. 48.594

LA BERCEUSE. Vincent van Gogh. *Bequest of John T. Spaulding. 48.548*

two Van Goghs were a *Street in Anvers* and the powerful *La Berceuse*. So the collection grew until even the ample walls of 99 Beacon Street — a high-ceilinged house designed by George M. Dexter and built in 1852 — were full to overflowing.

After Mrs. John T. Spaulding died on 11 June 1943, he stayed on alone in 99 Beacon Street, and, although he no longer lived in the great house high above the sea at Prides Crossing, he had it meticulously kept up, for he enjoyed going there and walking through the grounds, since, as Charles H. Pepper put it, "like a fine old picture, he loved it." When the construction of the Storrow Drive threatened the continued survival of 99 Beacon Street, John Spaulding moved to the Ritz-Carlton Hotel, where he died on 23 January 1948. He had twice declined the suggestion that he become a trustee of the Museum of Fine Arts; indeed he had never served on the Visiting Committee of either the Department of Painting or Asiatic Art. When he bought pictures, he brought them to the museum to be photographed and enjoyed by the staff, although he never sought their advice before making a purchase. He had lent all his French paintings for exhibition from 7 May 1931 to 27 October 1932. Although there were hopes, nothing of the future of the pictures was known until John Spaulding's will revealed that they were bequeathed to the Museum of Fine Arts.

With great rejoicing, the Spaulding Collection was displayed in the seven Special Galleries from 26 May to 7 November 1948. With the pictures were shown two Chinese ceramic statues of the seventeenth century, the Hokusai sketches, a rotating selection of Japanese prints, and some of the large group of Japanese sword-mounts that the brothers had given in 1937. A catalogue was published, with the essay "John T. Spaulding as a Collector" by Charles Hovey Pepper, from which I have quoted. Harold Edgell in his 1948 report noted:

> Mr. Spaulding was a collector of the finest taste and the keenest discernment. He exercised his own judgment and it seemed always unerring. Obviously, though he never said so, he had in mind complementing the Museum's collections. For example, we had received a superb male portrait by Van Gogh, *The Postman Roulin*, from Mr. Robert Treat Paine, 2nd. Mr. Spaulding left us an equally superb female portrait, *La Berceuse*, as well as a beautiful landscape. We already had a magnificent Tahitian Gauguin; Mr. Spaulding left us not only a small Tahitian painting but a Breton landscape which we needed, and a splendid still-life. One could elaborate on this theme almost indefinitely.

The background of the other great gift of the nineteen forties, the M. and M. Karolik Collection of American Paintings, 1815 to 1865, was almost the exact opposite. It was assembled with the foreknowledge and active cooperation of the Museum of Fine Arts. Indeed Maxim Karolik began his letter to the Director of 10 December 1945 offering the collection thus:

For the second time in seven years I am beginning my letter to you with the same exclamation: Our dream is becoming a reality!

The first time I wrote it to you on December 7th, 1938, when my wife and I were ready to offer our eighteenth century collection to the Museum of Fine Arts.

If you remember our general talk about nineteenth century American painting, you can see that our 1945 dream is simply a continuation of the 1938 one, with the only difference that this time I "Dreamt dreams" with Mr. Constable, instead of with Mr. Hipkiss. It is impossible for me to say which of the two dreams was the sweeter.

John Spaulding had enjoyed teasing the Museum of Fine Arts by holding his hand close to his chest. He bought pictures that not only pleased him, but would supplement the museum's holdings, and bequeathed them, knowing that they would be put to excellent use in decades when he could no longer enjoy them. Maxim Karolik's temperament was different. He had an idea, and it was a good one, but he wanted to be sure that everyone knew what it was. To be certain that the Museum of Fine Arts shared it, he collected in close consultation with the curators. As the decorative arts predominated in the first collection, Edwin J. Hipkiss was his chief ally in the years before 1938; as the second collection consisted exclusively of paintings, W. G. Constable succeeded to the role of guide, philosopher, friend, and — let us never forget — patient listener. For Maxim Karolik was an exuberant extrovert, who enjoyed the sound of his own voice so much that he seldom said a thing once if five times could be managed. But when you got used to his manner, you found a good deal of solid sense behind the rhetoric, as is the case in the following paragraphs of his letter to Harold Edgell.

You and Mr. Constable know well what our present collection of nineteenth century American paintings means. You know also the reason why it is made. Now, after we have finally removed the rigidity from the deadly word "permanent" and agreed that Father Time makes "stipulations" and "conditions" die a lingering death, I can tell you that my wife and I are ready to offer the collection to the people through the Museum of Fine Arts. But before doing so, we want the Trustees and the people of Boston also to know why this collection is made and what is its purpose. Here are our reasons:

It was made for one purpose only: To show what happened in this country in the art of painting in the period of half a century — from 1815 to 1865 — and to show the beginning and the growth of American landscape and genre painting. The aim was to make a collection not of "Americana" for the antiquarian, but of American art for the nation.

Our approach to this collection was primarily from the artistic point of view. It was the same approach as that to our eighteenth century collection — now belonging to your Museum. Each painting was judged and acquired on the basis of artistic merit. Names and history were of secondary importance.

We discarded the motto of the fashionable connoisseur: "Tell me who the painter is and I will tell you whether the painting is good." Our motto was: "Tell me whether the painting is good and I will not care who the painter is."

People who would like to see representative works by the well-known and much-praised painters will find them in this collection; but they are incidental to a larger purpose, which is to tell the whole story through that period — the story of the known, the little-known, and the unknown artists. Only an ensemble of all types of creative work, I believe, can adequately show what happened in that period. The well-known names — the popular Stars — are only part of the story.

I know there are some sensitive aesthetes who say that nothing of importance happened in the 1815–1865 period. I have had ardent debates with them on this subject during the past eight years. They usually grant that Copley and Stuart were "quite good" and then they jump to Homer, Whistler, and Eakins and accept them as "very fine." But what happened in between is lost to them.

Now that the collection is completed, I am inclined to let it speak for itself. I believe that it will show how wrong the doubters and sceptics were. Many of them, I am glad to say, now candidly admit that they had not known what happened in that period.

In accepting the 233 paintings of the second Karolik Collection, the trustees agreed to exhibit them as a whole for at least five years from the time they were first put upon display, so that the relations of the pictures to each other might show the nature of American

painting during the fifty years that the Karoliks were bent on eluci-
dating. Thereafter the pictures might be moved, occasionally lent, or
hung in other galleries in juxtaposition with other pictures. But as
there simply was not the space available, the paintings as received
were placed in storage while the architectural firm of Leland and
Larsen explored possible ways of gaining the necessary room. Their
first proposal, considered in June 1948, involved removing the present wall of the connecting link between the Huntington Avenue and
the Evans Wings and building out in the court an addition — rising
to the bottom of the clerestory of the Tapestry Gallery — that would
provide basement offices and two stories of roomy galleries. As the
necessity of making a prolonged study of artificial lighting involved
considerable delay, the Director, the architect, and various members
of the staff availed themselves of the generosity of the Metropolitan
Museum, which had appropriated $30,000 for experiments in light-
ing in some of their small galleries, to study the New York results
in detail. After doing so, the architect, Joseph D. Leland, and the
consultant electrical engineer, Willard W. Thompson, conducted
further studies which, Harold Edgell said in his 1949 report,

> went ahead and, I think it is fair to say, beyond what had been
> done in the Metropolitan. It was a long and arduous matter. Equip-
> ment had to be made specially, redesigned, and readjusted. The
> results, however, fully justified the expense and the delay. It is
> always dangerous to say that lighting is perfect but the resultant
> lighting seemed as nearly perfect as one is likely to attain. The
> coffering gives an impression of glass lighted by daylight, the lateral
> strips afford the maximum of cool light, bull's-eyes with incan-
> descent lighting can be directed at any wall or object and can afford
> the fullest of warm lighting if turned on to the maximum capacity
> or tempered with the rheostats if some warm lighting, but not too
> much, is required. One can, almost literally by electrical control,
> make the sun come out in the gallery or make it disappear beneath
> a cloud. Members of the Board, members of the Staff, experts from
> the Metropolitan and from the General Electric Company have
> all inspected the lighting and the Director has not heard one dis-
> senting voice in its general praise.

With this problem solved, plans changed, for it seemed illogical to make an addition to the building when so large an area as the one surviving Cast Court, to the east of the main staircase, was being inefficiently used. By getting rid of the last of the plaster casts, and relying entirely upon artificial lighting, the architects were able to propose in this space a new three-story structure, with four good galleries and a vestibule on both the first and second floors and with studios on the third that would accommodate a good many of the teaching activities of the Division of Education. At the same time, it was proposed to move the offices of the Department of Decorative Arts to space on the court level of the Decorative Arts Wing, thus releasing space on the first floor for the Leslie Lindsey Mason Collection of Musical Instruments, previously shown inadequately in a court floor gallery that had been closed since the war. The space that they vacated could, with redecoration, become a suitable gallery for the collection of rigged ship models, which had evolved chiefly through the gifts of J. Templeman Coolidge.

This construction was undertaken in 1950, and by the summer of 1951 the M. and M. Karolik Collection of American Paintings was being installed in the ten new galleries that had replaced the Cast Court. These were opened with a private view on 2 October 1951. Alas, one of the donors was absent, for Mrs. Karolik had died in April 1948, but her husband was at last able to see handsomely exhibited the paintings that they confidently believed would convince the world that the years 1815 to 1865 were something more than an extended *dies non* in the history of American art. The collection was immediately open to the public, which responded with enthusiasm. Attendance in November 1951 was more than ten thousand higher than in the same month the previous year. Harold Edgell reported: "Mr. Karolik's faith in the importance of what he had planned was more than fulfilled, and the Director hopes and believes that he realizes the gratitude of the Trustees and their appreciation of his imagination and his success."

The Karolik Collection brought together an extraordinary cross section of American painting, for it included the work of the esteemed and the unknown, the European-trained and the self-taught; the one common denominator was that each picture had some artistic quality that had excited the admiration of the Karoliks and of W. G. Constable. Here, to take the first three letters of the alphabet as a sample, were works by Washington Allston, Victor Gifford Audubon (son of John James Audubon the naturalist), the steamship painter James Bard, Albert Bierstadt, George Caleb Bingham, Thomas Birch, John S. Blunt, David Gilmour Blythe, the self-taught De Witt Clinton Boutelle, an almost unknown Edward Bowers and an equally hazy John Brewster, George Loring Brown, John Gadsby Chapman, Frederick Edwin Church, James Goodwin Clonney, Charles Codman, who began as a sign painter, Thomas Cole, and James Francis Cropsey, as well as a rich showing of that prolific artist, "Anonymous Painter," for Maxim Karolik and W. G. Constable did not disdain the more competent reaches of what is sometimes called "folk art." In Karolik's 1945 letter, he had remarked:

A STREET IN WINTER: EVENING. Anonymous, American, 19th century.
Karolik Collection. 47.1216

I cannot help laughing when I think of the time Mr. Constable and I discussed the Primitives. Before we worked out together our plan of procedure, we were doubtful whether we could find Primitives that would be accepted as works of art, as distinct from "Americana." Today you can see how our doubts were resolved!

I should not be surprised to hear that the paintings of the little-known and the unknown artists had "stolen the show"; they may even make the popular Stars, including Henri Rousseau, blush a little.

Before the Karolik Collection was opened, Fitz Hugh Lane and Robert Salmon were chiefly esteemed in maritime museums and local historical societies; now they are competitively scrambled for in the general art market. In addition to the large catalogue, Richard B. K. McLanathan prepared Museum of Fine Arts Picture Books on Lane, Martin J. Heade, and American Marine Paintings, as represented in the Karolik Collection.

In 1956, after the Karolik Collection had been exhibited as a whole for the stipulated five years, 136 paintings from it, together with 14 others from Karolik's personal holdings, were sent on traveling loan to twelve museums throughout the United States. A catalogue was specially prepared for the tour, which was to extend over two years. The 96 paintings not being circulated were rehung in the first-floor section of the new galleries, while the second floor was designated as a part of the Special Exhibition Galleries.

The years spent in rebuilding galleries had permitted the unusual phenomenon of a great catalogue's being completed long before the exhibition that it describes opened, for the 544-page folio volume, *M. and M. Karolik Collection of American Paintings, 1815 to 1865,* published for the museum by the Harvard University Press, bears the date 1949 on the title page and in the copyright notice. To this volume, prepared by W. G. Constable and his staff in which all the paintings are illustrated, John I. H. Baur contributed an introductory essay, "Trends in American Painting 1815 to 1865." As the general catalogues of the possessions of the Department of Paintings, hopefully begun in the thirties, were still far from complete, W. G. Constable published in 1955 as an interim measure a *Summary Catalogue of European Paintings in Oil, Tempera and Pastel.* Water

PAINTING GALLERY P–4 SUBDIVIDED INTO ALCOVES.

colors were excluded, for in 1945, to assure greater convenience in storage and ease of access, they had been transferred to the Department of Prints, which in 1949 had published a catalogue raisonné of all paintings and drawings in water color acquired before January 1948. For American oil paintings, one still had to resort to the *Catalogue of Paintings, Preliminary Edition*, published in 1921 as the result of Jean Guiffrey's work of nearly a decade earlier, or to *CCCXXXI Reproductions, Selected Oil and Tempera Paintings & Three Pastels* that Philip Hendy had prepared in 1932.

Even with the adaptation of the Cast Court to show the Karolik pictures, the Department of Paintings was seriously taxed for space. To find room for the Spaulding Collection as a unit and to bring it into proper relation with other Impressionist and Post-Impressionist paintings required a major reshuffling of the Evans Wing main galleries in 1950, and further changes in 1952. As long before as 1940 the galleries (P6 and P8) on either side of the Stone Room had been divided into compartments by low screens built out from the walls: although this device undoubtedly increased the area of available hanging space, it was hardly helpful to the general appearance of the rooms. Less than forty years after its completion, the Evans Wing was becoming distinctly overcrowded.

CHAPTER XV

The Second Golden Age
of the Asiatic Department

The Japanese galleries of the Asiatic Department, closed immediately after the Pearl Harbor attack as a precaution against possible vandalism, were used by the Museum School when dispossessed of its own building during the war. Although it was 1947 before this space was rehabilitated and again open to visitors, some of the department's finer paintings were included in the 1945 autumn exhibition, *A Thousand Years of Landscape East and West*, mentioned in the opening paragraph of the preceding chapter. In a similar collaborative exhibition in the autumn of 1946, entitled *Animals in the Arts* and arranged by Georg Swarzenski, the Department of Asiatic Art augmented the zoo by such works as Sesshū's *Monkey Screen* and the *Tiger and Dragon* screens of Kano Eitoku. Thus various works of Japanese art, stored in safety during the war, began to be seen again even before the Japanese galleries were reopened.

Although the great days of Bigelow, Weld, and Ross were decades in the past, the years immediately following World War II became a second golden age for the Department through the learning and skill of its curator, Kojiro Tomita. Having spent his entire adult life in the department, he had grown up with the collections committed to his charge, and had personally known the protagonists of the first golden age. Thus latter-day collectors of Oriental art who came to the department seeking information soon became helpful friends, and were drawn into the scene more closely through membership in the Visiting Committee. As an example, Gilbert E. Fuller, a Visitor to the department from 1925 until his death in 1960, made in 1939 a substantial contribution that made possible the posthumous publication of *Kiyonaga, A Study of His Life and Works*, by Chie Hirano (1879–1939), who had been librarian in charge of Chinese and Japanese books since 1916. Miss Hirano, who had been made Fellow for Research in Chinese and Japanese Art in 1936, had just completed this exhaustive work on a great printmaker before leaving for Japan in March 1939 on the trip during which she died.

In the years following the war a remarkable variety of gifts, of both objects and funds, gave evidence of the esteem in which the Department of Asiatic Art and its curator were held. The first of these was the John Gardner Coolidge Collection of Chinese Pottery and Porcelain, given by his widow in 1946. The collector, a younger brother of J. Randolph Coolidge, Jr., had gone to Japan in 1887, as was noted in Chapter IV. Thereafter he traveled widely in Asia and in Europe, as well as in Brazil and South Africa, until 1902 when he was appointed Secretary of Legation in China. During three years' residence in Peking, he developed a particular enthusiasm for Chinese porcelains, particularly of the blue and white variety. After serving as Secretary of Embassy in Mexico and as Minister to Nicaragua, John Gardner Coolidge resigned from the Foreign Service in 1908, returned to Boston, and the following year married Helen G. Stevens of North Andover. Although he served as Special Agent at the American Embassy in Paris from 1914 to 1917, most of Coolidge's later life revolved around collecting. As his wife fully shared this interest, they assembled in 171 Commonwealth Avenue, Boston, and in her family house in North Andover (now preserved by the Trustees of Reservations) a considerable variety of works of art; it was, however, in Chinese pottery and porcelains that his efforts were particularly concentrated. John Gardner Coolidge died in 1936. Although his widow maintained both houses until her death, she gave 115 of her husband's finest porcelains to the Museum of Fine Arts in 1946 in his memory.

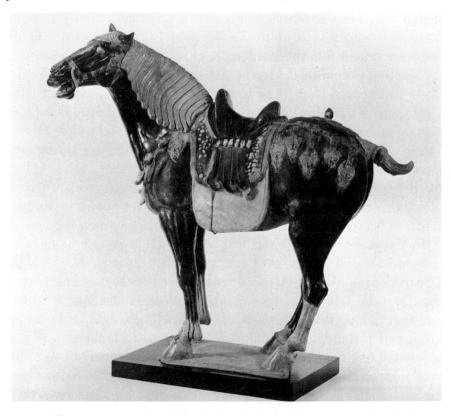

HORSE. Chinese pottery, glazed, T'ang dynasty. *John Gardner Coolidge Collection.*
46.478

The earliest piece in the collection is an unusually large and boldly modeled horse from a T'ang tomb, remarkable for its size and its strong black glaze. There is as well a striking unglazed T'ang horse's head. The strength of the collection, however, was in the porcelains, which extended from the Ming dynasty through the reign of Ch'ien-lung (1736–1795) but with particular emphasis on the K'ang-hsi period (1662–1722). As the John Gardner Coolidge Collection contained many fine specimens of types heretofore unrepresented in the museum, a special exhibition was held from 10 July to 6 October 1946, and it was described and illustrated by Robert T. Paine, Jr., in the December 1946 *Bulletin*. The following year Mrs. Coolidge added 23 objects that included not only Chinese porcelain, but Indian, Siamese, and Tibetan statuettes and small pieces of sculp-

ture in wood, bronze, silver, and gold. In 1950 she gave 4 pieces of
K'ang-hsi porcelain, as well as examples of Chinese amber, brass,
bronze, crystal, jade, lacquer, textiles, furniture, and an eighteenth-
century rug. Still other additions were made nearly every year until
her death in 1962, when she bequeathed $111,294, the income of
which was to be used "for the enhancement of the Asiatic Department."

In 1946 Miss Lucy T. Aldrich of Providence also began a continuing series of notable gifts to the department. Of the 97 Japanese
porcelains that were included in her initial gift, Kojiro Tomita observed that the museum was now able "for the first time to speak
with pride of its possession of Imari, Nabeshima, and Kakiemon
wares." In spite of Edward S. Morse's remarkable collection of
Japanese pottery, the museum had been relatively weak in examples
of the work of some of the porcelain factories that had been established in Japan in the seventeenth and eighteenth centuries under the
patronage of feudal lords. Some of Miss Aldrich's notable gifts in
this field were described by Robert T. Paine, Jr., in the June 1947
and February 1949 Bulletins. Like Mrs. Coolidge, Miss Aldrich
continued giving over the years; her gifts extended far beyond porcelains, for the 106 objects that she gave included Japanese prints,
Tibetan metalwork, Lamaist tankas, and Indian and Japanese paintings.

The devotion of President Holmes to the department remained
as constant as it had been for more than forty years. Moreover, his
keen interest in the ancient Near East and in the art of Persia and
other Islamic countries, enlarged the geographical extent of the
department's collections. In 1933, during his directorship, the museum joined with the University of Pennsylvania Museum in an
expedition to Persia to excavate under the direction of Dr. Erich
F. Schmidt the site of the ancient walled town of Rayy (Rhages),
six miles southeast of Teheran. The participation of the Museum of
Fine Arts in this excavation clearly represents Holmes's personal
enthusiasm. Rayy had been a city of importance under the Medes,
Achaemenids, Parthians, Sassanians, and Arabs; it had been sacked
in 1220 by Genghis Khan and a century later by Tamerlane. The
expenses of the excavation were shared equally by the two museums;

SILVER CANDLESTICK. Iran, dated 1129 A.D. and EWER. Brass inlaid with silver, Iran, early 13th century. *Holmes Collection. 48.1283* and *49.1901*

half the objects found were to be retained by the Persian Government and the other half divided equally between Philadelphia and Boston. Work began in 1934. The Museum of Fine Arts received from that year's campaign some 345 objects, including pottery, stucco, coins, and jewelry, ranging from prehistoric to Islamic times. Although excavation continued for two more years, the Boston museum withdrew in 1937, as it appeared that future discoveries would be of archaeological rather than aesthetic interest.

Edward and Mary Holmes were always eager to obtain any especially fine examples of Persian art that came on the market. In 1948 they gave a remarkable Persian candlestick of the twelfth century, wrought entirely of silver, engraved with scroll patterns and decorative Kufic writing, which had been presented to the shrine of Reza at Mashhad in A.D. 1137, during the reign of the great Sultan Sanjar. The following year he gave an outstanding Persian brass ewer, inlaid with silver, of the early thirteenth century. His death in 1950 deprived the department and the museum of a singularly valued friend, but Mrs. Holmes, who keenly shared his interest in Islamic art, continued to enlarge the collection. In 1950, for example, she gave an early thirteenth-century lusterware bowl, a large Mosul basin inlaid with gold and silver, a Turkestan pottery ewer, and a Sava pottery candlestick. Among her gifts in 1955 were a Persian bronze coffer dated 1197 and a Persian brass candlestick dated 1308. The silver post-Sassanian cup of the eighth century that she presented in 1956 was described by Kojiro Tomita as "the outstanding gift of the year." So the Holmes Collection grew year by year until her death in 1964. In the winter of 1965–66 the trustees established the category of Great Benefactor, in order to recognize in a permanent way those friends whose gifts of money or the equivalent in works of art amounted to $1,500,000 or more. Two of the twenty names in that list are, as one might suspect, Edward J. and Mary S. Holmes.

In the late forties other collectors added important Chinese objects to the Department of Asiatic Art. C. Adrian Rübel (Harvard A.B. 1926), who had long supported Oriental research at the Fogg Art Museum, gave in 1948 a beautifully glazed T'ang horse with a female rider. In 1950 he helped the department to acquire a copy of the 1633 first edition of the *Treatise on the Paintings and Writings of the Ten Bamboo Studio*, which is a masterpiece of Chinese color painting from wood blocks. Three third- or fourth-century Chinese mortuary figures of unusual merit were given in 1948 by Eugene, Paul, and George A. Bernat to honor the memory of their father, Eugene Bernat, who, as an expert restorer and consultant in the care of tapestries, had been associated with the museum from 1905 until his death in 1940. This touching gift consisted of a standing man, a kneeling woman, and a horse, fashioned in blackish clay, originally covered with a white slip over which were drawn various elements in black and red.

Charles Bain Hoyt, who died in 1949, ranks with Ross, Bigelow, Weld, and the Spaulding brothers as one of the Great Benefactors of the museum whose generosity especially assisted the Department of Asiatic Art. Born in Kenosha, Wisconsin, in 1889, he began collecting as a child, moving from shells to bookplates and engravings and etchings in his teens. At the age of twenty, when taken by his parents to Japan, he found his true field in oriental pottery and porcelains. As he followed no profession, and never married, collecting became the central interest in his life for the next forty years. The nature of his accomplishment will be best understood through the following paragraphs that Robert T. Paine wrote in 1964 in the preface to volume I of *The Charles B. Hoyt Collection in the Museum of Fine Arts, Boston*, by Hsien-Ch'i Tseng and Robert Paul Dart:

> The selection reveals both the esthetic perception and the extraordinary detachment of Mr. Hoyt. The one talent led him to collect whatever seemed desirable from any period, while the other saved him from the dictates of popular conventions. As his friend Rowland Burdon-Muller wrote in a letter shortly after Mr. Hoyt's death: "There was no arrogance or pettishness about his enjoyment of his possessions. His true feelings were for the objects themselves . . . He was a natural born curator and his attitude towards his own or any other objects was entirely objective, impartial, and professional."
>
> Though Mr. Hoyt's eye led him to the quiet rather than the spectacular, he must be reckoned a daring collector. At a time when most other collectors were dazzled by the gloss and color of the later Chinese porcelains, his favorites were the ancient potteries that still preserve the warmth of human craftsmanship with simple shapes and unobtrusive decoration. Even if this criterion might be denied in objects of tomb furniture, often representational in the Han dynasty or extravagant because of foreign influences in the T'ang dynasty, it was especially the sense of tactile value, so prized by the Oriental, that appealed to Mr. Hoyt.
>
> His collection was the result of an unusual combination of circumstances. While most collections are made by wealthy men starting in middle age, his was that of a young man with taste, capacity for study, and an adequate but not large fortune, who came of age at the moment when a form of art was appearing on the market for the first time. He was attracted to it, and pursued it assiduously from youth over a long period. Mr. Hoyt began collecting early Chinese objects in 1910, about five years after the first pieces became available as tombs were opened following the Boxer Rebellion. For the next fourteen years, preceding the death of his parents,

PAIR OF CLAY CANDLESTICKS. Chinese, T'ang dynasty. *Hoyt Collection.*
50.2150 and *50.2151*

he was living on an allowance; yet it was at this time that he bought
some of his best Han and T'ang pieces and most of the Korean
ones.

After having lived in New York for a time, Charles B. Hoyt moved
to Cambridge, settling in the pleasant Brattle Street house between
the Episcopal Theological School and Craigie House. His friendship
with the Museum of Fine Arts began in this period; from 1940 he
was a member of the Visiting Committee of the Department of
Asiatic Art, to which he frequently made gifts and loans. On his
death in 1949 he left his entire collection outright to the museum,
as well as a considerable portion of his estate, which will eventually
provide a substantial fund for the purchase of objects of Asiatic art.
Although his bequest of money being subject to certain life interests
has not yet been received, $86,238 realized from the sale of his
house in Switzerland was paid to the museum in 1950 and has for
nearly two decades provided useful income for Asiatic purchases.
From the fourteen hundred objects he bequeathed to the museum,

some eight hundred were shown in a memorial exhibition, held from 13 February to 30 March 1952, of which an illustrated catalogue was published. More detailed study of the Hoyt Collection continues. The first volume of a definitive catalogue, covering Chinese art from the neolithic period through the T'ang dynasty, appeared in 1964; another volume is now in press.

Of the eight hundred objects in the 1952 exhibition, four hundred and seventy-one were Chinese ceramics, ranging from the neolithic period through the eighteenth century. These were a superb addition to previous holdings because of the very personal taste shown in their assembly. Whereas John Gardner Coolidge instinctively sought the highly finished porcelains of the K'ang-hsi period, Charles B. Hoyt sought the very simple, in which beauty of form and color were of primary importance. Similar qualities had governed his acquisition of the one hundred and thirty Korean ceramics that were shown. Throughout the collection there was strong aesthetic unity, even though there was wide diversity of materials and countries of origin. There were fine Chinese bronze mirrors, Sino-Siberian bronze and gold ornaments and plaques (5th through 1st centuries, B.C.), Chinese, Korean, Japanese, and Persian bronzes, Chinese and Japanese paintings, Japanese, Annamese, Persian, and Greco-Roman ceramics, Syrian ceramics and glass, as well as Chinese sculpture in a variety of materials. But as the sculpture was always of modest dimensions, rather than monumental, it too complemented the earlier holdings of the museum. Kojiro Tomita well observed that, although Charles Hoyt had a sensitive and reserved nature, "he was never reticent nor hesitant in his aesthetic judgment." He continued: "It is apparent that to Charles Hoyt the historical or archaeological significance of a work was subsidiary to its artistic merit. In bequeathing his collection to the Museum, Charles Hoyt was not proposing to erect a monument to himself but rather to share with his fellow-men the joy in art which had enriched his own life."

The usefulness of Visiting Committees as a means of bringing collectors and curators into fruitful collaboration has never been more apparent than in the Department of Asiatic Art. From Marshall H. Gould, who joined the committee in 1933, there was received in 1948 a bequest of $100,000, the income of which was restricted to

MAITREYA GROUP. Chinese
marble, Northern Ch'i dynasty,
6th century. *Hoyt Collection.*
50.1074

purchases of Asiatic objects. Another member of the Visiting Com-
mittee, Frederick Lafayette Jack (Harvard M.D. 1884), who had
taught at the Tufts and Harvard medical schools left another
$100,000, similarly restricted, in 1951. In the same year Keith
McLeod (Harvard A.B. 1905, LL.B. 1909) died, leaving the Asiatic
Department the largest restricted purchase fund in its history. Mc-
Leod had practiced law in Boston until the First World War, but
in 1919 became a vice president of the Merchants National Bank.
He lent the museum two fine Chinese bronzes of the Chou dynasty
in 1928, and the following year became a member of the Visiting
Committee. Soon after, he retired from business and, although
sometimes engaged in research at the Radiation Laboratory at the
Massachusetts Institute of Technology, the Museum of Fine Arts
became his consuming interest. When he died, he left the museum
Vincent van Gogh's *The Ravine*, a fifteenth-century Aragonese altarpiece depicting the life of Saint Vincent, fine examples of early Chi-

nese bronzes and Cambodian sculpture, and a fund of $1,032,000, the income of which was restricted for the purchase of works of Asiatic art. With Edward and Mary Holmes and with Charles Hoyt he is reckoned as one of the Great Benefactors of the Museum.

Through these new funds, important purchases were made throughout the nineteen fifties. In 1951 the Marshall H. Gould Fund made possible the acquisition of an exquisite bronze mirror of the T'ang dynasty, decorated with gold- and silver-foil inlay, and an important Chinese scroll of calligraphy and painting entitled *Six Odes from Mao Shih*, the penmanship of which is ascribed to the Emperor Kao-tsung (1107–1187) and the illustrations to the twelfth-century artist Ma Ho-chih. The following year the new funds permitted the purchase of a Chinese scroll painting *Ch'i-tan Chieftain and Entourage on Horseback*, long attributed to Li Tsan-hua (900–937) and various early objects in bronze and pottery, as well as two porcelains and a silver filigree box of the Ming dynasty. From the McLeod, Gould, Jack, and Willard funds thirteen distinguished Chinese scrolls and one album of paintings were bought in 1956. These sources, together with the Morse, Hoyt, and Asiatic Curator's funds, brought eight distinguished Chinese paintings to the department in 1957. Among these were an early tenth-century landscape

SIX ODES (detail), HEAVY DEWS. Chinese scroll, ink and slight color on silk, painted by Ma Ho-chih, calligraphy attributed to Emperor Kao-tsung, 12th century. *Marshall H. Gould Fund. 51.698*

DRINKING AND SINGING AT THE FOOT OF A PRECIPITOUS
MOUNTAIN. Chinese landscape painting, by Kuan T'ung, Five
Dynasties, early 10th century. *Keith McLeod Fund.* 57.194

by Kuan T'ung, entitled *Drinking and Singing at the Foot of a
Precipitous Mountain* and a horizontal scroll of the late eleventh
century by Chao Ling-jang, *Summer Mist along Lake Shore*, both
purchased with the Keith McLeod Fund. The following year this
fund was the means of obtaining two extremely early Chinese paintings from Tun-huang; *Vimalakīrti Seated on a Dais*, dated 590, and
Buddha and Two Bodhisattvas, dated 715. Purchases of a painting
by Chao Mêng-fu (1254–1322) of *Dragon King Worshipping the
Buddha* and a scroll painting, *Red Cliffs* by Yang Shih-hsien, of the
early twelfth century, were made from it in 1959.

VIMALAKIRTI SEATED ON A
DAIS. Chinese painting, Sui
dynasty, dated 590 A.D. *Keith
McLeod Fund. 58.1003*

THE RED CLIFFS. Chinese scroll painting, by Yang Shih-hsien, Sung dynasty,
early 12th century. *Keith McLeod Fund. 59.960*

With the gift in 1957 of a superb Yung-chêng brush-holder with a painted landscape in sepia, Paul Bernat began a collection of exquisite decorative Chinese porcelains of the eighteenth century, to which he added in subsequent years. Kojiro Tomita, commenting in 1961 upon the latest of these gifts, wrote:

One is a dish (early 18th century) depicting in sepia enamel Mi Fei, a celebrated artist, paying homage to an unusual rock. This is one of the rare cases which shows that an artist, not a porcelain decorator, painted a picture on a porcelain surface. Mr. Bernat has already given to the Museum five other objects even more important than this dish, in which landscapes are treated on porcelain like paintings in ink. We believe that the Museum now possesses a group of this rare type unequalled anywhere under one roof outside the Chinese Government Collection. Another gift from Mr. Paul Bernat is a cup (Yung-chêng, 1723–1735) of eggshell thinness with a painted decoration of a blossoming hibiscus and a butterfly, the design spreading from the outside of the cup into the interior. One does not hesitate to state that this cup represents the acme of the Chinese enamel-decorated porcelain.

C. Adrian Rübel, who had given a Chinese pottery pillow of the Sung dynasty in 1935, added three extremely unusual examples of

PORCELAIN CUP. Chinese, Ch'ing dynasty, Yung-chêng period, 1723–1735. *Gift of Paul Bernat.*
61.1254

these objects in 1961; one was of the eighth or ninth century, another of the tenth, and the third was dated 1336. Another member of the Visiting Committee, Richard B. Hobart, gave in 1960 (in honor of Charles Sumner Bird) a large Ming dynasty porcelain bowl, with under-glaze red decoration of floral scrolls. With considerable frequency additions to the collection of ceramics were made through the income of the Charles B. Hoyt Fund.

Although ancient Chinese monumental sculpture has become all but unobtainable, a rare and beautiful coffin platform of the Wei dynasty was bought in 1962 through the Keith McLeod Fund. This early sixth-century piece, with elaborate relief and incised decorations, happily took its place among objects acquired more than half a century earlier through the efforts of Okakura-Kakuzo, Denman W. Ross, and Hervey E. Wetzel. But, as the political situation deteriorated, and it became possible to import into the United States only objects of Chinese art that had demonstrably left China before the Communist regime came into power, the Department of Asiatic Art increasingly turned its attention to Indian objects. Following the lamented death of Ananda K. Coomaraswamy in 1947, the department had had no staff member specifically concerned with Indian art, until in 1959 John Goelet (Harvard A.B. 1953) a keen collector who had traveled extensively in India and the Near East, was given the honorary title of Field Representative, which was changed in 1964 to Fellow for Research in Islamic Art. When in 1966 he was made a trustee there was, for the first time since the death of Denman Ross and Ned Holmes, a generous collector-member of the board who was specifically interested in the art of India and of Islam.

The Marshall H. Gould Fund was used in 1959 to buy a head of Śiva of the second century A.D. Through the same fund were acquired in 1960 and 1961 two very different examples of Indian sculpture: a Buddhist stele with *Khadiravaṇī Tarā and Attendants* from Bihar of the ninth or tenth century; and a black slate stele of the twelfth century, from Bihar or Bengal, of *Lokanātha,* "Lord of Worlds," or Khasarpana Lokeśvara. The latter is one of the new forms devised in Tantric Buddhism for Avalokitesvara, the most widely worshiped of the Mahāyāna Bodhisattvas. Again in 1962 the Gould Fund provided two pieces of Indian sculpture: a red stone figure of *Surasundārī,* Rājasthān of the tenth or eleventh century, and a brass statuette of the *Tirthankara,* Akotā of the eighth to tenth centuries.

A year after the Japanese galleries had been reopened in 1947, the department arranged in the Special Exhibition Galleries a showing of *The Art of Old Japan.* This exhibition, held from 5 February to 21 March 1948, was devised to remind Boston of the thousand-

STONE PLATFORM FOR A COFFIN. Chinese, Northern Wei dynasty, early 6th century. *Keith McLeod Fund.* 62.285 A-G

BUDDHIST STELE WITH KHADIRAVANĪ TARĀ AND ATTENDANTS. Indian, Bihar,
9th–10th centuries. BUDDHIST STELE WITH LOKANĀTHA OR KHASARPANA
LOKESVARA. Indian, black slate, Bihar or Bengal, 11th–12th centuries. *Marshall
H. Gould Fund. 60.924 and 61.129*

year-old tradition of Japanese art, extending from the eighth-century
Chinese artist Wu Tao-tzu to Ernest Fenollosa's friend Kano Hōgai,
that was represented in the collections that Fenollosa, Bigelow, Weld,
Morse, and Ross had formed for the Museum of Fine Arts in the last
decades of the nineteenth century. It gave an opportunity for a new
appreciation of the extraordinary richness of the department's collections, only a fraction of which could ever normally be on display at
one time.

During the fifties and early sixties several remarkable loan collections, sent to the United States by Asiatic governments, were shown
in Boston. From mid-November to mid-December of 1953 the *Exhibition of Japanese Painting and Sculpture*, sponsored by the Jap-

anese Government in cooperation with five American museums, reminded Bostonians of the great masterpieces that had come from Japan seventeen years earlier on the occasion of the Harvard Tercentenary. This comprised some 91 examples of pictorial and sculptural art from the sixth to the nineteenth century, many of which were of such importance that they could be seen in Japan only on very extraordinary occasions. In the twenty-five days that the exhibition was open, over twenty thousand visitors came to see it.

In the autumn of 1956 Robert T. Paine went to Korea in the company of Alan Priest, Curator of Far Eastern Art at the Metropolitan Museum, to make the selection for a similar exhibition of Korean art. There were problems, for, because of the division of the country, no objects from North Korea were available, while the whole of the Duksoo Palace Museum of Fine Arts in Seoul was devoted to an exhibition of *Atoms for Peace*, its great collection having been packed away as a security measure. Clearly monumental temple carvings could not be shipped across an ocean and a continent. Nevertheless, with the hearty cooperation of President Syngman Rhee and the Korean Government, some 187 gold objects, early stoneware, bronze and gilt-bronze small statues, ceramics, and paintings were selected, which were shown in Boston from 7 May through 15 June 1958 and besides in seven other American museums.

Kojiro Tomita went to Thailand in December 1959 as one of the four members of the Committee of Selection for an exhibition of the Art Treasures of that country, which its government agreed to send to the United States, at the instigation of Professor Theodore R. Bowie of Indiana University. This exhibition, shown at the Museum of Fine Arts from 11 March through 23 April 1961, contained works of sculptural and pictorial art, as well as of craftsmanship of all kinds, dating from the sixth to the nineteenth centuries. As it was designed to introduce to the American public the wide and varied artistic accomplishments of the Thai (Siamese) people, the National Museums and monasteries in Bangkok and other cities, as well as royal personages and other private collectors, lent their prized possessions with great generosity. The Museum of Fine Arts had a particular interest in the enterprise, not only because of Mr. Tomita's part in the selection, but because the exhibition catalogue — the only publication of its kind in English — was designed and its production supervised by Carl F. Zahn, Designer for the Museum.

The year 1961 ended with another even greater Asiatic loan exhibition, *Chinese Art Treasures*, a selection of 231 objects from the Chinese National Palace Museum and the Chinese National Central Museum, Taichung, Taiwan, sent by the Government of China to be shown at five American museums. Hsien-chi Tseng, Fellow for Research in the Asiatic Department, was one of the three American scholars who had gone to Taiwan to examine the thousands of works of art that had once constituted the Imperial treasure of China, and to select the 254 examples that were included in the exhibition. This was the greatest display of Chinese paintings ever seen in the Western world. When one considers the riches permanently owned in Boston, it is probable that from 30 November 1961 through 14 January 1962 there were under the roof of the Museum of Fine Arts a wealth of great Chinese paintings that will never again be matched in one place. Some 47,496 visitors crowded in to see the exhibition.

Still a fourth great exhibition, *7000 Years of Iranian Art*, loaned by the Government of Iran and circulated by the Smithsonian Institution, was shown in Boston during May and part of June 1965. Edward L. B. Terrace, Assistant Curator of Egyptian Art, was in charge of the installation, which included superb additional pieces lent for the Boston showing by Mr. and Mrs. Norbert Schimmel and Mr. and Mrs. Leon Pomerance of New York City.

Through an amendment of the naturalization laws, Kojiro Tomita was at last able in 1953 to become a citizen of the United States, where he had lived for forty-five years. He was, however, none the less esteemed in his native country, for in 1958, when, in grateful recognition of his half-century of distinguished service to the museum, he was given, with his wife, a three-months' trip to Japan, he was decorated with the Order of the Sacred Treasure, Third Class, and was received by the Emperor and Empress. This award, which is the highest honor given since the end of the war to a Japanese residing outside of Japan, was accorded for his outstanding contributions in introducing Japanese art and culture to the United States and for promoting friendly relations between the two countries. On

1 March 1963, after fifty-five years in the museum, for thirty-one of which he had been Curator of Asiatic Art, Kojiro Tomita became Curator Emeritus. He was succeeded by Robert Treat Paine, who had joined the staff as Assistant in the Department in 1932 and had been Associate Curator since 1957.

Unfortunately Paine's tenure of the curatorship was as brief as that of his predecessor had been lengthy, for he died prematurely on 11 July 1965 in his sixty-fifth year. His particular field of research was Japanese art, particularly wood-block prints. He was one of the international editors of the journal *Ukiyo-e Art* and co-author of the Pelican volume *History of Japanese Art and Architecture*. He was keenly interested in acquiring examples of painting and print-making of the period since the first formation of the Boston collection, and took pleasure in the twelve paintings by Tomioka Tessai (1836–1924), whose bold use of color has been likened to that of Cézanne or Van Gogh, that were given in 1955 by the Very Reverend Kōjō Sakamoto, Chief Abbot of Seichōji at Takarazuka. Paine himself, shortly before his death, gave the museum ninety-six Japanese wood-block prints of the twentieth century of the *sōsaku hanga*, or "self-created prints," type. In this method, which is considerably influenced by Western art, the artist is totally responsible for the creation of his print. By contrast the earlier Ukiyo-e School of the

PAINTING THE EYEBROWS. Japanese woodblock print by Shinsui Itō, 1928. *Gift of Robert Treat Paine.* 50.1425

seventeenth to nineteenth centuries limited the artist's contribution to the design, and a wood-block cutter, printer, and publisher completed the print.

Notwithstanding Robert T. Paine's strong interest in Japan, important additions of Indian sculpture and Islamic objects were made during his curatorship. These were illustrated in number 333 of the *Bulletin*, which contained a tribute to his memory. In 1963 he bought, through the Gould and Jack funds, a stone *Lokanātha*, 35 inches high, that shows the late Buddhist style in eleventh-century Orissa, and, from the Hoyt, Gould and Willard funds, an eighth-century seated *Buddha* in ivory, only 5½ inches high. The statuette when acquired was headless, but good detective work uncovered the missing portion in the Cleveland Museum of Art, which generously allowed the Museum of Fine Arts to acquire it by exchange. In the same year John Goelet gave an eighth-century Indian ivory plaque, less than 2 inches high, of a *Walking Buddha*, which admirably complements the seated statuette. A terra-cotta head of the Buddha from the Mon kingdom in what is now Thailand (sixth through eleventh centuries), purchased through the Justine F. Kershaw Fund, illustrated the influence of Indian Buddhist art in Southeast

SEATED BUDDHA. Indian, ivory, 8th century. *Charles B. Hoyt, Marshall H. Gould, and John Ware Willard funds. 63.1495*

BUDDHA WITH ATTENDANTS. Indian ivory. *Gift of John Goelet. 63.2673*

RSABHANĀTH. Indian stone sculpture, 10th century. *Keith McLeod Fund. 64.487*

Asia. A stone statue of *Rsabhanāth*, the first of a series of twenty-four Tirthamkaras, or saviors, of the Jain religion, which grew up contemporaneously with Buddhism in India, was bought with the Keith McLeod Fund in 1964. This figure, seated in a posture of meditation, being naked to indicate the Jain freedom from attachment to social form or material objects, is a contrast to the normally clothed Buddhist pantheon. Through the same fund was acquired an important addition to the museum's Indian bronzes, a large image of *Lakshmī*, the Hindu goddess of prosperity, from the Vijayanagar period in the fifteenth century.

Among the Islamic objects added were a superb eleventh-century plate, with inscription in plaited Kufic script, bought through the Jack Fund in 1954, a twelfth-century Mesopotamian jug added to the Hoyt Collection in that year, a late twelfth- or early thirteenth-century Persian bowl and jar, and two gold earrings of similar origin, given by Miss Helen Norton, in memory of Harry A. Norton, in

GLASS VASE AND BOTTLES. Persian, Gurgan(?), 10th–12th centuries. *Gift of the John Goelet Foundation. 65.241, 65.239, 65.238*

1963, and an outstanding group of Persian objects — eight pieces of pottery, eleven pieces of glass, and eleven pieces of gold — given by the John Goelet Foundation in 1965. The glass, dating from the ninth to the twelfth centuries, allowed the department to show important objects in a field not previously covered, while the gold objects add to its small but important holdings in Islamic jewelry.

Following Robert T. Paine's death, Milo C. Beach, who had become Assistant in Indian Art in 1964, held the fort until the arrival on 1 July 1966 of the new Curator, Dr. Jan Fontein, a graduate of the University of Leyden, who had been Curator of Asiatic Art at the Rijksmuseum in Amsterdam since 1955. The following December, Milo Beach resigned to continue his studies in India, and in May 1967, Dr. Pradapaditya Pal, formerly Research Associate of the American Academy of Benares, arrived as Keeper of the Indian Collections. At the end of 1967 Robert P. Dart, Senior Assistant in the Department of Asiatic Art, who had joined the staff in 1929, retired.

The great collection of the *Arts of India and Nepal*, assembled by Nasli and Alice Heeramaneck, was shown at the Museum of Fine Arts from 21 November 1966 until 8 January 1967. Subsequently it went on to the Los Angeles County Museum, the Detroit Institute of Arts, and the Virginia Museum of Fine Arts in Richmond. The immediate reason for the exhibition was an agreement reached between the museum and Mr. and Mrs. Heeramaneck by which the

Department of Asiatic Art obtained an option to purchase important pieces from the collection over a period of years. By the exercise of the first option in February 1966 four Indian sculptures and one Kashmiri bronze were purchased through the Keith McLeod Fund. These were the large fifth-century Mathurā head and chest of a monumental sandstone lion; an eleventh- or twelfth-century Rājasthān statue of *Sūrya*, the Sun God; a Rājasthān statue of *Hari-Hara*; a tenth-century central Indian statue of *Varāhī*, who is one of the seven mothers and the female aspect of Varāha, or Vishnu in his boar incarnation; and the bronze seated *Bodhisattva*, probably Maitreya, of the first half of the tenth century. In the same year John Goelet added to the collection some fifty-eight Indian paintings and three fine Nepalese gilt bronzes. Although a second exercise of the

DĪPAKA RĀGA. Indian painting, Rājasthān, Kotah, about A.D. 1740. GUJARĪ RĀGINĪ. Indian painting, Rājasthān, Kotah, about A.D. 1740. *Gifts of John Goelet.* 66.137 and 66.138

TANKA OF BUDDHA AMITABHA. Nepal, 13th century. *Gift of John Goelet. 67.818*

Heeramaneck option resulted in the acquisition in 1967 of a late first- or early second-century Indian stone head of *Buddha*, a ninth-century stone statue of the goddess *Yamunā*, and an Indian and a Nepalese bronze, it was decided later in the year by mutual agreement that the contract would not be continued.

An exhibition of Indian paintings representing musical modes held in 1967 was permanently recorded in a catalogue *Rāgamālā Paintings in the Museum of Fine Arts Boston* by Pratapaditya Pal. The comprehensive nature of the exhibition was made possible by the numerous gifts by John Goelet over the previous seven years of paintings of this type, which brought to ninety the strong holdings received in 1917 in the Ross-Coomaraswamy collection. The forty-three illustrations of this catalogue, conceived as a supplement to Ananda Coomaraswamy's 1925 *Catalogue of Rajput Paintings*, reproduced chiefly the recent additions. Dr. Pal is currently at work on a similar publication of works of Islamic art in the department.

The striking reconstruction of the Indian and Islamic galleries of the Department of Asiatic Art, completed in 1965, which will be described in detail in a later chapter, symbolizes the accomplishments of recent decades in these fields. By 1970 a similar recreation of the Chinese galleries will be completed. Thanks to enlightened curators who have made admirable use of the funds placed at their disposal by generous friends, living and dead, the years following the end of World War II have constituted a second Golden Age for the Department of Asiatic Art.

CHAPTER XVI

The Varieties of Artistic Experience

The death of John Templeman Coolidge on 16 November 1945 severed a long link with the past. Born in 1856, he was the senior trustee of the museum, having been appointed annually by Harvard College since 1902. When Visiting Committees were instituted in 1906 he became chairman of Western Art (except Textiles) and continued in that office until 1917; from 1933 to 1942 he was chairman of the Visiting Committee of the Department of Textiles. Although on a more modest scale than Denman Ross, Templeman Coolidge collected in many fields, following his painter's eye; he too constantly lent his purchases, which soon became gifts. For many years he was the chief protagonist of the Middle Ages in the museum, giving sculptures and tapestries that were the basis of the old Gothic Room in which I heard Benjamin Ives Gilman speak on 31 December 1919. Coolidge had a major hand in the creation of the Department of Decorative Arts, and in the planning and installation of its wing, although he did not advertise the fact, for, as Edward W. Forbes observed, "his work was done not with the flourish of trumpets, but modestly, quietly, effectively, with fine intelligence, excellent taste, and sound judgment."

Upon Templeman Coolidge's death, Edwin J. Hipkiss noted that his own appointment as working head of the department went back twenty-six years, but Mr. Coolidge's influence had been at work long before that and even before galleries for the decorative arts had been built. It is interesting to recall that the beginnings of our Gothic and Renaissance collections were once exhibited in the space between the library and Asiatic Arts and such American arts as we had were shown beneath pictures in three reserve galleries of the Department of Paintings. There has been a remarkable change during the past twenty-five years and for the share Mr. Coolidge had in it he will long be remembered — remembered with the fond good will which was his by nature.

Hipkiss had already been Curator long enough for the Decorative Arts Wing to have lost its pristine freshness. Its Tudor Room, dismantled in 1942 to make way for the McCann Collection of Chinese Export Porcelain and moved to the second floor of the addition built for the Karolik Collection, had not been reinstalled because of wartime conditions, while the entire court floor of the wing had been closed throughout the war for reasons of economy. Finally on 3 October 1945 a new Late Gothic Gallery was opened, in which the Tudor Room was not only better shown than before, but took its proper place chronologically. The fifteen early American period rooms and galleries on the court floor had, during their long closing, as the Curator put it, "drifted from good order and required both careful grooming and some rearrangement," which was completed in time for reopening on 15 January 1946.

When the Decorative Arts Wing was opened in 1928, Templeman Coolidge had placed on loan in one of the galleries his collection of some twenty rigged ship models. Most of these were European, contemporaneous with the vessels, although the group included a fine modern model of the frigate *Constitution* by Lieutenant Colonel William F. Spicer, U.S.M.C. (ret.), with engaging figures of the crew carved by J. Gregory Wiggins. This collection sprang from Coolidge's love of the sea, for he passed his summers in the old Wentworth Mansion at Little Harbor, New Hampshire, near Portsmouth, where he had made fast to his wharf an old pinkie schooner, available as an extra guest house for his children's friends; moreover he often cruised the coast of Maine in a small knockabout. He once wrote: "It seems especially fitting that our coast-line states should

SHIP GALLERY IN DECORATIVE ARTS WING. As arranged by J. Templeman Coolidge at the opening of the wing.

store memories, fast fading, of the splendid sailing vessels which
brought them renown and riches; and that an era of courage and
romance should be kept alive in the models and pictures of those
ships."

Although the Peabody Museum of Salem (founded in 1799 by
the shipmasters of the East India Marine Society) and the Whaling
Museum in New Bedford were specifically devoted to the task of
keeping alive the memory of the era of sail, Templeman Coolidge
wished the Museum of Fine Arts to add its witness. Therefore, when
he offered in 1932 to convert the loan of his collection into a gift, his
fellow trustees, who loved him, concurred. And as like attracts like,
Frederick C. Fletcher gave in 1935 a superb Admiralty model of
the ship-of-the-line *Royal George* of 1715, and a modern Boucher
model of the clipper ship *Flying Cloud*. In describing this gift in the
April 1935 *Bulletin* J. T. Coolidge remarked that the 1928 loan

exhibition "was probably the first time that such a collection was included with others on a permanent basis in a Museum of Fine Arts in this country," and, as if to silence doubters, continued:

> It has been asked if a model of a full rigged ship could be considered a work of art! The best ones so testify; and if John Ruskin could rightly say that "The mind of man never conceived and the hand of man never contrived a work of more exquisite beauty than that wonderful creation of oak and hemp known as a Ship of the Line," it may also be rightly claimed that the models from which these old ships were built are, in beauty of design and of craftsmanship, indeed works of art. They are the prototypes of actual vessels and have survived to tell their story, while the ships from which they were built have disappeared fifty, a hundred, or over two hundred years ago.

In 1947 Frederick C. Fletcher gave a modern model of the *Prynce Royal* of 1610, recently completed by John R. Whittemore of Santa Barbara, California, after twelve years of research and construction. Because of the presence of the collection, Mary Albena Bodemer, daughter of the great shipbuilder Donald McKay, bequeathed in 1933 the half-hull model of her father's clipper ship *Great Republic* (1853), while in 1939 Templeman Coolidge gave the half-hull model of McKay's *Romance of the Seas* (1854). In the years that followed Templeman Coolidge's death, ship models have been a peripheral, and sometimes difficult to explain, adjunct of the Department of Decorative Arts, while his enthusiasm for the Middle Ages has borne continuous fruit in the remarkably imaginative collecting of Dr. Georg Swarzenski and of Miss Gertrude Townsend in the Department of Textiles.

In the Department of Decorative Arts especially, one sees the way in which a wide miscellany of objects of high quality, lent or given by kind friends in the early years of the museum, has been transformed, through the activities of skillful curators, into a series of well-ordered collections. In the early years in Copley Square, pottery, porcelain, glass, metalwork, textiles, and the like were exhibited by materials, in a manner inspired by South Kensington. With the move to Huntington Avenue in 1909 such collections as did not fall within the provinces of the Egyptian, Classical, or Asiatic departments were divided between Europe and the Nearer Orient, and arranged chronologically in order to bring works of a period, rather than a material, together. With the construction of the Decorative Arts Wing, and with the creation of departments of Decorative Arts and of Textiles, each with its own curator, the area of collecting widened. In the first quarter-century of the museum's life there had been a few examples of a great many kinds of objects. In the fourth quarter, which opened in 1945, there were sizable holdings in many fields, some stronger than others, but there were also learned and experienced curators, conscious of deficiencies and eager to strengthen their departments wherever possible. Although the development of continuing friendships with individual collectors, who over the years came to lend, give, or bequeath their possessions, had contributed immeasurably to the growth of the Museum of Fine Arts, objects that would be invaluable for the enlargement of existing collections rarely came on the market and had to be purchased quickly or foregone. Over the years funds restricted to the purchase of paintings and prints had been received; in the last chapter the good fortune of the Department of Asiatic Art during the fifties in receiving several such restricted funds has been noted. The largest fund of the present day whose income is simply designated for the purchase of works of art, without indication of the kind, resulted from the generous bequest of William Francis Warden, who died in 1946. Its principal in 1969 amounts to $1,269,084. As an effort is made to allocate the income equitably among curators, objects purchased through the Warden Fund appear in many departments.

Sometimes strong collections have been built through the gifts of collectors of successive generations. The 664 pieces of pottery, earthenware, and porcelain received by gift and bequest in 1895 and 1903 from Mr. and Mrs. George W. Wales, pioneer collectors of ceramics from many countries and periods, had included some fine examples of English porcelain Chelsea figures of the eighteenth century. Richard C. Paine made the museum's collection of Chelsea figures and groups outstanding by adding in 1930 and 1953 over a hundred pieces, most of which had formed part of the Alfred E. Hutton Collection in England. Richard Paine's gifts enriched the department in many directions. With his sisters, Mrs. Alan Cunningham and Mrs. Thomas N. Metcalf, he gave in 1945 a Louis XV commode of 1769, decorated with lacquer and ormulu, bearing the signature of its maker, Jean-Henri Riesener; a Regency gilded fire screen, a pair of Louis XIV carved and gilded torchères, and a pair of French crystal candelabra. His gifts were made with a modesty that was diametrically opposed to the magnificence of the objects being presented. An instance of the quietness with which he helped was reported thus by the Curator:

> The works of English silversmiths have a wide representation here chiefly due to the Charlotte Beebe Wilbour Collection consisting of about three hundred and twenty-five carefully selected examples which range in date from the year 1504 to 1820. With all this richness we lacked a good piece of the Elizabethan period, but one day a fine rose-water dish in silver-gilt was, so to speak, left on our doorstep. In quality and skill of workmanship it is eloquent of its period; it has the floral motifs, sea monsters, masks, and griffins engraved, chased, and embossed within the strapwork patterns characteristic of its time, for it bears London hall-marks for 1599 with the stamp of its maker known only by his mark, a device in a shield. Its diameter is nineteen and three-quarter inches and its weight is approximately ninety-four ounces and ten pennyweights. On its central boss are the arms of the Cholmondeley family in colored enamels. The modest donor who generously left it in passing with the hope that we "might find it acceptable" was Mr. Richard C. Paine.

A related rose-water dish and ewer, made in London in 1604, was purchased in New York in 1947 when silver owned by J. P. Morgan was sold at public auction. This became possible through the income of a restricted fund established by the will of an even more reticent benefactor, Miss Theodora Wilbour of New York City, who had never even seen the Museum of Fine Arts. Although only after her death in January 1947 was her name ever publicly mentioned in the museum, it was she who had in 1933 begun to give the Charlotte Beebe Wilbour Collection of English silver in memory of her mother, and remarkable coins and medallions often in gold, in memory of her long-dead sister, Zoë Wilbour.

This very extraordinary collector, with a passion for anonymity,

SILVER-GILT ROSEWATER DISH. English, London, 1599. *Gift of Richard C. Paine. 46.845*

was one of the daughters of Charles Edwin Wilbour (1833–1896), a native of Little Compton, Rhode Island, who, after studying at Brown University, moved to New York City, where he was admitted to the bar in 1859. He embraced various careers in the course of his sixty-three years. He was for a time associated with Horace Greeley and Charles A. Dana on the *Tribune*, soon becoming the leading court reporter. Subsequently, as president of the New York Printing Company, owned by William March ("Boss") Tweed, he conducted a large printing and engraving business, as well as publishing a daily legal newspaper, *The Transcript*. Although the circulation of this periodical seldom reached more than a hundred copies, it was a profitable venture, thanks to the amount of city advertising that it carried at very high rates. In addition Wilbour at one time held three city positions simultaneously: Stenographer in the Bureau of Elections, Stenographer in the Superior Court, and Examiner of Accounts. Although always a literary man, who was somewhat less unknown than other members of the Tweed Ring, he apparently was the recipient of Tweed patronage.

Charlotte Beebe (1833–1914), whom Wilbour married in 1858, was the daughter of a Springfield, Massachusetts, clergyman, the Reverend Edmund M. Beebe. In 1868 she joined Mrs. Jane Cunningham Croly, the first American professional newspaper woman, in founding Sorosis, the first incorporated woman's club in the United States, and in 1870 became its president, a post that she held for five years. Although her daughter Evangeline became the wife of the mural painter Edwin H. Blashfield in 1881, the two daughters endowed with the names of Byzantine empresses — Zoë and Theodora — never married.

After the Tweed Ring came to grief, Charles E. Wilbour went to Europe in 1874 and devoted himself enthusiastically to Egyptology. He spent the winters from 1880 until his death in 1896 in Egypt working with Professor Gaston Maspero, making extensive studies and discoveries of inscriptions and monuments. Zoë Wilbour died in 1885, during the family's extended stay abroad; Mrs. Charles E. Wilbour returned to New York after her husband's death, and in 1903 resumed the presidency of Sorosis. After her death in 1914, her daughters Theodora and Mrs. Blashfield and her son, Victor Wilbour, carried out her desire to present her husband's collections and library to an American institution by choosing the Brooklyn Museum as the most suitable depository. That institution published in 1924 a *Catalogue of the Egyptological Library and other books from the collection of the late Charles Edwin Wilbour*, compiled by William Burt Cook, Jr., and in 1936 a selection of his letters, edited by Jean Capart, entitled *Travels in Egypt* [*December 1880 to May 1891*]. On his death in 1932, Victor Wilbour bequeathed funds to the Brooklyn Museum to maintain and augment his father's collections. The four folio volumes of Sir Alan Gardiner's *The Wilbour*

Papyrus, published for the Brooklyn Museum at the Oxford University Press in 1948, are an impressive monument to Charles E. Wilbour's later interests.

As Evangeline Wilbour Blashfield had died in 1918, her brother's death in 1932 left Theodora as the last of the family. Her father being adequately commemorated in Brooklyn, she began in 1933 the series of superb anonymous gifts to the Museum of Fine Arts of English silver in memory of her mother, and of coins and medallions in memory of her sister, Zoë, then dead nearly a half-century. As she had never visited Boston, one can only assume that the fact that her mother, Charlotte Beebe Wilbour, had spent part of her youth there, determined her choice of institution. The forthright yet courteous treatment that she received in her correspondence with the museum's curators won her confidence, for when she sent her first offering of Greek and Roman coins in memory of Zoë, Lacey D. Caskey, Curator of Classical Art, quite simply told her that some of them were forgeries. Many museums dealing with rich and eccentric collectors take whatever is offered, in the hope of more reputable benefits to come. As Caskey did not follow this dubious practice, he soon convinced Miss Wilbour that the Museum of Fine Arts was an institution to be trusted.

Gifts of English silver and of coins and medals of the highest quality consequently continued to arrive in Boston until her death, to the great enrichment both of the Classical and Decorative Arts Departments. As Leonard Forrer, Sr., the greatly respected classical numismatist of Spink and Son in London, was her adviser and agent at European sales in the thirties, the purchases that were sent to Boston were of the highest quality. With his assistance she acquired at the Prince Waldek sale at Basel in 1935 a rich variety of medallions, gold aurei, silver denarii, and rare bronze coins, in brilliant condition, showing many admirable portraits of Hellenistic rulers and Roman emperors. Although Theodora Wilbour never came to Boston, her will provided two funds, each of some $350,000, the income of one being restricted to the purchase of English silver and the other for rare and distinguished coins and medallions. The 1969 principal of each is close to $650,000. Few bequests have ever proved more helpful than this far cry from the New York of a century ago.

While Theodora Wilbour's bequest gave the Department of Decorative Arts a competitive advantage when fine pieces of English silver came on the market, it could not be used when the Paul Revere Liberty Bowl unexpectedly was offered for sale in New York in June 1948. This silver punch bowl bore the inscription:

To the Memory of the glorious NINETY-TWO: Members of the Hon'bl House of Representatives of the Massachusetts-Bay, who, undaunted by the insolent Menaces of Villains in Power, from a strict regard to Conscience, and the LIBERTIES of their Constituents, on the 30th of June 1768, voted NOT TO RESCIND.

It had been made by Revere for fifteen "Sons of Liberty," whose names were engraved around the outer rim. Although the ownership was originally shared, eventually one of the number, William Mackay, bought the interests of the other fourteen; it remained among his heirs for over a century. In 1902 it was bought by Mrs. Marsden Perry of Providence, a great-great-granddaughter of John Marston, one of the fifteen original owners. Forty-six years later,

THE LIBERTY BOWL. American silver, by Paul Revere, Boston, 1768. *Purchased by Public Subscription and the Francis Bartlett Fund.* 49.45

when her son, Marsden J. Perry, the last private owner, put the bowl on the market, the Museum of Fine Arts obtained an option. As the price was $52,500, it could not be bought from ordinary museum funds. Sixty years earlier, when something like the William Blake drawings or the Morse Collection came on the market, General Loring would quietly raise a subscription fund among friends, who often carefully safeguarded their anonymity. The Director and Edwin J. Hipkiss assembled three lunch parties with such a purpose in mind, but reached the conclusion that the purchase could not be undertaken. At this point Mark Bortman, a plastics dealer who was an enthusiastic collector of American silver, entered the picture. Having come to Boston from Rumania as a child, he had embraced with a convert's fervor everything concerning the history of the American Revolution. The beauty of the bowl, combined with its associations, made him determined that it should be acquired for the Museum of Fine Arts. He became chairman of a "Paul Revere Liberty Bowl Fund for Securing for the City of its Origin a Symbol of American Freedom," which described itself as "Acting Independently for the Museum of Fine Arts." This committee, equipped with a letterhead bearing the names of fifty-five distinguished sponsors, moved into a high-pressure campaign — the first with which the museum had ever been connected — that eventually raised $44,414 from 719 various contributors, of whom Mr. and Mrs. Edwin S. Webster and Frederick C. Fletcher were particularly generous. When the limit of popular response had been reached, the Museum of Fine Arts contributed $11,036 from the Francis Bartlett Fund to meet the balance of the purchase price and the $2950 expense of the campaign. Thus the Liberty Bowl of 1768 found its permanent home in the Department of Decorative Arts with the museum's great collection of Revere silver and portraits.

The department's most lasting accomplishment of the decade following the war came from the perceptive and often economical collecting of Dr. Swarzenski in the medieval and renaissance field. Through his efforts were purchased the Daucher Prophet from the Fugger Chapel, Augsburg, the St. Christopher bronze of 1407 attributed to Brunelleschi, and the Romanesque Salzburg Crucifix — while Mrs. Charles Gaston Smith's Group gave a particularly win-

ST. BARBARA. German, polychromed wood, about 1510. *Gift of Mrs. Charles Gaston Smith's Group. 45.474*

some wooden statue of *St. Barbara*, carved in Lower Bavaria about 1510. The ladies of the same group in 1947 gave another *St. Barbara* in limewood, this one Alsatian of about 1470. In this year the Curator reported that "our Director and Trustees, well aware of an unusual opportunity, drew heavily on their resources to make purchases of objects for this Department which are notable in their qualities and significance" and which "go far toward improving our collections

STONE ROUNDELS OF A NOBLEMAN AND A LADY. French, 16th century. 47.1452

representing continental Europe." These included Arnolfo di Cambio's group of three clerics from the Arca di San Domenico in Bologna, marble heads attributed to Nicola and Giovanni Pisano, two sculptured French roundels of a nobleman and a lady of about 1530, and examples of twelfth-century metal work and enamels. Similar purchases were made in 1948, while a sixteenth-century French sculptured chimney piece, attributed to Jean Goujon, was given in memory of the distinguished art dealer Joseph Brummer by his widow and by his brother, Ernest Brummer. In 1949 were purchased, mostly from the stock of the Brummer Gallery, fifteen pieces of sculpture, nineteen examples of ecclesiastical and secular metal work, four ivories, thirteen English Apostle spoons (1504–1660), three Elizabethan jugs with silver mountings, nine Renaissance coins, and a page of a Carolingian manuscript with an illumination of Saint Gregory. The huge fourteenth-century French gargoyles that were acquired in this year were among the objects described by Georg Swarzenski in an article in the December 1949 *Bulletin,* "Profane Work in the High Middle Ages."

Two masterpieces of thirteenth-century Limoges enamel were bought: a *Eucharistic Dove* in 1949, and an applied relief representing the *Baptism of Christ* in 1950. Of great significance was the purchase in the latter year of a hitherto unknown Ottonian ivory of the late ninth century representing the *Apparition of Christ*, for in the years that had passed since the 1914 publication of Adolph Goldschmidt's *Die Elfenbeinsculpturen aus dez Zeit der karolingischen und Sachisischen Kaiser*, "no more than half a dozen new plaques, which one can be certain are not spurious, have come to light." This rare acquisition provided company for the early thirteenth-century Italian ivory *The Descent from the Cross* and the eleventh-century Spanish ivory plaque from the San Millán de la Cogolla reliquary, purchased in 1934 and 1937 respectively, both of which were described in Goldschmidt's work. Such purchases bore out the *confessio fidei* in Ned Hipkiss' report for 1951.

Since 1919 your Curator has served toward the building up of this department and with good assistance the work continues. In a time of diverse thinking our main purpose is ever kept in mind.

THE APPARITION OF CHRIST. Ottonian ivory plaque, northern France, late 9th century. *William E. Nickerson Fund. 50.819*

THE DEATH OF ST. AEMILIANUS. Spanish ivory plaque (fragment), from San Millán de la Cogolla, 11th century. *36.626*

THE DESCENT FROM THE CROSS. Italian ivory, 13th century. *34.1462*

That is, in my belief, the acquisition of worthy objects through critical taste and judgment, a planned order of exhibitions, and the personal care of amassed treasure charged with interest, enjoyment, and even enlightenment.

Among the gifts of the year was a silver-gilt and enamel pendant by a sixteenth-century Augsburg goldsmith, presented by Emil Delmar in honor of Georg Swarzenski's seventy-fifth birthday.

An eighth-century Anglo-Irish portable shrine, known as the *Emly Shrine* — a yew-wood box encased in metal of delicate ajouré work in silver, with applications of gold cloisonné enamel — was purchased from the Theodora Wilbour Fund in 1952, thus carrying the Charlotte Beebe Wilbour Collection back into the Dark Ages. In November 1953 as both the Curator and Georg Swarzenski were none too well, the latter's son, Hanns, was transferred from the Department of Paintings to act as a Fellow for Research. The following year Edwin J. Hipkiss retired because of ill health after thirty-five years' service, and was named Curator Emeritus. Richard McLanathan, who after returning from his Roman fellowship in 1949, had become Assistant Curator of Decorative Arts, became Curator upon Hipkiss' retirement, while Mrs. Buhler was promoted to Assistant Curator. In the course of 1955 Hipkiss died, and at the end of the year Georg Swarzenski resigned on account of his health. During his fifteen fruitful years as Fellow for Research in Sculpture and Mediaeval Art he had remarkably enlarged the holdings of the Department of Decorative Arts. After his death on 14 June 1957 a double issue of the *Bulletin* (numbers 301–302) was devoted to the acquisitions for which he was responsible. Once again, as at General Loring's death in 1902, Sir Christopher Wren's epitaph — SI MONUMENTUM REQUIRIS, CIRCUMSPICE — was appropriately evoked. Happily his son was still in the department to carry on this great tradition.

In the Department of Textiles, Miss Townsend was on occasion acquiring objects that were remarkable counterparts to Georg Swarzenski's medieval discoveries. Among her 1947 purchases she reported:

A fragment of French embroidery of the twelfth century, from the chasuble of Raoul de Beaumont, Bishop of Angers, who died in 1190, a piece of Spanish-Arabic silk and gold weaving, dating from the thirteenth century, and a piece of Italian silk weaving of the fourteenth century are among other important additions by purchase to our collection of textiles.

She was, however, quite as likely to be adding to the remarkable collection of pre-Columbian Peruvian textiles, accepting a flounce of eighteenth-century *point d'Alençon* lace, the coat and waistcoat that Ebenezer Storer wore when he was graduated from Harvard College in 1752, pieces of sixth-century Coptic tapestry weaving, crewelwork valances for the collection of New England embroidery. There was no limit to Miss Townsend's omnivorous interest to acquire, study, and classify anything and everything that could be considered a textile.

Because of her varied and ever-growing interests, new friends and collections constantly came to the department. The costumes and costume accessories of the Elizabeth Day McCormick Collection, mentioned in an earlier chapter, which probably would never have left Chicago had it not been for Gertrude Townsend's presence in Boston, were first shown in their new home in an exhibition held between 10 April and 13 May 1945. English Spitalfields brocade dresses of the second quarter of the eighteenth century, slightly later French dresses of Chinese painted silk and *chinoiserie* brocade, early nineteenth-century French gowns of Indian embroidered mull or silk gauze shot with silver, were displayed on artificial ladies skillfully constructed by William J. Young.

In memory of their mother, Mrs. Horatio A. Lamb, a daughter of Benjamin Smith Rotch, one of the 1870 Founders of the Museum of Fine Arts, the Misses Aimée and Rosamond Lamb in 1951 gave twenty-five dresses with appropriate accessories, ranging in date from 1825 to the early twentieth century. Of these Miss Townsend wrote:

Exquisite examples of lace and embroidery, and floral headdresses with matching bouquets, make this distinguished group of costumes

DRESSES OF CHINESE EMBROIDERED SATIN AND OF ENGLISH BROCADE. English,
18th century. *Elizabeth Day McCormick Collection. 43.1645, 43.1641*

especially interesting as a reflection of the development of taste in
dress over a century. When just eighty years ago the first objects in
the Museum's collection were recorded and the first registered
number given to a tapestry, the founders of the Museum could
hardly have realized how soon the use of synthetic fibres would
revolutionize the whole textile industry. Looking back over the first
half of the twentieth century during which this revolution has
taken place the value and significance of the collection of costumes
and costume accessories now being assembled in the Museum become increasingly clear.

The following year the same donors added forty-seven costumes
with accessories and other pieces of textiles. Indeed their generosity,
combined with the saving habits of their family, have benefited many
departments of the museum and provided a record of New England
life in furniture and elegant examples of decoration.

The collection of tapestries grew more representative as well as
larger during the decade following the war. A great Brussels

DRESS OF CHINESE PAINTED SILK,
English, about 1760. *Elizabeth Day
McCormick Collection. 43.1644*

tapestry of *Vertumnus Disguised as a Fisherman* — illustrating an
incident from Ovid's *Metamorphoses*, book XV — was given in 1948
by Mrs. Ernest B. Dane of Brookline. The following year two outstanding textiles, in age a millennium apart, were bought with the
Kling Fund. The first was a fifth-century loop-woven hanging from
the Coptic period in Egypt, the design of which,

> a single figure standing under a pediment supported by columns, is
> woven with loops of wool of warm, rich colors on a neutral ground,
> a technique which suggests interesting comparisons with both
> painting and mosaic. The other wall hanging, woven about a thou-
> sand years later, illustrates the high degree of skill attained by
> tapestry weavers in Europe during the late fifteenth century.

It is a small panel, depicting the *Adoration of the Magi*, whose dimensions suggest that it might have been intended as a Gothic altar
frontal. Mrs. Solomon R. Guggenheim of New York gave in 1950 a
Flemish tapestry of *Zeus and Danae* of the second quarter of the sixteenth century, while Eugene L. Garbáty of New York gave, between
1950 and 1952, in memory of his parents Josef and Rosa Garbáty,

THE ADORATION OF THE MAGI. Flemish tapestry, possibly Brussels, part of an altar frontal, late 15th century. *Charles Potter Kling Fund. 49.505*

four panels woven in the Barberini tapestry manufactory (1650–1700) from the series *The Life of Pope Urban VIII.*

Visitors to the museum since 1913 had become familiar with a Flemish tapestry of *Alexander Refusing Water*, that had long been lent by Hon. George von Lengerke Meyer. This became the property of the Museum of Fine Arts in 1953 through the generosity of his heirs. A huge Flemish tapestry (1500–1525), depicting scenes from the manhood of Christ and from Christian allegory, was presented in 1954 by the Hearst Foundation in memory of William Randolph Hearst, from whose collection it came. This great hanging, very similar to one in the cathedral at Palencia, was one of six from the collection of the Duque de Berwick y Alba that were sold at auction in Paris in 1877; another of the series, a *Last Judgment*, was acquired by the Louvre in 1912.

The riches of the Department of Textiles are difficult to describe for they are largely hidden away, save for the small number of great pieces that in turn adorn the Tapestry Gallery. The Department of Prints presents an even more difficult problem, for it has no equivalent of the Tapestry Gallery. Its resources, neatly matted and carefully stowed in boxes, are the reservoir from which flow constantly changing exhibitions in a series of galleries on the ground floor of the Evans Wing. But unless one visits the Print rooms constantly, or frequents the department for serious study, it is difficult to compass the collections that Koehler, Richter, Carrington, and then Henry P. Rossiter, assembled. Here, as in the two other departments described in this chapter, there had been over a quarter of a century of curatorial continuity. The year 1919 had been a fruitful one in such appointments, for in March, Henry P. Rossiter had become Assistant Curator of the Department of Prints; in May, Edwin J. Hipkiss was appointed Keeper in the Department of Western Art; while in September, Gertrude Townsend became Assistant in Charge of Textiles.

By 1945 Rossiter had spent twenty-six years in his department, for twenty-two of which he had been Curator. His senior Assistant, Miss Anna C. Hoyt, had been there even longer, for she had joined the staff on 25 June 1917 in FitzRoy Carrington's time. After two and a half years of war work, Francis W. Dolloff, the department's technical assistant, returned in September 1945 to the museum, and in the same year Miss Eleanor A. Sayre, a Bryn Mawr graduate (A.B. 1938) who had completed two years of graduate work at Radcliffe, was appointed to the staff. Peter Arms Wick (Harvard A.M. 1951) became an Assistant in the department in August 1952.

The following paragraph from the Curator's report for 1946 gives a typical example of what the department might offer visitors in the course of twelve months.

During the year there have been twenty-one exhibitions in the Print Galleries. These have covered a good deal of ground, to take in some of the great periods and great masters of graphic art; also once again they have called attention to the Department's multiple and growing resources. Following the exhibitions of Water Colors by Winslow Homer, American Portraits in Mezzotint, Woodcuts by Lucas Cranach, Sr., Etchings by Bellange, Lithographs and Woodcuts by Gaugin, all held over from December, 1945, there were shown Etchings by Rembrandt, Stefano della Bella, Etchings and Lithographs by Whistler, Photographs by Stieglitz, Water Colors by Sargent, Lithographs by Redon, Etchings and Lithographs by Picasso, Etchings by David C. Read, Italian Engravings of the Fifteenth Century, Engravings by Schongauer, by Dürer, and by Hogarth. In the Book Corridor an exhibition of prints and tools accompanied by explanatory labels to illustrate the History and Technique of Etching replaced a similarly informative display of the woodcutter's art. From May to September the Department had the pleasure of showing more than one hundred flower prints from the superb collection of Mr. and Mrs. George Phillips Dike. Some were extremely rare and known chiefly to specialists, but all very, very charming. On view at the same time in three of the Special Exhibition Galleries, drawings by Francis Dahl and Gluyas Williams helped entertain many summer visitors, and Goya's satires in the remaining galleries, while by no means mirth-provoking, were not less provocative.

Such a variety of exhibitions reflects the breadth of Henry Rossiter's collecting. In 1936, for example, he added to the department's drawings by old masters — "a collection," he noted, "whose existence at the moment belongs more to the realm of faith than to fact" — two celebrated studies by Albrecht Dürer, *The Prodigal Son* and *The Holy Trinity*, and an example of the Florentine school, *Youth seated on a stool*, from the circle of Filippino Lippi. In a mood far removed from the contemplation of *The Holy Trinity* is Jean-Honoré Fragonard's enchanting drawing *Les Pétards*, purchased in 1944, which offers the lively spectacle of three girls, startled from their beds by a bunch of lighted firecrackers let down through a trapdoor in the ceiling. Presumably when the smoke cleared the male author of this practical joke enjoyed contemplating the charming disarray of the young ladies. Rossiter appreciated quality wherever it was to be found, whether in *The Three Maries at the Tomb*, an etching of the mannered seventeenth-century Lorraine artist Jacques Bellange, pur-

LES PETARDS. France, drawing by Jean Honoré Fragonard. *Otis Norcross and Seth K. Sweetser funds. 44.815*

chased from the Otis Norcross Fund in 1942, or in François Janinet's aquatint in color of *Marie Antoinette*, complete with its excessively rare decorative border. The latter was bought in 1944 to replace a clever nineteenth-century copy of the print that had been received in 1917 with the John B. How Marie Antoinette Collection of over 500 prints; it was providentially paid for by a small sum left after mounting the original collection that had, by the loaves-and-fishes miracle of compound interest, increased in the passage of twenty-seven years to $6,000.

W. G. Russell Allen, chairman of the department's Visiting Committee since the death of George Peabody Gardner in 1939, constantly made gifts of the most varied sort. In 1945 he gave from his own collection four superb impressions of Giovanni Battista Tiepolo's *Scherzi di Fantasia,* as well as contributing to the purchase of seven more of like quality, which nearly completed the department's set of these famous plates. At the same time he further gave fifty

THE THREE MARIES AT THE TOMB. France, etching by
Jacques Bellange. *Otis Norcross Fund. 40.119*

lithographs by contemporary American artists "which reflect the current scene with candor and vigor." Four years later he gave five portfolios of lithographs and etchings and sixty-five lithotints, lithographs, woodcuts, and stencils of Mexican artists. Russell Allen was quite as likely to give a sixteenth-century Italian woodcut of *Suleiman the Magnificent*, in a high helmet with plume, a rare impression of Schongauer's *Saint Catherine* or engravings and woodcuts by

MARIE ANTOINETTE. France, color aquatint by François Janinet, with separate border. *John B. How Bequest. 44.794*

Albrecht Altdorfer, as he was to add Tiepolos or the work of contemporary Americans from both sides of the Rio Grande.

Another continuing friend of the Department of Prints was L. Aaron Lebowich, who in 1949 gave an expressive eclectic group of more than five hundred etchings, engravings, woodcuts, and lithographs, the work of many printmakers of the late nineteenth and early twentieth centuries, American, British, and French. The following year he added seven hundred examples in all mediums. In 1952 he gave more than one hundred prints and drawings that included, in addition to more modern artists, works of Altdorfer and Tiepolo, while in 1953 he gave still additional prints as well as drawings and water colors. Maxim Karolik began in 1950 to appear among the contributors to the Department of Prints, for he embarked upon the final section of his "triology of American arts," the M. and M. Karolik Collection of American Drawings, 1800–1875. As this, like the earlier collections, was assembled with the collaboration of the appropriate curators, Henry P. Rossiter was intimately involved in its formation. One hundred and forty-nine drawings by artists of the period, both primitive and academic, were received in 1950. Along with gifts that followed in succeeding years, this collection will be described in a later chapter.

Less massive accessions came from a great variety of collectors each year. The 1950 report, for example, notes the following:

> To the fine group of photographs by Stieglitz already in the Museum, Georgia O'Keefe had added twenty-eight later examples and seven photogravures. Mr. and Mrs. John D. MacDonald have presented a fine Rowlandson watercolor, fresh in coloring, an undoubted original and typical of Rowlandson at his most vulgar best; and Robert Treat Paine, Jr., with the gift of forty-two prints, has greatly helped our collection of modern German art and filled in occasional gaps in the older school.

Sometimes the gifts would include undescribed states of familiar prints, as in 1951, when Mrs. Samuel Cabot presented a hitherto unknown proof of a first state of Albrecht Dürer's *Christ Carrying the Cross* (B. 12) from the Passion on copper.

With the restricted funds that were at his disposal, the Curator was able to keep a keen eye upon European sales, and make important purchases of prints and drawings. In 1948 he reported:

> Not since the 1920's when several great European collections were dispersed at auction has the Department been able to purchase such an imposing group of early prints as those acquired within the past year. Representing a diversity of philosophies and outstanding for quality, the following may be specially mentioned: Venus and Cupid, by Nicoletto Rosex da Modena; The Entombment, upright plate, School of Mantegna, H. 7; David and Goliath by Marcantonio, D. 5, executed in Bologna, possibly after Francia,

FRIGATES TOWING A HULK. England, water color by
Thomas Rowlandson. *Gift of Mr. and Mrs. John D.
MacDonald.* 50.3897

or conceivably from the engraver's own design, and also The Virgin
Weeping over the Dead Christ, D. 20, made in Rome under
Raphael's influence; Woman and Child Riding to Market, by
Boldrini, Pass. 6; The Card Players, by Israhel van Meckenem, L.
510; Susanna and the Elders, by Jorg Breu II, Pass. 3, a woodcut on
four sheets; Mahomet and the Monk Sergius, by Lucas van Leyden,
and the same artist's superb portrait of Maximilian, 1520, the most
masterly of all the engraved portraits depicting the Emperor, and
technically a milestone, combining etching with engraving; a Self-
Portrait, by Jacob Binck, B. 95; Christ on the Cross, by Hans Bal-
dung, C. 36, one of the great sixteenth century woodcuts in chiaro-
scuro; Landscape with River and Church, by Hirschvogel, B. 63;

Marie de Medicis' woodcut self-portrait of 1587; Clement de Jonghe by Rembrandt in a remarkable printing of the third state; Le Pantalon, Le Capitan, and La Zani, by Callot, L. 288–290; Head of an Old Man, and the Magdalen, by Prince Rupert, the second earliest practitioner in mezzotint; and the Portrait of Titian, by Jan Thomas of Ypres, to whom the Prince is thought to have communicated some useful hints at first hand.

The purchases of 1951 included "two of the most impassioned series of engravings known to graphic art — Jean Duvet's twenty-four plates of the *Apocalypse,* and seventy-five proofs of Goya's *Disasters of War."* The *Apocalypse* engravings, which were early impressions, uniformly and richly inked, with full, uncut margins, were obtained from the Duke of Arenberg; the Goya proofs, acquired in 1863 by Sir William Stirling Maxwell from the painter Valentin Carderera, a young contemporary of Goya, had remained in the Stirling family at Keir Castle, Scotland, for almost ninety years. Of them Henry Rossiter observed:

THE DRAGON CAST OUT OF HEAVEN and DUVET STUDYING THE APOCALYPSE. France, engravings from *The Apocalypse* series of Jean Duvet, 16th century. 1951 *Purchase Fund. 51.715* and *51.704*

Although they were rarely seen, Campbell Dodgson made them known through his illustrated catalogue privately printed by the Roxburghe Club in 1933. Several of the proofs are touched in pencil, showing the extreme care Goya took to extract the utmost delicacy of tone from plates in which he bared the ruthlessness and barbarity of war as no artist has done before or since. For making all arrangements leading up to their purchase the Department is indebted to one of the Museum Trustees, Mr. Philip Hofer, whose ardent lifelong interest in the work of Goya has been constantly helpful. Through Mr. Hofer the Department was also able to secure from the Stirling family twenty-six etchings by Goya after Velazquez; nearly half are proofs or early states and a few show the titles on the lower margins as Goya wrote them in his own hand.

Miss Eleanor A. Sayre, who has specialized in the work of Goya, studied and catalogued this unique set of *Los Desastres de la Guerra*; a unique proof of one of the subjects is here reproduced. In 1955 the department hung in the Special Exhibition Galleries a series of Goya drawings and prints from the Prado and Lazaro Galdiano museums in Madrid, which was more than doubled in size during its Boston showing by additions from the museum's own collection.

Notable among drawings purchased were three acquisitions of 1946: crayon portraits by the school of François Clouet of the Seigneur de Sainte-Corneille, François Duc de Montmorency, Maréchal de France, and of Louis de Saint-Gelais, Seigneur de Lansac. These and five other drawings, now owned by Harvard University, belonged in the eighteenth century to Lord Bessborough. Philip Hofer had given the portraits of Mary, Queen of Scots, and of François II of France, to the Department of Printing and Graphic Arts in the Houghton Library, of which he was the founder and first Curator, while three others were acquired by the Fogg Museum. Prior to the Bessborough sale in 1801, the entire group had been engraved by Bartolozzi, who had been commissioned by John Chamberlaine to make plates for his *Imitations of Original Drawings by Hans Holbein* (London, 1792). In 1947 another enchanting purchase was the Giovanni Domenico Tiepolo wash drawing, *The Milliner's Shop*, which gives a delightful glimpse of eighteenth-century Venetian life.

INFAME PROVECHO. Spain, etching by Francisco Goya y Lucientes from
Los Desastres de la Guerra. 1951 Purchase Fund. 51.1697

THE MILLINER'S SHOP. Italy, pen and wash drawing by Giovanni Domenico
Tiepolo, 18th century. *William E. Nickerson Fund, 1947*

The care and preservation of its multitudinous holdings have always been a major concern of the Department of Prints. In 1950, for example, Francis W. Dolloff cut and made 1,145 mounts; treated 348 water colors, prints, and drawings in his laboratory; unframed and examined 200 water colors, and answered 27 requests on the care of prints. His skill in cleaning and repairing has improved the appearance and extended the life of innumerable prints and drawings, while his helpfulness to institutions and private collectors has made many friends for the Museum of Fine Arts.

FitzRoy Carrington, under whose guidance the Department of Prints flourished from 1913 to 1923, died in 1954. Another grave loss was sustained in June 1955 through the death of W. G. Russell Allen. In number 296 of the *Bulletin*, which described the memorial exhibition of prints from Allen's collection, held in 1956, Henry P. Rossiter wrote:

> Following the best traditions of early nineteenth century print collectors, W. G. Russell Allen formed his collection with sound knowledge, unremitting care, and an unusually keen eye. In the memorial exhibition now on view, chiaroscuro woodcuts have been somewhat emphasized, since they were very personal to him and one branch of print collecting he made particularly his own. For many years he examined, compared, and studied them in European museums, took innumerable notes, changed attributions as he found fresh evidence, and brought together one of the choicest, most representative collections of these woodcuts in private hands. It had long been his purpose to write the definitive catalogue on them; now that the prints have come to us, together with his notes, the Print Department hopes to finish his project.
>
> Among other artists for whose work he had a strong predilection might be mentioned Goya, Daumier, Gauguin, and the French Impressionists, but his graphic art interests really covered the whole field, from the great masters as well as little known men of earlier periods to the restless sprawling output of today.
>
> His flair for discerning merit in artists before their work became extravagantly acclaimed, and speculated in, stood him in good stead. Thus, when the economic strains after World War I brought many great collections into the market, he was able to make important purchases, exercising as always rare connoisseurship and a catholic

taste. At that time the flow of prints seemed inexhaustible. Actually it was a sudden flood, and soon over; so also was the era of print collecting on the broad, leisurely, generous scale he practiced, like enlightened amateurs before him. Not that his collecting stopped; on the contrary, in the contemporary field he found much to interest and amuse him, and he bought liberally.

Over a long period his gifts to the Department included many important pieces by the great print makers. Sometimes they reflected the observant student exploring byways on his own, and finding little publicized prints, which were desirable none the less. To a collection as extensive as ours they added a pleasant fillip and the charming modesty with which they were offered belied the erudition of the donor.

Russell Allen was another of the quiet, understated Bostonians who made study and collecting their chief occupation. Although his bachelor quarters at 112 Pinckney Street, overlooking the Charles River Basin, contained some fine pieces of Chippendale furniture, they had by the time I knew them become grievously overcrowded with catalogues and books, boxes of prints and cases of spirits — both of excellent quality — in such numbers that there was little room to move about freely. When after an evening at the Club of Odd Volumes, I might go there in the company of Professor Paul J. Sachs, William H. Nye, head of the Turner Construction Company, the Haverhill lawyer Willard G. Cogswell, and John Cutter, who, after retiring from the textile business, devoted himself to growing apples and fishing, there would be good talk, often lasting until a very late hour. Prints would emerge from the boxes and bottles from the cases. Although Paul Sachs was the only one of the company who collected in Russell Allen's league, Nye, Cogswell, Cutter, and I were always given the impression by our host that our thoughts were of equal moment. It was a scene in which a nineteenth-century French collector would have felt himself completely at home. And on one occasion, when the last day of the year fell upon a Saturday, this little marching company migrated to the Museum of Fine Arts after the Club of Odd Volumes luncheon to recall the occasion in 1919 when I had heard Benjamin Ives Gilman give his "Thoughts for St. Sylvester's Day." Thus the living and the dead are inextricably linked through

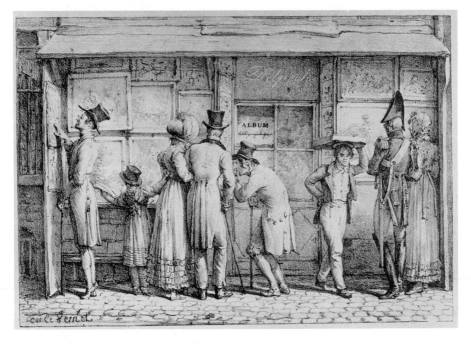

DELPECH'S LITHOGRAPH SHOP. France, lithograph by Carle Vernet, 19th century. *Gift of W. G. Russell Allen. 38.620*

ties with the Museum of Fine Arts. When his sister and niece came
to clear out Russell Allen's crowded quarters in Brimmer Chambers
they found that nothing, however unlikely, could be discarded
without careful examination, for a great pile of back issues of *Life*
might have been used to keep flat an unsuspected Rembrandt,
Tiepolo, or Toulouse-Lautrec print. A Carle Vernet view of Delpech's
early nineteenth-century lithographic establishment in Paris that
Russell Allen gave the museum depicts a scene in which he would
have instinctively been at home. He kept this tradition alive in the
Boston of the first half of the twentieth century, and greatly enriched
the Museum of Fine Arts into the bargain.

CHAPTER XVII

Research, Crowds, and Docentry

In annual summaries of the activities of various curatorial departments the name of William J. Young had been mentioned with respect and gratitude for fifteen years before anyone had the wit to ask him to publish an account of his own work. Only in 1947 did the annual report of the museum begin to contain a section devoted to the Research Laboratory, and the varied activities that he and his two assistants carried out. Much of it deserves quotation to show how closely the laboratory was allied with the work of various curators.

Basic research on Asiatic glazes was undertaken with encouraging results; further research in this field will be undertaken during the next year. Some research has been continued on the investigation of ancient dyes in textiles. As this project demands much concentrated time, it is planned to continue this research during the coming year. Many techniques and experiments have been carried out in the field of X-ray in the study of paintings with pleasing results. Considerable research in the identification of forgeries in paintings has been carried out by spectographic means with excellent results.

A three-meter spectograph was purchased and installed during the latter part of the year which will greatly increase the accuracy of analyses and greatly facilitate the work of detection of forgeries.

Two hundred and seventy-four objects passed through the laboratory for preservation, examination, or to be made ready for exhibition. A total of one hundred and fifty-five examinations were carried out by X-ray, Ultra-violet, Infra-red, Fluoroscopic, Microchemical, or Spectographic means. The Laboratory ceased the photographic work, by the reverse photographic method, of casts of coins for the Classical Catalogue for a period of time, as the question arose as to the type of plate needed for the work. It is hoped that satisfactory results have now been achieved and that this photographic work will be completed within the next few months. An automatic dehydrating case was designed and built by the Laboratory for the bust of Ankh-ha-ef. This was completed and the bust installed in the case for exhibition in the early part of the year. A colossal Archaic Vase was disassembled; this was reconstructed and restored. A marble Three-standing Figure Group from a font base, attributed to a Tuscan master of the thirteenth century, was drilled, dowelled, and restored ready for exhibition. This work was completed along with numerous other time-taking restorations.

The Departments calling for the most concentrated time during the year were the Classical, Asiatic, Painting, Egyptian, and Textile Departments.

These are, after all, five out of the seven departments. It should be noted that the Tuscan marble group came from the Department of Decorative Arts, and that the Department of Prints had its own laboratory in which Francis W. Dolloff was at work full time.

The following year William J. Young was devoting considerable time to detecting the nature of dyes and identifying the fibers in early Coptic textiles, studying the clay bodies and glazes of early Oriental ceramics to establish characteristic differences for dating, and to metallurgical analyses, both qualitative and quantitative, with the aid of his new spectograph. For ten weeks during the summer he continued these investigations in England and France, examining various collections of Oriental ceramics and Coptic textiles, and paying particular attention to ancient dyes.

Considerable research was done on tracking down the ancient Woad dye, with which the early Britains stained their bodies to make themselves look war-like, which was eventually applied to textile fibres. This was accomplished with the cooperation of the Botanical Laboratories of Oxford University and with the cooperation of the staff of the Herbareum at Kew Gardens at London, where samples of the Woad plant and seed were obtained for study.

Advantage was taken to visit some of the small Scottish family groups where fabrics were being produced, in many cases, by the use of old types of looms and dyes. Particularly interesting was "crottle" (or lichen dye) which is abundantly found clinging to rocks and seawalls. Samples of these various lichen dyes were obtained.

Through the interest of Monsieur R. Pfister, the authoritative dye expert and consultant to the Musée Guimet in Paris, much valuable information was obtained when he kindly demonstrated his analytical results and procedures of ancient dyes in his laboratory at Le Perreux. Samples were presented to the Laboratory by Monsieur Pfister of textile dyed with the *Murex Brandaris*, the true Tyrian purple, also a sample which was actually taken from the small bladder under the head of the *Murex Brandaris*, and a sample of *Purpura Lapillus*, the mollusks from which the royal samples were obtained and which are referred to by Pliny.

In addition to carrying on research on the fading of textile dyes and the chemistry of Chinese ceramics during 1949, new microscopic equipment was installed that permitted the study of "the various tell-tale layers which are formed in ancient patinas and are lacking in modern forgeries" of ancient bronzes. During this year a total of 669 objects passed through the laboratory, an increase of some 300 over 1948.

The shortest amount of time required by an object was fifteen minutes. The greatest was two and a half months, required for the restoration of a colossal black granite Egyptian statue. The restoration of this statue brought out many interesting problems, as it called for a period of forty-eight hours to drill four holes seven-eighths of an inch in diameter, and eight inches deep, with the aid of carbide tipped steel drills driven by an electric motor. This automatically gave rise to the question of what tools were at the command of the ancient Egyptians. As it is only possible to cut or abrade a substance with a material of greater hardness, experiments

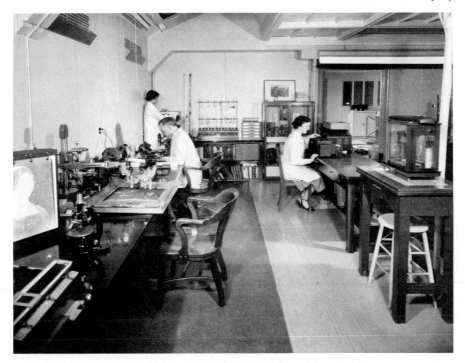

RESEARCH LABORATORY. Mr. Young at microscope, Miss Whitmore at spectrophotometer used in dye analysis, Miss Zacharias at heating apparatus for cross-sections.

were carried out on Egyptian granite with the aid of various mixtures of bronze of high tin content. When the tin content was increased to thirteen percent or over, the chisel fractured without having any decided effect on the granite.

In view of the high achievements of modern forgers in fabricating "ancient" bronzes, Young continued research in 1950 on ancient metals with the study of proven forgeries, as well as investigating ancient Egyptian stone and textile dyes. He spent two months in England, Greece, and Egypt, visiting museums and laboratories. No matter how involved his investigations became, he never forgot his basic British principle that a job can be done with a few toothpicks and a bit of string, provided one applies sufficient thought, intelligence, and experience. Normal American practice is to seek a large grant, purchase costly equipment, and assemble a staff before getting down to work. As Bill Young has never subscribed to this theory, he has often achieved remarkable results with comparative economy. In 1951 he wrote:

> Through the interest of Mr. Ernest Lucas, head of the Spectographic Laboratory, and the auspices of the American Steel and Wire Company of Worcester, the Department was most fortunate in obtaining an instrument, the densitometer. Although this instrument had been in use at their factory for ten years, it was possible by their gift and a comparatively small outlay of money to recondition this instrument whereby it is now possible to obtain far greater accuracy in quantitative spectographic work.

Similarly in 1952, through the help of Professor Clifford Frondel, Curator of the Harvard Mineralogical Museum, the Research Laboratory was able to buy an X-ray diffraction apparatus "at a considerable saving." This equipment permitted precise identification and analysis of most materials found in archaeological work, such as pigments, resins, dyes, metals, and ceramics, and might provide an answer where chemical and spectro-chemical means failed.

In addition to coping with the 510 objects that passed through his laboratory in the course of 1952, William J. Young's studies of Chinese ceramics led him to visit many museums, art dealers, and private collections, where he made a total of 1,179 photomicrographs from 369 objects. He noted with quiet satisfaction: "The Laboratory, with the addition of X-ray diffraction, is equipped to undertake most forms of analysis or research in the archaeological field. This brings the Laboratory to a standard comparable with any museum laboratory here or abroad, and has been possible only through the interest and encouragement of the Director."

The Research Laboratory was operating at capacity in 1953, with full use being made of the X-ray diffraction equipment. After three years' research Young had devised and published a method of dating Chinese Kuan and related wares by the microscopic study of their subsurface structures, as well as a means of distinguishing genuine red-decorated black mortuary figures from Hui-hsien from the numerous forgeries that had appeared on the market. For all its prodigies of research, the laboratory was constantly converting dilapidated

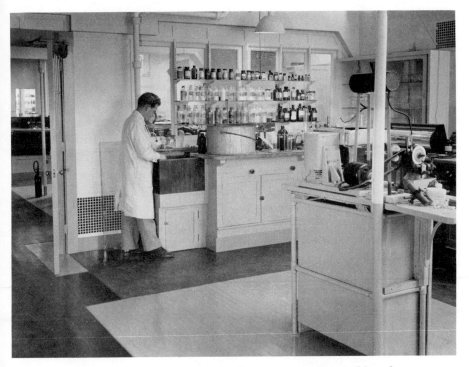

RESEARCH LABORATORY. Mr. Harrington at chemical bench.

fragments that had long reposed in storerooms into handsome objects for exhibition. The silver and electrum mask and trappings for the mummy of Princess Mernua (ca. 623–568 B.C.) that reached the museum in 1923 were thirty years later electrolytically cleaned, and a facsimile of a wrapped mummy made upon which they could be mounted for display.

The detection of forgeries continued to be a constant preoccupation of the Research Laboratory. Thus in 1954 William J. Young reported:

> Because the forger is applying modern methods of fabrication, in the case of Greek gold coins it was felt that microscopic methods were inadequate. After much experimentation and with the cooperation of Professor J. T. Norton, Department of Metallurgy, Massachusetts Institute of Technology, a more positive method of examination was obtained by the use of the Geiger Counter X-ray

Diffractometer. This non-destructive method whereby the coin is bombarded with X-rays and the results charted automatically by a mechanical pen indicates definite structural differences between ancient and modern gold coins. The X-ray method was also found practical in the identification of Greek pottery in establishing the origin of the clays. The curves, mechanically obtained from pottery of known localities, were in themselves characteristic. The results of the X-ray diffraction method have proved so successful in the study of ancient works of art that it is now planned to study the various sources of clays from which Chinese porcelains originated, bringing the pottery into more definite categories where it is hoped that the differences in shape and design will prove characteristic. This machine, which has now been installed in the Laboratory, can also be applied in the analysis of pigments and ancient patinas, thereby greatly facilitating the work of definitely establishing ancient objects and modern forgeries.

Behind the scenes in many parts of the Museum of Fine Arts great skill and ingenuity, unsuspected by the average visitor, are constantly applied. The presence of thousands of objects, handsomely placed in orderly galleries, is taken for granted, without much thought of the processes by which they came there. Yet walls have to be painted, roofs mended, works of art moved, and a thousand and one duties carried out even when no radical changes are in progress. All this falls within the province of the Superintendent of Buildings and Grounds, who began to be heard from in annual reports only in 1941 when Howard K. Alden assumed that post, with Walter F. Orech as his assistant. The installation of large and heavy new objects, such as the French Renaissance chimney piece given by the Brummers in 1948, posed many problems, as did the handling of objects in great loan exhibitions, Typical of the kind of competence demanded is a 1949 performance, reported by the Superintendent:

A large Egyptian sarcophagus which had been in general storage several years was sold to the Brooklyn Museum for exhibition in one of its main galleries. This sarcophagus with its cover, weighing about 10,000 lbs., was removed from general storage by a Cambridge rigger, Mr. Gordon Harnum, who rolled it out through a basement corridor underneath the Lecture Hall, through the painting storages of the Evans Wing, and out through one of the rear doors into the courtyard adjacent to the Administration office. It was then loaded onto a truck, hauled to Brooklyn, New York, carried into the Brooklyn Museum over several hundred feet of marble floor, and placed on exhibition. A grateful letter from the Museum director indicated that the service rendered was thoroughly appreciated.

Keeping track of thousands of objects in the museum has been, since the early years of this century, the function of the Registrar. After Matthew S. Prichard was demoted from Assistant Director to Bursar in 1906, he devised the present system of recording and cataloguing objects of art in the museum. When this went into effect, Morris Carter, the Librarian, was given the additional title of Registrar, although the duties of that office were never formally defined until a July 1920 revision of the by-laws. In 1920 it was stated that it shall be the duty of the Registrar

> on behalf of the Director to receive and record all works of art entering the Museum, and to release all works of art leaving the Museum; to assist those in charge of departments in the registration of objects in their care; to keep a record of the source of all works of art secured by purchase or gift or loan, together with a list of donors and lenders; to record any restrictions; and to render such other assistance in the work of the Museum as the Director, with the approval of the Committee on the Museum may determine.

Such a vigilant Cerberus was highly necessary in view of the number of valuable objects that entered and left the museum as loans or on approval, or remained there as part of the permanent collection. Morris Carter carried out these duties until 1912 when he became Assistant Director. Hanford Lyman Story, who was often holding the fort in the Egyptian Department, filled the post until his death in 1939, when Robert G. Rosegrant, who had been Morris Carter's Assistant Director at the Isabella Stewart Gardner Museum, took it over. As Rosegrant resigned in 1942, when qualified people were hard to find, the office remained vacant until 1946, when David Britton Little returned from almost five years of active duty in the

Navy. As he was a Chinese scholar, who had been one of Kojiro Tomita's assistants in the Asiatic Department before he commanded naval vessels in the Pacific, David Little had an admirable combination of scholarly knowledge and administrative competence. Such a man was indispensable at a time when a considerable increase in loan exhibitions was causing other people's valuable property to wander in and out of the museum doors with increasing frequency. For twenty years he was an effective Cerberus, although to sustain that role he often had to growl at his more relaxed learned colleagues as well as at shipping and insurance firms. But if anything were ever lost or damaged in shipment, it was not through any want of proper precautions on the part of the Registrar.

Immediately after the war the Paintings Department reported a great increase in the number of pictures lent to other institutions. The passion for founding museums that overtook the United States in the nineteen twenties had created many institutions that, lacking adequate collections of their own, attempted to compensate by borrowing the possessions of others. The Museum of Fine Arts was frequently the target of such importunities. It also received requests for important pictures that were wanted for more elevated purposes. Thus in 1946, when W. G. Constable reported "heavy drafts on the Museum for loans" that resulted in ninety-nine pictures going to thirty-eight different exhibitions, six were sent to the Tate Gallery in London for their exhibition of American paintings. When one considers the packing and paper work involved, not to mention the possibility of damage in transit, one appreciates W. G. Constable's 1948 remark: "Loans by the Museum have been numerous, but mercifully less than last year." In reading the Director's comments on the subject, however, one is reminded of Julia in Byron's *Don Juan*, who "whispering, 'I will ne'er consent,' consented." In describing the "highly unusual loan" of 1949 by which the great Gauguin and the smaller Gauguin from the Spaulding Collection were sent to Paris during the summer, Edgell noted:

> To do so required a special vote of the Trustees but since the request had come from the French Government, and the exhibition without our great piece would have seemed really crippled, an exception

was made. The prominence given to our paintings in the catalogue is proof that the magnanimity of the Trustees was appreciated.

In 1950 the Gauguin went traveling again, for Harold Edgell reported:

Although normally the Museum hesitates to lend things abroad, it made an exception and sent a Copley, a Sargent, and a typical Currier and Ives lithograph to the exhibition of American painting in Amsterdam. For the Diamond Jubilee of the Philadelphia Museum, this Museum broke all its rules and precedents and sent the large Gauguin, "D'où venons-nous? Que sommes-nous? Où allons nous?," and the Renoir "La Bal à Bougival." Philadelphia had made a supreme effort to bring together the greatest paintings and drawings in the United States and the Committee on the Museum felt that we should send our very best even though ordinarily we should not think of lending such paintings anywhere. The Diamond Jubilee Exhibition opened November third and in the opinion of the Director was the most distinguished exhibition of works of art ever held in the United States. It gave visual proof of the richness of American collections and the necessity for preserving them intact for posterity.

There is a certain contradiction in this statement, for the best way of keeping anything "intact for posterity" is to keep it inflexibly in one place under the best obtainable atmospheric conditions. People may enjoy traveling, but objects do not, as David Little often pointed out.

A year later Edgell reported:

Loans always present a difficult problem as they are constantly requested from other institutions and we cannot well refuse when we so frequently borrow from other museums ourselves. The Museum has to be particularly careful about loans abroad but every year it yields to some importunity. Thus, in 1951, we loaned to Thomas Agnew and Sons of London the very beautiful "William Locke" by Lawrence. From Agnew the painting went to the City Art Gallery at Bristol. The Walker Art Gallery of Liverpool borrowed our painting of a "Lion and Lioness" by Stubbs. The painting by Lawrence is safely back in the Museum and the Stubbs is on its way. The American Federation of Art borrowed two paintings,

"Mrs. Goldthwait" by Copley and "Portrait of an Old Man" by Joseph Hirsch, for exhibitions that were held in Munich, Berlin, and Vienna. Though the Federation was the sponsor, the request was made by the State Department and the loan really was to the United States Government officials in Europe. The Comune di Venezia requested and obtained for an exhibition in June our small sketch in oils by Tiepolo. To the Art Gallery of Toronto, Canada, we sent "The Slave Ship" by Turner and three watercolors for a special exhibition and subsequently these went to Ottawa for an exhibition there.

Another category of loans that we generally try to avoid are travelling ones, but the Museum made an exception in the case of the Matisse which went to a number of American Museums and the same was true of the very beautiful painting by Yates that was presented to the Museum by Mr. Henry L. Shattuck.

In spite of the ambiguities in his remarks about loans, Harold Edgell loved a full-dress international exhibition. The Japanese treasures shown during the Harvard Tercentenary had inspired him to attempt a similar Italian exhibition; although he spent much time in 1938 visiting Italian officials in this connection, the prospect of war prevented its accomplishment. Not even the memories of gallery floors looking like "the tan bark of a circus ring after the show is over," after the departure of the mobs attracted by the Thorne Miniature Rooms, deterred him from seeking the paintings from the Berlin Museum in 1948. These pictures, captured by General Patton's army and shipped to the National Gallery in Washington for safekeeping, were to be circulated among a number of American museums before being returned to the American Zone in Germany. They went first to New York, then to Philadelphia, to Chicago, and to Boston, the dates set for the Museum of Fine Arts being 14 to 31 August 1948. "The difficulties were obvious," Edgell wrote.

Each museum wanted to keep the paintings on view as long as possible and, therefore, to expedite the shipping, packing and hanging. The Registrar and the Assistant Superintendent went to Chicago to see the paintings packed and to make preparations for their reception in Boston. Mr. Constable returned from England to attend to the hanging. Mr. Alden and his assistants had installed special ventilation and arranged the necessary turnstiles and details of circulation. Everything went smoothly. The paintings arrived in the morning, were on the landing platform by noon, and by two o'clock were in the large gallery P-10 which we had arranged for unpacking. Meanwhile, the other major Evans Wing galleries had been stripped of their regular exhibitions and were waiting with empty walls. By 9 p.m. every box was open and every painting was leaning against the wall in the particular position in the particular gallery designated by a chart arranged by Mr. Constable. The hanging proceeded apace and actually we could have opened a day earlier than we had planned.

By order of the Army, each Museum was required to charge an admission fee, the money thus obtained, after the Government tax had been subtracted, to be used for the relief of babies in the American Zone of Occupation. The amount of the fee was left to the discretion of each Museum. Boston charged fifty cents but decided to have free admission from one until five and seven till ten on three Tuesdays. Meanwhile, Mr. Dooley had written many articles for the papers and the public imagination caught fire. The evening of the first Tuesday the crowds were so great that we were forced to close our doors long before the official time for closing lest somebody be hurt or some work be damaged. On subsequent Tuesdays, by changing the control, by routing the visitors downstairs on exit so that they would not collide with the incoming crowds, by arranging a line which ran sometimes from the base of the main staircase to the top, around by the Library, and back on the other side to the Tapestry Hall entrance, and by other expedients, we were able to handle the crowds without incident. On one Tuesday we had nearly 16,000 visitors, eclipsing by 4,000 the largest daily attendance in the history of the museum.

All rules were broken; the museum was kept open for a seven-day week, with the innovation of an evening opening. Vacations were disrupted and everyone worked overtime, but with good humor. When it was over, Edgell wrote: "So much credit is due to so many people that it seems invidious to name names but the Director, nevertheless, would like to emphasize the splendid work done by Mr. David B. Little and his staff."

Although it was three years before another extravaganza of this magnitude occurred, the exhibition of Paul Revere's Liberty Bowl in the Rotunda from 17 February to 31 December 1949 attracted many visitors because of the campaign that had led to its acquisition. The bowl was placed on a pedestal, flanked by the flags of the Nation and Commonwealth, with the Copley portrait of Revere on a screen behind and above it. Edgell remarked in his 1949 report: "Whether or not this priceless relic of our history should remain forever in so conspicuous a place is a matter for the Trustees to decide. It is shown so well, however, that one is reluctant to remove it to other quarters no matter how dignified." Mercifully it was in due time removed to its proper place in the exhibition of Revere silver, and reverted from its temporary duty as a sacred relic to its customary status as a work of art.

While the Liberty Bowl was still in the Rotunda, a counter attraction was from 5 October to 6 November 1949 exhibited in the Tapestry Gallery. This was Donatello's superb 9-foot gilded statue of San Ludovico, which had been sent for exhibition in New York to raise funds for the restoration of the Ponte Trinità in Florence.

When the Director saw it in New York he wrote the Superintendent of the Monuments of Tuscany asking if it might be exhibited in Boston, and received a favorable answer . . . On account of its scale, it posed a problem which taxed the ingenuity of Mr. Hipkiss and he conceived the rather grandiose scheme of making a plywood screen stretching from side to side at the end of the Tapestry Hall and carrying it as high as the main cornice. This he pointed out could be done cheaply and could be made to simulate the fifteenth century architecture of Florence. For a time we were defeated by the problem of blocking the major circulation of the Museum from the Huntington Avenue to the Evans wings to all who would not pay a fee, but this difficulty was overcome by the simple expedient of cleaning the west loggia outside the Tapestry Hall [which had never been used since it was built more than thirty years earlier] and allowing persons to circulate in the open though under cover from one side of the building to the other. Mr. Hipkiss designed his screen in a manner worthy of Michelozzo, painted the pilasters and the entablatures the color of *pietra serena*, the panels the color of light gray plaster, designed a niche in the center, and placed the statue in a setting as purely Florentine as could be devised in an American building. Discreetly lighted with spots, the golden statue was sensational and all agreed that its exhibition was a success. Twenty-five cents admission was charged on Tuesdays through Fridays, and admission on Saturdays and Sundays was free.

A brief but intense mob scene developed on three days in 1950 when the Museum of Fine Arts put on display in the Rotunda a carpet embroidered by Dowager Queen Mary of England. Harold Edgell reported: "Enormous publicity had been given to this piece which had toured the country and in three days 29,434 people came to see it. On Sunday alone there were over 16,000 visitors. It is amusing to note that this completely eclipsed the record of the 10,000 people who came years ago on Mother's Day to see the portrait of Whistler's *Mother*." The Superintendent of Buildings and Grounds, who had had to rope off a passage from the Huntington Avenue entrance to the Rotunda and back to the entrance again to keep the crowds under control, claimed that the total attendance "was in excess of 35,000." It probably seemed that there were that many, although the Director's figure, being of an exact number, has a greater ring of truth.

Parenthetically, it is diverting to recall that the earlier attendance record was an unanticipated folk reaction to the *Portrait of the Artist's Mother*, that was included in an extremely serious exhibition of paintings, drawings, and prints by Whistler, arranged by Henry P. Rossiter, that had been held from 24 April to 13 May 1934. Possibly the fact that this painting, having been lent by the French Government, was escorted from the South Station to the museum by motorcycle policemen added to the popular frenzy excited by its subject matter. In any case, this was the first time that police guards had ever entered the affairs of the Museum of Fine Arts. The entire move from Copley Square to Huntington Avenue had been quietly though extendedly accomplished in 1909 without special protection of the law.

Although the opening of the Karolik Collection of paintings in its newly created galleries brought a considerable number of visitors, the great attraction of 1951, which the Director thought "it fair to say the greatest special exhibition the Museum has ever held" was of the *Art Treasures from the Vienna Collections lent by the Austrian Government.* As everyone wanted it, a deal of in-fighting went on among various American museums, the account of which fills two rather uninteresting pages in Edgell's annual report. He having been successful in this scrimmage, the exhibition was shown at the Museum of Fine Arts from 31 October to 30 December 1951. As it filled not only the main floor Special Exhibition Galleries but the Tapestry Hall and all the main galleries of the Evans Wing, an extraordinary amount of clearance and storage was required. The installation, which was handsome, was under the direction of Dr. Ernst Buschbeck, the Viennese curator who accompanied the exhibition. He paid the Boston staff "the compliment of saying that he had never had in another museum as many men, as competent men, or as good equipment for installation as he found here."

An admission of fifty cents for adults and twenty-five for students was charged. Edgell reflected thus on the attendance figures: "Attendance in the building during the two months of the exhibition was 230,617. Paid admissions to the exhibition amounted to 83,276. There were, therefore, some 147,341 persons attracted to the Museum by the attendant publicity who did not enter it." I observed one of this number, Charles Francis Adams (1866–1954), moving away from the turnstile when he discovered that fifty cents was required, to contemplate, without charge, the Copley portrait of his great-grandfather John Quincy Adams. In doing so, he bore out an observation of the late Mrs. Edward Cunningham to Chiang Yee, quoted in *The Silent Traveller in Boston;*

> On hearing that I was going to the Museum of Fine Arts, she chuckled and told me to be sure to go to see the American room, for there I would see something which I never could see in any other museum in the world. I would find a group of people under a certain portrait and their family name would be that of the person in the portrait. All Bostonians were like that. They went to the museum to see their ancestors' portraits and never wanted to see any other picture.

LOOKING AT THE FAMILY PORTRAITS. Drawing by Chiang Yee, 1959, for *The Silent Traveller in Boston*, owned by the Boston Athenæum.

Although Mr. Adams' withdrawal did not surprise me, for there was a horrendous crush in the galleries containing the Vienna pictures, such general behavior did surprise Harold Edgell, who continued:

This is difficult to understand. One can easily understand a person not being interested in the Fine Arts and not coming to the Museum at all, but it is hard to understand the psychology of a person who would come to the Museum when such an exhibition was on view and not be inquisitive enough even to look at it. The real reason probably was the fee of fifty cents which was charged to enter the exhibition. In 1918 the Trustees voted to abolish all admission fees and we have prided ourselves ever since on offering our treasures free to the public. Speaking as a Trustee, the Director has always been proud of this attitude. The figures revealed by the Vienna Exhibition, however, may shed a new light on the whole matter. Have we not possibly educated a large bulk of the public into the belief that great art is not worth anything? The same people who would cheerfully pay a dollar or more to view an indifferent motion picture, would not pay fifty cents to see one of the greatest collections of artistic treasures in the world. We shall, I believe and I hope, continue to offer our collections free to the public, but I reveal these figures as something that the Trustees might want to ponder.

There was a good deal to ponder that was never fully resolved. Crowds make pleasing statistics but they cost money. Only twice in the museum's first seventy-five years did the annual attendance exceed half a million: 512,854 in 1941 and 546,564 in 1942. These records are clearly attributable to the two exhibitions of Mrs.

KUAN YIN SLIPS OUT OF THE BOSTON MUSEUM FOR MEDITATION. Drawing by Chiang Yee, 1959, for *The Silent Traveller in Boston*, owned by the Boston Athenæum.

Thorne's Miniature Rooms. In seven out of the nine years from 1937 through 1945, William H. Claflin and Robert Baldwin as treasurers achieved the beatific miracle of a balanced budget with a modest excess of income over operating expenses. While it may be coincidence, the two years whose operations resulted in a deficit were 1941 and 1942. Since 1946 deficits have been as constant a feature as they were before 1937. The Berlin pictures brought 1948 attendance to a new record, while the deficit — $9,570 in 1946 and $1,462 in 1947 — leaped to the new record of $69,280. Attendance fell to 476,522 in 1949; rose to 501,913 in 1950, and, with the Vienna pictures in 1951, reached the new high of 642, 911. The 1951 deficit, charged to the principal of an unrestricted fund, was $43,826. After 1951 attendance steadily dropped, year by year, to 390,635 in 1955. In 1952, thanks to roofs needing repair and a $57,858 deficit of the Museum School, the deficit amounted to $208,453, a sum not exceeded until 1968. Over the past quarter-century operating income has steadily increased through gifts, bequests, and skillful investment, but operating expenses invariably seem to increase a little more rapidly.

In the nineteen forties sociability, not immediately concerned with works of art, began to increase. The Director reported in 1942:

> The Museum continued its custom of occasionally holding a tea in connection with a private view. A very successful and well attended tea was held at the private view of Mrs. Thorne's Miniature Rooms. Another marked the opening of the Exhibition of the Work of the Guild of Boston Artists. On these and other occasions the Museum owes a great debt to Mr. Edwin S. Webster who lavishly loaned shrubs and flowering plants from his greenhouses to make the Trustees' Room a bower of beauty. The Museum participated in another very distinguished entertainment during the summer when it offered its hospitality to His Excellency Governor Saltonstall for a banquet which he gave in honor of Her Majesty Queen Wilhelmina of Holland. The banquet was held in the great Tapestry Hall, decorated with tapestries, flowers, and seven-branched candlesticks. A small stringed orchestra played Dutch folk music during the meal, and all seemed to agree that the effect was dignified and baronial.

The Governor's entertainment of Queen Wilhelmina was un-crowded in comparison with the evening of 8 September 1952 when a reception was given by the Right Reverend Norman B. Nash, Bishop of Massachusetts, for the Archbishop of Canterbury and the Presiding Bishop of the Episcopal Church, the Right Reverend Henry Knox Sherrill. Although the Director simply noted that "it filled the Tapestry Hall with appreciative clergy," the Superinten-dent of Buildings and Grounds reported more specifically: "About 10,500 people jammed the Museum during this Monday evening. The crowd was so large that it extended from the main entrance around the horseshoe and down Huntington Avenue to Forsyth Street. A first-aid station was set up in the Recent Accessions Gallery but luckily it was not used during the entire evening." Apparently the reception held in the same year, at the request of Commissioner Kelleher, by the Boston Fire Department, for the wives of visiting fire chiefs holding their annual convention in Boston, was of more modest proportions, for the Superintendent made no comment.

All this increase in activity had relatively little effect upon the subscriptions received from the two thousand or slightly more annual members whose names in columns filled a considerable number of pages in each annual report, much as they had since 1889. Their contributions, which formed a useful but not spectacular part of the museum's annual income, amounted to $40,031 in 1945. They dropped the following year to $35,891; although the amount fluctu-ated as individuals changed, the income from this source remained below $40,000 until 1955.

After the arrival of William Germain Dooley in 1941, the Direc-tor increasingly pointed with pride to the burgeoning activities of the Division of Education. With the end of the war a great many in-creases took place. In 1945 Dooley reported that the work of his division "has increased to the capacity of the present staff, and a study is being made for a definite long-term policy regarding this contribu-tion to community education." But as his senior staff was soon doubled from three to six, he observed in 1947 that "the activities in education by the Museum have in some cases almost doubled over two years ago and in every case have increased to some degree." From 1948 his reports tended to begin with a remark about the division's activities having reached a new all-time peak.

As the Victory Concerts given in connection with the USO, "to bring fine music to members of the armed forces," were becoming increasingly attended by civilians as the end of the war came in sight, which was contrary to the purpose of the series, it was in 1945 decided to withdraw from membership in the Committee for Victory Concerts. In the autumn of 1945 the Division of Education was free to start a new policy concerning music, in which an attempt was made to integrate music and the arts which the museum represented by offering concerts whose programs were carefully planned to supplement either a current exhibition or a lecture or gallery talk by some distinguished authority. The autumn program of 1945 included such combinations as a concert of pastoral music by the Boston Woodwind Ensemble accompanying W. G. Constable's lecture, "Reflections on a Landscape Exhibition," or a piano recital by Mary Michna, "Impressionism in Music," paralleling a lecture by Professor Frederick B. Deknatel of Harvard on "Aspects of Impressionism in Painting." Dr. Emmanuel Winternitz's discussion of "Musical Instruments in Paintings of the Seventeenth Century" was illustrated by seventeenth-century music played by the harpsichordist Daniel Pinkham and a string trio. By the end of the year attendance at the series had reached the three thousand mark. Eight or ten of such imaginative combinations of instruction and music, held on Sunday afternoons in the Tapestry Gallery, were offered for the next decade, Miss Eleanor E. Randall, Senior Museum Instructor, being responsible for the programs.

The liveliness and literacy of this series made friends from other institutions glad to pitch in and help. Two eminent Harvard art historians lectured in the 1949 series: Jakob Rosenberg speaking on "The Baroque and Rococo in European Art," and the medievalist Wilhelm R. W. Koehler expressing another side of his learning in a lecture on "Romanticism in Paintings," — each with related music. In the same year Philip Hofer lectured on the prints of Goya, accompanied by eighteenth-century music by the Boston Conservatory String Quartet; Professor Esther I. Seaver, then at Wheaton College, offered "Lutes and Lovers," after which Suzanne Bloch played the lute; I attempted to rationalize Templeman Coolidge's ship models by lecturing on "Maritime Arts," after which a male chorus directed by Eliot I. Wirling sang sea chanties, while the Boston String Quartet played contemporary music after a lecture on "Twentieth Century Art" by Professor Oliver W. Larkin of Smith College. When Miss Randall asked a lecturer or musician to appear, she did so in such a pleasant way that he readily agreed; thus on 16 December 1951 I was back, saying I recall not what about the "Vienna Collections: Religious and Secular Arts," followed by religious music by the boys choir of the Cathedral Church of St. Paul, directed by George Faxon.

The combined lectures and concerts were enthusiastically received. By 1947 William G. Dooley remarked, "the fact that on almost every occasion people have been turned away from the concert hall brings up the problem for the future of larger space for these concerts, although the Tapestry Gallery at present provides a distinguished and very beautiful setting." Two years later so many people were being turned away from both lectures and concerts for lack of space that, beginning in the autumn of 1949, "the entire Tapestry Gallery has been reserved first for those attending the lecture preceding the concert, thus assuring them of seats, and then, those who come for the concert only are seated." After six of these concerts had been given in 1954, they were, in spite of their popularity, abandoned, "a casualty of the current budget curtailment."

A series of Wednesday lectures by art historians offered an opportunity not only to hear museum curators and scholars from other American institutions but a variety of distinguished European authorities. Among the British visitors were Trenchard Cox, Alan J. B. Wace, Arthur M. Hind, Bernard Leach, Roger P. Hinks, and James Wardrop, while Osvald Siren spoke on "Chinese Gardens" in 1947 and the French medievalist Georges Gaillard on "Mozarabic Art in Spain" the following year. Gallery talks were, as always, given by instructors in the division and by curators. Such offerings were clearly related to the museum collections; there was, moreover, no limit to their possibilities beyond space and human endurance. An attempt, begun in 1944, to attract casual visitors by showing free movies in connection with current exhibitions, on Saturday afternoons and holidays, proved abortive. The October–December 1944 exhibition, "Sport in American Art," readily lent itself to such a plan, and short films on various sports were shown every Saturday afternoon, climaxing on 9 December with the feature film "Ski Chase."

As not all exhibitions offered such obvious possibilities, documentary and travel films were used in 1945. In the spring of 1946 this practice was discontinued "because of the difficulty of obtaining a sufficient number of good films on art or related subjects suitable for presentation, and also because the few superior films available were in poor condition from constant use. It was felt that it was better to show none, than to show inferior material."

As early as 1914, when Huger Elliott, Supervisor of Educational Work, was dividing his time between the museum and the Museum School, a class in vocational drawing, as part-time training for pupils in Boston high schools, was established. At least from the early nineteen twenties, Saturday morning drawing classes for children from eight to eighteen were an established fixture. In 1945 these had overreached the limit of space available, for nearly five hundred children were enrolled during the year in the four summer and ten Saturday classes, while adult classes in drawing, painting, and design — two in the summer and three in the autumn — were filled to capacity. Although their popularity was so great that in 1947 there was a waiting list of over a hundred, lack of space was a problem, for in that year the Division of Education lost one of its classrooms, which was urgently needed by the Egyptian Department to accommodate records recently arrived from Egypt. In compensation, some of the classes were moved into the high-ceilinged Cast Court, where the noise of various groups greatly disturbed each other, not to mention the general peace of adjacent exhibition galleries. The Superintendent of Buildings and Grounds valiantly attempted to abate this nuisance by hanging from the ceiling eighty sound-absorbing drums formed of Ozite, a foot in diameter and a yard long, at irregular intervals starting twelve feet above the floor. Although these, and other acoustical devices suggested by Dr. R. H. Bolt of the Massachusetts Institute of Technology, made the Cast Court somewhat more bearable, it was not the ideal location. This was part of a broader dilemma, for in 1948 William G. Dooley reported:

> This welcome flood of activities presents many inherent embarrassments, including lack of work and study space, extraordinary demands on the staff, and the problems of attendance. To name but

a few of the latter, we have exhausted all potential classroom space, even to corners of the basement and under the roof skylights. Our Sunday concerts have had "standing room only" signs up for the past year, and some of the Sunday gallery talks are so popular that they attract as high a number as 150, obviously too large a group to handle with good results. Our circulating exhibits, too, are in such demand that production, in the face of swiftly rising costs, cannot hope to keep up. We have in effect instituted an informal rationing system. All these problems are the happy result of a busy Division and an awakening public demand.

There was still a waiting list for the Saturday children's classes in 1949, with lack of classroom space as the limiting factor. The following year, when the Cast Court began to be reconstructed to provide galleries for the Karolik Collection, classrooms were mercifully rigged in the basement near the Huntington Avenue entrance, where teaching could be done with comparative freedom from outside distraction and with less disturbance to museum visitors. When the Karolik Galleries were completed in 1951, the Division of Education gained excellent new studios on the third floor above them. Nevertheless, in 1952 the attendance at the Saturday classes, like that of the Sunday concerts, "remained static" for "lack of space." That year there were 353 children in twelve classes, and ten classes containing 170 adults, with many turned away for lack of accommodation. Although drastic budget reductions in 1953 unfortunately killed off the admirable Sunday lecture and concert series, the drawing classes for children and adults continued at full speed, and were "filled to capacity" in 1954.

The experimental Children's Gallery was, for want of better space elsewhere, installed in "an inadequate, inaccessible room in the depths of the basement" where, on occasion it offered amusement-cum-babysitting. Its operation in 1946 was thus described by Bill Dooley:

> During July and mid-August, the Children's Room was open weekday afternoons under supervision. Boys and girls from four to twelve came down to read and look at the picture books, to use crayons, colored beads, and other art materials. One morning a

week a Story Hour was given, and another morning a motion picture
shown. Some children were younger brothers or sisters of boys and
girls in the drawing classes, some near neighbors to the Museum,
others, whose parents were attending an adult guidance or visiting
the galleries, were from out-of-town or even out-of-state.

Parenthetically, it was the *lack* of such a supervised playpen
earlier in the century that resulted in my having been acquainted
with many of the greatest works in the Museum of Fine Arts for more
than sixty years, for my mother simply took me with her on her visits
to the galleries. Although I remember nothing of the Copley Square
building, I believe that I was in it on several occasions. Most parts of
the Huntington Avenue building, from its earliest days, remain
vividly in my memory, including a gallery talk on Sienese painting
by Edward W. Forbes, whose orange Shantung silk necktie had
strayed out of place until it was more nearly under his left ear than
his chin. Of my years while still in the Boston Latin School, I recall
not only Benjamin Ives Gilman's gallery talks, but pleasant conversations with FitzRoy Carrington in the print rooms. But that was an
era when figuratively, you threw the baby into the pond and let him
swim or sink.

On 1 October 1948, however, the Children's Room moved into
superior quarters in the former Classroom C and an adjoining room,
under the direction of Miss Elizabeth Mixter.

> There is a splendid entrance stairway and a corridor for exhibitions.
> There is in process of preparation children's exhibit space and a
> workroom and library of their own. These rooms face onto the
> Garden Court and there is a temporary stairway giving access to
> the garden which will make it very pleasant for the children in
> good weather. Miss Mixter is experimenting with various types of
> activities interpreting the Museum's collections to the children and
> already a good deal of outside interest and support have been shown
> in this appealing activity.

It was duly reported in 1949 that the new room was "brimful of
activities and, in many cases, pioneering work," and that "the children have come through reading, games, treasure hunts, and story

hours (to mention but a few of the things done) to enjoy and understand the great arts of the past." Be that as it may, the Children's
Room was so much a going concern in 1950 that it had reached the
limit of its capacity. "Our problem now," remarked Bill Dooley, "is
not how to entice children in, but rather, how best to handle those
we can accommodate, so that the widest interest in our collections is
implanted." Although a "full house" was reported in 1951, some
misgivings about the quality of the audience appear in the 1952
statement:

> Though there has been a natural tendency for the room to be most
> frequented by children in the immediate neighborhood of the Mu-
> seum, this has been counteracted by a policy of inviting groups
> from all over the community. Thus constantly there are new faces
> from the Girl and Boy Scouts, day camps, settlement houses, and
> private schools. These eagerly seek afternoon and week-end recrea-
> tion at the room and in the galleries in a planned but informal
> stimulation of their interest.

The total attendance for 1953 was over 7,000 children between the
ages of five and fifteen, with weekly totals averaging 150 to 175. It
was noted, however, that the groups of Scouts, campers, and the like
were "often greatly outnumbered by the ever-growing nucleus of
neighborhood children." Miss Annette B. Cottrell, a graduate of
Bennington College, who took over the Children's Room in 1954,
was reported to have "inaugurated a new and promising system of
selected groups" for its activities.

Another project designed to lure in children was the Treasure
Hunt, first attempted in 1940 in collaboration with the Works
Progress Administration. The participants would seek some object
in the museum, and after discovery, study it and make a drawing
from memory, with materials supplied by the WPA. Of the first
year's experiment, Harold Edgell wrote:

> In the course of seven weeks, this brought 2,392 boys and girls to
> the Museum who spent at least an hour in the galleries, and a
> longer time in the Garden drawing. These came from the many
> playgrounds of Boston, 103 being represented, and the Art Project

had five instructors throughout the period. It was a novel way of interesting the young in the Museum, and, considering the youth and inexperience of the visitors, their behavior was exemplary.

The Treasure Hunt Competition continued later in the forties in cooperation with the Museums Council of Boston. Another old standby, the Annual Museum Competition in English, History, and Art, which offered prizes for essays from Boston high school students, was in its nineteenth year in 1953, when the subject was "Man's Story in Sculpture through the Ages." Of this it was reported:

> Thousands of Boston public high school students came to the Museum to study selected examples of Egyptian, classical, mediaeval, and eighteenth century European sculpture. An essay on the Snake Goddess written by Thomas D. McCarthy, a senior at South Boston High School, was judged the best submitted from the sixteen schools competing. The Grand Prize, a full-scale reproduction of a Greek Fifth Century B.C. bronze horse in the Metropolitan Museum, was awarded at a special assembly at the school. In addition to the Grand Prize for the best paper from the whole city, the Museum presented prizes of small sculpture reproductions for the best essay from each competing school.

Still another dragnet was provided when the Junior League of Boston in 1948 revived a prewar program of bringing children from settlement houses to the museum for Saturday morning programs.

The Division of Education began on 4 December 1946 to have its first regular radio program over the new station WBMS, which devoted its entire time to serious programs, chiefly of music, with a minimum of obtrusive advertising. From 11:05 to 11:15 A.M. each Wednesday, Mrs. Patricia Barnard, the Senior Assistant of the division, presented a program designed to bring activities, exhibitions, and treasures of the museum to a wide audience. Often she interviewed not only members of the staff, but foreign visitors and local friends, as in 1947 when Trenchard Cox, James T. Flexner, G. Wallace Woodworth, and I were brought into the act. This experiment came to an end in May 1951, after four and a half years of uninterrupted weekly programs. Beginning in January 1950, a series of fifteen-minute weekly programs entitled "Trips to Treasure House" were broadcast over Boston University's new FM station, WBUR. These dramatizations prepared by Boston University students for in-school listening on the junior-high level undertook to present "Museum treasures through the eyes of a group of teen-agers visiting the various departments under the guidance of a knowledgeable friend."

The techniques of advertising were summoned to drum up trade. Through the generosity of National Transitads Company, two thousand cards (normally costing $4,000) were installed in the MTA system cars in 1951 at the time of the Vienna exhibition for only $300, while the three railroads that served Boston offered special rates for school and club groups coming to Boston over their lines to see the exhibition. Forty thousand illustrated leaflets were distributed to libraries, schools, colleges, railroads, and bus lines throughout New England. When Tuesday evening openings were inaugurated in 1953, the word was spread not only by streetcar advertising but through billboards on Boston Common and at Brigham Circle, donated by the Donnelly Advertising Company.

In addition to all these devices for luring people in, the Division of Education carried on a great deal of missionary activity beyond the museum's walls. The Slide Library constantly lent its materials to lecturers and teachers in many institutions. In 1945, when the collection had reached almost twenty-seven thousand, over twenty thousand were borrowed in the course of the year. Well over a thousand new slides would be added each year, with an effort made to supplement the old collection on glass by new 2 by 2 inch color slides. The Illustrative Sets, described in Chapter XIII, were lent to 1,385 colleges and schools in 1945, the highest number ever. Color plates began to be inserted whenever they could be obtained. The division in 1947 became the headquarters and base for circulating exhibitions for the Arts Association of New England Preparatory Schools. The preparation of new material had to be accomplished in odd moments until January 1948, when Miss Narcissa Williamson was transferred from the Department of Textiles, where she had been since 1945, to carry on research and editorial work that had lapsed since the resignation of Dr. Catherine Boyd seven years before.

Miss Barbara Wriston and other members of the staff frequently went to schools and other organizations to lecture in connection with circulating exhibits.

Although the Division of Education was pursuing its missionary efforts with fervor, problems of staff, space, and money were perennial. After "all-time peaks" in the two previous years, in 1950, which was described as "the most active year in Education in the Museum's history," William G. Dooley reported:

> Our immensely vital lecture and lending services could be doubled and redoubled at will, had we the funds and the available staff. Our problem there is to determine just how far the Museum can go, to do the most good with what we have available. Much thought has been given to drawing a line in our Extension activities beyond which the Museum should not be expected to perform services which by right are the duties of the school. This question must be met in time.

Nearly two decades later it is still unresolved. A hopeful possibility was mentioned later in his report.

> This is possibly the last year in which television will not be mentioned extensively in an annual report. Tentative negotiations have been begun with two organizations as to possible use of our materials, but at this writing it looks as though the Federal Communications Commission will allocate the remaining Very High Frequency wave lengths to commercial telecasting. They were particularly intended for educational institutions, but because of the very high expense in operating and maintaining a station, it seems as though the opportunity will go by default. Our hope is that at least portions of television viewing time will not degenerate into the low standards that have marked radio, and that a place can be found for a higher type of program. If so, Museum participation is a definite possibility.

The death of Edward Jackson Holmes on 29 May 1950 accidentally helped to increase that possibility. Richard Cary Curtis, who had been Vice President of the museum since 1936, would have been a logical successor had he not suffered from a rare and menacing disease of the blood from which he died on 20 January 1951 at the early age of fifty-six. Consequently, at the annual meeting on 18 January 1951 Ralph Lowell, who, as Trustee of the Lowell Institute had been an *ex officio* member of the board since 1943, was elected the ninth President of the Museum of Fine Arts. Ned Holmes, although ostensibly a lawyer and private trustee, was at heart a collector, whose deepest interest was the growth and curatorial care of the museum's collections. His successor was, by contrast, the very active President of the Boston Safe Deposit and Trust Company, who sat on more boards, both eleemosynary and concerned with business, than anyone has been able to count. In a world tour that followed much of the proposed itinerary of John Lowell, Jr., founder of the Lowell Institute, eighty years earlier, Ralph Lowell had, after his graduation from Harvard in 1912, traveled in Egypt. There he visited George A. Reisner, with whom he had taken a course in his senior year, and had the good fortune to be present at Reisner's discovery of the Sixth-Dynasty wooden statue of Senezem-ib Mehy. Although fascinated by Egyptology, Ralph Lowell was not a collector by temperament; thus he approached the problems of the museum with more administrative abstraction than had his predecessor. To Ned Holmes the Museum of Fine Arts was the consuming passion of his life; to Ralph Lowell it was an institution whose affairs should be handled in the able way in which he was accustomed to dealing with banks, corporations, colleges, hospitals, and a great variety of commercial and benevolent organizations. For more than a century the Lowell Institute had sponsored in Boston series of free public lectures of remarkable distinction. As the passion for lecture-going began to wane, Ralph Lowell became intrigued by the possibilities of FM broadcasting. In cooperation with several local colleges and universities and the Boston Symphony Orchestra, he established the Lowell Institute Cooperative Broadcasting Council, which in due course created an FM radio station on Great Blue Hill, called because of its location, WGBH. When he became President, it was natural that the Museum of Fine Arts should become a partner in the venture. The new station went on the air on 6 October 1951, and the "standing room only" problem of the museum's Sunday concerts was solved, so long as they survived, by broadcasting them live over WGBH-FM.

To give the museum a continuous Sunday afternoon hour on WGBH, a series of tape-recorded discussions between Miss Williamson and Miss Morna E. Crawford, Museum Instructor in the Division of Education, correlating music and art, was broadcast on the days when there was no live concert. They would, for example, discuss the relation between the Romanesque church and Gregorian chant, or Gothic art and early polyphonic music, using recordings for the musical illustrations. A series of fifteen-minute radio talks, called "This Week at the Museum of Fine Arts," began to be broadcast over WGBH on Tuesday evenings at seven o'clock, with Mrs. Barnard, or the Misses Crawford, Randall, Williamson, or Alice M. Maginnis, another Museum Instructor, alternating as speakers. In addition to a weekly half-hour story program for children, and a ten-week summer program, "Let's See New England," various lectures given at the Museum of Fine Arts were tape-recorded for later broadcasting. Mrs. Barnard acted as coordinator for these museum activities. With the regretted demise of the Sunday lecture-concert series in 1953, Miss Williamson arranged an informal Tuesday evening series of little-known classical and contemporary music, which was tape-recorded by WGBH for subsequent broadcast.

Narcissa Williamson's musical interests constantly led her across the boundaries between museum departments. In 1949 she assisted the Department of Paintings in a complete reorganization of the recorded music played in the Catalan Chapel that contained the Romanesque mural paintings from Santa Maria de Mur, adding new and improved recordings in successive years. By her devising a choir directed by Dr. Paul Giuliana in 1953 sang a series of the Mozarabic chants used in such churches, from scores provided by Dr. Willis Wager of Boston University. These too were recorded for subsequent use. At her instigation the instruments in the Leslie Lindsey Mason Collection began to be taken out of their cases in their court floor gallery in the Department of Decorative Arts and actually played, as their collector, Canon Galpin, had so strongly hoped they would be. Having attracted the interest of fellow musicians, she conceived the idea of creating the Camerata of the Museum of Fine Arts, a permanent concert ensemble for early music, consisting of six instrumentalists, of which she was one, and two singers, a tenor and a soprano. In the autumn of 1954 she organized the Museum Friends of Early Music to underwrite, by annual subscriptions of $10.00, a series of concerts by the Camerata in the museum, using instruments from the Mason Collection or similar modern replicas. The name of this new organization soon spread far beyond Boston through the publication in *The New Yorker* of John Updike's poem "Vow (On Discovering Oneself listed on the Back of a Concert Program as a 'Museum Friend of Early Music')" and its inclusion in his 1969 volume, *Midpoint and other poems.* The Camerata concerts got off to a flying start in the winter of 1954–55 with the Oxford musicologist Thurston Dart, who was at Harvard that year, assisting both in directing and in playing the viols and harpsichord. Thus individual ingenuity, imagination, and energy triumphed over the budget cuts that had eliminated the earlier series of Sunday concerts. Moreover, Miss Williamson's activity made the Mason Collection a living attraction to many musicians and instrument makers in the region.

The museum's first serious excursion into television occurred on 28 December 1952, when it took part, as William G. Dooley reported,

> by invitation in the half-hour "Our Believing World" television program, a regular Sunday morning feature of WBZ-TV, conducted by Richard V. McCann. By special permission of the Trustees, a number of Museum objects including paintings, small sculptures from the Department of Decorative Arts, and prints were taken to the studio. The objects were selected to illustrate the Christmas Story and were scanned by the cameras as Mr. McCann read the appropriate Bible passages. After the Scriptural reading, the rest of the program was devoted to a discussion of Museum objects with three members of the Museum staff — Morna Crawford, Richard B. K. McLanathan and Peter Wick.

Clearly trucking valuable objects about in this way was unacceptable general practice. Thus in 1953, WNAC-TV telecast two programs directly from the museum galleries: on 16 February a half-hour tour of the loan exhibition of *Early American Jewish Portraits and Silver,* and on 28 November a full hour's tour of the *Japanese Art Masterpieces*, and outstanding works of art from various departments. The latter program had involved the undesirable necessity of moving extremely fragile and valuable objects to the Rotunda for filming. Consequently, when WGBH expanded from radio into television, the museum trustees undertook in 1954 the considerable expense of re-wiring much of the building to provide a 50,000-watt installation, feeding power to outlets covering all exhibition floors, with a control room linked directly to the WGBH-TV studios, and all necessary lighting equipment. This would permit television broadcasts directly from museum galleries with a minimum of improvisation.

After an experimental series of five programs from the WGBH-TV studios in May 1955, broadcasting direct from the museum galleries began the following October. Three regular programs were initially scheduled: "Adventures in Art," a half-hour show for children presented on Tuesdays at 6:00 P.M.; "Open House," a program for adults on Tuesday evenings from 8:00 to 9:00, in which Richard B. K. McLanathan interviewed curators and guest experts in the galleries; and a Thursday evening "Images," planned by Miss Williamson and Mrs. Nancy Hartford, in which slides, photographs, and music were used to develop such themes as "Daumier's Paris," "The Arena Chapel," or "The City."

The prospect of such regular telecasting required considerable investigation by the Research Laboratory early in 1955 to determine the effect of television lights on various types of objects, a field hitherto unknown to the staffs of both the museum and WGBH. It was found that lower wattage lamps could be used for television than was at first anticipated, and that heat absorbed by objects could be more readily dissipated under controlled conditions than was initially believed. William J. Young reported:

> After testing a number of objects of different construction under various lighting conditions, it was found that by situating the objects so that air space exists at the back of the objects and a current of air passed directly over the objects, heat and humidity were controllable to the extent whereby objects could be kept within a safe temperature and humidity range. The humidity was controlled by circulating air from other galleries. This air was then blown over the objects from a series of fans. Objects were removed from the Museum to the air-conditioned studio of WGBH where it was found that the temperature rise was considerably lessened under air conditioning.

The last remark relates closely to a further paragraph in the 1955 report of the Research Laboratory.

> The atmospheric conditions of this last summer were such that a great number of bronzes in the Museum suffered from bronze disease. The Laboratory treated over three hundred objects for bronze disease during this period. Bronze disease is caused from a corrosion product, cuprous chloride, formed during burial conditions. Cuprous chloride becomes very unstable above 70% relative humidity causing the bronze to powder and a small area to completely disintegrate. The ideal method by which this condition could be kept under control would be by complete air conditioning of the galleries.

Although nearly fifteen years have passed, this warning is still unheeded. It raises in some minds the question as to whether the careful preservation of invaluable and irreplaceable objects, assembled at great pains over a century, is not a consideration that should take precedence, given the financial necessity of a choice, over many of the activities, however worthy and admirably intended, that have been described in the preceding pages.

Turning to the Museum School during the decade of 1945–1954, one finds peaks of optimism followed by valleys of doubt. Enrollment rose in 1945, while the school was still in wartime exile in the museum, to a five-year peak of 230. The following year, with an enrollment of 224 and an operating cash surplus of $14.80, Russell T. Smith was reflecting on the advantages of the exile, in bringing closer affiliation between the school and the museum departments, which he hoped would prove "the beginning of a development which will make the School unique among art schools"; in short, the return under the museum's roof had somewhat revived the old mood of Copley Square that had been steadily dissipated since 1909. The building at 230 The Fenway, when turned back by the Navy on 30 June 1946, required such extensive repairs that the school did not completely return to it for another year. Nevertheless, it opened in the autumn of 1946 with 306 day and 147 evening students, an obvious reflection of veterans returning under the GI Bill of Rights.

In the summer of 1947 a session was held in Pittsfield during the

Berkshire Music Festival, reviving in a more formal way summer expeditions of the 1880's to the adjacent town of Richmond, Massachusetts. Twenty-nine students enrolled: approximately a third from the winter school, a third from Pittsfield, and a third from other schools throughout the country. Nine entered under the GI Bill. Although 34 students were enrolled in 1958 and 48 in 1959, the number fell to 32 in 1960, and the summer school was regretfully discontinued "due to lack of financial success."

Enrollment in the winter sessions caused no anxiety until the autumn of 1951 — the seventy-fifth anniversary year — when there was a marked drop in applications from veterans. The following year the discontinuance of the Government's program reduced the student body by 68. With 215 students during the day and 76 enrolled in the evening school, the faculty not only increased the tuition to $350 a year, but did their best to rebuild the loss. Although the numbers increased slightly in 1953, there was the thumping deficit of $61,562 that had to be met by the museum, largely because of the need for extensive repairs on a building that was a quarter of a century old. As a means of attracting students more readily, the thought of awarding a degree was considered, for, as Russell Smith noted, "the Museum School was the last of the professional schools in the country to offer a degree either in its own right or in affiliation." Thanks to the new Korean Veterans Bill, the prospect was a little brighter in 1954, for the enrollment, which had been declining ever since 1950, showed a small increase, but there was still a deficit of $24,916.

The Library of the Museum of Fine Arts has seldom been mentioned in the preceding chapters, for, like all useful libraries, it acquired the requisite books, made them available when needed by the staff or by interested visitors, and did nothing spectacular. Ashton Sanborn had become its Librarian in February 1922 and continued for thirty years, even though he quietly and uncomplainingly assumed a great many additional duties when no other hands were available. From 1936 to 1942 he had doubled as Supervisor of the Division of Instruction. From the retirement of Benjamin Ives Gilman in 1925, he had been Secretary of the Museum, as well as being, through that office, in charge of publications. When Ashton Sanborn retired in 1952, these duties were redistributed. Miss Marjorie W. Childs, who had worked with him for twenty-eight years as cataloguer, was appointed Librarian, as of 1 September 1952. In her first report she noted that,

> Through his farsightedness and able discrimination, the Library has expanded from 50,000 volumes to its present capacity of over 100,000 books and pamphlets. This noteworthy record has been achieved, in spite of several difficult years, by making the best use of funds available, by filling in gaps of important serials or out-of-print books as they became obtainable, and by purchasing as many as possible of the current publications which seemed to be essential.

Upon Miss Childs's accession, she passed the care of the extensive series of mounted photographs, housed next to the reading room, into the semiautonomous custody of Mrs. Elizabeth L. Lucy, who was designated Keeper of the Collection of Photographs.

The Library had long since outgrown the pleasant room, furnished, on completion of the museum in 1909, by Mrs. Horatio Nelson Slater as a memorial to her father, William Morris Hunt. As its overflow stacks were placed in the attic above, chiefly accessible by an iron spiral staircase in a corner of the Librarian's diminutive office, convenience was at a minimum. Space, even in the attic, having long been at a premium, a new stack room was constructed there in 1953, permitting a long-desired rearrangement of various sections of books the following year.

On Ashton Sanborn's retirement, Richard McLanathan, then Assistant Curator of Decorative Arts, was appointed Secretary of the Museum and placed in charge of publications. The secretaryship had been intended for David Little, to combine with his duties as Registrar, but as he had been recalled to active duty by the Navy during the Korean Emergency, it was otherwise filled for a few years. A pleasant innovation of Richard McLanathan's responsibility for publications was a series of Museum of Fine Arts Picture Books, the first of which began to appear in 1954. Admirably printed in offset by the Meriden Gravure Company, they made reproductions of museum objects widely available at a modest cost, to a considerable extent eliminating the need for continuing the printing of the far larger and greatly more expensive Illustrative Sets of the Division of Education. The earlier portfolios of collotype plates had been prepared for classroom exhibition, with commentary. The picture books were so inexpensive and attractive that, while useful in organized instruction, they were readily bought in large numbers for individual pleasure. The first was a selection of thirty portraits and busts, entitled *Great Americans from the Revolution to the Civil War*. William Stevenson Smith's delightful *Country Life in Ancient Egypt* was the second, while the third was Kathryn C. Buhler's *English Porcelain Figures, 1750–1775*, which charmingly illustrated some of the Chelsea figures, given by George W. Wales and Richard C. Paine, mentioned in Chapter XVI. The series has continued ever since to provide useful reproductions of important collections in different departments. Beyond the retirement of Ashton Sanborn, other administrative changes occurred in 1952, the saddest of which was occasioned by the sudden death of Dr. George H. Chase, who had been Acting Curator of Classical Antiquities since the death of Lacey D. Caskey in 1944. During these eight years George Chase, greatly loved by everyone, had worked on the numismatic collection, adding some fine coins in memory of Zoë Wilbour after that fund became available, and in 1950 had purchased three fine seventh-century B.C. griffins' heads from a large bronze cauldron. He had revised and improved Arthur Fairbanks' *Greek Gods and Heroes* in 1948, and in 1950 wrote a wholly new *Guide to the Classical Collection*. Few men have started a new job when almost fifty years out of college and have done as much with it as he did. Upon his death the care of the department passed for several years to Miss Hazel Palmer, who was appointed Assistant Curator. In 1952 Howard K. Alden, Superintendent of Buildings and Grounds, retired and was succeeded by his former assistant, Walter F. Orech, who, according to the Director, "had soundly proved his efficiency and who was *persona gratissima* to the Curators, a valuable asset in his position."

Upon the death of Edward Jackson Holmes, he was succeeded as a trustee by a man equally concerned with the arts, but in quite a different way: Bartlett Harding Hayes, Jr. (Harvard A.B. 1926), elected 18 January 1951, Director of the Addison Gallery, Andover, an instructor in art at Phillips Academy who was constantly engaged in experimentation with methods of teaching and exciting the interest of schoolboys. Several changes occurred among the appointed trustees. Following the retirement of Donald Scott from the directorship of the Peabody Museum of Archaeology and Ethnology, Harvard College in 1949 appointed John Coolidge, Director of the Fogg Art Museum, to the Museum of Fine Arts board. To replace Richard Cary Curtis, Harvard in 1950 designated Francis Keppel, Dean of its Faculty of Education. Keppel was, incidentally, a grandson of the pioneer print dealer, who had been the friend and partner of FitzRoy Carrington. In 1950 the Massachusetts Institute of Technology appointed the architect Walter Humphreys following the death of Edwin S. Webster, and in 1953 the Boston Athenæum designated me in the place of Charles Kimball Cummings.

For eighty-three years no change had been made in the organization of the Trustees of the Museum of Fine Arts. The 1870 act of incorporation limited their number to thirty; as it provided for the annual appointments of nine and the service *ex officiis* of five, this left (after the death of the twelve Founders named in the act) sixteen places to be filled by election. In earlier chapters it has been shown how meticulously new trustees had been chosen over the years to provide qualities and abilities that approximated those of the men they were replacing. The original board had represented a subtle balance of concern with learning, teaching, collecting, solvency, and financial competence. Although no sex disqualification appeared in the charter or by-laws, the trustees had always been men. Then, with Ralph Lowell in the chair, changes began to occur, designed to make the board of the Museum of Fine Arts more like those of other institutions of the third quarter of the twentieth century. On 9 April 1953 the Massachusetts Legislature approved an amendment to the 1870 act of incorporation, raising the limit on the number of trustees from thirty to thirty-five. With five new spaces to be filled, the board on 18 February 1954 elected Nelson Wilmarth Aldrich (Harvard A.B. 1934, M.Arch. 1938), like his trustee-father, William T. Aldrich, an architect, and Mrs. Henry Mather Bliss and Mrs. Roger Haydock Hallowell.

Change was in the air, but it came from more directions than had been anticipated, for on 29 June 1954 George Harold Edgell unexpectedly died after a brief illness. A few days later Henry P. Rossiter, Curator of Prints, was appointed Acting Director, and a committee appointed to seek a permanent successor. The choice fell upon Perry Townsend Rathbone, since 1940 Director of the City Art Museum, St. Louis. Although he was unable to come to Boston until the spring of 1955, he was on 15 February of that year elected a trustee of the Museum of Fine Arts. Thus the museum remained in the hands of its third Acting Director some ten months.

For a quarter of a century Henry P. Rossiter had been making superb and adventurous acquisitions for the Print Department. The cares of general administration in no way diminished his skill in that respect, for in 1954 he acquired the only known impression of an *Annunciation* by an anonymous fifteenth-century Ferrarese artist, a superb impression of Dürer's *Great Fortune*, a group of rare sixteenth-century German woodcuts, and the lovely though rarely seen full-length series of Hollar's *Four Seasons*. And during his tenure as

MOSES AFTER STRIKING THE ROCK IN THE WILDERNESS. Netherlands School, by Lucas van Leyden, 16th century. *William King Richardson Fund. 54.1432*

Acting Director two very spectacular acquisitions were made in other departments. The first of these was Lucas van Leyden's *Moses after Striking the Rock in the Wilderness*, a superlative painting with a long and fully documented history. Of it, he wrote:

> Even in 1657 when Francesco Scanelli da Forli saw it in the Villa Borghese, he wrote "an impressive narrative work of rare talent, very well preserved, of highly individual style, full of invention and revealing great beauty . . ." For over two centuries it remained in the Borghese Gallery until the Villa Borghese became municipal property in 1892, when the picture went to the Principessa Piombino. In 1900 the Germanisches Nationalmuseum at Nuremberg bought it and there it has hung ever since, giving pleasure to countless visitors, students, and scholars.

WILD MEN AND MOORS (details). South German linen and wool tapestry, about 1400. *Charles Potter Kling Fund. 54.1431*

This purchase was made possible by the generous bequest of William King Richardson (Harvard A.B. 1880, A.M. 1886, Oxford B.A. 1884), a Boston patent lawyer who, on his death in 1951 when well into his nineties, had left the museum $500,000. Although no restrictions were placed upon the principal or income, he had expressed the wish that the money be spent, if the museum considered it proper, on paintings of the fifteenth and sixteenth centuries. The acquisition of the great Lucas van Leyden would have given singular pleasure to its posthumous donor.

Another notable acquisition was the earliest tapestry in the collection which was bought in 1954 through the Charles Potter Kling Fund. This remarkable tapestry woven in south Germany about 1400, being 3¼ feet high and 16 feet long, was probably designed to hang above a row of choir stalls or benches. It represents *Wild Men and Moors*, coping in woods with a remarkable menagerie of animals.

ST. MARGARET. Upper Rhine, dotted print, about 1450–1460. *William A. Sargent and Stephen Bullard funds.* 55.626

Wild men armed with treetrunks, held as clubs, attack a turreted castle that is defended by dark-skinned men armed with bows and arrows. Another wild man, or woodwose as he might more properly be called, raises his club to strike a lion that he grasps by the mane. Still others attack a dragon and attempt to capture a unicorn. This marvelous medieval scene of heraldic combat and confusion had been at one time in the collection of Prince Hohenzollern-Sigmaringen at Sigmaringen. It presents a world that William Morris, C. S. Lewis, or E. R. Eddison might well have imagined, as well as being the first German tapestry to enter the Museum of Fine Arts and the earliest European one from any country. Another German evocation of such a "wood beyond the world" came to the Print Department the following year when Henry Rossiter bought a particularly beguiling anonymous print of *St. Margaret* in the dotted manner, executed in the Upper Rhine region about 1450–1460.

CHAPTER XVIII

The New Deal

When Perry Townsend Rathbone, the sixth Director of the Museum of Fine Arts, took over his new post on 1 May 1955, he was returning to a region that he had not known intimately since his days as an undergraduate in the Harvard class of 1933. Although he had remained in Cambridge for a year's graduate work, which included Paul Sachs's museum training course, he had gone in 1934 to the Detroit Institute of Arts. After two years as an educational assistant, and as curator of a branch museum known as Alger House, he became general research assistant to its Director, Dr. William R. Valentiner, continuing in that capacity until 1939 when he went to the New York World's Fair. There he first assisted, and then succeeded, Dr. Valentiner in directing the exhibition of masterpieces of art from various parts of the world. When he became Director of the City Art Museum in St. Louis in 1940, he was still only twenty-nine.

Now on his arrival in Boston he was forty-four years old, while the institution that he headed was eighty-five. Its building, having been opened to visitors two years before he was born, was crowded to the gunwales, for no major addition had been made for more than twenty-five years. While the President, Ralph Lowell, and four trustees had been elected within the past five years, Edward W. Forbes, the senior member, had been on the board for fifty-two. Of the remaining trustees, other than those appointed or present *ex officiis*, four had served more than thirty years, four more than twenty, and four more than ten. Four of six of the departments of the museum were manned by scholars of long experience. The curatorship of the Classical Department had not been permanently filled for more than a decade, and Edwin J. Hipkiss, who had created the Department of Decorative Arts, had retired the previous year. But curators of Prints and of Textiles had been in the service of the museum for over thirty-five years, the Curator of Asiatic Art more than forty-five, and the Curator of Paintings some seventeen years. The new Director was new not only to his post but to Boston, for although he was a Harvard man, his entire career had been in the Middle West, and at the New York World's Fair.

During the ten months of Henry P. Rossiter's acting directorship the usual activities of the Museum of Fine Arts had progressed smoothly; important purchases had been made, and plans laid out for much of the year 1955. Consequently, Perry T. Rathbone's first report laid principal emphasis upon his initial view of the scene and his intentions for the future. He began this with the statement: "In the twenty years since I entered the profession, museums have assumed an increasingly important place in the cultural life of our country." This is, so far as I have observed, the first suggestion in the eighty-five years of the Museum of Fine Arts that there was such a thing as a "museum profession." Hitherto it had been assumed that members of museum staffs were competent as scholars or teachers in some particular branch of knowledge, or possessed scientific, technical, or artistic skills that specially qualified them for the care and exhibition of collections. The second and third directors, Edward Robinson and Arthur Fairbanks, had been competent classical archaeologists over and beyond their connection with the museum. The other three, having been initially trustees, had agreed to assume the chief responsibility for the institution only when asked to do so by their colleagues on the board. Loring and Holmes were native Bostonians, collectors and amateurs, in the literal sense of the word; Edgell had spent twenty years as a Harvard teacher and dean before turning curator and museum director. In 1922 Professor Paul J. Sachs had inaugurated in the Harvard Department of Fine Arts a graduate course on Museum Work and Museum Problems. Designed as an emergency measure, like the wartime naval training courses that converted land-based civilians into "ninety-day wonders" to man a rapidly expanding fleet, this Harvard program undertook to provide directors for the tremendous number of new art museums that were springing up throughout the United States. Its immediate acceptance led to a generation of men who, without necessary specialization in any other branch of learning, regarded museum administration as their chosen career. Like librarians half a century earlier, they found it convenient to believe that they were members of a profession, uniquely qualified for their tasks, and developed a kind of standard doctrine and operating procedure.

This approach is clearly reflected in Perry T. Rathbone's 1955 statement of purpose, which continued:

A generation ago museums in America had begun to liberalize their policies and were less often jeeringly referred to as warehouses of art; but the transition from static depository to dynamic institution is a recent accomplishment. Through unremitting educational programs for children as well as adults — a development native to the United States — countless popular books on art, a multitude of color reproductions, many great exhibitions skilfully promoted, through the mediums of the press, radio and now of television, the art museum has taken its place as an essential of cultural existence.

In this missionary effort the Boston Museum has pioneered. It was the first to offer free educational services for children, first to provide docent service for adults. Boston's most recent manifestation of this art mission to the public is the most ambitious, the most costly, and again a first in the country: a full-fledged live television project from the galleries of the Museum. In other words, museums have been consistently using many resourceful means to attract the public for a generation or more, and the Boston Museum is no exception.

Meanwhile, the public, responding to these invitations and inducements to enjoy art and make fuller use of the great collections held in trust for them, have come to expect more of their museums. They have come to expect more exhibitions of high quality, more special services and activities; works of art they expect to be displayed with the fresh beauty and effectiveness that modern techniques permit. They look upon their museums not only as places for the study and contemplation of art, but also as places where physical comforts are provided so that the recreation of the mind can be combined with the relaxation of the body. They have come to think of museums as places beautiful in themselves, where the dispiriting earmarks of the public institution have been obliterated. In other words, the museum, like the successful and popular host, has had to meet new obligations in providing for the pleasure and comfort of its guests.

Now, while our Museum has been in the vanguard of popularization through education and can take pride in this aspect of its modernization, not a few of the services and amenities so widely expected of museums remain to be supplied. To do so will take time, thought and money. But, it is my belief that there will be ample justification for the changes required, for through them the influence of the Museum will be broadened and the experiences it provides will be deepened and enriched.

It is therefore proposed that the program of exhibitions be accelerated and that it be punctuated more frequently by important exhibitions organized by the Museum staff; that a more active program of special events, both for the general public and Museum members, be inaugurated. It is also indicated that as a long-term project the staff will have to turn its attention to the reinstallation of many Museum galleries and displays, employing new lighting and new case designs. Some suites of galleries will have to be reorganized on a more logical and comprehensible plan. Likewise, in combating the outmoded institutionalism of an old museum building we must look forward to providing for visitors the ordinary creature comforts more abundantly and attractively. Essentially, this calls for a public reading and smoking lounge equipped with comfortable chairs and lamps; a similar facility for Museum Members where special functions can take place; a new restaurant on the ground floor, perhaps overlooking the garden court; a larger and more fully equipped auditorium; and an expanded sales room redesigned so that Museum materials can be adequately displayed and conveniently handled. Finally, we must bend our efforts to making every part of the Museum a place of harmony, agreeable and refreshing in atmosphere.

While all these proposals would require considerable outlay of money, they would not automatically bring in an increased income.

While the operating deficit had dropped from its 1952 record of $245,707 to $219,838 in 1953, and $118,643 in 1954, it was clearly necessary to find some new source of funds. The method that immediately suggested itself to Perry Rathbone was a substantial increase in membership. The annual subscriptions instituted in 1889 had steadily risen for forty years to a peak of $94,487; thereafter they declined with almost equal constancy. The $38,289 received from 2,152 members in 1954 helped relatively little in meeting operating expenses of $747,004. The standard statement of recent years had indicated that

> A subscription of $10.00 or upwards entitles the subscriber to an invitation to all general receptions and private views held at the Museum during the current year, with copies of the Annual Report and of the quarterly Bulletin of the Museum; also upon application to the Division of Education, to guidance in the galleries by a Docent of the Museum; also upon application to the Secretary of the Museum, to a copy of the Handbook of the Museum in the current edition.

As subscriptions at the minimum rate, of which there were over five hundred, barely met the cost of the printing and mailing involved, little would be gained by a mere increase in numbers. Consequently in 1955 the system was reorganized, with ascending grades of Annual Membership from $10 to $250 and new categories of Life Membership, involving a single payment of $1,000 or $5,000.

To round up more members, the trustees established in principle in June 1955, a month after Perry Rathbone's arrival, a Women's Committee, appointing as its Chairman Mrs. Roger H. Hallowell, who had been elected a trustee the previous year. In November by-laws had been drawn up for this new group, which the following year dignified its title to the Ladies' Committee. By the end of the year Mrs. Hallowell had enlisted from Boston and surrounding communities a committee of sixty-five members, with Mrs. Thomas B. Gannett as Vice Chairman, Mrs. Richard P. Chapman as Secretary-Treasurer, Mrs. Frank S. Christian as Assistant Secretary-Treasurer, and an executive committee of ten. The first organized membership campaign in the history of the museum began in January 1956. To handle the considerable paperwork involved, Mrs. Isabella Halsted, a daughter of the painter Charles Hopkinson, was appointed to the new post of Membership Secretary, as a member of the Treasurer's office, although closely allied with the Ladies' Committee. Mrs. Hallowell's committee, as the Director reported, "brought the first intensive phase of this drive to a climax with a reception and tea for new members, which was held in the Rotunda February 7, 1956. While the great majority of new members had joined by this date, membership continued to climb throughout the year, as indicated on the graphic symbols that were placed at both entrances of the Museum." By the end of the year members, and their contributions, had more than doubled, for in 1955, 2,201 persons had contributed $40,344, while in 1956 a total of 4,924 had given $94,837. The additional funds thus obtained were allocated to an augmented program of activities and exhibitions, to the creation of a new Members' Room and membership office, and to the rehabilitation of certain galleries and displays.

This was no flash-in-the-pan. Through the constant and unrelenting activity of the Ladies' Committee, membership doubled, tripled, quadrupled, and so on, until in 1967 there were 14,148 members who had paid annual subscriptions of $321,474. As these members had, in addition, contributed $80,110 to a Year End Appeal, the total for 1967 was $401,584, a sum almost ten times the $40,344 that was received in 1955 before the Ladies' Committee went to work. Such a result was attained only by periodical drives, with a constantly increasing series of attractions and inducements offered to those who joined. Beginning in 1956, all social activities of the museum were placed in charge of the Ladies' Committee and the Membership Secretary, who made themselves responsible for the arrangements of parties preceding the public opening of exhibitions, teas for new members, and similar entertainments.

To sustain the interest of the growing membership, it became essential to supply new dress for the printed materials that were sent to them. Illustrations had first been introduced to the annual report in 1954 when Henry P. Rossiter was Acting Director. Hitherto these reports had been pedestrian in typography and uninviting in binding. The tall, thin, double-columned *Bulletin* — 7⅜ by 11½ inches in size — had changed hardly at all since March 1903 when Benjamin Ives Gilman had produced the first number. Henry P. Rossiter, soon after his arrival in 1919, had fallen afoul of Gilman by inquiring: "Don't you think the *Bulletin* type is about the worst you've ever seen in your life?" Gilman's friend and contemporary Henry W. Kent, Secretary of the Metropolitan Museum, whose life was similarly involved in publications and docentry, was a far better typographer. Through Kent's friendship with the best printers of his time, the Metropolitan Museum developed a typographical consistency in its publications, labels, signs, and everything that had to be printed that was far superior to the Boston standard. With Bruce Rogers, Daniel Berkeley Updike, T. M. Cleland, and William A. Dwiggins within easy reach, it is unfortunate that the Museum of Fine Arts had not availed itself of remarkable typographic opportunities. The *Bulletin* might easily have been printed at the Merrymount Press from the beginning, for Updike was a friend of many of the trustees. Unfortunately it was not, and Gilman's rather austere and uncomfortable format survived virtually unchanged through the summer of 1955.

The annual reports of the new administration soon became more attractive in design and more fully illustrated; each had a striking colored cover that reproduced some handsome object recently acquired. Although the size remained unaltered for the decade following 1955, the design of the interior changed four times during this period. To me at least the format of the 1958–1960 reports was more pleasing than its predecessors and successors. As the names of the 6,385 members for 1957 had filled fifty-one pages of that year's report, the practice was adopted the following year of listing only the names of those that had contributed "over and above the basic cost of membership," but even these filled eight pages of small type in double columns. In 1963 it became necessary to reduce membership listings to Permanent Fellows, Fellows for Life, and contributors of $100 or more. From the autumn of 1955 the *Bulletin* acquired colored covers and a new format, with rather less text and more illustrations, although the page size remained unchanged. This continued until 1966 when a squarer format (7¾ by 9 inches), more reminiscent of advertising literature, was adopted both for the

Bulletin and the annual report, which was renamed *1965 — The Museum Year, The Ninetieth Annual Report of the Museum of Fine Arts Boston.* In this new dress, the space provided for the individual reports of the departments was greatly reduced. Where curators had previously been allotted eight to twelve pages each to use as they wished, they now reported in a pattern that called for a few short paragraphs of text, followed by a brief listing of accessions. Moreover the restlessness of the museum in the late sixties became apparent even in the new format of the annual report, for after only two years the type face was changed and lines ceased to be justified.

In 1956 a new monthly *Calendar of Events* was instituted to bring to all members brief illustrated articles on new acquisitions and loan exhibitions, as well as notice of the constantly increasing programs and activities of each month. In that year the membership offerings included a puppet show for members' children, a concert of early music by the Camerata, a lecture each on Egyptology and on flower arrangement, and a benefit performance of the Van Gogh film *Lust for Life.* In addition there began a continuing series of "Know Your Museum" tours of the various departments, which provided, after a brief talk in the lecture hall by the appropriate curator, a guided visit to the galleries, as well as to study rooms, storage, and laboratories that were usually closed to the public. The guided tour principle was gradually extended, in 1958 to a "Know Your Boston" series of bus tours of architectural and historical monuments of the city, correlated with the American collections of the Department of Decorative Arts, and in 1960 to organized group visits to European museums and private collections.

Constant effort was required to sustain this phenomenal growth, for without drives for new members the number might have lessened. In the earlier campaigns advertising methods, originally designed to sell breakfast food or cigarettes, were employed, crossed with the tear-jerking and repetitious techniques of the professional fundraiser. Direct-mail appeals, abounding in mass "personalizations," might bear such postal-meter cancellations as

VISIT   ENJOY   JOIN!
    SUPPORT   ITS
YOUR ART MUSEUM   YOUR MUSEUM

I recall one such offering whose cover was equally divided between the title "Your Museum of Fine Arts" and a photograph of a young mother holding up little daughter to admire the diminutive ivory and gold Minoan *Snake Goddess* of 1500 B.C. On page 2 came the assertion:

THIS IS

. . . a recreation center

. . . a place to learn

. . . a collector's paradise

. . . a research laboratory

. . . a craftsman's mecca

. . . a "World's Fair" of art

THIS is YOUR family's PERSONAL Museum of Fine Arts.

On page 3 were listed the classes of membership by which the recipient might make it HIS or HER family's PERSONAL Museum. The inducements listed included free admission to paid exhibitions; invitations to previews; programs for children; concerts, tours, and lectures; discounts on publications and art classes; as well as "use of attractive New MEMBERS' ROOM."

This last attraction, completed in the autumn of 1958, opened from the Crypt. It was created through the remodeling of the former Secretary's office and part of an Egyptian gallery, long known as the "mummy room." Including space for the Membership Secretary, a kitchenette for the preparation of light refreshments, and a lavatory, it became a focal point for the activities of the Ladies' Committee. There was, in consequence, a deal of sociability, and a marked increase in casual coming and going throughout the museum corridors. Volunteers did their best to make everyone feel at home. Being new to the scene themselves, they did not always recognize old inhabitants, as on the occasion when a lady attempted to direct David B. Little, long a member of the staff, to a tea for new members. He courteously asked if she could tell him where the glass flowers were! By the time that she had returned from discovering that they were in the Museum of Comparative Zoology in Cambridge, he had reached the safety of his office. Although some of these admirably intentioned efforts often confused, puzzled, and annoyed old friends of the museum, they brought in over the years a number of new and valuable friends, as will be seen in later chapters.

The Ladies' Committee was not a static body in which people became permanently entrenched, for its members and officers had definite terms. The Chairman, for example, changed every two years. On 15 May 1957 Mrs. Hallowell, who had set it all in motion, was succeeded by Mrs. Frank S. Christian, who has been followed by Mrs. Thomas B. Gannett (1959–1961), Mrs. William B. Chace (1961–1963), Mrs. Robert M. Morgan (1963–1965), Mrs. John W. White (1965–1967), Mrs. Claude E. Welch (1967–1969), and Mrs. George A. Marks (elected in 1969). Beginning in 1964, the Chairman of the Ladies' Committee became a trustee *ex officio* during her term of office, and the committee was given the right to appoint another of its members to the board for the current year. Thus, in addition to Mrs. Morgan, Mrs. White, Mrs. Welch, and Mrs. Marks, who were trustees *ex officiis*, Mrs. Paul Bernat, Mrs. George N. Proctor, and Mrs. Harvey H. Bundy, Jr., have also in succession served on the board by appointment of the Ladies' Committee. Moreover, Mrs. Frank S. Christian (Chairman, 1957–1959) was elected to a regular place on the board of trustees on 18 February 1965, as was Mrs. Paul Bernat on 17 February 1966. Mrs. Bernat was, of course, no recent recruit, for she and her husband had been keenly interested in the museum for a good thirty years, while her father-in-law's association with it went back to the early years of this century.

The attraction of new members and the retention of those already enlisted required both acceleration and dramatization of temporary exhibitions. Perry Rathbone, who combines rare artistic perception and knowledge with the instincts of a showman, especially enjoyed the confection of happy surprises. His first dramatic venture, which made it clear to most Bostonians that a new breeze was blowing through the Museum of Fine Arts, occurred in November 1955 in connection with an exhibition entitled *Sport in Art*. For the opening he arranged in the Rotunda a fashion show, sponsored by Filene's, as well as a dazzling performance by the enchanting young skater Tenley E. Albright (now Mrs. Tudor Gardiner) on a temporary ice rink installed for the occasion. This was an un-

equivocal declaration of change. Perry Rathbone's first major exhibition, *Sargent's Boston*, which commemorated the centennial of
the birth of John Singer Sargent, was largely drawn from the local
scene. Rather than attempting to present all aspects of the artist's
career, it illustrated in an intimate and personal way the fruitful relation between a great artistic personality and the friendly patronage of
Bostonians over forty years. From 4 January to 7 February 1956 the
temporary exhibition galleries of the museum presented quite a new
face. It will be recalled that in 1934 the Renaissance Cast Court
had been converted into two floors of galleries, and that in 1951 the
Classical Cast Court had been similarly sacrificed, without tears, to
provide two levels of new galleries for the M. and M. Karolik Collection of American Paintings. Now that the five-year exhibition of the
Karolik pictures in the form specified by the donors had come to an
end, Perry Rathbone brought the second floor galleries that had been
designed for them into the area available for temporary exhibitions.

So far as *Sargent's Boston* was concerned, this was a brilliant inspiration, for it brought the Sargent mural paintings of the main stairway, completed in 1925, squarely into the middle of the exhibition.
Visitors mounting the stairway to the Rotunda went first to the older
temporary exhibition galleries to the west, where oil portraits of Bostonians were hung, with embellishments of plants, pieces of furniture, and a huge bearskin rug that created a vaguely Edwardian atmosphere. By the great portrait of the daughters of Edward D. Boit,
painted in Paris in 1882, stood a vase similar to one that appeared in
the picture. On leaving these rooms, instead of going down the interior stairway to the temporary galleries below, visitors continued
around the main stairway, passed the library entrance, and went
on to the galleries created out of the Classical Cast Court, where a
profusion of water colors and drawings were exhibited. Among the
charcoal sketches made in Boston in 1917 were portraits of William Sturgis Bigelow and Denman W. Ross; the latter had remarked emphatically on seeing the result: "I have the greatest respect for Mr. Sargent. I am sure I *look* exactly like that, but I assure
you I do not *feel* at all like that." Visitors then returned to the Rotunda, having had the opportunity, if they chose to look up, to see the
Sargent murals in sequence. This was an admirable innovation so far

as traffic circulation was concerned, for when admission was charged to a special exhibition, as came to be the case, visitors paid at the southwest opening from the Rotunda, made the circuit, and left by an automatic turnstile at the southeast opening. This was soon adopted as the standard pattern for large exhibitions.

Its only inconvenience was that it blocked the principal entrance to the Library, for as that space, when covered with hangings, was a dramatic location for a large painting that could be seen across the stairwell from the Rotunda, the door was blocked a good deal of the time in future years. During large exhibitions, of which there were many, anyone seized with the desire to read had to pass the turnstile, work his way through exhibition visitors, and crawl behind a curtain to reach the Library, or, alternatively, to seek an inaccessible service stairway and sneak in through the photograph collection. It sometimes seemed on crowded days that this was a symbol of a new dispensation that subordinated learning to showmanship, for the Library had been deliberately put in this conspicuous and central position in the hope of tempting to further reading those visitors whose curiosity had been aroused by objects in the galleries. Although as Chairman of the Visiting Committee of the Library I felt bound to point this out every now and then, the arrangement was too logical as far as large exhibitions were concerned to be seriously questioned. This was the first of many instances in which a building carefully planned in the first decade of the century was to creak and groan under new demands placed upon it in the sixth.

David McKibbin of the Boston Athenæum, who had for many years studied Sargent's portraiture, prepared a book, *Sargent's Boston with an Essay and a complete Check List of Sargent's Portraits*, that was published by the museum at the time of the exhibition as a permanent commemoration of the centennial of the artist's birth. Designed and composed by The Stinehour Press at Lunenberg, Vermont, and printed in fine-screen offset by the Meriden Gravure Company, this volume had a typographical distinction that had not always characterized earlier publications of the museum.

In his 1956 report, Perry Rathbone thus described another exhibition of the year that was of similar interest and significance to the region:

The practice of celebrating anniversaries laid an obligation upon the Museum to observe yet another important date in Boston's cultural history. In 1906 the first exhibition of early American silver ever held took place at the Boston Museum. In the intervening years interest in the subject has grown to such a degree and research in this field has yielded such a harvest of factual knowledge of the craft and its craftsmen that the significance of the first exhibition deserved to be recognized anew. Much that we now know about American silver is due to the devoted labors of Mrs. Yves Henry Buhler. She organized the brilliant anniversary exhibition, "Colonial Silversmiths, Masters and Apprentices," which took place in November and December and wrote the catalogue. Mrs. Buhler and Mr. Carl Zahn collaborated on the arrangements and installation of the silver which numbered more than three hundred and fifty pieces. The catalogue containing much unpublished material is an important contribution to the subject and, like the exhibition, has been enthusiastically received.

Although its contents were permanently useful, the format of this catalogue, which — to be the *dernier cri* of contemporary typography — was square, with huge margins at the top and minute ones at the bottom of pages, exasperated some visitors to the exhibition, whose thumbs invariably obscured the final sentences of any pages they attempted to read. Such subordination of convenience to design was happily not permanent, for the later work of Carl F. Zahn has been admirably appropriate to its purpose. Over the past thirteen years he has produced an extraordinary number of brilliantly designed exhibition catalogues and other museum publications of high typographical distinction.

In the course of 1956, twenty-four special exhibitions were held, in addition to fifteen in the Print Department. Such a pattern furthered a lively interest in the museum, for unless one went there constantly there was a strong chance of missing opportunities to see works of art seldom visible in Boston. The 1956 purchase of Claude Monet's huge *La Japonaise*, painted in 1876, inspired an exhibition the following year that included not only all thirty-three of the museum's Monet landscapes — many of which had been in storage in recent years — but fourteen others from local private collections.

LA JAPONAISE. Claude Monet, 1876. *1951 Purchase Fund.*
56.147

The acquisition of *La Japonaise* represented a strong personal conviction on the part of Perry Rathbone, who had admired and coveted the painting long before he came to Boston. Of it he wrote in his 1956 report: "This fantastic large picture, gorgeous in color and original in conception, was Monet's tribute to the *Japonerie* which swept Europe in the last decades of the nineteenth century and changed the course of modern art. The painting is especially appropriate to our Museum as it brings the only figure painting by Monet to a collection of thirty-three of his landscapes and, at the same time, forms a dramatic link between the extensive collection of modern French paintings and our enviable holdings in the field of Japanese art."

In the same year the Director successfully recommended the purchase of Rembrandt's full-length, life-sized portraits of the Reverend Johannes Elison and his wife, Maria Bockenolle, which are signed and dated 1634. These paintings, which Wilhelm Bode had wished to buy for the Berlin Museum as early as 1876, when the Schneider Collection was offered for sale, were purchased with the William King Richardson Fund. They were specially exhibited from 6 February through 8 September 1957. A showing in March of paintings and modern sculptures from the collection of Walter P. Chrysler, Jr., attracted 32,000 visitors, of whom 27,197 paid admission. It now became the practice to charge admission to special exhibitions, save for museum members, thus providing some return for the considerable expense of shipping and insuring objects, as well as furnishing an inducement to become a member. Later in the spring of 1957 was held the first comprehensive exhibition of New England miniatures, organized by Mrs. Haven Parker, whose essay and catalogue *New England Miniatures, 1750–1850*, is still a useful work of reference. The Department of Textiles arranged four showings of New England costumes of different periods as a complement to the miniatures.

Like Serge Koussevitzky, who often made Bostonians listen to contemporary music whether they wished to do so or not, Perry Rathbone rubbed their noses in contemporary art. In his 1956 report, he had written:

> The need of the Institute of Contemporary Art to find new and more adequate quarters and the desire of both the Museum and the Institute to interrelate their programs and to develop a working arrangement of mutual benefit led to making space provision for the Institute in the building of the Museum School, which was ready in September.

TWENTIETH CENTURY GALLERY OPENED IN 1956.

In August a new gallery for twentieth century art was opened on the ground floor of the Evans Wing. Here there was added to a nucleus of modern works already owned by the Museum a number of recent acquisitions of painting and sculpture and several important loans. The purpose of the gallery is to provide a suitable space in the Museum where the visitor may count on seeing important examples of the art of our time always on view.

To supplement this modest permanent showing, he arranged in the autumn of 1957 *European Masters of Our Time*, a loan exhibition drawn from eighty-two collections in Europe and America, which occupied nine galleries, including the Rotunda and stair gallery. Of this he wrote:

The first exhibition of modern art ever organized by the Museum, it was received with widespread favorable comment both in this country and abroad. The impressive display . . . was intended as a comprehensive witness of the major achievements in painting and sculpture in the twentieth century. From our point of view the exhibition also served several purposes peculiar to our problem in Boston. First, it proclaimed the concern of the Museum henceforth with the art of our time as well as with that of the past; second it provided our public with a broad foundation of experience in modern art which will give meaning to future exhibitions of a more specialized nature, as well as the modern acquisitions of the Museum; third — and we admit hopefully — it will contribute to a revival of the collecting of contemporary art by private individuals, a pursuit which distinguished Boston in previous generations and which has immeasureably enriched the Museum that we know today.

This exhibition owed much to the collaboration of Hanns Swarzenski of the Department of Decorative Arts, who had always, side by side with his medieval studies, maintained a lively interest in contemporary art. To supplement the display, the Print Department organized a remarkable showing of modern graphic work from its own collections; 27,804 visitors, of which number 23,115 had paid admission, attended the exhibition. The Ladies' Committee arranged receptions for the previews of the Chrysler and the *European Masters* exhibitions, the former being attended by 2,239 and the latter by 2,513 members. In conjunction with the Museum School, a comprehensive exhibition of oils, water colors, prints, and drawings by Jan Cox was arranged early in 1957, in honor of his first season as Instructor in Advanced Painting, while in October the Asiatic Department organized a one-man show of the Japanese artist Tomoika Tessai (1836–1924).

The extraordinary sequence of Asiatic loan exhibitions has been described in Chapter XV, but in 1958, the year when the *Masterpieces of Korean Art* was shown, Perry Rathbone organized a *Masterpieces of Primitive Art*, in collaboration with Professor John Otis Brew, then Director of the Peabody Museum of Archaeology and Ethnology, Harvard University. With the help of the collector Eliot Elisofon, Robert G. Gardner, and Hanns Swarzenski, this first exhibition of primitive art ever held in Boston was brilliantly mounted in five galleries. The interest it aroused led to a continuing arrangement whereby for the next ten years the Peabody Museum lent objects from its collections for rotating exhibits of primitive art in a first-floor gallery, cleared for the purpose in 1959. Unfortunately this useful practice was suspended, temporarily one hopes, in 1968, when the gallery fell a victim to the demand for office space, gene-

ANNE, LADY DE LA POLE. George Romney. *Given in Memory of Governor Alvan T. Fuller by the Fuller Foundation.* 61.392

rated in strict accordance with Parkinson's Law by the increased activities of the museum.

The Hon. Alvan Tufts Fuller, who had been a trustee of the museum for thirty years, died in 1958. Through Perry Rathbone's efforts, the Fuller collection of paintings was shown from 6 February

through 22 March 1959 and a catalogue of it published. Nine of
the pictures including Romney's portraits of Anne, Lady de la
Pole, and Master Thornhill, Monet's *Nymphéas et le Pont*, and
two Renoirs were given by the Fuller Foundation in memory of the
Governor in 1961. Happily his Rembrandt portrait of a man, which
Perry Rathbone characterized as "perhaps the greatest privately
owned work of art in Boston," has remained on exhibition in the museum as a loan from the Fuller Foundation. The year 1959 was
marked also by a splendid exhibition of Winslow Homer, a showing
of a cross section of the collections of the recently opened Solomon
R. Guggenheim Museum in New York, the first important exhibition
in Boston of Paul Klee and of America's earliest abstractionist,

NYMPHEAS ET LE PONT. Claude Monet. *Given in Memory of Governor Alvan T.
Fuller by the Fuller Foundation. 61.959*

Arthur Dove, and the only showing in an American museum of Picasso's recently created bronze sculptural group, *The Bathers*. To demonstrate the two-hundred-year-old tradition of Boston painting, *Four Boston Masters: Copley, Allston, Prendergast, and Bloom,* planned by Professor John McAndrew of Wellesley College, was shown from 19 May through 26 June 1959.

A great exhibition of Gustave Courbet, organized in collaboration with the Philadelphia Museum of Art, and a Maurice Prendergast Centennial Exhibition were the largest efforts of 1960, although a remarkable selection of the Buddhist sculpture of Gandhara, lent from museums in Pakistan, through Asia House in New York and the Smithsonian Institution, a Feininger exhibition organized by the Cleveland Museum of Art, a Museum of Modern Art showing of *Recent Sculpture, U.S.A.*, were notable among the twenty-nine special exhibitions, beyond those of the Print Department, held in that year. Attendance, which had been steadily climbing from 390,635 in 1955, reached 627,826 — the second highest in the museum's history — in 1961, for this was the year of the Chinese and Thai exhibitions, as well as of a great Modigliani show, *The Artist and the Book: 1860–1960*, jointly arranged with Philip Hofer of the Houghton Library, and *25 Centuries of Peruvian Art, 700 B.C. to 1800 A.D.* which was a continuing instance of productive collaboration with Harvard's Peabody Museum.

A Van Gogh exhibition in 1936 had drawn such crowds that Harold Edgell remarked that "the people came as though the Museum were exhibiting the Sistine Chapel." On the closing day 9,488 visitors swarmed in, and over 100,000 came to the museum during the month the show was on. A similar phenomenon occurred between 22 March and 29 April 1962 when eighty oils and sixty drawings of Van Gogh, owned by the artist's nephew, V. W. van Gogh of Amsterdam, were exhibited. Perry Rathbone thus described it:

> In order to accommodate comfortably the very large turnout expected for the preview, two members' receptions were held for the first time, one in the afternoon without charge, the other in the evening, a champagne gala at a charge of five dollars a person. A crowd of some 1,869 attended in the afternoon and 650 were

present in the evening on which occasion the grandnephew of the artist, Mr. Johan van Gogh, and Mrs. van Gogh were guests of honor. Anticipating the unprecedented popular enthusiasm for the exhibition, the galleries remained open from 10:00 a.m. to 10:00 p.m. every day but Sundays throughout the duration of the show. When in the not-distant future the entire collection of V. W. van Gogh passes into the possession of the Dutch government, it is unlikely that a van Gogh loan exhibition so large and so rich in masterpieces both of painting and drawing will be possible ever again. Fortunate then are the 121,967 visitors who saw the exhibition during its five week stay. Of these 104,750 were paid admissions. The total exceeds by some 30,000 the attendance at any previous exhibition at the Museum. Over 26,000 catalogues and 7,855 color reproductions were sold during the show.

A centennial exhibition called *The Civil War: The Artists' Record*, arranged in collaboration with the Corcoran Gallery of Art, was enlivened by an attempt to play soldier in the Forecourt with a Civil War cannon, whose reverberations broke windows in neighboring apartment houses. As 1962 began with the *Chinese National Art Treasures*, which had opened in December, and closed with the final part of the Karolik trilogy, the M. and M. Karolik Collection of American Water Colors and Drawings, 1800–1875, it is small wonder that the attendance leaped to 754,161, surpassing by 112,000 the record produced in 1951 by the Vienna treasures. The following year with *She Walks in Splendor, Great Costumes, 1550–1950, Old Master Drawings from Chatsworth*, the *Treasures of Tutankhamum, Barbizon Revisited*, and *The Arts of India*, as major attractions, almost as many visitors came, for the 1963 figure was 731,299.

Membership drives were always enhanced when it could be reported in the press that eminent persons had signed the pledge. Mrs. Franklin Delano Roosevelt, at the urging of the Ladies' Committee, made a special trip to Boston in November 1959 to see the Museum of Fine Arts for the first time and to enroll as a member. It gave similar pleasure when President and Mrs. John F. Kennedy became members in June 1963. Soon after the President's death, a uniquely moving portrait bust of a man of about 1500, in the glazed terra cotta known as Hafner ware, was given in his memory by R. Thorn-

SHE WALKS IN SPLENDOR EXHIBITION, 1963.

PORTRAIT BUST. Glazed polychromed terra cotta (Hafner
Ware), Salzburg, about 1500.
*Gift of R. Thornton Wilson in
memory of the late John Fitzgerald Kennedy, thirty-fifth
President of the United States.*
64.1

ton Wilson of New York City. This memorial gift was formally accepted at a ceremony in the Rotunda on 2 January 1964. A *Kennedy Memorial Exhibition*, consisting of illustrated color enlargements, memorabilia of the late President, and documents of his administration, attracted unprecedented numbers of people, many of whom were visiting the museum for the first time. It was opened on 18 August 1964 with a special preview attended by Governor and Mrs. Endicott Peabody and Mrs. Edward M. Kennedy. Although it only lasted for four days, the museum remained open for twelve hours each day, thus permitting 139,689 people to visit it. In consequence, the 1964 attendance set a new record of 830,007, an increase of 98,708 over the previous all-time record of the previous year.

Mercifully nothing has since produced the concentrated crowds of the *Kennedy Memorial Exhibition*. The spectacular and dramatically exhibited *Greek Gold: Jewelry from the Age of Alexander*, shown from 23 November 1965 through 2 January 1966 before going on to the Brooklyn Museum and the Virginia Museum of Fine Arts, attracted 20,057 visitors, although when one tried to get near the cases it often seemed that there must have been nearly that number present every day. Opening with the *John Singleton Copley Exhibition* (25,994), the major 1966 offerings were *Dürer and His Time* (10,594), *Henri Matisse Retrospective* (101,880), *Painting and Sculpture Today: Selections from the Collection of Susan Morse Hilles* (10,447), and *The Arts of India and Nepal: The Nasli and Alice Heeramaneck Collection* (18,645).

The first important exhibition of Dutch painting ever shown in Boston, *The Age of Rembrandt*, organized by the Museum of Fine Arts in collaboration with the Toledo Museum of Art and the California Palace of the Legion of Honor in San Francisco, proved to be the most popular in the museum's history. Opening with a dinner in honor of the Ambassador from The Netherlands to the United States and his wife on 21 January 1967, a record of 201,000 visitors came to the exhibition during the next six weeks. Crowds waited in line for hours inside and outside the building, even though the galleries remained open on Tuesdays and Fridays until 10:00 P.M. and opened on Sundays at 10:00 A.M. Groups made special trips from

SCENE DURING THE AGE OF REMBRANDT EXHIBITION OF 1967.

New York, Philadelphia, Hartford, and New Haven, as well as numerous Massachusetts towns and cities, while other visitors were accommodated on Mondays, during hours when the museum was normally closed. During the exhibition 13,000 catalogues and over 50,000 postcards and reproductions were sold. But, even with 26,732 visitors viewing the *Art Treasures of Turkey*, at the end of the year the 1967 attendance was 680,197. This hopefully suggests that the 1964 record of 830,007 is unlikely to be repeated without an emotional stimulus of the intensity produced by the death of President Kennedy. When the temperature goes higher than the degrees marked on the thermometer, there is danger of the mercury breaking the glass. Equally there is a point beyond which a building cannot accommodate crowds, or curatorial and maintenance staffs stretch themselves to accomplish the extraordinary labors imposed by a continuous rotation of great loan exhibitions. Yet problems of this kind are the reverse of the coin, so far as a vastly increased membership and continuing income from fourteen thousand rather than two thousand contributors are concerned.

CHAPTER XIX

The Renaissance of the Classical Department

To a historian considering the first hundred years of the Museum of Fine Arts, the most significant contribution made by Perry T. Rathbone since his arrival in 1955 has been his skillful choice of scholarly curators, who have made admirable use of the riches assembled by those who went before, while building even stronger collections for the century to come. In some cases candidates sprang to the eye; in others they had to be sought from a distance. But in every instance the museum departments over the past fifteen years have been placed in the charge of scholars fully able to carry on a great tradition, while adding to knowledge in a manner that commands the respect of the learned world. In this Boston has more closely resembled the practice of the British Museum than that of any American art museum other than the Metropolitan in New York.

Fortunately when Georg Swarzenski retired at the end of 1955, his son Hanns was already on duty in the Department of Decorative Arts. When Dows Dunham simultaneously sought early retirement from his administrative duties to devote all his time to preparing excavation reports for publication, William Stevenson Smith was readily at hand. Through fifteen years' experience in the department and in Egypt with Dunham and Reisner, he was admirably qualified to become Curator of Egyptian Art. On the other hand, the vacancy created by the sudden death in 1965 of Robert Treat Paine, Jr., who had become Curator of Asiatic Art in 1963 after more than thirty years in the department, was only filled when Jan Fontein was persuaded to come to Boston from the Rijksmuseum in Amsterdam. The most pressing curatorial problem facing Perry Rathbone lay in the Department of Classical Art, which had been in the care of a *locum tenens* since the death of Lacey D. Caskey in 1944.

In Boston and Cambridge in the nineteen twenties classical studies were shrouded in a dignified but melancholy twilight. With the abrogation of compulsory requirements for the study of ancient languages in schools and colleges, most classical scholars, feeling that the world no longer appreciated what they had to offer, became increasingly withdrawn. There were, of course, notable exceptions like the Harvard Latinist and medievalist Edward Kennard Rand, whose learning and genial humanism surmounted all buffets of administrative fate or popular nonsense, and like George H. Chase, who cheerfully and energetically became the museum's Acting Curator of Classical Art when entering his seventies. In the forties and fifties the situation changed completely as a new generation of Harvard classicists attracted first-rate students who pursued ancient languages not from compulsion but from positive desire. Although undergraduates concentrating in Classics were few in number, compared to the mobs that flocked to English, History, Government, Economics, and Social Relations, they carried off a disproportionate share of degrees *summa cum laude*, traveling fellowships, and similar honors. Having had to master the discipline of ancient languages in their stride, their learning was beyond question. Thus, they could eschew the protective jargon of the literary critic or sociologist, and be as lively, witty, and disrespectful as they pleased. In actions fought on behalf of humane learning, these new classicists became the shock troops, situated in the van, rather than fighting a rear guard action as their predecessors had so few decades before.

Toward the end of 1956, Perry Rathbone announced that Cornelius Clarkson Vermeule, III, Assistant Professor of Classical Archaeology at Bryn Mawr College, would become Curator of the Classical Department on 1 October 1957. Cornelius Vermeule was an especially lively, energetic, and productive specimen of this new breed of Harvard classicist. A member of the class of 1947, he had gone into the Army during his freshman year. Returning to Cambridge in the autumn of 1947, he completed the requirements for his A.B. in two years, and took an A.M. in 1951 before going to London, where he spent two years cataloguing the Greek and Roman antiquities in Sir John Soane's Museum, that enchantingly crystallized prototype of our own Isabella Stewart Gardner Museum. After receiving his Ph.D. from the University of London in 1953, he taught for two years at the University of Michigan before going to Bryn Mawr. His appointment doubly strengthened the museum's Classical Department, for eight months before taking over his new post in Boston, he had married another very able classical archaeologist, Emily Dickinson Townsend (Bryn Mawr A.B. 1950, Ph.D. 1956, Harvard A.M. 1954).

From the moment of Cornelius Vermeule's arrival in the autumn of 1957, he was busily reorganizing both galleries and storerooms, while continuing to publish an incredible amount in learned journals. His first full year as Curator — 1958 — coincided with the thirtieth anniversary of the deaths of Edward Perry Warren and John Marshall and the fiftieth of the arrival of the Greek fifth-century relief known as the Boston Throne. The Classical Department's acquisitions for that year would have gladdened Warren's heart, for they included a gold votive double-axe of about 1500 B.C., inscribed in the Minoan script known as Linear A. The syllables of this superlative offering to a Cretan sanctuary contemporary with the Boston Snake Goddess may be a votive inscription to Demeter, a pre-Hellenic record of a goddess greatly esteemed in the classical Greek world. There was also purchased in 1958 a masterpiece of Hellenistic craftsmanship in gold, perhaps as early as 400 B.C.: a pendant about 2 inches high in the form of a bull's head, found in western Asia Minor. This may well have been worn on a chain around the neck by a devotee of the cult of Artemis.

In 1958 Cornelius Vermeule observed that, while "people often think that a museum's collections are like an iceberg, twenty per cent on display, eighty per cent in storage," in his department the figures were necessarily reversed, and should remain so. This theme entered into the statement of the aims of the Classical Department that he prefaced to his 1960 annual report.

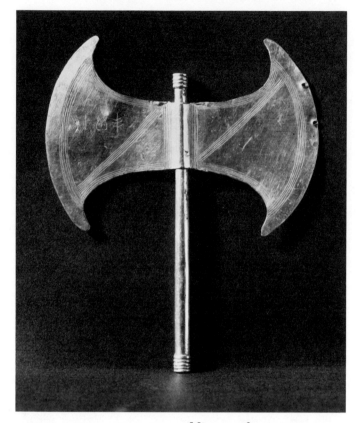

GOLD VOTIVE DOUBLE-AXE. Minoan, about 1500 B.C.
Theodora Wilbour Fund in memory of Zoë Wilbour. 58.1009

The Museum of Fine Arts has certain responsibilities peculiar to the first-class museums of the world. In terms of our Department, this means a maximum number of objects of every class must be displayed as attractively as possible. Smaller collections of Greek and Roman art can afford to have one masterpiece of each major category bathed in handsome lights and fabrics in near empty galleries, but not the collections in Boston and New York. The public, whether laymen or specialists, come to our Museum to see good examples of Greek and Roman art in every category and in depth within these categories. We are, in effect, a part of what James Rorimer admirably termed an "encyclopedic museum."

Is our Department meeting these responsibilities? The geography of our wing of the building is such that unless the building as a whole expands we can never hope for the gallery space we desperately need . . . We scheme and scheme to arrange and rearrange our works of art so as to show the best without relegating too much of that best to our study storage. In another two years we can fully measure the success of complete reorganization without destruction of aesthetic effect by overcrowding and without succumbing to an "iceberg" policy of a few objects on view and masses in storage.

The responsibilities of the "encyclopedic" Department in terms of acquisitions are different from those of the general museum of art. We naturally do not hesitate to build on strength. Thus, if an Attic red-figured vase enters our collections, it must keep company with perhaps the best assembly of such painted vases on this earth. On the other hand, this past year I have tried to develop our group of Attic black-figured vases, and the relative weakness in this class puts these earlier Greek painted vases at the top of our list of desiderata in years to come. I hope the breakdown to follow of our 1960 acquisitions will show that we have tried, and will keep trying to make our exhibits as comprehensive as possible, never losing sight of the fact that this Museum cannot display or harbor rubbish.

In terms of "encyclopedic" acquisitions, our Department must live to some extent by its wits. The total purchase funds of the Museum are not so large that a curator can go on annual "gap-filling" sprees. On the contrary, each entry to the collections, whether by gift or purchase, must be given the triple scrutiny of aesthetic worth, balance among its immediate neighbors, and current market value. We must not surrender to desire to buy "space-fillers" merely because they are cheap, and, like certain securities, might go up in value as fashions change. At the other extreme, Cycladic art is very much in vogue and very expensive. We possess one mediocre Cycladic idol and one recently purchased Cycladic marble vessel, a pitiful representation. I do not feel, however, that we should go into the current market to purchase better Cycladic idols while the market is so high. We must wait, perhaps for a generation, until tastes change, and, meanwhile, we can hope for gifts and loans so that the public, especially students, are not cheated by our poverty in a field so spiritually linked with modern art. These are some of the negatives of acquisition; they are meant to show that the positives are not taken lightly.

It will be easier to appreciate the positive elements in this policy by considering a few outstanding acquisitions of the past decade in

PORTRAIT OF SOCRATES. Greek marble, 2nd century A.D. after an original of about 330 B.C. *Frederick Brown Fund. 60.45*

HEAD OF THE CYCLOPS POLYPHEMOS. Hellenistic marble, about 150 B.C. *Gift in honor of Edward W. Forbes from his friends. 63.120*

ETRUSCAN LEOPARD. Volcanic stone, about 560 B.C. *William Francis Warden Fund. 61.130*

various fields. In sculpture, for example, a Greek marble portrait head of Socrates was purchased in 1960 through the Frederick Brown Fund. This perceptive rendering of the philosopher's "ugly but not ignoble features," the first monumental portrait of him to enter an American collection, was carved in Pentelic marble in the second century A.D. after an original of about 340 B.C., often attributed to Lysippos. The friends of Edward W. Forbes, to honor the sixtieth anniversary of his election as a trustee, gave in 1963 a Hellenistic marble head of Polyphemus. This nearly colossal representation shows the Cyclops, whom the wily Odysseus blinded to escape from his cave, "in the Jovian disarray of a Pergamene centaur or satyr; the giant's one eye is set, curiously enough, on the bridge of his nose."

The department's Classical zoo was enlarged by a variety of superior animals. The first of these, a lifesized Etruscan leopard of about 560 B.C., carved in volcanic stone of the type associated with Vulci, arrived in 1961 in the company of a fragmentary winged lion. Of him, Cornelius Vermeule wrote:

> This svelte beast evidently was one of a pair adorning the lintel of a tomb. His companion, a roaring lion, stood either in the entryway of a similar tomb, or on top of the monument as a monumental talisman. The leopard catches the simple line and contemplative spirit of archaic Greek pedimental or funerary sculptures, while the lion transmits the boisterousness of decorative animals transmitted to the Greeks from the early art of the Near East.

When this beast, purchased through the invaluable William Francis Warden Fund, was unveiled, the Museum of Fine Arts rejoiced in having what was then thought to be the only Etruscan archaic stone leopard in existence. Then, within two years, Horace L. Mayer, until his regretted death in 1968 a generous friend of both the Classical and Egyptian departments, gave *two* more! One was a pendant to the leopard bought in 1961, perhaps from the same tomb of about 550 B.C. in the great necropolis at Vulci.

> If this alone were not gift enough in the realm of monumental Etruscan sculpture [Cornelius Vermeule wrote in his 1963 report],

Mr. Mayer has provided a second leopard, making us the only Museum in the world with *three* such beasts. The second newcomer faces left like the original leopard, but he is no contented, gently purring cat. A malevolent, snarling beast, twice the size of the other two, he derives from the ferocious rather than the contemplative leopards in Corinthian vase painting and archaic Greek minor art. When first publishing "Pard I," as we term the animal bought in 1961, I made the assertion, dangerous for an archaeologist, that he was unique. Mr. Mayer's surprise has happily proven my error to all. To cap this coup in early Etruscan sculpture, Horace Mayer has given us two Etruscan nenfro sphinxes. One of these mythological creatures has head, wings, and body preserved, a Peloponnesian-style counterpart of the famous centaur from Vulci, while the second is headless and of quality sufficient to indicate derivation from excellent Corinthian and Attic funerary painting and sculpture of around 550 B.C. This sphinx will make a wonderful didactic contrast to the sphinx of the Attic stele that was Lacey Caskey's last purchase.

Of a remarkable Greek addition to the zoo, a marble lion from Attica of about 390 B.C., purchased through the Warden Fund, Cornelius Vermeule wrote in his 1965 report:

> Greek love of sculpture outdoors and interest in an ideal form, whether human or animal, are blended in the marble lions that were

FUNERARY LION. Greek marble, from Attica, about 390 B.C. *William Francis Warden Fund.* 65.563

produced in the century from 420 to 320 B.C., the greatest age of Attic funerary reliefs. Like the sculptors working at Xanthos in Lycia, artists in Greece could have seen small mountain lions, but in the late fifth and fourth centuries their vision of the king of beasts was distilled from generations of using motifs from Syria and Mesopotamia and by actual contemplation of large dogs and precocious cats. Their lions crouch like dogs over bones. Their lions' bodies are as well proportioned and smoothly ideal as those of Hegeso herself and her servant girl. Manes are like ruffs, and it is only close to the beginning of the Hellenistic Age, that is around 330 B.C., that they begin to look like the hair on lions seen nowadays in zoos and circuses. Round eyes, broad canine snouts, and ears like those of a Doberman pinscher add to the image of friendly conceptualism. Toward the end of the hundred years of Attic funerary lions, some beasts look as if they might bite, but most of them are placid, occasionally even playful. The emotional faces which can be identified with the style of Skopas around 350 B.C. enter the repertory of lion sculpture, and the elongation of athletes by Lysippos in the generation after 340 is even translated into feline anatomy. Among the other animals that also guarded Attic tombs (large butting bulls, colossal mastiffs, mild leopards, and even griffins) the lion remained the favorite, and his decimation by the anti-luxury decree of 317 B.C. was an irreparable loss not only to Attic art but to that of all Greece. Hellenistic lions are nebulous and Roman lions are dull by comparison with the masterpieces of Attic funerary sculpture before the closing years of the fourth century. It is only really with Antonio Canova in Italy in the Neo-Classic epoch of art that the king of beasts becomes a worthy monument in sculpture.

Another purchase made possible by the Warden Fund was the highly polished and deeply drilled marble group of a dancing satyr and maenad, watched by a small Eros, that was added in 1962. This half-sized group, evidently designed to be seen in an architectural setting, was found years ago at Carian Aphrodisias in southwestern Asia Minor. Carved about 225 A.D., it represents "a stunning exercise in the continuity of Hellenistic decorative emotion into the third century of the Roman Empire." Another maenad came to Boston in a group of eight marbles and terracottas that were given in 1968 by Paul Manheim of New York City, a new friend of the depart-

SATYR, MAENAD, AND EROS. Marble group from Aphrodisias in Caria, about
225 A.D. *William Francis Warden Fund. 62.1*
PRIAPUS AND A MAENAD. Greco-Roman marble copy of a Hellenistic composition.
Gift of Paul E. Manheim. 68.770

ment. She with Priapus was represented in a Greco-Roman marble
group that had been in the Smith Barry (Lord Barrymore) collection
at Marbury Hall, Cheshire, since the late eighteenth century. Although the original group had not often been seen for many years,
bronze replicas of it, made before the sculpture was taken from Italy
to England, had spread all over Europe. One of these groups, loosely
interpreted, may well have inspired the central section of Delacroix's
Liberty Leading the People during the Revolution of 1830.

A notable addition of very recent date is the East Greek head of a
kouros of about 510 B.C., probably from Asia Minor, given in June
1969 by Landon T. Clay (Harvard A.B. 1949). This member of the
Massachusetts Investors Trust and the brokerage house of Vance,
Sanders and Company, is known for his interest in and support of
field excavations, including the University of Pennsylvania – Boston
University expedition to Müskebi (Episkopi) in Caria, led by Emily
Vermeule in the summer of 1963. He joined the Visiting Committee
of the Classical Department in 1963; following his election as a
trustee of the museum on 18 February 1965, he became chairman

of that committee, succeeding the venerable and greatly loved Edward W. Forbes, who had held that post for two decades. In a very few years, Landon Clay has demonstrated the same generous concern and helpfulness to the Department of Classical Art that his fellow-trustee and contemporary John Goelet has shown in other parts of the museum.

A south Italian or Sicilian Greek group of a young man on horseback, accompanied by his dog, of around 500 B.C., thought to be "probably the only complete, non architectural Greek archaic terracotta horse and rider of larger than miniature dimensions that has come down to us from classical antiquity," was purchased in 1965 through the William Francis Warden Fund. The group, which is over two feet high, consists of a young rider trotting a sturdy stallion, while his hound runs alongside. The young man wears a light tunic that extends to just below the waist, and sports a *petasos*, or sun hat, suspended by a chin strap on the back of his neck, much in the man-

YOUNG MAN ON HORSEBACK WITH RUNNING HOUND. Greek terra cotta, about 510 B.C. *William Francis Warden Fund. 65.464*

ner of a Rough Rider campaign hat in the Spanish-American War of 1898. The *petasos* today hangs from a shoelace from one of the Curator's ski boots, for the hat seems too small when placed on the head, and Attic vases furnish precedent for this form of millinery. The group was undoubtedly placed as a votive offering in a tomb, probably of some dashing young hunter who regrettably crossed Styx in the prime of life.

The collection of Attic black-figured vases was strengthened in 1962 by a hydria, or water jar, of about 530 B.C., with a scene of Herakles wrestling with Triton in the presence of Nereus and a Nereid, given by Horace L. Mayer. Another large hydria of about 510 B.C., with Achilles dragging the corpse of Hector at Troy on the major panel and the duel between Herakles and Kyknos represented on the shoulder, was bought in 1963 through the Warden Fund. In the same year was purchased from the H. L. Pierce and Francis Bartlett funds, an Attic black-figured amphora some thirty years older, that Cornelius Vermeule described thus:

HERAKLES AND TRITON. Attic black-figured hydria, about 530 B.C. *Gift of Horace L. Mayer. 62.1185*
ACHILLES DRAGGING THE BODY OF HECTOR AROUND THE WALLS OF TROY. Attic black-figured hydria, about 510 B.C. *William Francis Warden Fund. 63.473*

A generation earlier, about 540 B.C., the great Exekias made a large amphora with exuberantly decorated handles. One side parallels his famous amphora in the Vatican, with a scene of the heavenly twins Castor and Pollux and their sister Helen tending to a chariot and horses. On the other side, the wine-god Dionysos, so labelled, sips the fruits of the vineyard from a large kantharos, while his followers the satyrs or Silens gather the grapes for pressing. Dionysos has the impish dignity of his representation in a pirate ship on the famous Exekias cup in Munich, while the daring use of the intertwined vines to form an overall pattern around him is best paralleled in the linear carving of late antique, early Byzantine reliefs or the mosaics in the vault of Santa Constanza in Rome.

Another important Attic black-figured vase was acquired in 1968: a hydria decorated with a representation of Achilles and Automedon in a quadriga.

The year 1963 was an *annus mirabilis* for purchases of vases, for during it five of the largest and most significant Attic vases ever to be

DIONYSOS AMID SATYRS. Attic black-figured amphora from the workshop of Exekias, about 540 B.C. *H. L. Pierce and Francis Bartlett funds. 63.952*
ACHILLES AND AUTOMEDON IN QUADRIGA. Attic black-figured hydria, about 540 B.C. *J. H. and E. A. Payne Fund. 68.105*

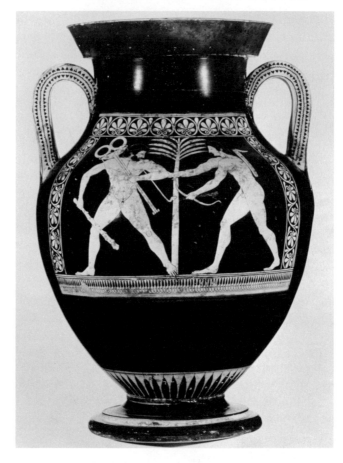

APOLLO AND HERAKLES STRUGGLING FOR THE DELPHIC
TRIPOD. Attic red-figured amphora. *Warden, Perkins, and
James funds.* 63.1515

on the market at one time were bought over a period of eight months.
In addition to the black-figure hydria and the Exekias amphora just
described, three extraordinary red-figured vases were purchased. A
giant amphora, among the largest vases ever made, in the severe Attic
red-figure style of the late sixth to early fifth century B.C., from the
circle of Euthymides, depicts Apollo and Herakles struggling for the
Delphic tripod in front of a tapering palm tree. On the other side is
depicted a friendly revel in which a maenad is beating off with two
trailing vines a pair of well-endowed and exuberant satyrs. The
second was a kalyx-krater that the Curator described as "exceeding

in size and rivalling in importance of subject the krater with scenes of the Fall of Troy, purchased in 1959."

The 1959 kalyx-krater of about 465 B.C., which Sir John Beazley had identified as the work of the artist known as the Altamura Painter, was superlative as illustration of the greatest Greek epics, for it showed three episodes in the fall of Troy: "Neoptolemus hurling Hector's son Astyanax at the aged Trojan King Priam, seated in refuge on the palace altar; Ajax the Less seizing Cassandra, Priam's daughter, beside the image of Athena; and Aeneas carrying his aged father Anchises from burning Troy, with Creusa following behind." The 1963 kalyx-krater, executed about 460 B.C., by the Dokimasia Painter, who usually decorated cups, illustrates scenes from the Oresteia.

On the chronologically earlier side, Agamemnon in his transparent bath garment bleeds under the slaying hands of Aigisthos, while the adulteress Klytaimnestra rushes from the left into the scene of tragic confusion. On the second side, the children have their revenge: Orestes and Elektra murder Aigisthos while he plays the lyre and Klytaimnestra runs up with her double axe. The scene of Agamemnon surprised in his bath is without parallel in Greek art and has thought-provoking connections with the Oresteia in Greek literature.

The fifth in the quintet of great 1963 vase purchases was a pelike from the workshop of the Niobid Painter, of about 450 B.C. The scene shows the princess Andromeda being tied to a stake, while her father Cepheus, King of the Ethiopians, watches his Negro attendants arrange her costume and her possessions. Andromeda is dressed in Persian tights, for Greek vase painters frequently characterized foreigners by depicting them in Persian dress. As Cornelius Vermeule observed: "Aside from its connections with contemporary theatre, the scene documents an artist's valiant attempt to portray black-skinned men on a black-glazed surface. The drawing of the negroes' faces is particularly charming and sympathetic." The faces are outlined in white, which is also used to represent their woolly hair and, together with pale red, for their garments. In Euripides' later play, Andromeda was chained to a cliff by the sea; the earlier

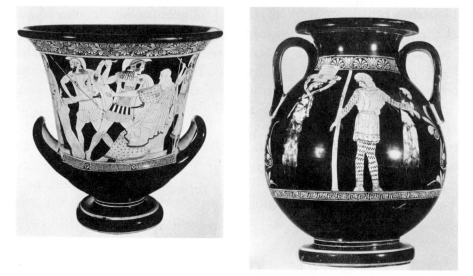

THE DEATH OF PRIAM; CASSANDRA AT THE PALLADIUM. Attic red-figured krater, about 465 B.C. *William Francis Warden Fund. 59.178*
ANDROMEDA TIED TO A STAKE. Attic red-figured pelike, about 450 B.C. *Arthur Tracy Cabot Fund. 63.2663*

painter of this pelike, who clearly has her tethered to a stake, represented another version of the myth; perhaps his source was the lost *Andromeda* of Sophocles, of which a few fragments have survived.

A south Italian bell krater, purchased in June 1969, has considerable dramatic interest, for on one side men are hurrying to the theater, while on the other is represented a farcical scene from Old Comedy, in which the actors wear flesh-colored tights, ornamented with a sizable phallus, and well padded fore and aft to produce a comical redundancy of belly and backside. Seemingly a rural policeman is apprehending, red-handed, a thief whose stolen goose and kids are ill-concealed in a basket. Mention should also be made of a red-figure kalpis, added in 1968, with the representation of Danaë and the shower of gold, which admirably augments the museum's holdings of other manifestations of the myth of Danaë and Perseus.

Two Etruscan painted plaques of about 470 B.C. with representations of a man playing double-flutes and a lady with a lyre, were purchased through the Warden Fund in 1962. Etruscan tombs in the great century from 550 to 450 B.C. were frequently adorned with scenes painted directly upon their walls, but terra-cotta plaques (*pinakes*) such as these, attached to the walls of tombs by metal pegs, have always been a great rarity.

Thanks to one of the Theodora Wilbour Funds, classical coins and medallions of high artistic importance have been purchased in considerable numbers, in memory of Zoë Wilbour. In 1959, for example, there was acquired a significant part of a Mediterranean treasure that included fifteen gold aurei and four multiple aurei or medallions of the Emperors Maximianus Herculeus and his son Maxentius, who

LADY WITH A LYRE and MAN WITH A DOUBLE FLUTE. Etruscan painted terra-cotta plaques, about 470 B.C. *William Francis Warden Fund.* 62.362 and 62.363

TWO GOLD MEDALLIONS OF MAXIMIANUS HERCULEUS, REVERSE AND OBVERSE.
Theodora Wilbour Fund in memory of Zoë Wilbour. 59.497 and 59.495

contested for power in the decade before Constantine the Great's defeat of Maxentius and the edict of religious toleration in 312 A.D. The condition of all nineteen pieces was superb; the medallions were characterized as "without parallel as examples of Roman portraiture in these years of transition to Late Antiquity." Also of remarkable quality is an aureus of Numerianus, purchased in 1968.

AUREUS OF NUMERIANUS, OBVERSE
AND REVERSE. *Theodora Wilbour Fund
in memory of Zoë Wilbour.* 68.752

A silver tetradrachm of Carthage of about 350 B.C. was acquired in 1962. The obverse portrays the head of a woman wearing a Phrygian cap, perhaps a personification of Libya; on the reverse a lion with lowered head stands before a palm tree, with a Punic inscription below. This masterpiece of fourth-century die cutting, undoubtedly influenced by the earlier Greek coins of Sicily, had a long history in French private collections. Miss Mary B. Comstock, who published it in number 322 of the *Bulletin*, noted that "Delacroix sketched the obverse a number of times and the head of Liberty

TETRADRACHM OF CARTHAGE. SILVER OCTODRACHM OF PTOLEMY V OF EGYPT.
Theodora Wilbour Fund in memory of Zoë Wilbour. 62.656 and 67.290

in *Liberty Leading the People* was derived from his study of this particular piece." A notable silver octodrachm of Ptolemy V of Egypt (204–180 B.C.) was purchased in 1967. Especially notable among the bronzes is the medallion of Clodius Albinus, a little-known Roman Emperor (193–197 A.D.) with a very limited coinage. On the obverse of this superb medallion, acquired in 1968, Albinus is portrayed as Caesar, wearing the appropriate drapery and cuirass although without the imperial laurel wreath. A seated personification of Fortuna, with a cornucopia and rudder in hand, and a wheel resting beside her throne, is depicted on the reverse.

A number of cameo and intaglio gems have been sought to strengthen a collection known throughout the world for possessing many of the Duke of Marlborough's stones, sold at auction at the end of the last century, and many of the gems that were the particular delight of Edward P. Warren at Lewes House until the last years of his life. Some of the recent additions were acquired in 1962 after the untimely death of Dr. L. Lahut Uzman, native of Turkey who had become a professor at the Harvard Medical School and a Visitor to the Classical Department. Dr. Uzman, who bought his first gem during his student days in Istanbul, eventually added seventeen others, as an adjunct to his collection of late Roman and Byzantine coins. Still other cameos and intaglios — early Greek, Hellenistic, Italic, early Roman, Greco-Roman, and neo-Classic — were bought in 1959, 1963, and 1964 through the Theodora Wilbour Fund. While such additions were made specifically to strengthen collections that went back many decades to the Warren era, in the 1960 report Cornelius Vermeule described an accession that was the first of its kind.

DONKEY NURSING TWO LION CUBS. Roman mosaic, 4th or 5th centuries, A.D. *Gift of the Class of the Museum of Fine Arts, Mrs. Arthur L. Devens, Chairman. 60.531*

The Class of the Museum, Mrs. Arthur L. Devens, Chairman, presented us with the first mosaic of importance to enter the building. Ever since the pre-war Antioch excavations, mosaics have drifted about American museums by the dozens. We wanted something "smashing," and I think the *Donkey Nursing Two Lion Cubs* fills the bill. The scene, the remainder of a larger floor area, comes from Tunisia in North Africa and belongs in the later fourth or fifth centuries A.D. The subject is fraught with political and religious symbolism. The composition recalls the Lupa Romana, the Wolf and Twins who were the emblem of imperial Rome, but worship of Bacchus, god of wine, and his consort, Cretan Ariadne, is also implied. The lion cubs are always associated with the two divinities and the she-ass is the beast of Silenus, their principal attendant. The mosaic, then, may well be a document of dying paganism, or a Christian parody of Roman imperial traditions. The tesserae of the mosaic are small, and the colors are rich, varying from black to golden yellow.

The Assistant Curator, Miss Hazel Palmer, a fine scholar of the vases of Corinth and a meticulous record-keeper, who had been in acting charge of the Classical Department during the years after the death of George H. Chase, left the Museum late in 1960 to become one of the select professional librarians of ancient art. Miss Mary B. Comstock, who came as a volunteer in May 1960, so rapidly proved her usefulness in many directions that she was formally appointed an Assistant in the department on 1 January 1961. As a result of her numismatic studies and publications she was appropriately designated as Keeper of Coins in 1965. Although Dr. Herbert Hoffmann, who became Assistant Curator in the autumn of 1962 only continued in that post for two years, he planned the Greek gold exhibition of the winter of 1965–66, and with Patricia F. Davidson, a practicing goldsmith on the staff of the Brooklyn Museum, wrote the catalogue, *Greek Gold: Jewelry from the Age of Alexander*, that is a permanent record of that memorable event. Mrs. Penelope von Kersburg (later Mrs. Penelope Truitt), joined the department as a second Assistant in 1964, while in 1965, Mrs. Vermeule, who had taught at Boston University and is now Professor of Art and Greek at Wellesley College, was appointed Fellow for Research on the museum staff. A succession of departmental secretaries — the Misses Mary Cairns, Collette Flynn, Julia T. Green, Alice Graves, and Sarah C. Dublin — have turned their hands to curatorial, editorial, and archaeological work as help was needed in one direction and another. The Curator has at various times lectured in courses at Smith and Wellesley colleges and at Harvard, Boston, and Yale universities, while his wife has excavated extensively in Asia Minor, Greece, and the Aegean islands. In 1964 the Harvard University Press published his 1959 Lowell Lectures under the title of *European Art and the Classical Past*, while the University of Chicago Press published her *Greece in the Bronze Age*, which went into a fourth revised edition in 1969. In 1968 the Harvard University Press published Cornelius Vermeule's *Roman Imperial Art in Greece and Asia Minor*, the result of fifteen years' work in the field.

Remarking that "a yearly paean of self-congratulation makes dull reading," Cornelius Vermeule began his 1961 report with the following revelation of current "inner thoughts":

> Ours is a teaching department, and it should always remain oriented on that level. Few, too few, people own works of Greek, Etruscan and Roman art (despite their availability at reasonable

670 MUSEUM OF FINE ARTS, BOSTON

prices), but everyone revels in our debt to classical civilization and wants the visual aspect of this heritage passed on to the broadest audience, old and young. The reinstallation of our galleries is our first duty, to physically attract visitors to the best of the ancient world, well displayed and intelligently labelled.

Publications on all levels, from the picture book to the highly-footnoted article in a learned journal, are equally vital to all. The illustrated calendar, the postcard or the flowery news release are end products of a process in cataloguing that goes on continually in its efforts to make many aware of the full truths in works of art under our care. This year Hazel Palmer's *Greek Gods and Heroes* appeared. The new guide to the Department is on the presses; the plates to Sir John Beazley's final volume of the large-scale publication of *Attic Red-Figured Vases* have been printed; and the catalogue of *Roman Medallions* will have circulated before this report is out. As the staff bibliography reveals, our Department tries very hard to project its message via the printed word.

These paragraphs led to the crux of the matter — the Classical Department's library, and the museum's Library as a whole. The departmental library

is the only classical library in the greater Boston area which is a constantly available tool for working museum people, archaeologists, classicists, advanced students or the serious general public. Our Department must grow largely by its wits, and curatorial accuracy in display or acquisitions, in publicity and publication, can only come with the backing of a topflight Library . . . We of the Department, and our loyal friends, must lead the way in making sure we do not drift backwards, by standing still in developing the most basic tools of our trade, books and the space to use them properly.

Although space, on or off stage, has continued to be at a premium, what there is has been skillfully manipulated. When the Treasurer's office moved to new quarters near the Sales Desk in 1961, the Classical Department retrieved an area on the ground floor facing Huntington Avenue that was converted into a handsome Etruscan Gallery, completed in 1965. The present museum had been planned with the thought that the ground floor would be confined to offices, classrooms, and study-storage, while all major galleries would be on the main floor above. Had the building been promptly completed, according to Guy Lowell's original plan, this might well have worked admirably. As wings had been added only at a snail's pace, Perry Rathbone early concluded that the original concept must be abandoned, and handsome exhibition galleries created on both floors. While a more detailed discussion of his plan of renovation will follow in a subsequent chapter, its specific reference to the Classical exhibition problem must be noted. In the first stage of this general transformation, a new and handsome Ancient Near East Gallery had been created in 1958 in the ground floor area leading from the Sales Desk to the classical wing. The Etruscan Gallery was another step in this direction, and the 1964 completion at the east end of the ground floor of the wing of a new Minoan, Mycenaean, and Early Greek Art Gallery a third. This plan involved an almost complete reversal of

CLASSICAL GALLERIES AS RENOVATED IN 1967.

CLASSICAL GALLERIES AS RENOVATED IN 1967.

the contents of the classical wing to achieve a new chronological sequence that would begin on the ground floor and proceed upstairs. By December 1967 the ground floor had been completely renovated, with new cases and new lighting that transformed a dim "cave of the Cyclops" into a series of handsome galleries in which were exhibited some 550 objects, extending from 2500 to about 460 B.C. At the moment of writing, the second-floor Classical galleries are still awaiting transformation, although $85,000 toward that work was contributed by members in response to the 1967 Year End Appeal.

It is instructive to note the combination of popular and scholarly publications produced by the department in the past decade. *Greek and Roman Portraits, 470 B.C.–A.D. 500,* prepared by the Curator, appeared in 1959 in the Picture Book series. *Greek Gods and Heroes,* originally written by Arthur Fairbanks in 1915 and revised by George H. Chase in 1948, was published in a fifth edition, extensively revised by Hazel Palmer, in 1962. A completely new design by Carl F. Zahn, executed by the Stinehour Press and the Meriden

Gravure Company, eliminated all trace of the high-minded pedagogical aspect that had characterized the original work. This has become one of the most inviting of museum publications; handsome to look at and instructive alike to adults and children. *The Trojan War in Greek Art: A Picture Book* prepared in 1965 by Mary Comstock, Alice Graves, and Emily and Cornelius Vermeule, is another brilliant example of *haute vulgarization.* Cornelius Vermeule has also prepared *Greek and Roman Art*, a handbook for school children, printed initially in 1967 in an edition of 30,000 copies. Earlier he had revised a general handbook to the department prepared in 1950 by George H. Chase; this was published in a new format in 1963 under the title *Greek, Etruscan and Roman Art: The Classical Collections of the Museum of Fine Arts, Boston.*

The possession of great collections imposes the obligation of definitive scholarly publication, such as the series of *Attic Vase Paintings in the Museum of Fine Arts, Boston*, that had begun some forty years earlier. Sir John Beazley's part III, which completed the description of the red-figured vases, appeared in 1963 in an edition of four hundred copies. It was in the form of a huge portfolio with 94 pages of text and 26 collotype plates containing 122 illustrations. To meet a similar obligation, Cornelius Vermeule and Mary Comstock collaborated in two volumes that supplement Agnes B. Brett's 1955 *Catalogue of Greek Coins: Roman Medallions* (1963) and *Greek Coins, 1950 to 1963.* These were illustrated by direct photographs made by Edward J. Moore, the museum photographer, rather than from plaster casts of the coins, as had formerly been the practice in many numismatic publications. The fine plates, made by the Meriden Gravure Company, bear out the contention that "it is better to capture the real life of a natural piece of metal instead of the bland and almost ghostly shadow of the original." Furthermore this change relieved William J. Young of the considerable labor of making casts of innumerable coins.

An intermediate stage between popularization and the definitive catalogue is represented by a 1968 publication, *Ancient Glass in the Museum of Fine Arts Boston*, by Axel von Saldern of the Kunstmuseum, Düsseldorf. This attractive volume reproduces seventy examples from the collection, with a brief introductory essay. Although a large part of the ancient glass in the museum came through the purchases of Edward P. Warren, a Roman glass cup and beaker had been bought as early as 1872 with General di Cesnola's collection, while other pieces had been given in the eighties and nineties by such local friends as Martin Brimmer, Mrs. S. D. Warren, Mrs. Henry Whitman, and Dr. William Norton Bullard. During the second, third, and fourth decades of this century other pieces had been given to the M. Elizabeth Carter Collection, while a few fine examples were received more recently by bequest of Charles B. Hoyt.

In spite of the fig leaves diligently affixed by Dr. Henry J. Bigelow before the opening of the Copley Square museum in 1876, Classical sculpture still worried some local puritans. In June 1901, for example, a lively controversy broke out in Boston newspapers over the proposal to hold a YMCA reception in the Museum of Fine Arts, which was, in the view of some, obviously no place for a mixed social gathering because of the presence of nude male statues. Two years later when Edward P. Warren submitted photographs of five fragments of an archaic grave stele of a nude youth from Thebes, Edward Robinson wrote: "The lower fragment of that could not be exhibited publicly, and I should be better pleased if it were not included." When the sculpture arrived in Boston, Robinson observed: "It is certainly a more interesting sort of archaic than I thought, and if the lower piece would be treated in any way so as to make it possible to exhibit in a public gallery, I should withdraw the opinion I expressed, though I do not see how this could be done without mutilation." Although the museum did not choose to buy the stele, it was accepted in 1908 as a gift from E. P. Warren's brother, Fiske. It languished in fragments for a good half century before William J. Young and Miss Florence Whitmore fitted the pieces together, and without mutilation, made it a much admired exhibit in one of the recently renovated classical galleries.

In the "nasty-nice" beginning of the twentieth century, many of the greatest red-figured Greek vases were "expurgated" by an application of black paint in an effort to curb the sexual exuberance of boisterous satyrs. Greek vases indeed presented a problem to the prudish by their ingenuous mixtures of subjects. The bell-krater by the Pan Painter, acquired in 1910, displays on one side the moralistic

GRAVE STELE OF A YOUNG ATHLETE. Greek,
from Boeotia, about 550 B.C. *Gift of Fiske
Warren. 08.288*

THE PAN KRATER. Attic red-figured krater, about 470 B.C. *James Fund and Special Contribution. 10.185*

death of Aktaion, who had indiscreetly violated the privacy of Artemis, while on the other a very ill-behaved Pan is pursuing a young
goatherd. Not even this — one of the great vases of the world —
was exempted from retouching. Fortunately the black paint could be
removed, as it was, with the expert help of William J. Young, in the
early years of Cornelius Vermeule's curatorship. Similarly certain
bronzes and vase fragments with erotic subjects from Edward P.
Warren's personal collection languished in dark storage for half a
century after he gave them in 1908. As they were of the same artistic
quality as other Greek objects that he acquired, they caused no
commotion when restored to their proper places in the collection in
1964, or when published by Professor Emily T. Vermeule in 1969.

What *did* cause a commotion of international magnitude was the
theft in September 1963 of the fourth-century gold earring, *Nike
Driving a Two-horsed Chariot* that had been one of the great glories
of the Classical collection since its acquisition in 1898. Soon after
this diminutive masterpiece had been featured on a museum television program, it disappeared from its case. Nearly eight months of
exhaustive detective work on the part of the Boston Police, the FBI,
and the museum staff followed. In an anonymous pamphlet entitled
Bodrum, 1963, Minority Report of an "Expedition," privately printed

in 1964 to present the lighter side of Emily Vermeule's expedition to Asia Minor, her husband had written:

> Having achieved the most glorious museum director's office in Asia Minor, Haluk Bey told us in all seriousness he wants to have bars placed across his picture windows, "in case they tried to come over from Kos at night to steal something." We suggested gently the depot was secure enough for anything of value he might keep around his office. The picture of Greeks from Kos swarming over to loot the Bodrum museum seemed ludicrous.
>
> We did not laugh so hard two weeks later when we had to return in a rush from the Greek islands to Boston, because the famous early fourth-century golden earring, Nike driving her chariot, had been stolen from the Boston museum.

The important difference was that the treasures of the Bodrum museum in Asia Minor were not being televised to attract the attention of miscreants and crackpots as well as the intended audience.

The theft was widely announced, circulars describing in intricate detail the missing object being airmailed to museums, art dealers, and pawnbrokers throughout the world. A $5,000 reward for its return was offered, and the museum waited — and hoped against hope — while the police and detectives continued their search. Nothing promising developed until January 1964, when a new theft unexpectedly provided a clue. The second object stolen — a Millet still life of three pears from the Quincy Adams Shaw collection — was traced to a patient in a mental institution, who not only admitted his crime but confessed that he had also stolen the earring, burying it under a tree in the Fenway near the Muddy River, not far from the museum, in a hole five inches deep, dug with his shoe. He volunteered the information that the object was inside a Campbell's soup tin, to which the lid of a paper cup was tied with a string. This clue could not immediately be verified, for the ground in the Fenway was frozen too hard for digging.

Although various probes of the suspected region were made, nothing came to light until spring when Professor Emily Vermeule took her Boston University Archaeology 354 class for systematic excavation on the grid system made famous by Sir Mortimer Wheeler. Beer cans and bottles in plenty came to light, together with the corpses of two dogs, before one of the students, Mrs. Florence Wolsky, the wife of a Woburn doctor, encountered the correct soup can. It was brought back to the museum in triumph, where William J. Young took over. Nike had survived her winter under ground unharmed, but she was found in the nick of time, for the soup can would soon have started to disintegrate. Had that occurred, it could have crushed the delicate gold beyond redemption. The practical value of archaeology was as strikingly demonstrated as was the risk involved in the indiscriminate publicizing of valuable objects which otherwise would hardly come to the attention of thieves.

CHAPTER XX

The Expansion of European Sculpture

At the end of 1956, after something over two years as Curator of Decorative Arts, Richard B. K. McLanathan was given a leave of absence, during which he accepted the directorship of the Community Arts Program at the Munson-Williams-Proctor Institute in Utica, New York. In February 1956 he had been succeeded as Secretary of the Museum of Fine Arts by David B. Little, who combined that post with his previous duties as Registrar. Dr. Hanns Swarzenski, Fellow for Research in Medieval Art and Sculpture, became Acting Curator of the Department of Decorative Arts at the beginning of 1957, and, upon the termination of his predecessor's leave of absence, its Curator in November. Having been in the museum for nine years, the later ones of which had been spent collaborating with his father in the building up of collections, the new Curator had had ample time to assess the problems that were to face him. Consequently, in his 1957 report he analyzed the directions and needs of his department:

Created and continuously enriched by the generosity of four generations of Bostonians and donors from outside, its first Curator, Edwin J. Hipkiss, established the universal historical program of cultivating all possible crafts of European and American tradition:

gold, silver, bronze, enamel, ivory, ceramics, furniture and other interior decoration, and, in certain limits, even sculpture.

The needs and directions of the Department can now shortly be described in three programmatic sentences. First, a more severe concentration on the artistic content and quality of its overwhelming, but also somehow confusing wealth of objects displayed on all three floors or in storage. Second, a more balanced integration and expansion of the materials already represented and a strengthening of neglected categories of work and techniques, such as earthenware, faience, Continental porcelain, crystal, leather, furniture and modern sculpture. Third, a reorganization of the galleries in a more comprehensible sequence, and a more effective use of modern lighting and installation devices. Only then will our galleries disclose the palpable and intimate personal contact with the individual object, and convey the stimulating experience of the uniqueness of artistic creation. Only then will our collection be more than a static repository that has served chiefly the specialized interests of the antiquarian and the collector. And only then will the artistic content of the Department be recognized in its cultural potentialities as equal to the other great collections of the Museum.

More than a quarter of a century's work with American silver had brought the senior Assistant Curator, Mrs. Yves Henry Buhler, an international reputation in her field. In 1964, for example, she was granted six months' leave to catalogue the Garvan Collection of American Silver in the Yale University Art Gallery. In November 1964 she exchanged her previous curatorial duties for an appointment as Fellow for Research in American Silver; although she retired in September 1966, she continues work on a definitive catalogue of the museum's collection in this field. The extent of the department's American collections, which continued to arouse wide popular interest, required the employment of a second Assistant Curator, who would provide scholarly knowledge of the American decorative arts. In this post there has, alas, been little continuity, for the first holder, Paul Whitman Etter, who arrived on 1 October 1957, was killed less than eight months later. His unnecessary death on 23 May 1958 at the age of twenty-eight, when his automobile was accidentally struck by a police car in hot pursuit of a criminal, deprived the

Museum of Fine Arts of a very promising scholar. His successor, Richard H. Randall, Jr., formerly Associate Curator of The Cloisters of the Metropolitan Museum, became Assistant Curator of this department on 1 July 1959, but resigned in November 1963 to go to the Walters Art Gallery in Baltimore. Although originally a medievalist like Hanns Swarzenski, Richard Randall transformed his long-standing personal interest in American handcraftsmanship and design into professional curatorial knowledge. His *American Furniture in the Museum of Fine Arts, Boston,* a scholarly catalogue of all holdings not already described in the earlier volume on the Karolik Collection, published by the museum in 1965, is a permanent reminder of his four years in the Department of Decorative Arts. David T. Owsley, who became Assistant Curator on 1 September 1964, resigned at the end of 1965 to pursue further study at the Victoria and Albert Museum. He was succeeded by Harry H. Schnabel, Jr., who came to Boston in April 1966 after two and a half years as Assistant Director of The American Museum in Britain at Bath, and resigned in 1969.

The policies that Hanns Swarzenski set forth on becoming Curator in 1957 led to developments that became formal in 1963 when the name of his province was enlarged to Department of Decorative Arts and Sculpture. This recognition of the broadening of the limits of its artistic content, led him to make a further statement in the 1963 report.

Its collecting policy now encompasses not only the so-called decorative arts — metalwork, ceramics, furniture — in all its ramifications, but also sculpture from the Early Christian period to the present. The new title of the Department, however, indicates more than the widening of its range. It intimates a basic change in our approach and evaluation of the decorative arts — often also called "useful," "applied," "technical" or "minor" arts. By combining sculpture and decorative arts under a single heading and displaying both together we regard them as equals and so relinquish the still prevailing distinction between "major" and "minor" arts, which we feel is based on a confusion of values. True, our concept of a style and period is chiefly formed by the paintings and sculpture of the accepted great masters. Yet even their unrivalled works reveal only certain individual aspects and stylistic elements and never the whole potentiality of a period in its great moments. We also need the smaller and often less ostentatious production of the so-called minor arts if we wish fully to comprehend the genius of a period and a country, the richness, originality and spontaneity of their artistic ideas.

In making this statement we do not, of course, wish to propagate an historical statistical completeness of every craft in all its technical and formal aspects. Today such an encyclopaedic aim would hardly be possible to accomplish without a sacrifice in quality. It would also be undesirable. Classified collections of this sort have certainly contributed much to specialized study and knowledge, but, no doubt, they have also contributed to the deplorable decrease of interest in the decorative arts. We are most fortunate in owning superb collections of American and English silver and English porcelain, and as distinct categories they are justly installed in special galleries. However, in order to comprehend fully their artistic spirit and historical contribution, we must separate certain pieces of singular importance, and display them in appropriate relation to works of other media produced in the same style and period, because their value and interest extends far beyond the material of which they are made. Technical mastery and utilitarian purpose alone are never sufficient to justify permanent exhibition of an object. After all, the purpose of our Department is not merely to teach the public the various developments of a particular craft. With our growing and maturing collections we shall have to bring the "minor" arts into closer correspondence and harmony with the "major" arts, concentrating more and more on the essentially artistic and inspiring qualities of the individual object, rather than on the typical and the exemplary. For the same reason, the M. and M. Karolik Collection of American Art, especially the furniture, must be more closely integrated with our other rich holdings in this field.

In this ambitious program, which can only be continued with success when the long-planned addition to the Department is undertaken, we must feel a more impartial responsibility towards all creative periods. We must not disregard the creativeness of those works of art which are unpopular now, unpopular because they do not conform to the taste or fashion of our time, or simply because the general public is not sufficiently familiar with them. They might easily strike the unaccustomed eye as too finicky, elaborate or just

"plain bad taste," or at the other extreme, too "scholarly and austere." However, history has taught that art museums of universal
standards and obligations cannot afford to omit or to neglect for
those reasons whole areas of artistic production. And this lesson
holds good for contemporary art as well. But if we apply rigorous
standards of quality and try to collect independent of fluctuating
taste and fashion, the objects we acquire will eventually develop in
the public a contemplative faculty and a sensibility for historical
aesthetic evaluation. And with this sensibility it will become easier
to experience and to enjoy the artistic accomplishment, the creative
spirit of an object that at first seems to have no aesthetic appeal.
Moreover, in collecting this way, we shall not only preserve but
communicate a heritage on which future generations can draw.

The first year of Hanns Swarzenski's curatorship was marked by
the purchase of two hitherto unrecorded Italian Romanesque works
of the twelfth century that carried on the great medieval tradition
of his father. One was a south Italian *Oliphant*, an elephant tusk of
majestic dimensions, lavishly carved with fantastic animals and
mythological scenes; the other a polychromed stone *Madonna and*

OLIPHANT. South Italy, ivory, late 11th century. *Frederick Brown and H. E. Bolles funds. 50.3425*

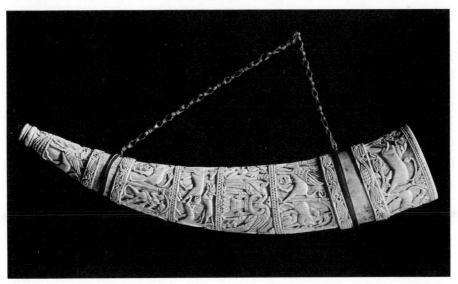

MADONNA AND CHILD. Lombardy, polychromed stone, late 12th century. *Maria Antoinette Evans Fund.* 57.583

Child that is a masterpiece of Lombard sculpture. When offered to the museum for consideration, the full beauty of the Madonna was disguised by a coat of gaudy nineteenth-century paint, intended to give the group the appearance of a Renaissance stucco or terracotta; when this was painfully removed, layer by layer, in the Research Laboratory, the original coloring of the sculpture was revealed. Two years later, this stone Italian Romanesque *Madonna* was joined by an early Gothic French *Virgin and Child* in polychromed oak, carved in the Ile-de-France about 1200. After discovering the group in a Norman belfry near Conflans in the late eighteen nineties, the sculptor Joseph Mezzara had taken it to Paris, where he kept it for many years. Carried to Germany during World War II, the group was ultimately returned to the discoverer's daughter, in whose Paris apartment the Curator and Director succeeded in seeing and studying the sculpture. The owner, however, unconditionally refused to have the sculpture sent to Boston for examination. It is a credit to the courage of Perry Rathbone's artistic convictions that he succeeded in recommending to the trustees the purchase of the sculpture, sight unseen, at what was then a record price. It was, with the aid of the William Francis Warden Fund, purchased by the Museum of Fine Arts in 1959.

As recently as 1966 another polychromed Romanesque sculpture was bought: a limestone *Praying Angel*, carved in extremely high relief about 1160, probably in the region of Maastricht. Although

VIRGIN AND CHILD. Ile-de-France, polychromed oak, early 13th century. *William Francis Warden Fund. 59.701*

PRAYING ANGEL. Maastricht(?), polychromed limestone, about 1160.
Charles Amos Cummings Bequest Fund. 66.458

no other figure from the same monument is known, the triangular shape suggests that it was a spandrel, perhaps one of four used to decorate the pendentives of a circular dome. In such a case it might have been either part of a quartet of angels, or the symbol of the Evangelist Saint Matthew. But whatever its subject, its acquisition was welcome, for, as Hanns Swarzenski pointed out, "in all likelihood its export would have been stopped had its true origin been recognized at the time when it was purchased."

Later medieval sculpture was acquired both by gift and purchase. A wood statue of *St. Joseph Kneeling in Adoration* (then attributed to Niccolo dell'Arca, now thought to be by Pietro d'Allemania, a German Gothic sculptor active in Naples), was given in 1958 from a fund contributed by friends in memory of Georg Swarzenski. As this doubtless formed part of a highly realistic Nativity group, it was appropriately first exhibited in the Rotunda during the 1958 Christmas season, in the company of two recently purchased polychromed wooden angels by the eminent Augsburg sculptor, Ehrgott Bernhard Bendl (1660–1738). When purchased in England these angels were thoroughly disguised in whitewash that had been applied to make them conform to the neoclassic taste; when cleaned in the Research Laboratory by Joseph W. Harrington, under the direction of William J. Young, enough of the original polychrome and gilding was revealed to make it clear that they are beyond question the most important representations of Bavarian monumental sculpture of the Baroque period outside of Germany.

A cheerful alabaster trumpeting angel, carved in the fourteenth century in the Ile-de-France, was bought in 1961, and in 1967 a Burgundian limestone *Pleurant* of the early fifteenth century, carved in the atelier of Claus Sluter, was purchased. The New York manufacturer of office supplies and collector Jack Linsky gave in 1966 three exquisite Spanish Gothic alabaster reliefs of a *Procession of*

THE ROTUNDA IN 1958. In the center ST. JOSEPH, attributed to Pietro d'Allemania. *Georg Swarzenski Memorial Fund.* 58.719 To the right and left TWO ANGELS, polychromed wood, by Ehrgott Bernhard Bendl, Augsburg, 1660–1738. *Francis Bartlett Fund.* 58.43–4

PLEURANT. Burgundy, lime-
stone, about 1430. *Frederick
Brown Fund.* 67.764

Mourners, set against a deep blue background of églomisé glass. They
are part of a tomb monument that is close enough in style to one in
the sanctuary of Belloch de Santa Colonna de Queralt, known to
have been carved by Pedro Aguilar of Lérida (ca. 1337–1370) to
suggest the attribution of these reliefs to that great Catalan Gothic
sculptor. Jack Linsky's generosity to the Department of Decorative
Arts and Sculpture has strengthened other galleries than the medieval, for in 1964 he gave an exquisitely lacquered and powerfully
modeled sixteenth-century bronze group, *Centaur Attacked by a
Lion*, "the work of a Florentine contemporary of Giambologna, who
rightly should be called a Pollaiolo of the Cinquecento." The variety
of Mr. Linsky's interests is evidenced by his 1967 gift of a French
commode, ornamented with marquetry and ormolu, made and signed

by Jacques van Oostenryk, called Dautriche, who was active as a cabinet maker in Paris between 1743 and 1778.

German Gothic sculpture in polychromed wood, a field poorly represented hitherto, was enhanced in 1963 by the bequest of Dr. Siegfried J. Thannhauser, in memory of his wife, Franziska Reiner Thannhauser. This gift included a polychromed walnut *St. Sebastian* of about 1470, from the Dangolsheim altar shrine, Strasbourg, which is one of the great Alsatian carvings made in the time of Master E. S. and Martin Schongauer; the *Pietà* of Glottertal in Baden; a seated *Virgin and Child* from the Pacher workshop in the Tyrol, and a *St. Barbara* by Hans Leinberger that is in style closely related to Albrecht Altdorfer. The polychromy of all these works was brought to light during patient restoration by Joseph W. Harrington in the Research Laboratory.

The fund bequeathed by Theodora Wilbour for English silver, in memory of her mother, Charlotte Beebe Wilbour, procured in 1964 an English fourteenth-century marriage casket with engraved silver mounts for fifteen panels of carved ivory, that, on all sides and on the lid, depict episodes from the Romance of Tristan and Isolde

PROCESSION OF MOURNERS FROM A TOMB. Catalan, alabaster, attributed to Pedro Aguilar of Lérida. *Gift of Jack Linsky.* 66.384–386

PIETA FROM CHAPEL OF GLOTTERTAL. Upper Rhine (Black Forest), poly-chromed wood, late 14th century. ST. SEBASTIAN. Strasbourg, polychromed wal-nut, from the Dangolsheim altar shrine, about 1470. *Bequest of Dr. Siegfried J. Thannhauser in memory of his wife, Franziska Reiner Thannhauser.* 63.590 and 63.589

and other amorous subjects. Another remarkable Gothic purchase of 1965 was the *Aquamanile* in the form of a man's bust, cast in bronze in the thirteenth century in one of the great foundries of Lower Saxony, probably Magdeburg, that worked for the newly Christian-ized countries east of the Elbe. It was, in fact, dug up in Borsow at the Dniester River in Poland.

The department's willingness to recognize the creativeness of works of art representing the taste of other times is illustrated by the purchase in 1964 of the lifesized bronze *Bust of Cleopatra* by Pier Jacopo Alari Bonacolsi, the classicizing Mantuan sculptor popu-

GOTHIC MARRIAGE CASKET. English, ivory with engraved silver mounts, 14th century. *Theodora Wilbour Fund in memory of Charlotte Beebe Wilbour. 64.1467*

AQUAMANILE IN FORM OF A MAN'S BUST. Lower Saxony, bronze, 13th century. *Decorative Arts Special Fund. 65.465*

CLEOPATRA. Mantua, bronze, by Pier Jacopo Alari Bonacolsi, called Antico, about 1460–1528. *William Francis Warden Fund. 64.2174*

larly known as Antico (ca. 1460–1528). When this highly finished
Renaissance bronze, perhaps made for Isabella d'Este, which once
adorned her studio in the Palazzo Ducale at Mantua, was submitted
for purchase, the Committee on the Museum greeted it with a notable
lack of enthusiasm. Various members contrasted it unfavorably with
a late Egyptian wooden statue of a young woman that had simultaneously been submitted by William Stevenson Smith (illustrated
on page 281). In its stark impressionistic simplicity the Egyptian
sculpture immediately appealed to current taste. By running down
Cleopatra, the Committee soon sold itself the wooden Egyptian girl.
But it also had the good sense to buy the totally different Renaissance
bronze, for when as perceptive a curator as Hanns Swarzenski recom-
mends a purchase, and the money is available, only a very stupid
and obstinate group of laymen would interpose a veto. In my experience, at least, Museum of Fine Arts committees have only
disappointed curators when there simply was no money in the till.
Also in the Italian Renaissance, the department's obliviousness to
an arbitrary line between "major" and "minor" arts is indicated by
the purchase in 1962 of a mid-sixteenth-century *bancone* (a desk for
the Municipal Money Exchange) from Palermo, which displays in

BANCONE (MONEY EXCHANGE DESK). Italy, walnut, after Montorsoli, about
1550. *William Francis Warden Fund.* 62.7

POSEIDON AND AMPHITRITE.
Austria, Salzburg, 18th century.
57.665

its architectural proportions and multiplicity of festoons and mer-
maids the spirit of Florentine Mannerism at its best. As Montorsoli,
who was one of the leading masters of this particular style, was
active in Palermo from 1547 to 1557, the desk may reasonably be
attributed to him.

The Baroque and Rococo styles of Germany and Austria began for
the first time to appear in the department's galleries. A carved group
of *Poseidon and Amphitrite* from Salzburg, "highly symbolical of the
spirit of the age of Mozart," and a console table designed by Effner,
the architect of the Munich *Residenz*, enlivened the galleries in
1957. There soon followed the previously mentioned polychromed
angels from Augsburg; a marble statue of the great patron of Bavarian
Baroque, the Elector Prince Max Emmanuel II (1662–1726),
carved after 1714 by W. de Groff, fortunately acquired in 1959
from the collections of the National Museum, Munich; a Bavarian
polychromed wood *God the Father* of about 1750, bought in 1960,
and the next year a superb faience figure in monumental size. Of this
glorious *Madonna of the Immaculate Conception*, the Curator wrote:

MAX EMANUEL II OF BAVARIA. German, marble, by W. de Groff, after 1714.
William E. Nickerson Fund. 59.177

Resplendent in its lustrous white glaze, the contours and certain
details left in the golden brown clay, this miraculously preserved
statue is more than a feat of brilliant technical skill. Signed and
dated 1771 by the Bamberg sculptor Johan Martin Mutschele and
fired in the kilns of the factory of Schretzheim, it is a unique creation of the ecclesiastical art of Franconian Baroque, full of dramatic
movement in an undefined space charged with the Divine Presence.

This statue, called by Dr. Rainer Rückert, Curator of Ceramics at
the Bavarian National Museum, "the most important faience sculpture ever made in a German factory," was commissioned in 1771 by
a Freiherr von Lehrbach, then commander of the Teutonic Knights
at Wolframs-Eschenbach, to occupy as *Haus-Madonna* a niche over
the front door of the Manor House of the Knights.

No greater contrast can be imagined than that obtained by confronting the faience *Madonna of the Immaculate Conception* and the highly polished metal sculpture of *The Golden Fish* by Constantin Brancusi, bought in 1957, of which Hanns Swarzenski wrote: "The Rumanian-born artist exploits here the light-reflecting effect of the polished surface of a static object to the utmost degree and thus arrives at an abstraction, or better, an evocation of an organic shape that is at once aesthetically convincing and technically perfect." In the same year as the Lombard Romanesque *Madonna* and the Brancusi, the department bought Gauguin's monumental wood carving with the moving inscription: *Soyez amoureuses, vous serez heureuses.* This was exhibited in the Stone Room of the Evans Wing with the great Gauguin painting, where it was before long joined by

GOD THE FATHER ENTHRONED ON A CLOUD. Bavaria, polychromed wood with gold and silver, second half 18th century. *Arthur Tracy Cabot Fund. 60.1455*

MADONNA IMMACULATA. German, Schrezheim faience, white glazed, signed and dated by Johann Martin Mutschele, Bamberg, 1771. *William Francis Warden Fund. 61.1185*

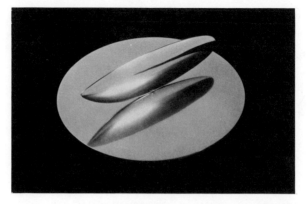

THE GOLDEN FISH. Constantin Brancusi, 1876–
1957. *William Francis Warden Fund.* 57.739

Gauguin's reliefs *La Guerre et La Paix*, lent by Mr. and Mrs. Laurence K. Marshall.

Carved at Tahiti early in 1901, from two specially selected panels
of Tamanuja hardwood of a beautiful reddish brown and enhanced
with polychromy, for Gustave Fayet, an avant-garde collector of
French Impressionists, the work is clearly related in its careful
technical execution and exploitation of the wood to our relief *Soyez
amoureuses et vous serez heureuses*, done twelve years earlier in
Brittany. Although the meaning of all the elements in this highly
symbolic narrative, whose title is taken from Tolstoy's *War and
Peace*, defies concrete rational interpretation, it symbolizes the suffering religious state of the great artist during his second stay on
the island. His features are reflected in the face of Christ in the
lower panel. Some of the figures are walking in the shadow of
the Tree of Knowledge. Parts of the representation as well as the
superimposition and the shape of two reliefs — their principle of
continuous rhythm and design — are taken from the friezes at the
Buddhist Temple of Borobudur, Java; other details of the composition, from a section of Trajan's Column. Photographs of both monuments were found in Gauguin's possession.

When Mr. and Mrs. Marshall made their loan a gift in 1963, it
seemed possible that their generosity might well have been motivated

SOYEZ AMOUREUSES, VOUS SEREZ HEUREUSES. French, painted wood sculpture
by Paul Gauguin. *Arthur Tracy Cabot Fund. 57.582*
LA GUERRE ET LA PAIX. French, polychromed tamanuja wood, by Paul Gauguin,
Tahiti, 1901. *Gift of Mr. and Mrs. Laurence K. Marshall. 63.2764-5*

by the happy proximity in the Stone Room of their reliefs and the
museum's, opposite the great *D'où venons nous? Que sommes nous?
Où allons nous?*

Following the purchase of the Gauguin and Brancusi, the department devoted great effort to assembling representative examples of
modern sculpture, a task that would not have been possible before
Perry T. Rathbone's appointment. It seems worth recording that in
1940 the recommended purchase of a great Maillol bronze, the *Ile
de France*, was refused. Happily at the close of the exhibition of
his collection in the spring of 1957, Walter P. Chrysler left on
view on an annual loan basis Lehmbruck's monumental work, *Kneeling Woman*. The following year the museum bought one of Henry
Moore's most original creations, the *Seated Figure against a Curved
Wall* (1956–57) and Gerhard Marcks' *Pomona*, carved in 1932,
while Hyman Swetzoff gave Kaethe Kollwitz's original plaster model
of a deeply moving group of *Mother and Son* that was never cast in
the artist's lifetime. In 1959 were bought Rodin's group *Les Pre-
mières Funerailles* (also called *La Purgatoire* or *La Tombée d'une
Ame dans les Limbes*) and the powerful *Head of a Horse*, cast in

bronze in 1937 by the French sculptor André Beaudin. These were followed in 1960 by the purchase of Oskar Kokoschka's 1908 polychromed clay *Bust of a Warrior*, Reg Butler's *Girl on a Wheel*, cast in Paris in 1959, and three exceedingly rare and imaginative creations by Alexander Calder: a brass wire *Cow* of about 1926; a mobile in black painted sheet steel, about 1935; and *Diana*, constructed of four sensitively carved pieces of walnut, about 1934. A second Renoir sculpture was given in 1961 by Mr. and Mrs. Abraham A. Sonna-

DIANA. American, sculpture in walnut, by Alexander Calder, about 1934. *Frederick Brown Fund. 60.956*
FEMME QUI MARCHE. Bronze by Alberto Giacometti, 1933–1934. *Henry Lee Higginson and William Francis Warden funds. 64.520*

bend, a plaster model of a table clock, signed and dated 1915, adorned with allegorical figures signifying the triumph of human procreation over the despotism of time. In 1964, along with the English Gothic ivory marriage casket, was purchased Alberto Giacometti's bronze *Femme qui marche* — "striving toward an entirely revised sense of human representation, it is one of the noblest and purest creations of our time" — and the monumental bronze *Torso Romano* of 1963 by the young American, Gilbert Franklin. In the same year Mrs. Peggy Guggenheim gave four examples of nonfigurative sculpture, including abstract compositions in metal by Arnaldo Pomodoro and Berto Lardera. Henry Gaudier-Brzeska's 1914 plaster relief, *The Wrestlers*, was bought in 1965; George Rickey's polychromed stainless steel *Red Vine* in 1966 (aided by a gift from Mr. and Mrs. Stephen A. Stone); and Robert Eshoo's *Echo 2* (painted wood, plastic, and aluminum) in 1967. And, lest the primitive American aspect of the department be overlooked, a polychromed wood figure of *Uncle Sam* from Ossipee, New Hampshire, about 1840, was purchased in the latter year. This, Harry H. Schnabel, Jr., considered "perhaps the outstanding folk art discovery of the decade."

Ceramics were constantly augmented through the generosity of collectors. The long projected gift of the Jessie and Sigmund J. Katz Collection of English porcelains came to a sad fruition with his untimely death in 1957. By the terms of his will, the museum received one half of each piece of this remarkable assembly of specimens of Langdon Hall, Chelsea, Bow, Derby, and Worcester, with a life interest to his widow. The following year Mrs. Katz gave her interest in thirty-two pieces of Bow and two of Chelsea porcelain; in succeeding years she annually augmented the collection by similar gifts.

R. Thornton Wilson of New York City, whose gift in memory of President Kennedy has earlier been noted, had steadily from 1959 been adding important ceramics to the department. His generosity to the Museum of Fine Arts sprang from his attachment to Boston since his youth, and was rekindled by the happy accident of Hanns Swarzenski's and his simultaneous coveting of a piece of German Hafner ware in the New York shop of Leopold Blumka. His gift in

UNCLE SAM. American, polychromed
wood, Ossipee, New Hampshire, about
1840. *Harriet Otis Cruft Fund.*
67.763

JUG   DECORATED   WITH   ANIMALS.
Portuguese majolica, late 16th century.
*Gift of R. Thornton Wilson in memory
of his brother, Orme Wilson.* 67.613

1959 of an Austrian plaque in green glaze of the *Crucifixion*, dated 1600 and signed with the initials of the potter, and a Staffordshire faïence dish, painted in Holland in the eighteenth century with *The Flight into Egypt*, "filled a sore gap" in the department's collections. So for that matter did his gifts the following year of examples of Hafner and Habaner wares and a Christ from a Crucifixion group by J. P. Melchior, the famous porcelain sculptor of Hochst, about 1770–1775. These welcome objects were given in memory of Florence Ellsworth Wilson. Many similar gifts and loans have followed. During the summer of 1969 several rooms were filled with masterpieces from Thornton Wilson's collection that included Hafner, Leeds, Delft, Sèvres, Meissen, Italian majolica, and the delicate products of the Russian Imperial Porcelain Factory at St. Petersburg.

While special mention has been made of the development of sculpture, and of other less familiar collections, many important accessions in silver, furniture, and other types of materials have been received, both by gift and by purchase. The Theodora Wilbour funds have permitted constant additions to the English silver, while American examples have been added in respectable numbers, even without the help of such restricted funds. The Curator noted in 1960 how improved display of the American silver introduced "an added burden and responsibility for Mrs. Buhler, for in order to show every aspect of the craft a selective rotation program has to be set up. As the conscientious guardian of her treasures she prevented the sale of Paul Revere's unique tea service, made in 1793 for Burrell Carnes, on loan at the Museum since 1916, and secured it for our collection through the disposal of less important items."

Richard Randall's particular concern with American furniture, and his work in preparing the catalogue, resulted in extending the scope of the department's holdings. Having arranged an exhibition of *The Furniture of H. H. Richardson* at the beginning of 1962, he inspired the gift of a distinguished group of "Golden Oak" pieces designed by that architect for the Crane Memorial Library of Quincy and the Ames Free Library in North Easton. Similar extensions of field were prepared by his work, for the Shaker Collection of Ralph E. and Myra T. Tibbetts, given by Mr. and Mrs. Russell W. Knight in 1967, provided an opportunity for a comprehensive study

SILVER COFFEE URN. American, by Paul Revere, 1793, made for Burrell Carnes. *Gift of Henry Davis Sleeper in memory of his mother, Maria Westcote Sleeper, by exchange.* 60.1419

not only of Shaker cabinet work, but of basketry, textiles, metalwork, and small wooden wares.

There have been innumerable directions for acquisition without loss of artistic quality. An unexpected example given in 1963 by the Misses Aimée and Rosamond Lamb is furnished by three superb sets of jewelry: two brooches of blue and black enamels, diamonds, and sapphires, which can be separated to form earrings and pins, made in Paris in 1850 from designs by their grandfather, Benjamin Smith Rotch, one of the museum's founding trustees of 1870, and a diamond spray in two parts of flowers which vibrate by means of springs, made in Paris about 1890. These pieces were given in memory of their mother, Mrs. Horatio Appleton Lamb. The greatest single gift ever received by the Department of Decorative Arts and Sculpture — the Forsyth Wickes Collection of eighteenth-century French objects — will, however, be described in a subsequent chapter because of the chain of events set in motion by its receipt in 1965.

Over the past decade many changes have been made in the installations of the Department of Decorative Arts and Sculpture. When its wing was built in the late twenties, most American museums were in hot pursuit of "period rooms," created by the installation of doors, windows, mantlepieces, and paneling from some building of the past. Such rooms were, in theory at least, furnished with the objects they might have contained when first built. In theory they evoked the past. There was always the possibility that, to obtain a desired spread of periods and styles, an institution might accept inferior woodwork simply because it was the only thing available. Moreover such installations, when made by committees of tasteful amateurs and architects, succeeded better in pleasing the contemporary eye than in presenting a thoroughly documented record of the taste of the past. In practice period rooms were often a considerable nuisance, for visitors — unless confined to very small groups as at Winterthur — had to view their contents only from a carefully confined channel or passage, or, at worst, simply peer through the door. Thus such installations encouraged gaping at the ensemble rather than careful study of the details that created it.

Three small Louis XV rooms on the ground floor of the Decorative Arts Wing, whose *boiseries* had seemed adequate enough when

BROOCHES. Paris, gold, black enamel, and diamonds, 1850, designed by Benjamin Smith Rotch. *Gift of the Misses Aimee and Rosamond Lamb in memory of their mother, Mrs. Horatio Appleton Lamb. 63.665–666*

WOODCOTE PARK ROOM IN DECORATIVE ARTS WING.

installed in 1928, failed to meet the more exacting standards of three decades later; thus they were removed and sold in 1959 to create additional space for more systematic exhibitions. When the fine mid-eighteenth-century English room from Woodcote Park had been installed, the white paint on its woodwork troubled no one. Yet in 1962 it was found that the frames of the room's overdoors and the moldings of the panels had originally been gilded, and that the panels had not been white, but of two shades of green. When the original color scheme was restored, the effect of the room was entirely different, and considerably handsomer into the bargain.

The American period rooms remain today much as they were on installation in 1928, as do the French and English ones given by Mrs. Bradbury in memory of her brother, George Robert White. But the Tudor Room now forms part of a Gothic gallery containing painting and sculpture; its exterior window adorns one wall of the gallery, but visitors also may go inside to view its paneling and furnishings. The new galleries, however, are freed from the confining limitations of period rooms. They show not only the sculpture, furniture, ceramics, and metalwork of their time, but frequently paintings and textiles drawn from other departments. Thus portraits by Smibert and Copley hang above American furniture of the eighteenth century, while Gainsborough's *The Mushroom Girl* accompanies English furniture. The Hôtel de Montmorency panels and the Boucher paintings from the Deacon house, among the earliest acquisitions of the museum, hang in the department's eighteenth-century French gallery with the Beauvais tapestry of *The Luncheon*, bought by the Department of Textiles in 1940, as a background for superb French furniture, acquired in Paris soon after the Revolution by Colonel James Swan and continuously donated by descendants of his family.

A dramatic instance of such juxtaposition of the arts, still under way at the moment of writing, has been the installation on the ceiling of one of the department's galleries of Tiepolo's *Aurora Dispersing the Clouds of Night*. From the moment of its purchase in 1930, this irregularly shaped canvas of slightly over 10 by 11 feet, from a ceiling in the Mocenigo Palace in Venice, had been awkwardly displayed. As it would have been overwhelming to its neighbors if hung flat against a wall, it was for some years canted between the wall and ceiling of one of the larger galleries in the Evans Wing (as illustrated in Chapter XXII). Moreover, its original gilded rococo frame, having come to Boston in numerous unmarked fragments, seemed unusable. Early in 1969 the museum's master cabinetmaker, Vincent Cerbone, began fitting this jigsaw puzzle together; by late spring the huge canvas, cleaned and restored by the conservator Richard Finlayson, was fitted into its reassembled frame and installed on the ceiling of gallery D-7. When seen as it was intended to be, the Tiepolo acquires vastly increased importance; furthermore it will enhance the objects soon to be placed below it.

In addition to the chronological sequence of rooms exhibiting the varied arts of different periods, old galleries have been renovated for the improved display of American and English silver, of Continental and English porcelain, and of glass. A singularly cheerless and dreary ground floor corridor, running from the Crypt to the

CEILING DECORATION FROM MOCENIGO PALACE, VENICE, WITH FRAME.
Giovanni Battista Tiepolo. *Maria Antoinette Evans Fund.* 30.539

Decorative Arts Wing, was transformed in 1960 for American silver. A carved and painted eighteenth-century door frame from Hatfield, Massachusetts, was installed at the entrance, and the Copley portrait of Paul Revere at work was hung on the end wall. New wall cases, designed by Carl F. Zahn, were built in walnut, with interior lighting, to display the silver. Thus a handsome and arresting gallery was achieved out of an awkward passageway. This is one of the many instances where recent improvements in lighting have made possible new uses of old space.

The increased emphasis upon sculpture, which led to the 1964 renaming of the department, drew in a number of new visitors, individuals as well as groups of students from schools and universities, who came especially to see sculpture. Hanns Swarzenski commented upon this phenomenon in his 1964 report, where he wrote:

> We realize, however, that these new visitors are rarely arrested by the artistically related objects of a more intimate and less showy nature which are displayed in the same gallery — the smaller and seemingly humble works in metal, enamel, ivory, boxwood, and pottery, made for religious and domestic use. Most certainly these visitors seldom come to the period rooms or the ceramic, silver, and furniture galleries. On the other hand, ever since the word "Sculpture" was added to the name of the Department, we are continually asked by mail, telephone, and in person, "Where is your collection of sculpture?" The question made us wonder how many visitors and friends of the Museum actually realize that this Department now has an important and systematically growing collection of sculpture — Medieval, Renaissance, Baroque, and Modern. We should have

AMERICAN SILVER GALLERY AFTER 1960.

TEXTILE CORRIDOR BEFORE 1960.

no illusions. Those who want to look at sculpture, and want to learn about it, generally go to the galleries of Classical, Egyptian, or Oriental art. Many of those who come to our Department, often highly specialized groups, expect to see and study the so-called decorative arts — silver, pewter, glass, pottery, and furniture. When these objects are assembled in period rooms they offer the added nostalgic attraction of homely human immediacy and a kind of assurance that certain standards are stable, evoking sentimental and ancestral memories of a more desirable age. Apparently, these are two distinct types of visitors that never seem to meet.

The fantastic variety and quality of the acquisitions mentioned in this chapter is an indication that the Department of Decorative Arts and Sculpture, like the Department of Classical Art as indicated in the preceding chapter, has immeasurably benefited by the learning and ingenuity of its Curator. Both departments have had to live by their wits, for although both have benefited from the Theodora Wilbour funds where gold and silver are involved, neither has had the good fortune of the Asiatic, Print, Textile, and Painting departments in receiving substantial bequests specifically restricted to the purchase of works of art that fall within their fields. Both have had to rely upon encouraging gifts from concerned collectors and upon their share of purchases from the William Francis Warden Fund and smaller funds with only the most general restrictions. This has produced its frustrations, as in 1962, when Hanns Swarzenski wrote:

This galaxy of accessions that we have proudly and gratefully recorded should not, however, give us illusions. The good fortune of obtaining works of art worthy of the Museum is becoming rarer every year. We must face the cruel, sad fact that our budget no longer permits us to compete with the other great institutions and private collections in this country and abroad. One example may suffice: the Metropolitan Museum was able to acquire this spring a miraculously perfect and beautiful Gothic reliquary altar of radiant gold and translucent enamel. This superb and little-known treasure, made for Queen Elizabeth of Hungary, was first offered to us. But our desperate attempts to secure it for the Museum, or for a Boston collector, failed. Because of this Museum's scholarly prestige and its sincere and determined efforts, it will for a while continue to be among the fortunate few to which such extraordinary and rare works of art will first be offered. But such privilege is bound to suffer in due course as a result of our limited funds. Where shall we go?

Such laments are by no means peculiar to the nineteen sixties, for readers of Chapter II will recall the 1881 observation of Charles C. Perkins, made as Chairman of the Committee on the Museum: "Knowing that other chances of equal importance may arise, we could wait with greater patience, did we not also know that every year increases the number of purchasers, and raises the scale of prices which objects of any merit will bring in London or Paris." This is a perennial dilemma that increases in magnitude each decade. The possession of large sums of money does not, in itself, lead to the most perceptive collecting. He who can readily buy, without counting his pennies, often does so without much reflection. When objects are sufficiently touted, the possessor of ready money may succumb to transient whims and fancies. The nineteenth-century American "big spenders," so lovingly chronicled by Lucius Beebe, were seldom men of any notable taste or education. Their delight lay in observing the startled admiration their extravagances aroused in waiters, shop clerks, journalists, and others as ignorant as themselves. The pursuit of books, manuscripts, and works of art, especially in very recent years, has created another race of "big spenders," who bask in the glory of press reports of inflated prices. But the true collector, whether buying for himself or for an institution, follows Edward Perry Warren's principle of 1893: "My policy is always to decide on a purchase from the point of view of its ultimate worth, not of present needs." But Warren also observed, in an 1895 letter to Martin Brimmer: "The museum must look ahead, seize occasions as they arise, and take into consideration the present opportunities and those likely to occur, adapting itself in short to the inevitable conditions of the situation." This means, in short, the ability to seize opportunities that will contribute to the accomplishment of a plan, thoughtfully devised for the distant future. It is in accordance with such a plan that the Department of Decorative

Arts and Sculpture acquired in 1968 (through the Otis Norcross Fund) a Frankish crosier head of the seventh or eighth century and other pieces of metal work of the Dark Ages, and, with the help of a 1968 Curator's Fund established by John Goelet, a Rhenish reliquary pendant of about 1500, decorated with a representation of Saint George and the Dragon.

CHAPTER XXI

Four Aspects of Curatorship

In July 1956 Adolph S. Cavallo, formerly on the staff of the Detroit Institute of Arts and the Brooklyn Museum, became Assistant Curator of Textiles. Three and a half years later, when Miss Gertrude Townsend resigned, as of 31 December 1959, he was appointed Curator to succeed her. In announcing this change, Perry T. Rathbone wrote:

> Presiding over this department for thirty years, Miss Townsend has long been the acknowledged "dean" of American textile curators. Under her guidance, the Boston collection developed into one of the foremost in the world with unexampled concentrations of embroidery, both European and American, Coptic and Pre-Columbian textiles, as well as distinguished representations in virtually every field and period of this universal art. The costume collection which Miss Townsend was entirely responsible for forming — and largely through an untold number of gifts — is an *embarras de richesse*. In quality, extent and in the surprises it still holds for nearly everyone, the collection can only be described as fabulous. The Trustees appointed Miss Townsend Fellow for Research in Textiles to enable her to carry on her research for the Museum and to complete work long delayed on her books on textiles. Thus, it is a pleasure to record that Miss Townsend will remain with us as a working member of the staff.

This she did for another four years. Following her resignation as Fellow for Research, she was in 1964 named Curator Emeritus. Miss Townsend's remarkable acquisitions continued until the end of her curatorship. One that requires special mention is a fifth-century panel of tapestry from the eastern Mediterranean, possibly woven in Egypt where it was found, that was purchased in 1957 through the Charles Potter Kling Fund. This large fragment of what must have been a wall covering, shows a man grasping the folds of a curtain that hangs below a narrow horseshoe arch connecting two twisted polychrome columns; it is significant, both in design and technique, as a forerunner of medieval European tapestry hangings.

The Department of Textiles has worked under severe handicaps of space. Aside from the Tapestry Gallery, its remarkable possessions have always been exhibited in widely separated odd corners and corridors, or, with other types of objects, in certain of the galleries of the Department of Decorative Arts and Sculpture. Moreover, to prevent undue fading from light, specimens frequently have to be rotated from exhibition to storage. The average museum visitor knows all too little about the rich holdings of the department; such knowledge is largely confined to the numerous scholars from other institutions, graduate students, professional costume and accessory designers, embroideresses, and weavers who come to study specific materials, and to the persons who attend lectures given by the department. In 1960, for example, Adolph Cavallo lectured on the history of lace to a group of lace collectors and on English and New England embroideries to groups of professional and amateur needlewomen. In February and October he gave introductory talks on the collection in the "Know Your Museum" series, and in November, at the request of the Ladies' Committee, a course of three lectures on textile art, as well as speaking during regularly scheduled gallery talks. He remarked, however, in his 1960 report that,

> It is difficult for anyone outside the Department to appreciate the long and often physically fatiguing work hours spent attending to the needs of visitors or preparing for lectures. Because of the delicate nature of the material with which we deal, only the specially trained professional members of the departmental staff are qualified

TAPESTRY PANEL (detail). Eastern Mediterranean, probably 5th century. *Charles Potter Kling Fund. 57.180*

MANTLE. Peruvian, south coast, transitional Ica-Inca style, 1300–1550 A.D. *Gift of the Class of the Museum. 62.1180*

to handle the textiles, which are often large and heavy and frequently stored in high places accessible only by ladder. The process of selecting, taking out and replacing textiles for a single visitor often takes one of us the better part of a day. Preparations for a single lecture can cost the Curator and an Assistant as much as two days' constant work. If costumes are to be shown on mannequins, more time is required. Other behind-the-scenes efforts which might be of interest to the reader in this brief digression include the time-consuming arrangments for the design, manufacture and delivery of special mannequins and wigs, the weeks spent mounting textiles for exhibition, and the plans, partially realized already, for installing special equipment in the Tapestry Gallery to suit it for continued use as a hall for public entertainments while providing maximum safety for the rare and costly tapestries hanging there. Twin exhaust fans in the clerestory windows will remove the cigarette smoke which accumulates during the evening. Specifications have been drawn up for pulley systems on which the tapestries can be raised for protection when the Gallery is crowded. The same rigging will enable us to change the tapestries in a quarter of the time now allotted to that complicated and painstaking task. The tapestries, as well as our visitors, find such a change refreshing.

To cope with textile mounting for the accelerated programs of changing exhibitions, and with conservation work, Mrs. Benjamin A. Markell joined the staff in 1960 as an Assistant. In 1964 she was given the title of Special Assistant, because of her augmented responsibilities in connection with the preservation and exhibition of the collections. When I recently wandered into the workroom of the Textile Department, I saw Mrs. Markell washing a great Persian carpet, with the assistance of Miss Suzanne Chapman, who had come over from the Egyptian Department to help. Miss Chapman was beating with a wire whisk what appeared to be a bowl of meringues; actually it was a decoction of soapwort (*Saponaria officinalis*), an herb used in the Middle Ages, and since, for washing fabrics. It is always cheering to see instances of the accomplishments of the remarkable artists and craftsmen who are hidden away in museum departments, as well as in the Research Laboratory, and to note how they adapt their talents to help each other in an incredible variety of problems.

In 1961 Mrs. Henry Ware Eliot, a Visitor to the department who was an expert needlewoman, was persuaded to take a part-time position as a regular member of the staff to help in the conservation of textiles. In the same year Mrs. Stuart Cary Welch offered her services as a volunteer in similar directions; she was joined the following year by Mrs. Jan Cox. For several years Mrs. Edward L. B. Terrace was a Research Assistant in the department. Robert Hall McCormick, who had served as Honorary Curator of the Elizabeth

Day McCormick Collection since 1943, died on 27 December 1963. He was succeeded by his sister, Miss Mildred McCormick.

Adolph Cavallo's thoughts on the problem of acquisitions in his department were presented in his 1960 report.

> Ours is now one of the world's most extensive and representative collections of textiles, ranging in date from the early Christian era to recent years. Taking this fact into account, together with the simple truth that our storages are seriously overcrowded, it appears to me that the only realistic program to follow is one of strictly selective acquisitions. This means that we must refuse, and have refused, many generous offers of gifts or objects for sale. We must use our limited purchase funds only to fill important gaps in the collection (we need medieval embroideries, Byzantine silks, early Gobelins tapestries) or to buy masterpieces in areas of the collection which are already strong.

He then described two recently purchased examples of Peruvian textile art that fully qualified in the last category.

The museum's Peruvian holdings went back to the earliest years in Copley Square, for in 1878 Edward W. Hooper gave 47 specimens of early textiles from that country. Denman W. Ross and Edward J. Holmes had made such important additions that in 1932 Philip Ainsworth Means had assessed the collection as "one of the largest and most representative collections of Peruvian textiles in the United States; indeed its only serious rivals are the collections of the Metropolitan Museum of Art, and the private collection of Mr. H. S. Ellsberg, of New York City." In addition to pre-Columbian textiles, Denman Ross had, around the turn of the century, given peerless examples of Peruvian tapestries of the Colonial period. Then in 1960 was acquired a sumptuous panel of featherwork from the front of a poncho, dating from the Tiahuanaco period or later (around 1000 to 1500 A.D.), which was the first piece of featherwork in the collection. Another Peruvian masterpiece was purchased in the same year; a small, tapestry-woven panel, with armorial bearings surrounded by a border of floral motifs, birds, and animals, rendered with the finest silk yarns, woven on cotton warps. "This jewel-like piece," the Curator wrote, "which probably dates from the seventeenth century,

SILK TAPESTRY PANEL. Peruvian, Colonial period, probably 17th century. *Charles Potter Kling Fund. 60.794*

will be the chief ornament of our extraordinary collection of Peruvian Colonial tapestries when they are shown again." That opportunity came in the 1961 exhibition, *Twenty-five Centuries of Peruvian Art, 700 B.C.–1800 A.D.*, jointly sponsored by the Museum of Fine Arts and the Peabody Museum, Harvard University, where the featherwork panel was reproduced in color on the cover of the catalogue.

Although the museum had remarkable holdings of pre-Inca Peruvian textiles and of Colonial tapestries, it was weak in Inca weaving. Consequently the gift of a man's mantle of the transitional Ica-Inca style (1300–1500 A.D.) by the Class of the Museum of Fine Arts in 1962 was particularly welcome. In the same year two remarkable tapestries were purchased through the Kling Fund. The first, a brilliantly woven and magnificently preserved seventeenth-century hanging of *Apollo Pursuing Daphne*, was the first great Parisian tapestry to enter the collection. The other was a long and narrow part of a valance, woven in northern Germany or Denmark in the late sixteenth or first half of the seventeenth century, with *Scenes from the Book of Genesis*, derived from a series of woodcuts by Virgil Solis of Nuremberg that appeared in various editions of German and Danish illustrated Bibles. The Sacrifice of Isaac, and

APOLLO PURSUING DAPHNE. French tapestry, 17th century. *Charles Potter Kling Fund.* 62.330

SCENES FROM THE BOOK OF GENESIS. North German or Danish tapestry, late 16th or first half of 17th century. *Charles Potter Kling Fund.* 62.1012

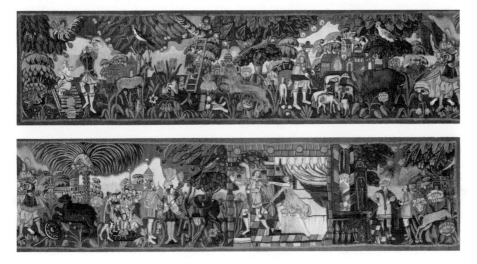

THE LAST SUPPER. French tapestry, 16th century. *Charles Potter Kling Fund.*
65.1033

scenes from the lives of Jacob and Joseph are represented, Potiphar's
wife being very decently covered by a knee-length nightgown.

Three rare English, Flemish, and French tapestries, acquired in
1965, represented periods or types previously lacking in the collection, while a fourth purchase of equal rarity complemented a tapestry bought in 1904. The latter, *The Last Supper*, woven in France
in the first third of the sixteenth century, was a companion piece to
the *Two Miracles of the Eucharist*, described in Chapter VI, which
had been one of the delights of my childhood. Both are believed to
have been part of a series given to the abbey of Notre-Dame-de-la-

THREE EPISODES IN THE LIFE OF ST. PAUL. Flemish tapestry, probably Brussels, 16th century.
Charles Potter Kling Fund. 65.596

ARABESQUES WITH BUST. English tapestry, 18th century. *Charles Potter Kling Fund. 65.1314*

Charité at Angers by Dame Loyse le Roux, who probably died in 1519. A Flemish *Three Episodes in the Life of St. Paul*, of the second third of the sixteenth century, and an English eighteenth-century tapestry, *Arabesques with Bust*, were, like *The Last Supper*, bought through the Kling Fund. *The Emperor on a Journey*, a Beauvais *chinoiserie* of the early eighteenth century, was the gift of Mrs. Henry U. Harris in the name of her mother, Mrs. Edwin S. Webster.

In 1963 Adolph Cavallo opened his report:

> The problems of making the material in a department such as this available and meaningful to our visitors are peculiar to the nature of the material itself. Our objects are for the most part very large or very small; very glamorous to all or dull to anyone but a specialist; and all of them are fragile. This year we concentrated on the problem of bringing some of our unsung treasures before the public eye and devoted most of the year's effort to offering sumptuous surprises from the costume collection in a special exhibition entitled *She Walks in Splendor: Great Costumes 1550–1950*. Although this collection is one of the oldest in the country, having been started in 1877, its contents have rarely been shown.

This exhibition, held from 3 October through 1 December 1963, was considered by Perry Rathbone as "one of the most remarkable in the history of the Museum." It was certainly one of the most dramatic, for the backgrounds were created and the lighting designed by Broadway theater designers Raymond Sovey and Horace Armistead. Against these settings eighty costumed mannequins were arranged in a series of period groups. Many of the fine examples from

THE EMPEROR ON A JOURNEY. French tapestry, Beauvais, late 17th or early 18th century. *Gift of Mrs. Henry U. Harris in the name of Mrs. Edwin S. Webster. 65.1352*

the Elizabeth Day McCormick Collection contributed to the brilliance of the exhibition.

She Walks in Splendor opened with a dinner in the Painting Galleries, with the Ambassador of France to the United States and Madame Hervé Alphand as guests of honor. As Perry Rathbone described the exhibition:

> Among the 210 guests at dinner, headed by His Excellency, the Governor of the Commonwealth, Endicott Peabody, and Mrs. Endicott Peabody, and including a number of former ambassadors and celebrities, were many from out-of-town, especially kinsmen of the late Elizabeth Day McCormick of Chicago whose renowned collection of costumes figured prominently in the exhibition. Two openings for the membership were held the following day: one in the afternoon, the other in the evening when Miss Cornelia Otis Skinner was our guest of honor. A total of 3,340 members attended.

SHE WALKS IN SPLENDOR EXHIBITION, 1963. American and French evening dresses, about 1926–1930. *51.685, 54.820, 52.1494*

During the two months' exhibition a dazzled and unbelieving public was attracted, a total of 41,550, of whom 31,600 nonmembers paid the $1.00 admission charge. Like the exhibition, the catalogue with twenty-four color plates inspired favorable comment everywhere. Over 2,500 copies were sold during the show. No less than five national magazines, including *Time*, *Vogue* and *Woman's Day*, carried feature stories on the exhibition. Needless to say, the exhibition stimulated the demand for a special costume gallery — a deficiency of many years standing — where selections from this, the choicest collection of costumes in America, would always be on display.

Yet behind these two dazzling months lay three years of planning and concentrated work in the Department of Textiles, with only a charming 61-page Picture Book, *Great Costumes 1550–1950*, as a permanent result.

The costume exhibition inadvertently brought to a head one long-term project in conservation: the cleaning of metal threads woven or embroidered into old textiles. The distinguished goldsmith, Mrs. Margret Craver Withers, agreed to join with the staff of the department and of the Research Laboratory in investigating this problem. After extensive experimentation, a safe and quick method of cleaning silver threads and wires was found. But much of the routine current work of the department had less satisfying permanent results, for storage was so uncomfortably crowded that it was never an easy matter to bring out materials for the increasing number of visitors who constantly came to the Textile Study Room. And as long as gallery space was so severely limited, a quarter million or so textiles could only be seen by appointment in this way. The lack of funds for acquisitions often proved frustrating. With the help of the Kling Fund, and through gifts from generous friends, many remarkable pieces were acquired, but many more disappointingly got away. In 1964 the Curator wrote:

> Competition from at least seven major museums in this country and many more in Europe, particularly in Switzerland, Germany and Holland, coupled with a corresponding scarcity of fine things in the market, has operated to raise the price of tapestries, em-

broideries, and weavings to the level of those for paintings and sculptures. It would be unrealistic to overlook the fact that major purchase funds for general use have been and will continue to be used for the purchase of major classes of art objects which are considered to be more necessary than textiles in a general collection. Consequently, we can only hope that in the future one or more patrons, devoted as our earliest patrons were to the ideal of maintaining a high level of quality for the Museum's collection as a whole, will earmark important gifts of money for the acquisition of textiles. In a number of departments it is only because such gifts were made in the past that curators have been able to maintain their collections on superlative levels in the face of growing competition.

Although such funds have not yet appeared, the department did receive in 1962 a grant from the Ford Foundation to assist the publication of a scholarly catalogue of its tapestry collection. Thus there came to be published in 1967 Adolph S. Cavallo's *Tapestries of Europe and of Colonial Peru in the Museum of Fine Arts*, a carefully studied and handsomely produced work that is a model of its kind. Sixty-six of the approximately one hundred tapestries in the department were selected for intensive study in the catalogue.

These pieces are the best in quality and condition; but their selection was also influenced by the author's wish to present as complete but unrepetitive a survey of European and Peruvian Colonial tapestry weaving as was possible with the materials in the collection. Tapestries judged to be of secondary interest within this frame of reference have not been described in the catalogue but the author has referred to them briefly in certain entries, in connection with the more important tapestries to which they are related in one way or another.

The work is in two volumes. The first, of 250 pages, contains a brief essay on the technique of tapestry weaving, followed by detailed analysis of the sixty-six major examples chosen for description; the second is a larger volume which reproduces admirably all sixty-six tapestries, with details and color plates of the most important, as well as with several plates of weavers' marks. These volumes are in the finest tradition of scholarship.

In the summer of 1966, preparations for a major building renovation required the removal of the entire Department of Textiles — offices, library, and storage space — to temporary quarters on the Court floor of the Decorative Arts Wing. On 1 June 1967 the staff moved back to the space that had long been assigned for its offices, Textile Study, and conservation room, but under vastly improved conditions, for the area had been rebuilt with new lighting, built-in bookcases, and other desirable changes. The Curator's 1967 report began:

> A problem with pleasant prospects conditioned the Department's activities during the past year. Except for a few examples retained on exhibition in the Asiatic and Decorative Arts galleries, the Coptic Corridor, and the Tapestry Gallery, the entire collection of textiles remained shut away in closed storage space awaiting the construction of specially designed storage space on the Court Floor of the new building block constituting Phase II of the Museum's Centennial reconstruction program. Because of this, the staff could not show visitors material in the collection, nor indeed could members of the staff reach most material needed for study. It is expected that by the end of 1968 the collection will be housed in its new quarters beneath a gallery designed for the display of textiles of all kinds, on the Main Floor of the Museum. Next door there will be a gallery for costume exhibitions.

These proposed improvements took longer than had been anticipated. In June 1969 the Department of Textiles was still in confusion, with most of its collection still inaccessible, although the opening of the much-needed new gallery was scheduled for the spring of 1970. It is greatly to be regretted that, in that same month, Adolph S. Cavallo resigned as Curator. For ten and a half years he had admirably upheld the standards and traditions established by Miss Gertrude Townsend during her thirty-year curatorship. Between them they had maintained extraordinary continuity in the department for well over a third of the museum's existence. His loss will be deeply felt by his fellow curators, and by many trustees and friends. At the moment of writing the department is in charge of Larry Raymond Salmon, who became Assistant Curator of Textiles in September 1968.

The Department of Prints and Drawings (as it came to be called in 1962) has been more fortunate in its continuity, for Henry P. Rossiter, who first joined the staff in 1919 — the year of Miss Townsend's initial appointment — only retired in 1967, after forty-seven years in the department, forty-four of them as Curator. He was succeeded by Miss Eleanor A. Sayre, who had joined the department in 1945 and had been appointed Assistant Curator as of 1 January 1960. In 1959 Miss Anna C. Hoyt, Assistant Curator, who had come to the department in 1917, resigned upon her marriage to James W. Mavor, and was, in view of her forty-two years of service, appointed Fellow for Research in Graphic Arts. Another Assistant Curator, Peter A. Wick, resigned on 1 December 1964, after twelve years' service in the department; he is now Curator of the Department of Printing and Graphic Arts in the Houghton Library, Harvard University.

The department has been equally fortunate in the generosity of its friends, who have provided funds restricted to the purchase of prints. When Miss Katherine Eliot Bullard, sister of Stephen, Francis, and Dr. William Norton Bullard, died in 1920, she left the greater part of her property in trust, with life interests to her sole surviving brother William and her cousin, Miss Ellen T. Bullard. Upon their deaths, a third of the principal was to go to the Museum of Fine Arts, with the thoughtful provision that the income be used "for purchase of prints valuable for their beauty, or for aiding the Curator of Prints in studying the subject of prints elsewhere than in the United States, or for both purposes, the same to be and remain a memorial to my late brother Francis." Dr. Bullard died in 1931; his cousin Ellen who fully shared the family passion for prints, lived until 1959. She was long a member of the Visiting Committee. On her death Henry Rossiter noted that the Department of Prints had "lost its oldest and greatest friend. Interested in everything that touched the Department, she was a constant visitor. Her last call was only a few days before she died." The Katherine E. Bullard Fund, which because of these life interests came to the museum nearly forty years after the death of its donor, has in 1969 a principal of $1,044,776.

Another Boston family without descendants substantially aided the Department of Prints and Drawings by generous bequests. Lee Max Friedman (Harvard A.B. 1893, LL.B. 1895), a bachelor lawyer greatly interested in Jewish history and in the graphic arts, lived in Bay State Road with his unmarried sisters, Sophie and Elsie. Under the wills of Lee and Sophie Friedman, who died in 1957 and 1958 respectively, the museum received bequests that were paid in the course of the next decade. The income of the Lee M. Friedman Fund, with a 1969 principal of $487,380, was restricted to the purchase of prints. Although the Sophie M. Friedman Fund, with a 1969 principal of $493,029, was announced upon its receipt to be similarly restricted, subsequent interpretation of the phrase in her will "for the purchase of modern pictures" has brought paintings, as well as prints, drawings, and water colors, within the permissive limits of the fund. In addition to the bequest of money, Lee Friedman's will also brought the museum some 205 prints, 8 drawings, and 1 water color from his own collection, for both he and Miss Sophie Friedman had been constant frequenters of the Department of Prints and Drawings and active collectors. With the help of the Lee M. Friedman Fund, a substantial number of twentieth-century prints by American, English, French, German, and Israeli artists have been added in very recent years: a striking example is Pablo Picasso's 1949 lithograph, *Le Crapaud*, purchased in 1966.

The shadow of W. G. Russell Allen grew rather than diminished in the years following his death in 1955. In addition to the memorial exhibition of 1956, the Department of Prints prepared a picture book, *The Raven*, dedicated to his memory, which reproduced Edouard Manet's illustrations to Stephane Mallarmé's translation of Poe's poem, from a copy of the 1875 edition, that Russell Allen had given the museum in 1932. It had been slow work hoeing out his crowded quarters at 112 Pinckney Street, where any pile of books or magazines might contain a rare print, but by 1960 some of the prints, drawings, and illustrated books that he had bequeathed to the museum had been received. Of this collection, which ranged from the early fifteenth century to the present day, Henry P. Rossiter wrote:

LE CRAPAUD. Lithograph on zinc by Pablo Picasso, 1949. *Lee M. Friedman Fund.*
66.955

The forming of such an extensive collection, involving as it did painstaking study and research, gave him a broad, long-range view of graphic art second to none in the honorable brotherhood of print connoisseurs. Knowing his subject thus intimately he was never misled by passing art fashions; neither was he taken in by rarity nor high prices, pitfalls for the credulous and inexperienced. Needless to say, his prints greatly reinforce our Museum collection in many ways, as he intended. Refreshing, and very personal too, was his choice of works by minor artists. His gift for finding excellence where least expected was almost a sixth sense. Some of the little-known men represented in the five hundred and twenty-six examples received from his bequest during this year include Boilly, Chadel, Chaplin, Coupin de la Couperie, Cross, Deroy, Forster, Grenier, Gudin, Hugo, Lambert, Leroux, Madaule, C. Nanteuil, Roger, Seguin, Serusier, and Wattier. But masterpieces are not lacking, by such outstanding painter-engravers as Bonnard, Cézanne, Degas,

Delacroix, Dufy, Gauguin, Ingres, Maillol, Manet, Matisse, Picasso, Redon, Renoir, Rouault and Vuillard.

Over 900 prints, including 750 by Daumier, were added in 1963 from Russell Allen's bequest, while in his memory his niece, Mrs. Christopher Tunnard, has continued most generously to give numerous prints and drawings of remarkable quality over succeeding years.

From 1950 Maxim Karolik's name appeared with considerable frequency among the contributors to the Department of Prints, for he had turned to assembling, in close collaboration with Henry P. Rossiter, the final part of his trilogy, the M. and M. Karolik Collection of American Water Colors and Drawings, 1800–1875. "The panorama of an unspoiled America as it looked to native born artists and to those visiting from abroad from 1800 to 1875 and the many stirring events marking her growth were never more eloquently recorded," as Henry Rossiter expressed it, than by this group of water colors and drawings which were first seen in the Special Exhibition galleries from 18 October 1962 through 6 January 1963. The third of Karolik's typical letters of transmittal, this one dated 2 October 1962, concluded with a tribute to the three curators — Hipkiss, Constable, and Rossiter — who had collaborated so closely in the formation of the trilogy.

> This collaboration has been a complete success, because we never behaved like petty men trying constantly to please each other. In all our discussions there never was a suggestion that could have been interpreted as seeking a bargain, or even a favor ("If I will do this for you, would you do that for me?"). Such language we never used. And this is the reason, I believe, why we did not need lawyers to confirm our trust in each other. In the highest sense of the word, this collaboration is a shining example of a real Gentleman's Agreement.
>
> I want the Museum authorities and the people of this nation to know that the twenty-seven years, from 1935 to 1962 of this collaboration are the brightest chapter in my life.

There had, indeed, been an absence of *quid pro quos* in the museum's relationship with Maxim Karolik. In most parts of the United

States, the donor of only one large collection might well have anticipated election as a trustee, or some similar recognition. That did not
accord with the New England temperament. The Karoliks gave their
first collection; as it had been assembled in collaboration with the
museum staff, it was obviously appropriate and wanted. The trustees
accepted it, and the Karoliks went on to their next. Such a method of
procedure seemed so strange to Perry Rathbone, that, at his urging,
the trustees in 1958 — seventeen years after the first collection had
been given — appointed Maxim Karolik Honorary Curator of American Arts. Once this had been done, the new Honorary Curator
began haranguing various trustees, both in person and by telephone,
at great length to express views on current museum policies and
operations that were often critical of the Director. As these were in
fields that the trustees felt were in the Director's province, not theirs,
little was accomplished by these conversations — which never had
occurred before 1958 — save a considerable loss of time and
expenditure of patience.

When interviewed by Dr. Brian O'Doherty on a museum television
program in 1959, Maxim Karolik made this forthright comment
upon current theories of showmanship and ingratiating entertainment that prevail in many American art museums.

What is the purpose of a Museum? A museum is an ideal, not a
reality. Science is practical, a Museum of Fine Arts is an ideal.
I am a collector driven by ideas, not by a hobby. A museum serves
the community not as an entertainment. You shouldn't sell the fine
arts like Coca-Cola and soap. It offends me to be invited to relax and
have a good time. No, a real museum lifts the public to the level of
the museum, not brings the museum down to them. A museum
preserves high standards and the meaning of the fine arts — rever-
ence for excellence, for creativity, for genuineness. That's the
meaning of the word education. You educate not for the sake of
teaching, but for enlightenment. If you want to be taught, you go
to an academy, not to a museum. The word *museum* has a lofty
meaning. You cannot just say "Come in, enjoy togetherness." A
museum cannot have a motto like a department store. Directors
who want to entertain with exhibition all the time, they are not
directors, they are exhibitionists!

Theory makes odd bedfellows, for Karolik's statement, in content, though not in style, has some of the ring of Matthew S. Prichard or Ananda K. Coomaraswamy.

The publication in 1962 of the liberally illustrated two-volume catalogue *M. and M. Karolik Collection of American Water Colors and Drawings, 1800–1875*, prepared by Henry P. Rossiter with the assistance of his staff, completed the permanent record of the Karolik trilogy. These volumes were selected by the American Institute of Graphic Arts for their "Fifty Books of the Year 1963," and included by the Institute in the representation of American bookmaking that they sent to the *Most Beautiful Books of the World* exhibition at the Leipzig Fair in September 1963. Fortunately this had occurred before Maxim Karolik's sudden death at the end of the year. In the previous quarter-century, he had done much to retrieve and elucidate aspects of the arts of his adopted country. It is appropriate that he and Martha Codman Karolik should be ranked among the Great Benefactors of the Museum of Fine Arts in its first century.

Although the 1860's are as little appreciated in British art as they were in American before the efforts of Maxim Karolik, when their day comes the Museum of Fine Arts will be grateful for Henry P. Rossiter's foresight in buying Sir Harold Hartley's great collection of English illustrators of that period in 1956. All the important British painters and illustrators of that time, including the Pre-Raphaelites, made drawings to be engraved on woodblocks for the magazines and gift-books then flourishing. The Hartley Collection of English Illustration, having been begun by Sir Harold's father, contains more than 1,000 proofs, most of them touched by the artists, many drawings, some 300 of the original woodblocks, and practically all the printed volumes and magazines in which these illustrations appeared. In magnitude, it is second only to that in the Victoria and Albert Museum. In 1956 excellent studies by Burne-Jones, Caldecott, Richard Doyle, Charles Greene, A. B. Houghton, Arthur Hughes, Charles Keene, Millais, Pinwell, Rossetti, Stothard, Thackeray, Fred Walker, and Whistler were bought by the Curator in Europe to add to the Hartley collection. Although the Print Department has not yet had staff or time to arrange, catalogue, or exhibit this mass of material, it will be a gold mine for future research. The best curators always operate *sub specie aeternitatis*.

EMPEROR AUGUSTUS AND THE SIBYL. German engraving by
Master E. S., 15th century, *Katherine E. Bullard Fund.*
61.1201

Henry P. Rossiter's acquisitions during the last dozen years of his
curatorship were as catholic and perceptive as always. In 1931 among
his numerous purchases at European auctions was the circular *St.
John the Baptist in the Wilderness*, dated 1466, by the German
engraver known as Master E. S. In 1961 he bought this artist's
Emperor Augustus and the Sibyl, and in 1963 a unique impression
of the first state of Master E. S.'s *Saint Barbara*, both through the
Katherine E. Bullard Fund. The same fund made possible the 1965
purchase of an extraordinary rarity, the tiny *Garden of Love* by an
unknown Burgundian engraver, active about 1440–1450, which
Rossiter described in these words:

ST. BARBARA. German engraving by Master E. S., unique impression of first state, 15th century. *Katherine E. Bullard Fund. 63.582*

THE LITTLE GARDEN OF LOVE. Netherlands, engraving by the Master of the Gardens of Love, active 1440–1450. *Katherine E. Bullard Fund. 65.594*

The *Garden of Love* shows a number of well-groomed young men and women over whom the Queen of Love is casting her spell. Staged in a meadow with animals, holiday tents, shady woods, and distant hills, the scene is sophisticated, yet pastoral. It savors of pleasure-loving Burgundy at the time of Philip the Good and was possibly inspired by the courtly verse of the period. The artist was enterprising to undertake a subject so at variance with the biblical themes then predominant. The print itself is unique, since the works of this artist survive only in single impressions.

"One of the most distinguished and gratifying acquisitions in the Department's eighty year history" was the purchase in 1966 of two prints of secular subjects by the unknown fifteenth-century engraver called the Master of the Amsterdam Cabinet, or the Housebook Master, who is thought to have been active from about 1480–1510 on the upper Rhine. These remarkable purchases represent scenes from the world that surrounded the artist. Of them the Curator wrote:

> Our two prints, *Mother, two children and shield*, and *Bearded man and shield*, are subtle character studies of tramps resting. The

MOTHER WITH TWO CHILDREN AND A BLANK SHIELD and BEARDED MAN WITH A BLANK SHIELD. German, drypoint by Master of the Amsterdam Cabinet. *Katherine E. Bullard Fund. 66.376–375*

CHRIST BEARING THE CROSS. Italy, woodcut, hand-colored, by anonymous Milanese artist, 15th century. *Katherine E. Bullard Fund. 63.2668*

wife, comely, neatly dressed, still mindful of appearance, has tied her hat under her chin to keep her hair tidy even though she and the children go barefoot. The man is glib and voluble. Prominently at his side, lies a mended hammer and a nail, as if to imply his being some sort of itinerant handyman on occasion. No sign anywhere of rags or begging. In an earlier single print showing this same family on the move, the wife carries a beggar's sack, the man a tall bow.

A Milanese fifteenth-century woodcut of *Christ Bearing the Cross,* colored by hand in pink, brown, and dark red, measuring 21 ¾ by

16 ½ inches and consequently almost lifesized, was bought in 1963. Only one other contemporary impression is known, a somewhat damaged one in the Berlin Print Room. This and the previously described purchases of the nineteen sixties, were made possible by the Katherine E. Bullard Fund. But even before its receipt, Henry Rossiter managed to seize opportunities when they arose. In 1957 he bought 119 proof woodcuts for *Der Weisskunig,*

the political history, largely autobiographical, of the Emperor Maximilian's reign in the guise of an historical romance. Accompanying the woodcuts, of which several are the only impressions known, are 52 preliminary sketches for further woodcuts in the series. Drawn by various hands under the watchful eye of Maximilian or his advisors, these designs, once approved, went to Augsburg for the final drawing on the blocks, usually by Hans Burgkmair or Leonard Beck. The actual cutting supervised by Jost de Negker probably dates about 1510–1516. For this elaborate work, left incomplete,

MAXIMILIAN I'S WEISSKUNIG. Volume of proof woodcuts and sketches by Hans Burgkmair, 1473–1531. *William Francis Warden Fund.* 57.40

PRESENTATION OF THE BOOK TO THE EMPEROR. Germany, woodcut (proof impression) from *Der Weisskunig*.

236 blocks were finished only to disappear after Maximilian's death. They were found at Graz in the eighteenth century and were first published in Vienna in 1775. Our proofs and sketches preserved in a bound volume, bear many manuscript notes, some by the Emperor himself. There is also a transcript of a letter signed by him to his friend Sigismund of Dietrichstein dated October 14, 1512, reporting that the *Weisskunig* is only half completed, since many of the blocks remain uncut. Before our volume of proofs and sketches became the property of Prince Leichtenstein from whose collection it was acquired, it belonged to Baron Richard Strain von Scwarzenau (d. 1600) and to Georg Christoph von Schallenberg. (1633).

The *Weisskunig* was obtained only because the Curator persuaded the Committee on the Museum to advance money from the William

FARM BUILDINGS AND POLLARDED MULBERRY TREE. Italian, pen and ink
   drawing by Fra Bartolommeo, 1472–1517. *Francis Bartlett Fund.* 58.1
LANDSCAPE WITH A LARGE TREE. France, red chalk drawing by Jean-Honoré
Fragonard, 1732–1806. *Gift of Elizabeth Paine Card and Richard C. Paine.*
63.282

Francis Warden Fund that normally would not have been received
for the use of his department until several years in the future. By
similar persuasiveness of the need for seizing opportunities as they
arose, he was also able to buy in 1958 some 38 etchings, woodcuts,
and lithographs by Edvard Munch (1863–1944). Munch's prints in
such numbers are rarely found in collections outside Norway.

The collection of drawings was augmented so far as possible both
by purchase and gift. A fine example of Rembrandt's early style,
Watchdog Sleeping in his Kennel, was bought in 1956, as was a
drawing of *Farm Buildings and Pollarded Mulberry Tree* by Fra
Bartolommeo (1475–1517) the following year. The department's
strength in Goya's prints, combined with Miss Sayre's scholarly concern with that artist, inspired the acquisition of his drawings whenever possible. His *Mucho sabes, y aun aprendes* (You know a lot and
you're still learning), showing an old man writing, was bought in
1958 from the Warden Fund, at the same time as Edgar Degas'
charcoal drawing *The Violinist*. Eleanor Sayre made the old man the

point of departure for her study of Goya's journal-albums that was published in number 305 of the *Bulletin* in the autumn of 1958. In 1959 Henry Rossiter reported:

In the nineteenth century two purchases stand out prominently, Goya's *La Madre Celestina*, brush with gray wash and black ink, and Gericault's *Horse Being Shod* in pencil, pen and sepia wash. Of this subject Gericault made a lithograph in 1823 (Del. 72), but little of the original sparkle was retained. The Goya drawing belongs to Journal-Album D which deals with people of ill repute and clergy. Another drawing of Goya, or possibly by his brother-in-law Francisco Bayeu, was discovered by Miss Sayre in a residuary group of English sporting prints bequeathed years ago to the Museum. Drawn in pencil heightened with white on blue paper, it is a study for two of the first tapestry cartoons which Goya executed under his brother-in-law and one of the few of this type which have survived.

MUCHO SABES, Y AUN APRENDES. Spanish, gray and black wash drawing by Francisco Goya y Lucientes. *William Francis Warden Fund.* 58.359

THE SKATERS. Spanish, brush drawing by Francisco Goya y Lucientes. *Otis Norcross Fund and gift of Mrs. Thomas B. Card.* 61.166

Two years later in 1961 when Goya's brush drawing *The Skaters,* which came from his Journal-Album F, appeared on the market and purchase funds were low, Mrs. Thomas B. Card generously contributed half the cost. In 1963 Mrs. Card, with her brother Richard C. Paine, gave a Fragonard *Landscape with a Large Tree* in red chalk, which handsomely complements his drawing of a figure subject, *Les Pétards,* which had been bought some years earlier. The purchase in 1963 of two double-sided sketchbook pages by Goya, which Miss Sayre identified as belonging to his Sanlúcar and Madrid albums, and commemorating his famous sojourn with the Duchess of Alba, added four early drawings in brush and gray wash of the period 1796–1798. One of these drawings Goya subsequently used as the basis of number 18 of his *Caprichos.*

The search for Goya drawings in no way diminished the effort to add prints when they became available. In 1965 it became possible to buy the extremely rare aquatint *Colossus,* a powerful brooding figure, who sits squarely on top of the world. This is again one of the acquisitions that would hardly have been managed without the resources of the Katherine E. Bullard Fund. In all the affairs of the Department of Prints and Drawings there are intricate patterns of acquisition, study, and exhibition. An anniversary loan exhibition commemorating the one hundred and fiftieth anniversary of the birth of Honoré Daumier was arranged in 1958 by Peter A. Wick, who prepared a catalogue of the material shown. An aspect of Daumier's work never previously exhibited in Boston was the sculpture in bronze, lent by the National Gallery of Art and by Lessing J. Rosenwald and other private collectors. The 750 Daumier lithographs and twenty-five books containing his illustrations that were received from the W. G. Russell Allen bequest in 1963 required careful study. Two departmental Assistants, Mrs. St. John Smith and Mrs. John S. Reed, and Mrs. John J. Glessner, a volunteer, immediately began the task of checking each print for state, quality, and duplication. By midwinter 1964, when their work was completed and Francis W. Dolloff had matted the new prints in the museum's standard sizes, the Daumier print collection was not only a coherent physical entity but one of the most complete and outstanding in the country. Moreover, in 1964 a hitherto unknown study by

COLOSSUS. Spanish, aquatint by Francisco Goya y Lucientes. *Katherine E. Bullard Fund. 65.1296*

Daumier, *Un omnibus en temps de grippe*, drawn about 1858 in
chalk, wash, and body colors, was purchased. This vivid representation of well-wrapped passengers, coughing and sneezing their way
to their destination, was only the third Daumier drawing to enter the
collection.

Henry Preston Rossiter retired as Curator of Prints in June 1967,
in his eighty-second year, and with his new leisure returned to
England for an extended visit. Fifty years earlier he had operated
machine guns considerably faster than his contemporaries; the passage of half a century had scarcely diminished the speed of his eye or

UN OMNIBUS EN TEMPS DE GRIPPE. France, black chalk and colored wash drawing by Honoré Daumier, 1808–1879. *Helen and Alice Colburn Fund.*
64.710

the accuracy of his aim, for he found in London that the incredible Dürer collection formed by Tomás Harris, a wealthy Spanish-American collector, was coming on the market. After spending some weeks studying it, he had it shipped to Boston so that his successor, Miss Eleanor A. Sayre, might make arrangements for submitting it to the Committee on the Museum. He wrote the Director, strongly urging its purchase, in spite of some duplication, for this was the last great collection of Dürer's prints in private hands. As it ranked with the one made by Sir Thomas Barlow some years previously that was sold after his death to New Zealand, Henry Rossiter felt that no other Centennial purchase by the Museum of Fine Arts could match it, especially with the five hundredth anniversary of Dürer's death coming in 1971. His recommendation was followed; in a foreword to number 341 of the *Bulletin*, devoted to some of the more remarkable prints and drawings acquired during Rossiter's 47 years in the Museum of Fine Arts, Perry T. Rathbone wrote:

In a congratulatory article addressed to Mr. Rossiter on the fiftieth anniversary of the Print Department and appearing in the Museum *Bulletin* for February 1937, Campbell Dodgson, the renowned Keeper of Prints and Drawings at the British Museum, spoke of the "skill and gallantry" with which the Print Department had been developed under the Curator's leadership. If to energy and enterprise, to skill and gallantry you add immense knowledge, deep humanity and the flair of a connoisseur, you will have an accurate profile of Henry Rossiter, the man and the curator.

I would add mention of literary sensitivity, for this Curator had a flair for the choice of words that enlivened even the most routine reports. In 1937, on the fiftieth anniversary of the department, he paid tribute to his predecessors, especially Sylvester R. Koehler, in this manner:

While fifty years of effort may tell against an individual by slowing his step or hardening his arteries, it has had the opposite effect on the Department of Prints. As time passed, its portfolios filled, its step and pulse grew livelier, and it became more efficient by widening its range. Liveliness and efficiency are purely relative terms, and it must be remembered that for over half its existence it was the one serious pioneer in its field in America. Nevertheless before others undertook to cultivate similar plots it had reached an established position and held the honorable ambition — an ambition now largely realized — of being pre-eminent in the country. Through the liberality of friends, through gifts, bequests, and by opportune purchases, the Department has continued to expand and improve its collections. Year in and year out it has demonstrated its value to students and to the community at large, and has earned admiration abroad because of the wisdom of its benefactors and supporters in making publicly available in originals thousands of the world's greatest masterpieces in graphic art. Nor do these numerous masterpieces tell the whole story. For prints by their millions have fluttered into the world during the past five hundred years. Even dullards and impenitent scapegraces have made them, as well as great creative geniuses, and there is no aspect of the dignity, pathos, or comedy of human life which they have not tried to express. A well endowed print room might truthfully be likened to a Gargantuan picture book of western civilization.

Thirty years later these words applied with even greater accuracy to the Department of Prints and Drawings than they did in 1937, when their writer, who had been at the helm for only fourteen years, was describing the accomplishments of his predecessors. And the manner in which his successor, Miss Eleanor A. Sayre, goes about her business indicates that the tradition is in no danger of running down.

The Department of Paintings has had a very different history, for since 1957 it has been without a curator. When W. G. Constable assumed that post on 1 April 1938, he had been Assistant Director of the National Gallery in London, Director of the Courtauld Institute of the University of London, and Slade Professor of Fine Art at the University of Cambridge. He knew the great galleries and private collections of Europe, the auction rooms and their records, and much else pertinent to his task, with an intimacy that is denied to an American curator who spends only a few weeks of each year in rapid travel between European capitals. Twice before the Museum of Fine Arts had sought a European Curator of Paintings, but after brief stays Jean Guiffrey and Philip Hendy had returned whence they came. W. G. Constable, however, remained for six months short of twenty years. During these two decades he brought a wholly new breadth and depth of learning to the Department of Paintings, and became as well a much liked and greatly valued figure in the Boston scene. On 1 October 1957, a few days before his seventieth birthday, he retired from the curatorship.

There was, unfortunately, to be no curatorial continuity, as there had been in the Textile and Print departments, for Mrs. Haven Parker, Assistant in American Painting, who had become a leading authority in that field during her nineteen years in the department, had resigned on 1 October 1956. Although Alfred E. Lowe, the Senior Restorer of Paintings, had retired in 1955 after twenty-five years of brilliant service, his colleague John A. Finlayson continued to care for the physical condition of the pictures with remarkable skill. But W. G. Constable's retirement left the Department of Paintings in interim charge of Thomas N. Maytham, who had been appointed a temporary Assistant only the previous year. No permanent curator has yet been found. Thomas Maytham, with the rank of

EXPULSION FROM PARADISE. Sienese School, by Benvenuto di Giovanni, 1436–1518? *Charles Potter Kling Fund.* 56.212

Assistant until 1965 when he was made Assistant Curator of Paintings, ably tended to the routine business of the department and published a number of excellent studies of recently acquired paintings. In the summer of 1957, for example, he contributed to number 300 of the *Bulletin* an account of the fine predella panel, bought the previous autumn, depicting the *Expulsion from Paradise* by the Sienese painter Benvenuto de Giovanni. Although Maytham continued in nominal charge of the department until the middle of 1967, when he resigned to become Associate Director of the Seattle Art Museum, its major decisions became an additional though unspecified duty of the Director, who already had quite enough to do in his own bailiwick.

To continue work upon the long delayed catalogues of paintings, Mrs. Neil L. Rudenstine was engaged in 1961 as a Research Assistant. In December 1964, when Peter A. Wick left the museum to go to Harvard, she took over, in addition, his work as Editor of Publications, but in 1968 she also resigned both posts. Thereafter the department was staffed by two Assistants, Miss Laura C. Luckey, appointed in 1964, and Mrs. Paul Giese, who came in April 1967, for John A. Finlayson had retired in May 1967 after twenty-five years of service. To carry on essential restoration and preservation, his brother Richard Finlayson undertook part-time work in March 1968, while Philip Vance, an able restorer formerly at the Metropolitan Museum, was appointed a full-time Assistant in Conservation that June.

A grant from the Ford Foundation's Program in the Humanities accelerated work on the catalogue of American paintings as effectively as similar subventions had aided in the publication of Richard Randall's work on American furniture, Adolph Cavallo's on tapestries, and the Classical Department's comprehensive study of Greek, Etruscan, and Roman bronzes. *American Paintings in the Museum of Fine Arts, Boston,* has now been published in two volumes, one of text and the other of illustrations. The preparation of the text had been the work of many hands over a considerable number of years. Begun by Mrs. Parker, it was continued by Miss Arianwen Howard, Miss Sarah Bullock, Miss Elizabeth Gwin, and Miss Luckey. Thomas N. Maytham helped at many stages, while Mrs. Rudenstine edited the catalogue and prepared the manuscript for the printer. The appearance of this catalogue fills a major need, for hitherto only the paintings of the Karolik Collection had been fully described in print. It is to be hoped that companion volumes on the European paintings will follow before too many years have passed.

Perry T. Rathbone was formally appointed Acting Curator of Paintings in May 1968, more than ten years after W. G. Constable's retirement. As the pursuit and exhibition of paintings had always been one of his chief delights, this designation simply confirmed what had prevailed since his arrival so far as fields of acquisition were concerned. But as no director of an institution — particularly of one that is seething with activity — ever has uninterrupted leisure for detailed investigation, it is hoped that the appointment of a full-time Curator of Paintings may not be far over the horizon. In the 1966 report of the Department of Paintings, Thomas N. Maytham spoke of the nearly four hundred paintings acquired since 1955:

They have spanned the past six centuries and have stressed the past two. On the one hand, our renowned nineteenth-century collections are even stronger and on the other, with very limited means we have made important advances in the formation of a sorely needed twentieth century collection.

Of greatest significance has been the acquisition of an extraordinary number of individual masterworks. Among them are the magnificent fifteenth-century Flemish altarpiece of the *Martyrdom of St. Hippolytus*, the *Dead Christ with Angels* by Rosso, the Rembrandt portraits of the *Elisons*, Ruisdael's *Rough Sea*, the Tiepolo, *Time Unveiling Truth*, Romney's *Anne, Lady de la Pole*, Monet's *La Japonaise*, and paintings by Renoir, Redon, Gauguin, Van Gogh, Munch, Kirchner, Feininger, Nicholson, De Staël, and Picasso. Of scarcely less importance are paintings by Lotto, Tintoretto, Veronese, Terbrugghen, Aert de Galder, Courbet, Bousin, Bernard, Braque, Kokoschka, Prendergast, and Appel. A host of American pictures of the eighteenth and nineteenth centuries include master works by Copley, Greenwood, Blackburn, Feke, C. W. Peale, Field, Darby, and Peto.

The earliest of these summarized acquisitions was described in Perry Rathbone's 1963 report:

Many exciting acquisitions were made during the year, but for one (if no other) of them alone, 1963 will not be forgotten in the annals of the Museum. This was the courageous and imaginative purchase of the altarpiece of the *Martyrdom of St. Hippolytus*. The

MARTYRDOM OF ST. HIPPOLYTUS. Flemish, last quarter of the 15th century. *Purchased. 63.660*

art world was stunned when in the spring of 1962, this unknown and totally unsuspected great work of the Flemish school appeared on the auction block in Paris. With a group of notable pictures it came into the market from the virtually secret collection of the late Claude Lafontaine who died over fifty years ago. The only other known fact of its history is that for a time it was in the collection of Emile Gavet of Paris and that he sold it to Lafontaine in 1888. Painted for Hippolyte de Berthoz, special counsellor to Philip the Good of Burgundy, in the last quarter of the fifteenth century, the altarpiece deals with a subject as difficult to handle as it is rare. The composition of dramatic action notable for its originality is brilliantly organized into three panels, and executed with masterful drawing and with colors that glow like enamels. The presence of a great artistic personality is evident here, but scholars have as yet been unable to identify the author with certainty. The preservation is almost flawless. One can be virtually certain that no other un-known works of comparable quality exist. The known works are in public collections. This unprecedented purchase was, therefore, the last opportunity for the Boston Museum to acquire a truly great work of early Flemish art, a field in which the Museum has been sadly undersupplied.

A panel by Paolo Veronese representing *Diana and Actaeon*, for-merly in the Holford Collection, was given in 1959 by Mrs. Edward

DIANA AND ACTAEON and VENUS AND JUPITER. Venetian, Paolo Veronese, 16th century. *Gift of Mrs. Edward Jackson Holmes. 59.260, 60.125*

Jackson Holmes. A second panel of *Venus and Jupiter* disporting themselves in a setting of classical architecture and fountained courtyards, was given by her the following year, while in 1964 two more decorative panels from the same series, *Atalanta and Meleager*, and a representation of *Olympus* were received through the provisions of her will. Although these panels, which greatly improved the museum's showing of Veronese, came as the gift of an old and valued friend, most of the significant additions to later Italian painting were purchased. In 1958 the Director described one of his earliest purchases:

DEAD CHRIST SUPPORTED BY ANGELS. Florentine, by Il Rosso Fiorentino, 1494–1540. *Charles Potter Kling Fund.* 58.527

It would be nothing less than false modesty to omit to mention first of all the panel painting by Il Rosso Fiorentino [Giovanni Battista Rosso] of the *Dead Christ Supported by Angels*, purchased from the Charles Potter Kling Fund. The acquisition of this imposing and startlingly original work brings to our shores the greatest example of Italian mannerism in America. Possessing the adventitious merit of having been mentioned by Vasari — a distinction rare amongst works of art that have changed hands in modern times — this signed picture immediately assumes a place of importance in art history. The painting reflects the monumental figure style of the Sistine ceiling, softened by the breath of Leonardo. Yet in it Rosso introduces a new and personal use of high-keyed color and a disparity in the scale of the figures which contributes to the strange tensions the picture possesses. Long given up as one of the "lost paintings" of the master, it emerged recently from a Spanish Bourbon collection where it had been secluded for over a century.

The *Madonna and Child with Saints* by Lorenzo Lotto, purchased through the Kling Fund in 1960, "came from the obscure collection of an Oxford don, its identity eclipsed by discolored varnish and dirt." When specially displayed at Christmas, for the first time after

MADONNA AND CHILD WITH ST. JEROME AND ST. ANTHONY OF PADUA. Venetian, Lorenzo Lotto, 16th century. *Charles Potter Kling Fund. 60.154*

cleaning, "it aroused the admiration of everyone, the humble and sophisticated alike." The Director characterized it as "a new discovery quite surpassing in quality and condition the nearly identical composition, long a possession of the National Gallery, London," and called it "the finest figure composition by the artist in any American collection."

Although the Lotto *Madonna* may not have been widely publicized before it came to Boston, its last private owner was far from obscure, for he was the eminent R. M. Dawkins, Fellow of Exeter College, Bywater and Sotheby Professor of Byzantine and Modern Greek Language and Literature in the University of Oxford, whose profound learning and remarkable eccentricity were admired far beyond the reaches of his university. His edition of the *Erotokritos*, the great Cretan medieval epic, and his *Modern Greek Folk Tales* were monuments of learning, while his collection of icons and Edward Lear water colors was admirable. It would not necessarily have followed that such a man would during the First World War have successfully carried out cloak-and-dagger operations in Athens and the Aegean in the disguise of a naval officer, or have known Baron Corvo. Had I not had the opportunity to meet Professor Dawkins in Oxford in 1927 and hear his "cackling laugh of great carrying

PROFESSOR R. M. DAWKINS PERCHED IN AN OXFORD TREE. Drawing by Osbert Lancaster in his *With an Eye to the Future.*

TIME UNVEILING TRUTH. Venetian, by Giovanni Battista
Tiepolo, 18th century. *Charles Potter Kling Fund. 61.1200*

power," I would less readily have believed the vision evoked of him
by Osbert Lancaster in *With an Eye to the Future*: "Once when
passing alongside the high wall of Exeter, startled by this extraordinary sound, I looked up and saw the Professor happily perched in
the higher branches of a large chestnut tree hooting like a demented
macaw." Such a provenance gives an added fillip to the presence of
this remarkable painting in Boston.

The spotlight played in 1961 on another Kling Fund purchase,
Giovanni Battista Tiepolo's *Time Unveiling Truth*, a monumental

allegory painted about 1745, which had been brought to the United States from France earlier in the year, and had been submitted to the museum for consideration before it was cleaned of the accumulated layers of varnish and dirt that obscured its brilliance. The distinction and beauty of this painting had inspired early anti-export regulations nearly a century before, for when the French diplomat Baron de Schwiter bought it in Venice in 1865 he was unable to obtain permission to ship it to France. When Venice was ceded by Austria to Italy in 1866, amnesty was granted Austrian diplomats to export their luggage without passing customs. The Tiepolo was apparently smuggled to Vienna in this way and was then sent to Baron de Schwiter's home in Paris. The nineteenth-century French critic Henri de Chennevières pronounced it as possibly "the most beautiful easel picture by Tiepolo." Subsequently it was an ornament to two Parisian collections, and has been frequently published by Tiepolo scholars. In June 1969 it at last proved possible to purchase, through the Kling Fund, Giuseppe Maria Crespi's *The Lute Player* that had for some time hung as a loan in the gallery with the *Time Unveiling Truth.*

Purchases of paintings in some instances supplemented strong collections of works by the same artist in the Department of Prints and Drawings. An extremely subtle miniature of a *Reclining Nude,* painted by Goya in the last year of his life, in black and white accented with colored washes, provided an unusual link between his painted and graphic work. Edvard Munch's vivid *Portrait of a Model,* painted in 1918, which today dominates a ground floor corridor in the Evans Wing, was purchased in 1957. This painting and his intense psychological study of 1893 entitled *The Voice,* purchased in 1958, probably represent Munch's work better in Boston than anywhere outside of Norway. Other acquisitions, like Courbet's *Stream in the Forest,* bought in 1955, and *Reclining Nude,* bought with the Eliza H. Oliver Fund in 1957, or Claude Monet's *La Japonaise,* purchased in 1956, were destined to strengthen the showing of nineteenth-century painters who had long been represented in the museum.

In the same year that Rosso's *Dead Christ Supported by Angels* came to the museum, there was purchased with the Robert J. Ed-

THE ARTIST'S MODEL,
INGEBORG ONSAGER.
Norwegian, Edvard Munch,
1863–1944. *Arthur Gordon
Tompkins Residuary Fund.*
57.744

wards Fund the first painting by Pablo Picasso to enter the collection, a *Standing Nude*, described in the 1958 Director's report as

> a modern masterpiece. A large painting of a standing female nude with upraised arms, it was created in 1908 — the year the term "cubism" was coined — when Picasso was evolving a new vocabulary of form inspired by primitive art. Impetuously executed with a rich palette of earth reds, rose tones, and electric blues, the picture by virtue of its dynamic design, forceful brushwork, and explosive energy proclaims a new age. It is the only important work of this crucial year in Picasso's career outside the famous collections of Russia.

A second painting by Picasso was purchased in 1964, somewhat "in view of the fact," as Perry Rathbone observed, "that we cannot anticipate the bequest of major works of Picasso from Boston collections." This was a recent work, completed the previous year, of the *Rape of the Sabines*, "inspired by," we are told, though hardly resembling "the painting by Jacques Louis David in the Louvre." To augment the twentieth-century collections, various works were purchased of Kirchner, De Staël, Feininger, Kokoschka, Beckmann, Morandi, Gatch, and Giacometti, as well as some of the artists that the late Francis Henry Taylor used to describe as "the Picassini."

Even more pictures have come through the gifts and bequests of old friends. The paintings received from Governor Fuller's collection have already been mentioned in Chapter XVIII. Although Maxim Karolik had theoretically turned to assembling water colors and drawings for the third part of his trilogy, he could never resist an outstanding "primitive" in oils when he found one. Thus in 1958 he gave Erastus Salisbury Field's magnificent group, *Joseph Moore and His*

THE VOICE. Norwegian, Edvard Munch. *Ernest Wadsworth Longfellow Fund.* 59.301

STANDING FIGURE. Spanish, Pablo Picasso. *Juliana Cheney Edwards Collection.*
58.976
THE RAPE OF THE SABINES. Spanish, Pablo Picasso. *Robert J. Edwards, Fanny
P. Mason, and Arthur G. Tompkins Residuary funds. 64.709*

Family, which attracted great attention when sent to the American
Primitives Exhibition at the Brussels World's Fair. In 1962 he added
twenty-three paintings from his personal collection to the M. and
M. Karolik Collection of American Painting, 1815–1865, while
ninety more pictures, predominantly nineteenth-century American,
were selected by the department in 1964 in accordance with the
generous provisions of his will.

Two gifts of very recent years exemplify the long ties of friendship
that have been woven through the history of the Museum of Fine
Arts. The portrait of *Mrs. Fiske Warren and Her Daughter*, which
came in 1964 from the daughter, Mrs. Rachel Warren Barton, is
one of the most distinguished works of John Singer Sargent. Painted
in the Gothic Room at Fenway Court during Sargent's stay in Boston
in 1903, it is a superb example of Edwardian portraiture, doubly of
interest because the two ladies are not only beautiful in themselves,

but were the sister-in-law and niece of Samuel D. Warren and Edward Perry Warren, who played such decisive roles in the history of the Museum of Fine Arts at the time when the picture was being completed. Edouard Manet's early masterpiece, *The Street Singer*, which came to the department in 1966 following the death of Mrs. J. D. Cameron Bradley, was an old friend returning home, for Mrs. Bradley's mother, Mrs. J. Montgomery Sears, who had brought the painting to Boston in the late nineties, had lent it for exhibition in the Copley Square museum in 1905, when Samuel D. Warren was president. Another magnificent Manet, *La leçon de musique*, painted in 1870, was given by Mrs. Richard E. Danielson in June 1969.

Curatorial continuity in the Museum of Fine Arts is nowhere better represented than in the Research Laboratory, for William J.

THE FAMILY OF JOSEPH MOORE. American, Erastus Salisbury Field, 19th century. *M. and M. Karolik Collection.* 58.25

SCENE IN A QUAKER MEETING HOUSE. American, anonymous. *Bequest of Maxim Karolik. 64.456*

Young, who established it in 1929, is still its learned, imaginative, and ingenious head forty years later. Of his two chief allies of 1955, the Conservator, Joseph W. Harrington, died in June 1967, but his Technical Assistant, Miss Florence W. Whitmore, remains actively at work. Year in and year out, the Research Laboratory constantly aids all departments in the restoration of objects and their preparation for exhibition. It carries out meticulous investigations that aid in dating bronzes and ceramics, and that are equally helpful in the prompt detection of forgeries. And it practices the kind of preventive medicine that is designed to insure the longest possible life of great works of art.

In 1956, when the Research Laboratory had become the finest equipped museum laboratory in the United States and on a par with outstanding ones abroad, a scientific advisory committee was established for it, comparable to the Visiting Committees of the various departments. Its chairman was the trustee-chemist Samuel Cabot, while Harvard and M.I.T. scientists, who had long cooperated with the laboratory's work, were among the members. Chemical, spectrophotometric, spectrographic, X-ray diffraction, and X-ray spectrographic analyses, along with the radiographic examination of paintings, were within the normal activities of the laboratory at this time. A recently installed X-ray spectrographic unit opened an entirely new world in museum research, for this very accurate method of analysis was both nondestructive but time saving. It could accomplish in fifteen minutes to an hour, without the removal of a sample, an analysis of a ceramic glaze or glass that by chemical methods would have demanded twelve hours to two days' work, according to the elements sought.

Additional possibilities began to be developed in 1959 through applying the electron-beam microprobe to museum objects. Such

MRS. FISKE WARREN AND HER DAUGHTER. American, John Singer Sargent, 1903. *Gift of Mrs. Rachel Warren Barton and the Emily L. Ainsley Fund.* 64.693

specific use of this apparatus, which is primarily a metallurgical tool, was developed in collaboration with M.I.T. scientists in that field, for Professor John T. Norton, Dr. Robert Ogilvie, and one of his graduate students successfully analyzed different paint strata with it, as well as colored sections of Roman glass. Of this, William J. Young wrote:

> In paintings, a boring is obtained by inserting the finest hypo-dermic needle (number 24) through the painting and into the ground. The section of the needle containing the core is then mount-ed in plastic and polished down to reveal the various paint layers. The micro-beam is then focused on the different paint layers, and a chemical analysis made. By micro-beam techniques, it will even-tually be possible to obtain a boring smaller than the size of a human hair. This approach will have definite advantages in such cases as the analysis of inscriptions and the comparison of the same color pigment in other sections of the painting. When such samples are taken, the puncture is not discernible to the human eye.

Commenting further on this process in 1960, Young observed that few techniques other than the electron micro-beam probe can analyze an area as small as 1 to 3 microns, and noted that a human hair averages between 50 and 70 microns. During the year the micro-probe had been used in the analyses of pigment strata, glass, bronze, and corrosion films. He noted, however, that "the electron micro-beam probe is at present out of the reach of the budget of even the large museum laboratory, as its cost is approximately that of an old master." Through the intervention of the Museum of Fine Arts, the Harvard geologist Professor Clifford Frondel — long a helpful ally of the Research Laboratory — obtained from the Prado Museum in Madrid small samples of a painting by Goya for electron micro-beam probe analysis. In 1965 Young mentioned new areas of research in Laser beam probe analysis and examinations by transmitted infra-red rays, made directly from the surfaces of paintings, Roman glass, and metals and their corrosion films. The Laser analyzer was the gift of the late Mrs. Samuel Cabot in memory of her husband who had been Chairman of the Laboratory's Visiting Committee from its organization in 1956 until his resignation as a trustee in 1963.

The Laser beam [Young wrote] removes a sample from the object, approximately 80–100 microns in diameter, from which the spectrochemical analysis is made. It was found that by transmitting infrared rays through a painting, the artist's original drawing in silverpoint or charcoal hidden under layers of paint was revealed, and in many cases greater clarity resulted than from the use of X-rays.

A seminar entitled *Application of Science in Examination of Works of Art*, arranged by the Research Laboratory on 15–18 September 1958, attracted delegates from various parts of the United States and from Brazil, Canada, and England. As it followed shortly after the eighty-fifth birthday of Edward Waldo Forbes, special tribute was paid to him for his achievements in the field of conservation at the Fogg Art Museum. The friends assembled on this occasion instituted an award in his honor for the most outstanding contribution in the field. This was in 1961 presented to Dr. Harold J. Plenderleith of the International Institute of Conservation in Rome during a seminar at which William J. Young lectured on "The Application of the Electron Microbeam Probe and Micro X-Ray in Non-Destructive Analysis."

A ten-day expansion of the theme of the 1958 seminar was held at the Museum of Fine Arts from 7–16 September 1965. The first week was devoted entirely to the study of metallurgy, while during the second, papers were presented on various aspects of new research in other fields. A total of 185 delegates from many countries made this the first such gathering on a truly international scale to be held in the United States. As with the 1958 seminar, the papers presented were subsequently published by the museum.

In a period dominated by Parkinson's Law, it is noteworthy that the Research Laboratory continued to be a small and tightly knit organization, which accomplished more and more each year, not by employing additional people, but by developing more efficient equipment with which the few could accomplish more. In remarking that 497 more objects had passed though the laboratory in 1964 than in the preceding year, William J. Young noted: "This additional work was accomplished not by additions to the staff but by the full cooperation of each of its members." This *esprit de corps* was particularly notable in November 1966 when the museum, in answer to an urgent call, sent William J. Young to Italy to assist the Florentines in first-aid to the innumerable works of art that had suffered during the recent floods that had inundated the city. He remained in Florence for a month, working in the Bargello Museum on statues, wooden and embossed leather shields, and a great number of other objects that had been completely submerged in water. In 1967, at the urging of Dr. Ugo Procaci, Soprintendente di Belle Art, he returned to Florence for six months to set up a chemical and conservation laboratory in the Palazzo Davanzati under the support of CRIA and the British and German relief funds. While engaged in these international labors of mercy, the Boston Research Laboratory continued to function efficiently "under the expert, if overtaxed, guidance of Miss Florence Whitmore."

The labors of the Research laboratory resemble those of Herakles in their variety and difficulty. At one moment the staff are establishing the authenticity of a work of ancient art by examining crystals completely invisible to the naked eye that could only have formed in the course of millennia. At another they are coping with immensely large and heavy objects, like the Attic funerary lion of about 390 B.C. purchased by the Classical Department in 1965. When this animal arrived, it had only one leg in contact with the base. As the body weighed a little over a ton, it was a challenge to position the lion in a proper pose while making the supports on which it would rest. As Young reported it:

> What made this a particularly difficult task was the fact that less than half of the original base existed. In order to eliminate a heavy support directly under the abdomen of the lion, which would have aesthetically disturbed its appearance, a chain tackle was suspended from the ceiling of the laboratory to help position the lion which was further supported from beneath by wooden blocks. This allowed the missing legs and base to be modeled in clay while the lion was in position. When the clay restorations were felt to be acceptable, armatures were designed that would run up through the restored areas of the legs and into the marble itself. Plaster molds were then made of the clay restorations. The armatures were positioned in the marble, the plaster molds were then carefully placed around the

armatures, and the missing areas of the legs cast in position. The entire operation took a period of two and one half months to accomplish.

Yet when the lion, or the 1800-pound archaic grave stele on which Miss Whitmore was engaged during the winter of 1961–62, went to their places in the newly renovated galleries of the Department of Classical Art, only the staff realized the immense labor and artistry that had been involved in their presentation. They *looked* right; consequently the thousands of visitors who have annually passed them have simply taken them for granted.

William J. Young's warning of 1955 about damage to objects from changes of humidity has been repeated in succeeding years. In 1962, after coping with Greek bronzes whose green patina was turning black, he wrote:

> The Laboratory cannot overemphasize the importance of proper control of humidity in the galleries along with air-washing and air-filtering. High humidity along with rapid changes in temperature and humidity has proven to be one of the most destructive factors in the preservation of any work of art. The climatic extremes are greater in Boston than in many cities in Europe. The mean range between the coldest and the warmest month is approximately 24°C., whereas Rome has a mean range of 17°C. between the coldest and the warmest month and Vienna has a mean range of 18°C. The highest humidity of the year in the Museum is found to be approximately 90 percent in August and again in the early part of October when the heat is first turned on in the building. In winter months it is very often found that the galleries have a relative humidity between 20 percent and 30 percent. While high humidity and rapid changes in temperature create bronze disease, prolonged dryness and rapid changes in temperature within the building create shrinkage in both panel paintings and furniture. Therefore, the ideal means, if we are to keep objects of art in the Museum in a static condition, will be air-conditioning. In the not too distant future, the super highways being contemplated in the Museum's direct vicinity will automatically create an atmospheric hazard from carbon dioxide and rubber dust containing sulphur. Although this can be accomplished only at tremendous cost, air-conditioning will be the only recourse.

Again in 1964, after repeating the same warning in very similar terms, Young concluded: "Great works of art are rapidly becoming more scarce and are increasingly difficult to obtain. If we are to preserve the objects we now have in our museums, we must not ignore the very important area of research into the disintegration of art objects caused by atmospheric conditions and pollution. The time is late."

CHAPTER XXII

A Decade of Facelifting

From the moment of Perry T. Rathbone's arrival in Boston in May 1955, he was full of plans to provide a "new look" to a building that was almost fifty years old, as well as to add blandishments for the additional visitors that he set out so successfully to attract. There were, alas, a great many unglamourous and necessary repairs that had to be made first. As time catches up particularly rapidly with slanted skylights, roofs required great expenditure of time and effort during the nineteen fifties. A plan was devised for installing plexiglass domes and plastic roof panes to reduce the areas of vulnerable skylight without sacrificing natural daylight in galleries where it was genuinely needed, and in those where it was not, like the recent Library stack, to eliminate skylights entirely and cover the whole area with solid 2-inch gypsum planking. Such work began in 1954 on the Decorative Arts Wing and moved on to the Evans Wing in 1956. Until it was completed in 1960 any major renovation of the painting galleries was impossible. Nevertheless, a considerable number of changes were made in other parts of the building.

Toward the end of 1955 the main staircase and the Rotunda were repainted and relighted, and various niches closed to provide "more flexible display space." In August 1956 a new gallery of twentieth-century art was created on the ground floor of the Evans Wing. Such space as was available near the Huntington Avenue entrance and in the corridors leading to the Crypt had long been devoted to memorials like marble busts of Martin Brimmer and Morris Gray and the not very exciting portraits by Theobald Chartran of George Robert White and his sister, Harriet White Bradbury. These were soon banished into storage to permit the display of portraits of earlier worthies by Copley, Blackburn, and Trumbull, accompanied by fine pieces of early American furniture. The 1957 Director's report contained a new section entitled "Rehabilitation of the Interior," which began:

> Largely thanks to the devoted labor and enterprising spirit of the Ladies' Committee we are well launched in our program of popularizing the Museum and of bringing it to a position where it will more deeply penetrate the life of the community and the nation. The potential of the Museum as a means of education and recreation, as an agent for the refinement of the eye, and as a source for the nourishment of the spirit, is immense. To advance the Museum's role as a civilizing element in society is one of our major responsibilities. We are concerned, therefore, with the number of people who come to the Museum and with the quality of experience they meet here. But can we hope to enlarge these factors and maintain them at a higher level so long as much of the interior is badly lit, some of the collections are illogically arranged and too often inadequately labelled; where there is not sufficient comfort, and while we cling to installations that were up to the minute in 1910? It may seem a simple matter to correct these conditions, but I assure you that it is not. To do the job properly will require a great deal of money, it will take time, it will tax the ingenuity of the most ingenious, it will require endless patience.

The architectural planning for these changes was entrusted to Nathaniel Saltonstall, who had been elected a trustee of the museum on 16 February 1956, and to his partner, Oliver Morton. Saltonstall had long been a leading spirit in the Institute of Contemporary Art, which had moved into quarters on the second floor of the Museum School in 1956, where it remained for three years before going on to a calamitous "arts center" created on the Brighton shore of the Charles River beyond the Harvard Stadium. Devising of the new installations was initially the responsibility of Carl F. Zahn of the

Institute of Contemporary Art, who was in 1956 appointed to a new post of Designer for the museum on a half-time basis. As he had the responsibility for the design of all publications and printed matter, it was not long before he had to give all his time to the museum. In 1966 work had increased to such a point that Carl Zahn became purely the Graphics Designer, while Duncan Smith joined the staff as Exhibits Designer. Both designers have ranked as Administrative Assistants to the Director, introducing a hitherto unfamiliar centralization into matters of exhibition, which had previously been in the province of the Curators.

The new Members' Room, that was to be the stamping ground of the Ladies' Committee, and a new Sales Desk and Lounge, which Saltonstall and Morton began planning in 1957, were opened for use in October 1958. The latter posed a considerable architectural problem for it involved merging an inadequate room looking into the Forecourt with a corridor that led from the Huntington Avenue entrance to the Classical Wing. By replacing the wall that divided these spaces with four round posts, the sales area was tripled in size, with great gain in flexibility for display. The asymmetry of the new room was disguised by building display tables around the posts, and by a polyangular plastic ceiling, through which the area was lighted. Near the entrance a smoking area was created with a few comfortable chairs; at the far end a new Treasurer's office was provided. Between these there was what then seemed ample space for the display of museum publications, postcards, photographs, color reproductions, and a wide selection of paperback books about the arts. The attractiveness of the Sales Desk immediately increased business, for gross receipts of the last three months of 1958 amounted to $33,794, as compared with $25,763 in the old salesroom for the same period the previous year.

Between the Sales Desk and the entrance to the Classical Wing a new Ancient East Gallery was at the same time created out of an equally unpromising combination of old gallery and corridor. Of the new gallery, the Director wrote:

> The new installation of ancient art has had a similar popular effect. Enticed by the striking display of our glazed tile lion from

THE SALES DESK IN 1957.

THE SALES DESK IN 1958.

the Ishtar Gate of Babylon, visible from the Salesroom, our visitors now find themselves in a gallery where lighted cases and effectively illuminated monumental sculpture spaciously placed against a rich red wall generate a new response to splendid works of art which were almost forgotten in their former drab setting. This stimulating introduction to the ancient world has encouraged visitors to venture further in the same direction. Our Greek and Egyptian galleries have been markedly more populous since October 15.

Like many changes in the museum, this was accomplished only by robbing Peter to pay Paul, for it deprived the Department of Textiles of one of the only two galleries, apart from corridors, that it had ever been able to call its own. Perry Rathbone further noted,

> However inadequate these display areas, and notwithstanding their inappropriate location, it is a distinct hardship for the Department to do without them. This is a temporary condition which has been borne with exemplary patience. Our future planning will provide new display galleries specially designed for the great riches of the Textile Department and in every way worthy of its distinction.

But it has been a long wait, for Miss Townsend has retired and her successor has resigned after a decade of service, and the new display galleries, although built, have not yet been opened at the moment of writing.

The Director's 1959 report described the next state of rehabilitation in these words:

> The most conspicuous improvement to our building has been at the Huntington Avenue entrance. Here, the prison-like effect of low ceilings, heavy masonry, and dim light has been eradicated. Instead, upon entering the Museum one feels immediately the effect of spacious simplicity, of light, of the cheerful sights of works of art and of illuminated panels for the purposes of orientation. It can be argued that a museum contains no room more important than its entrance hall. It was with this conviction that the committee felt justified in the expenditure of about $11,000 to work the change. The fact that the clear, bright and inviting aspect of the new Sales Desk, completed in 1958, offered a most unflattering comparison

with the old entrance was not to be ignored. Consequently in consultation with the Director and our Designer, our architects, Messrs. Saltonstall and Morton, drew plans for enclosing the checking area so as to conceal the dreary view of miscellaneous coats, hats and umbrellas. Lighted cases were let into the new walls for changing displays of objects of special distinction from various departments.

It could also be argued that the "low ceilings, heavy masonry, and dim light" of the 1909 entrance had been deliberately planned to enhance the attraction of the monumental stairway that was intended to draw the visitor directly to the main floor, where from the light and lofty Rotunda, adorned with Sargent's murals, roads led straight to the principal exhibition galleries of the various departments. By such a theory the visitor's first act would be to look at works of art, rather than buy colored postcards of or books about them. Be that as it may, the resplendent Sales Desk now established the predominant mood, and it was as well to be consistent. Many visitors, not being bright

HUNTINGTON AVENUE LOBBY AND SALES DESK IN 1960.

enough to go upstairs as they were intended to, had long strayed off into the ground-floor areas intended for offices and study storage, only to bother Dows Dunham in the Egyptian Department with the plaintive inquiry: "Where is the art?"

So in 1959 the Recent Accessions Gallery, opposite the Sales Desk on the other side of the entrance hall, was remodeled to present a more attractive appearance. Its three windows that once looked on the Forecourt were blocked and plastered over, to provide increased hanging space and permit more dramatic lighting than that of the sun. The room beyond, which had in recent years housed the art of the Ancient East, being vacant, was transformed into a Primitive Art Gallery to display the rotating exhibitions lent by Harvard's Peabody Museum. The two checkrooms by the Huntington Avenue entrance were not only enclosed but equipped with new racks to accommodate the wraps of 425 people, while a third, opening from the Crypt was created, designed for students and groups of children with a capacity of nearly 600. In the same year, 18,000 square feet of lawn between the museum and Museum Road were black-topped to enlarge parking capacity from 190 to 260 cars. This still left a grass plot of approximately 10,000 square feet to be violated by overflow crowds.

To increase the brightness of the Huntington Avenue entrance, the dark mortar joints in the limestone masonry were painted out, and the passages on either side of the main staircase remodeled to provide an enhanced setting for the eighteenth-century American portraits and furniture that now attracted the visitor to the new Members' room. The Crypt, which was the traffic center for the Lecture Hall, the administrative offices, and the Members' Coat Room, was repainted in 1960. At the same time the vast Egyptian sarcophagus in the center, which had, as Perry Rathbone put it, "become in the minds of many more of an obstruction than a work of art," became a dramatic point of interest by focusing four spotlights on its sides to illuminate the delicate relief carvings and subtle color of the granite. Four Rodin marbles and two bronzes, each with their individual spotlights, were placed on pedestals around the walls. In this new guise, the Crypt became a place where the Ladies' Committee served tea every afternoon from 3:00 to 4:30.

THE CRYPT IN 1960.

Perry Rathbone gave in 1960 an extended rationale of future changes proposed in the long range planning for the museum, which began,

One of the most important goals is to achieve greater clarity and logic in the disposition of the major collections, to provide for the first time appropriate display space for the Textile Department, and increased space for the display of paintings, both European and American. The general plan of the galleries on a departmental basis is by and large a good one. Nevertheless, owing to the original concept of the arrangement of the collection in two categories, to accidents of growth and the adjustments resulting from them — often merely expedient — needless confusion still exists. Our building is large and complex, the collections highly developed and much ramified. To promote clarity and order under these conditions is an obvious *sine qua non*. The problem that faces us in this objective is threefold: 1) to consolidate the arrangement of the collections and to eliminate the illogical sequences of display that remain, 2) to withdraw study collections from public view thus releasing areas for more useful purposes, 3) to redesign existing space for new galleries.

In reviewing the history of the building, which had been designed to house two categories of collections, major works and study pieces, he quoted Arthur Fairbanks' remarks of 1909: "The plans further provided for a principal exhibition on the main floor with rooms for compact exhibition and study on the floor below" and "as the installation has proceeded, the wisdom of these provisions has become more and more evident." To the observations of the third Director, the sixth countered forty-one years later: "While this arrangement may have simplified the installation problems that faced the staff in 1909 when the building was first occupied, it has long been clear that the wisdom referred to was theoretical rather than practical." Perry Rathbone continued:

It would seem then that study collections open to the public were a mistake in the first place. In the second place, from a practical point of view, the Museum can no longer afford to use its limited space for a display of secondary or merely study material. Forty years have brought an immense expansion not only to every department but to the functions and activities of the Museum as well. Like water seeking its own level, the multiplication of objects no less than the broadening of the Museum program has had to find accommodation. Without the Museum officially abandoning the policy of maintaining public study collections, these "compact displays" have nevertheless quietly eroded away.

Thus the Morse collection of Japanese pottery, originally placed on the ground floor where the Recent Accessions and Primitive Art galleries stood in 1960, had migrated to the obscurity of the attic, while the two courts of plaster casts had been transformed in two levels of special exhibition rooms. Then an Egyptian study room was ceded to the Textile Department to display some of the Elizabeth Day McCormick Collection until 1959 when the space was incorporated in the new Ancient East Gallery. In 1956 the study gallery of the Paintings Department was converted into new use for the exhibition of twentieth-century painting and sculpture, while in 1958 the Pre-Dynastic Egyptian study collection gave way to the enlarged Sales Desk and Treasurer's office, and part of the Late Egyptian study room was pre-empted by the new Membership office. So for all practical purposes, the theories that Prichard and Gilman had so painstakingly evolved decades before were deader than a mackerel, and the sooner they were forgotten the better.

The new gospel provided for concentrating on one floor whenever possible every major subdivision of the museum's collection.

> For the visitor it provides a pattern of arrangement that has clarity and logic in the over-all plan of the Museum and, for the individual collection, it offers a maximum continuity of related material. The resulting simplification will be an untold relief to those of the staff who are under constant obligation to answer questions as to location and to direct the unacquainted visitor.

Thus all American collections, paintings and decorative arts alike, would be in tolerable proximity on the first floor, or on the court floor that lay below it in the Decorative Arts Wing. The Director further indicated that

> it is only a matter of time before textiles, with the exception of tapestries, will be exhibited on the first floor, and all the Egyptian collections will be gathered together on the second floor. This will leave only two subdivisions permanently divided between the first and second floors, the Japanese collections and the collections of Greek and Roman art. Fortunately, in both cases these major concentrations, the former occupying twelve galleries, the latter fifteen galleries, are connected by staircases within each department.
>
> Yet putting aside the advisability of discontinuing study collections and the obvious desirability of achieving greater clarity of arrangement, it must be admitted that a very considerable factor in undertaking the current relocations is the urgent need for increased area for the adequate display of paintings, both American and European. This could only be achieved by breaking out of the boundaries assigned to the Painting Department when the Evans Wing was opened in 1915. The transfer to the Painting Department of five galleries from the Decorative Arts Department, formerly occupied by American silver and musical instruments, has made this possible. One of the major galleries on the second floor, Gallery P-10, formerly occupied by American paintings, can now be devoted to our truly great collection of French Impressionists.

There ensued a game of musical chairs, which continued between departments a process that had begun within the Department of Paintings more than twenty years earlier. One of W. G. Constable's earliest innovations had been to hang in the Hemicycle of the Evans Wing in 1938 a group of portraits of eighteenth-century Boston patriots and founders of the Republic. The Athenæum portraits of George and Martha Washington were hung nearby in alcoves to the left and right of the entrance to the Stone Room, which was allotted to five of the principal masterpieces of the collection, irrespective of country or period. In 1939 Constable moved to the first floor all other American paintings, save for those of the Colonial period and the early nineteenth century, which occupied gallery P–10. To complete in 1960 the concentration of all American pictures on the first floor, it became necessary to pre-empt the rather unattractive rooms in the Decorative Arts Wing, previously devoted to American silver, for which new provision had to be made, as described in Chapter XX, in a corridor requisitioned from the already sorely contracted Department of Textiles. And to clear the Hemicycle for European pictures, the portraits of patriots and founders were in 1962 moved from the conspicuous second-floor walls surrounding the Evans Wing staircase to a less dignified passageway directly below, that had formerly been within the province of the Department of Prints. "Correspondingly," the Director wrote in the same year,

the celebrated Athenæum portraits of George and Martha Washington were brought to the same level and placed on either side of the staircase so that these "national monuments," these symbols of Boston, are the first works of art the visitor beholds on entering the Museum [provided he comes in from the Fenway]. Opposite these are placed two of our Houdon busts, the marble of Thomas Jefferson, the original plaster of John Paul Jones. Mounting the stairs the visitor will find himself surrounded by a galaxy of great Monets, a "half-crown" of them appearing through the columns of the Hemicycle and seen now against a becoming color and flooded with new light. Altogether twenty-one paintings (of the total collection of thirty-four) are gathered here, thus emphasizing one of the major strengths of the collection. Beyond them and seen through the entrance to the Stone Room is Gauguin's masterpiece *D'où*

THE EVANS WING HEMICYCLE REHUNG WITH MONETS IN 1962.

venons-nous, que sommes nous, où allons nous?, a work closely related to the Impressionism of Monet.

If the American paintings suffered by their logical demotion to the artificially or side-lighted rooms on the first floor, the European pictures immeasurably benefited by their new sole occupation of the second-floor skylighted galleries of the Evans Wing. When in 1960 the roof of the wing was at last completely rebuilt, Perry Rathbone began a complete renovation of the galleries. In the course of forty-five years there had been a considerable amount of tinkering with the internal arrangements of the wing, occasioned by the growth of the collections and by the changing taste of curators. To accommodate the Catalan Romanesque mural paintings in the twenties, the southern part of the large westernmost gallery had been walled off to create a simulation of a chapel. In the thirties, as noted in Chapter XII, the three small oak-paneled rooms designed for the hanging of

THE FENWAY STAIRCASE IN 1962. Through the door to the Stone Room may be seen the great Gauguin.

THE STONE ROOM IN 1962 WITH THE GAUGUIN.

early Italian paintings were merged into a single gallery with plaster walls and simulated groin vaults, while the awkwardly long and narrow east and west corridors were subdivided by projecting partitions that provided increased hanging space for small pictures. When Mr. and Mrs. Edward J. Holmes gave up their Beacon Street house in 1943, a large Renaissance fireplace was moved from it to the center of the Italian Primitives Gallery. While this enhanced the somewhat plaster-of-Paris-ish medievalism of this vaulted apartment, it eliminated one window and reduced both hanging space and daylight. Consequently, trapezes of fluorescent lights were soon hung from the center of the vaults to provide increased illumination. Also in the early forties the two large galleries (P–6 and P–8) on either side of the Stone Room had been subdivided into compartments by screens projecting from the walls. This, W. G. Constable noted in 1940, allowed pictures "to be seen to much greater advantage, as well as providing more hanging space."

GALLERY P–3 IN MAY 1962 BEFORE RENOVATION.

GALLERY P–8 WITH ALCOVES BEFORE RENOVATION.

During the first century of the Museum of Fine Arts taste and habit in the hanging of pictures have considerably changed. In Copley Square paintings had solidly covered the walls of the galleries, as in Pannini's *Roman Picture Gallery* (reproduced in Chapter I), for a nineteenth-century art museum was instinctively modeled upon a palace, whose great walls required symmetrical adornment. Just as the music of Bach and Mozart was written for use in church or palace rather than for the concert hall, paintings were normally considered, like tapestries and mirrors, as objects of appropriate color and size that provided a handsome background in great rooms. Private and public collectors alike, until well into the present century, treated their paintings as decorative elements in large galleries rather than considering them as chronological milestones in art history that should be reduced to the didactic uniformity of neat rows of dead butterflies, impaled upon pins. In Copley Square as many as five levels of pictures might be fitted onto a wall by ingenious balancing of sizes. Although the Evans Wing galleries were conceived of in the palatial nineteenth-century tradition, they seldom showed pictures

EAST WALL OF GALLERY P–10 IN 1930.

on more than three levels. Not long after they were completed, however, a taste developed for hanging everything, large and small, in a single row at eye level, so that visitors might concentrate more intensely on individual pictures. Thus tall handsome galleries became something of a liability. Although projecting partitions made eye-level hanging easier, as well as somewhat increasing the running feet available for it, they hardly enhanced the appearance of the galleries in which they were inserted.

Photographs of gallery P–10 in various manifestations over the past forty years indicate as clearly as anything the shifts of taste and practice within the Evans Wing. The long east wall in 1930 was devoted to American paintings of the late nineteenth century. A dark oak dado 3 feet high indicated a uniform level for the bottoms of the lowest pictures, while a bronze handrail of similar height, placed 2½ feet from the wall, kept visitors at a safe distance. Although paintings were hung on two or three levels, there was considerable vacant space between the highest of them and the cornice, which was 18 feet from the floor. Hanging was governed by a certain symmetry of pattern for the wall as a whole, in which a large painting would be balanced by superimposed smaller ones. Thus John W. Alexander's tall *Isabella and the Pot of Basil*, which was immensely popular for decades following its purchase in 1898, was flanked on one side by Winslow Homer's *The Lookout – "All's Well"* with Mary Cassatt's *At the Opera* above, and on the other, Homer's *The Fog Warning*, topped by Walter Gay's *Interior of the Palazzo Barbaro*. Next came Abbot H. Thayer's *Caritas* (84½ inches high and 38½ wide) and Sargent's *Daughters of Edward D. Boit* (87½ inches square), with pairs of smaller pictures on either side. Loans were

interspersed, for immediately to the left of the door leading to the
Louis XVI Room in the Decorative Arts Wing were two Sargent portraits not owned by the museum: General Charles J. Paine below
and Mrs. Charles E. Inches above.

The end walls of this gallery were confused by superfluous doors;
at the northern end a glazed door led to a balcony overlooking the
Fenway, and two doors at the southern end gave access to a service
closet for the storage of copyists' easels and painting materials. By
1930 the balcony door had been closed, and George de Forest
Brush's *Mother and Child* hung over it. In the same year Regnault's
Automedon with the Horses of Achilles nearly filled the space
between the closet doors in the south wall. It was the right size, although from the wrong country, and had no conceivable relation to
the portraits of children that balanced the wall.

When W. G. Constable moved American paintings of this period
to the first floor in 1938, P–10 was completely allocated to the
Colonial period and to Gilbert Stuart and contemporaries. The
arrival of John T. Spaulding's pictures brought about a major reorganization of the Evans Wing; to bring that collection together as
a unit, in reasonable proximity to other Impressionist and Post-
Impressionist paintings, British pictures were in 1950 ejected from
gallery P–9. The southern end of P–10 was partitioned off to make

NORTH WALL OF GALLERY P–10 IN 1930.

SOUTH WALL OF GALLERY P–10 IN 1930.

a refuge for the large British paintings. Thus by the construction of a sturdy two-faced division wall, covered with fabric similar to that used on the walls of the room, gallery P–10A came into being. As the smaller number of early American paintings was to be rehung in a single line at eye level, a secondary cornice was installed to reduce the apparent height of both galleries. The dark wall fabric was carried only high enough to permit the hanging of John Neagle's huge *Pat Lyon the Blacksmith at his Forge*, which, ignored by the men of 1876 because of its proletarian subject, had only recently been borrowed from the Boston Athenæum by W. G. Constable. Against a deep red fabric, paintings like this, Copley's *Watson and the Shark*, and the Stuart portraits of Mayor Quincy and Bishop Cheverus looked comfortably at home, but in 1961 they too migrated downstairs to make way for the flower of the French Impressionists. Perry Rathbone removed the oak dado and intermediate cornice and reduced the size of the dark marble doorframes. The bronze guardrails and the obnoxious doorways in the end walls had earlier disappeared. With the walls covered with a soft gray fabric, P–10 made a handsome setting for thirty-nine Impressionist paintings. Here were hung Renoir's *Bal à Bougival*, Degas' *Duke and*

GALLERY P–10 IN ITS 1950–1961 FORM.

GALLERY P–10 AS RENOVATED IN 1961.

GALLERY P–10A AS RENOVATED IN 1961.

Duchess of Morbilli, Monet's *La Japonaise*, and Manet's *Street Singer*, together with other paintings and pastels by those artists as well as by Sisley, Pissarro, and Berthe Morisot. The effect was so striking that the Director and the Ladies' Committee could hardly resist using this room as a setting for dinners given before the opening of loan exhibitions. The smaller adjacent gallery P–10A, which led to the Louis XVI room, was rebuilt to house all the Millets in the Quincy Adams Shaw Collection in an arrangement suggesting the cabinet of a nineteenth-century collector. "This was," as Perry Rathbone put it,

> in part dictated by the terms of the gift, which requires that the entire collection of fifty-three oils and pastels be kept together at all times, and partly by our limited space. But it is also true that given the factor of the heavy Victorian frames and the restraint of Millet's color, the pictures gain in effectiveness by the muted green tone of the walls and the dense, double hanging which the

large scale of the room easily permits. Lighted alcoves in one wall have allowed an informal and pleasing arrangement of sixteen of the pastels.

Fortunately it had proved possible to hang the Shaw examples of Italian Renaissance sculpture in the appropriate gallery in the Department of Decorative Arts and Sculpture, and to remove to storage a few that, like the museum's "Mino da Fiesole" purchase of 1924, had been shown, on examination in the Research Laboratory, to have been the work of later forgers.

Actually the first step in the redecoration of the Evans Wing had been taken in the adjacent gallery P–9, which was completed with similar simplifications in the course of 1960. This provided a spacious setting for the harmonious display of large nineteenth-century French and English paintings of the Romantic and Realist schools. The new roof and the introduction of more translucent lights in the ceiling increased the amount of natural light available, while for the first time an adequate system of artificial lighting was provided. In 1961 gallery P–8, between P–9 and the Stone Room, was cleared of its subdividing alcoves and rehung with a golden fabric, which provided a handsome setting for French and English Baroque paintings. Here works of Poussin, Claude, LeSueur, Watteau, Fragonard, Chardin, Gainsborough, Reynolds, Romney, Raeburn, Wilson, and their like were grouped handsomely in relation to the shape of the gallery, rather than being strung along strictly at eye level in a didactic sequence. This change essentially restored the architectural dignity that the room had had when first occupied in 1915. Two smaller galleries (P–11 and P–12), newly covered with an off-white fabric, were devoted to Impressionist and Post-Impressionist works. The 1930 subdivisions of the long eastern corridor (P–13) were removed, and "instead the walls at the center have been projected at parallel angles," as Perry Rathbone described it, "to interrupt the excessive length of the gallery and to permit certain pictures, hanging on these projections, to be seen at a distance as the visitor approaches." Essentially this amounted to using another method to obtain a similar result. In this corridor were hung smaller paintings relating to the English and French works in P–9: Corot,

EVANS WING EASTERN CORRIDOR AS RENOVATED.

Constable, Crome, Gros, the Barbizon painters, and a small group of Impressionist works.

With the transfer of the Shaw Collection of Millet pastels to P–10A, the ground floor room that they had formerly occupied (P–19) was made available to expand the collection of contemporary paintings and sculpture that had been installed in P–20 in 1956. In the same year, 1961, the two large Bouchers from the Deacon House, for which there was no room (without overcrowding) in P–8, were installed in the new eighteenth-century French gallery in the Department of Decorative Arts and Sculpture. This began a practice, increasingly followed in subsequent years, of intermingling paintings in the exhibitions of that department. Conversely a few fine pieces of furniture found their way to the picture galleries of the Evans Wing. Simultaneously rehabilitation and relighting were going on in other parts of the museum, for in 1961 a new gallery for English silver was created, other Decorative Arts galleries refurbished, and a new gallery of Etruscan art created in the Classical Department.

In 1962, when the Monets had been installed in the Hemicycle and the great Gauguin in the Stone Room, the renovation of the western half of the Evans Wing proceeded. With the removal of its subdividing partitions, gallery P–6, adjoining the Stone Room, recovered its original character and became a fine setting for the Baroque paintings of the Netherlands. Here, against a soft gray fabric, Rubens' *Queen Tomyris with the Head of Cyrus* dominated one long wall, and the recently purchased Rembrandts of Pastor Elison and his wife the other. The size and height of the room, as well as the height of some of the largest pictures, permitted a harmonious double hanging of smaller ones, thus accommodating thirty-two paintings without a sense of crowding. As in gallery P–8, the oak dado was not removed, but simply painted a light color to harmonize with the fabric above it. The adjacent gallery P–5, as-

GALLERY P–6 AS RENOVATED IN 1962.

GALLERY P–5 AS RENOVATED IN 1962.

signed to Spanish paintings, was entirely relieved of its dado, and an unnecessary doorway eliminated. El Greco's *Fray Felix Hortensio Paravicino* was hung on the principal axis, with another El Greco, works of Murillo, Ribera, and the eighteenth-century still-lifes of Luis Menendez for company. There were also three Velázquez works, although not the portrait of *Philip IV*. That royal portrait, so bravely defended after its purchase in 1904, seems now by general agreement to be counted as a work from the studio rather than the hand of Velázquez. The great Gothic *Retablo of St. Peter* by Martín de Soria handsomely dominates the north wall of the room.

The largest of all the picture galleries, P–4, devoted to Italian painting of the High Renaissance and the Baroque, gained wall space by the closing of the doors that had originally connected it with P–5 and with a never-used balcony overlooking the Fenway. Here the oak dado was removed, two projecting screens dismantled, and a heavy figured wall covering replaced with a plain terra-cotta color fabric. The Tiepolo *Aurora Dispersing the Clouds of Night* was re-

GALLERY P–4 WITH SCREENS BEFORE RENOVATION.

moved from its awkward position above the cornice, and stored pending its 1969 installation as a ceiling in the Decorative Arts Wing.
Tiepolo's *Time Unveiling Truth*, purchased the previous year, occupied the center of the north wall, and Tintoretto's great *Adoration
of the Magi* was hung in the center of the west wall. Near the
Tintoretto on the axis of the entrance was dramatically placed Il
Rosso's *Dead Christ Flanked by Angels*.

The renovation of the Evans Wing was completed in 1963. In the
vaulted gallery (P–3) of early Italian painting, the fireplace
from the Holmes house was removed, thus increasing natural light.
For the suspended trapezes of fluorescent tubes were substituted
spotlights recessed in the vaults. In the adjacent Catalan chapel, the
frescoes from San Baudelio de Berlanga were moved back from the
apse to avoid competing with the vault painting from Santa Maria
de Mur. The French twelfth-century frescoes of *The Visitation* and
The Flight into Egypt, bought in 1949, were installed on the wall
opposite the apse, above the door. An elevator entrance outside P–3

GALLERY P-3 IN APRIL 1964 AFTER RENOVATION.

THE CATALAN CHAPEL AFTER RENOVATION.

was converted into an additional tiny exhibition room by covering a recessed wall hydrant and a large electric control box with a sizable hinged panel, which in turn becomes a background for paintings.

In the long western corridor (P–2) the projecting partitions of 1930 were removed, and the area divided midway in its length by a ceiling-high central panel, fitted with floor-length curtains, with passage room on both sides. This device, the Director reported in 1963,

> provided two excellent focal points or "vista stoppers" for master-works. The walls have been covered with a specially dyed fabric and the five original lights which primarily illuminated the floor have been replaced by no less than twenty-five lamps aimed at the walls. Two well-illuminated "semi-galleries" result. The one nearest the Hemicycle now houses our small collection of late medieval and early Renaissance northern paintings, Flemish, Dutch, French and German. The central panel provides a long needed *place d'honneur* for one of the Museum's most beautiful and celebrated works, *St. Luke Painting the Virgin*, by Rogier van der Weyden. The other "semi-gallery" contains the smaller paintings of the seventeenth century Dutch and Flemish school.

Ingenious as is this use of space, such mini-galleries emphasize the extreme overcrowding of the Department of Paintings, even when minor works are relegated to storage. Van der Weyden's *St. Luke* is indeed emphasized, but the width of P–2 is too narrow to provide an adequate setting for Wohlgemut's somewhat larger *Death of the Virgin*, while the 72-by-90-inch Lucas van Leyden, *Moses after Striking the Rock in the Wilderness*, being covered by glass, is all but invisible in this restricted space. Moreover, the gallery was barely finished when the long Flemish triptych of the *Martyrdom of St. Hippolytus* was purchased. Once this had had its fling in the Recent Accessions Gallery, it was placed, for want of room else-where, in the center of P–4, among Italian High Renaissance and Baroque paintings, where it very obviously does not belong. This suggests the evanescent nature of museum installation; no sooner is an exhibition completed than it begins to become crowded or shabby.

Between 1957 and the end of 1963 forty-one galleries in three departments had been completely renovated: eighteen in the Department of Decorative Arts and Sculpture, seventeen in the Department of Paintings, and six (including the Ancient East) in the Egyptian Department. Plans for eight more — one in the Egyptian and seven in the Asiatic Department — were ready to move from the drawing board into action whenever the necessary money could be found. While six other Egyptian galleries had been completed with only moderate expenditures for paint, lights, and improved cases, the proposed scheme for E–3 involved heaving about many tons of stone from positions specially prepared for them when the building was under construction more than half a century earlier. As has already been described in Chapter VIII, the Old Kingdom mastaba chapels, logically placed in 1909, were out of sequence in the greatly expanded Egyptian collection of 1963. Although perfectly visible and entirely safe, they seemed somewhat drab in comparison with the newly renovated galleries. The cost of reinforcing floors was so great that there seemed strong likelihood that the plan for E–3 would be indefinitely postponed. When the matter came before the trustees, one suggested with some firmness that as mummies were dead, they could wait. Another replied with equal firmness that as curators were not mummies, they could not be kept waiting indefinitely. After a few minutes of typical Boston shouting, a compromise was reached: the plan would proceed, but a year-end appeal would be sent to members asking for gifts for this specific purpose. Consequently, by the end of 1965, E–3 and all the other Egyptian galleries on the second floor were completely renovated, with lighting dramatic enough to make the mummies stir.

Simultaneous work on seven galleries of the Asiatic Department was stimulated by a pledge of $50,000 from John Goelet, provided a similar sum would be matched from museum funds. The Indian collections had long been housed in a corridor leading from the Rotunda to the Asiatic Wing, and in two galleries that, before the construction of the Decorative Arts Wing, had housed medieval and Renaissance objects from western Europe. The corridor, although dimly lighted, contained sculptured fragments from Sanci and archaeological specimens arranged with undramatic logic by the late

Ananda K. Coomaraswamy, who had come to Boston forty years before and had been dead for ten. In the next room, a bronze of Siva Nataraja had replaced the chasuble with the Barberini bees, and bits of Renaissance metalwork had been displaced by cabinets containing the exquisite Rajput miniatures of the Ross-Coomaraswamy Collection. Next door Indian and Cambodian sculpture had followed French Gothic fragments, without change of background or lighting. And the Iranian objects that had grown so markedly through the interest of Edward and Mary Holmes had no adequate abode anywhere. With a promise of help, this seemed a good place to begin, so far as the Asiatic Department was concerned.

Unlike E–3, the Indian and Iranian exhibition contained no objects as recalcitrant as the mastaba tombs, but the Director and the architects had far-reaching plans that involved formidable structural alteration in that part of the museum. Perry Rathbone's report of the "spectacular changes" in progress during 1964 noted:

> Throughout the year most of you must have noticed that gallery entrances in both departments were closed off, the display of Chinese bronzes was disrupted, and that one of the main corridors was being used to store tons of limestone blocks from the Egyptian tomb chapels. And no one entering on the Huntington side could fail to notice the long chute from the second floor window, down which load upon load of old plaster was dumped into waiting trucks. The staff has stoically put up with hours of pounding from pneumatic drills, and our sweepers have fought without complaint against blankets of rubble dust.
>
> The aim of our reconstruction has been to beautify existing space, to enhance the light, both natural and artificial, and to gain display area. In the galleries that will house the Persian and Indian collections, new proportions have been achieved, giving the effect of great spaciousness and heightened dignity. The Indian Corridor, a long gloomy passage lined with stone sculpture, has been reduced in length, its walls have been recessed at intervals and pierced with lighted cases, and its ceiling has been interrupted with circular plastic domes to admit natural light.
>
> This new space flows into a lofty gallery that scarcely recalls the original fabric. In turn, the second gallery gives into the largest

LOOKING FROM THE INDIAN
CORRIDOR INTO GALLERY A-2
AFTER RENOVATION.

gallery in the sequence for the display of monumental works of Indian sculpture. New ceilings, new skylights, and new floors, both wood and stone, are part of this renovation program still in progress.

When bearing walls are pierced or obliterated, when lighted exhibition cases are recessed into those that remain, when the whole shape and appearance of part of an old building are transformed beyond recognition, costs inevitably mount beyond expectation. One thing leads to another. In this case, anticipated expenses quintupled between the beginning and the opening on 3 November 1965. After paying tribute in his report for that year to architects, contractors, and staff, Perry Rathbone concluded:

These long delayed improvements — most of the galleries had seen little change in fifty years — could only be accomplished with the help of the Museum's members, three special gifts and, for the first time, contributions from Boston corporations. The special gifts came from John Goelet of Paris, Mrs. Susan Morse Hilles of New Haven, and the Charles E. Merrill Trust. To two year-end appeals about twenty-two percent of the membership responded and twenty Boston corporations. From all these sources a total of $251,677 was gathered. To this the Museum allocated an additional $249,450 from unrestricted capital, thus incurring a serious deficit.

The reward is the satisfaction of bringing new life to some of our greatest collections: of revealing the hidden beauty and the deeper meaning of many noble works that had long been obscured. The reward is also the acclamation that has greeted the accomplishment.

As satisfaction and acclamation butter no parsnips, something had to be done about finances, for the Museum of Fine Arts was living beyond its means. The immediate answer had been reported by the Director in the first paragraph of his report of the preceding year:

A decision was taken in 1964 that will affect the development of the Museum, every department, division, office and shop, as well as the School of the Museum. This was the vote of the Trustees to establish the Centennial Development Fund. The Museum of Fine Arts will reach its one hundredth anniversary on February 4, 1970. The vote is the first measure to implement our long-standing desire to expand the Museum and improve its facilities; to increase our endowment; and to do so in honor of our centennial, completing the work by the anniversary date. The President appointed a Centennial Development Fund Committee whose first responsibility is to explore ways and means of raising the Fund and to determine its magnitude. Mr. Lowell was nominated Chairman unanimously.

The possibility of continuing the renovation of the building on the scale undertaken clearly required a great deal of new money. Moreover, there was, just over the horizon, the possibility of an important addition to the collections that could not by any flight of the imagination be accommodated within the existing structure.

For several years directors of American art museums, Boston not included, had been paying assiduous court to an elderly New York lawyer, Forsyth Wickes, who had assembled an extraordinary collection of French eighteenth-century works of art in nearly every medium. Born in New York on 26 October 1876, he attended St. Mark's School and was graduated from Yale University in 1898.

After attending Columbia Law School he practiced law in New York City, but legal work in Europe, combined with the emotions of the First World War, brought about an intense love affair with the life and art of France. René Huyghe and Pierre Verlet of the Louvre, Georges Haummont of the Sèvres Museum, and François Boucher, Director of the Musée Carnavallet, whom he met in the French Army, became his close friends. In 1925 he bought a house in the rue Weber in Paris, which he furnished with what became the basis of his collection. In the late twenties he acquired the Château de Courmoulin at Gaillon in Normandy, where other parts of his possessions were installed. But in 1945, when approaching his seventieth birthday, Forsyth Wickes brought together the eight hundred pieces that comprised his collection in Starbord House, an 1850 structure in Newport, Rhode Island, whose interior he reconstructed to provide a compatible background for the result of forty years of intensive collecting.

Sir Kenneth Clark in his introduction to *Great Private Collections* (New York, 1963) — which included that of Forsyth Wickes — wrote: "The collection of a *grand amateur* should not be too big or too systematic; it must look completely at home in its surroundings and must be related even to the food and the wine on the sideboard. It must, above all, be personal, an extension of the character of the collector." In April 1964 Perry T. Rathbone, who had been lunching in Newport with a friend, was taken to Starbord House for the first time. Forsyth Wickes, who had never seen the Museum of Fine Arts, asked its Director various questions about the institution, and was sufficiently attracted by Perry Rathbone's answers to invite him to return in the near future, bringing with him, if he wished, some of the trustees of the museum.

In consequence, the Committee on the Museum migrated in a body to Starbord House for its stated meeting on 8 June 1964. Although Mr. Wickes had already left for Normandy, he had instructed his servants to provide lunch and give the guests the complete freedom of the house. This was incidentally the first time that Ralph Lowell, a summer resident of Nahant, had been in Newport. Even without their collector, the objects in Starbord House spoke for themselves. Furniture, porcelains, sculpture, drawings, and paintings were grouped with subtle harmony. I lost my heart to a diminutive Nanteuil drawing and a tiny terra-cotta bust of Fénélon by Lemoyne that were enchantingly placed in a narrow spot beside a door. When the committee left Newport there was little doubt that everyone shared Perry Rathbone's intense desire to secure the collection if humanly possibly. It was equally clear, as it had been a quarter of a century earlier with the first Karolik gift, that the existing Decorative Arts Wing would not hold it without a reasonable addition.

Although Forsyth Wickes died only a few months later, without having made any definite commitment, the Museum of Fine Arts received just before the end of 1965 the grateful news from his heirs that it had become the recipient of the entire collection. So Perry Rathbone reported with especial satisfaction that

> Not since 1948 when the collection of nineteenth and twentieth century paintings formed by John T. Spaulding was received has the Museum been so lavishly endowed with works of art from one benefactor. The Wickes Collection consists of some 800 items altogether, including forty-one pieces of furniture, among them noteworthy signed examples of the cabinet-maker's art; twenty-four sculptures in bronze, terra-cotta, porcelain, and wood; twenty paintings; eighty-five drawings, watercolors, and pastels; forty-five ornamental bronzes and ormolu; 391 pieces of porcelain and faience, and miscellaneous other *objets de vertu* including six important clocks. The collections form a stunning ensemble, a many-sided testimony to the creative genius of France during the Age of the Enlightenment.

So once again, as with Theodora Wilbour twenty years earlier, a New Yorker became a Great Benefactor of the Museum of Fine Arts without ever having set foot inside its door. But the proper housing of this great gift underlined the need of getting more money at the earliest possible date.

CHAPTER XXIII

Financial Crises

Perry Rathbone's fourth report as Director, for the year 1958, provided "the opportunity of pointing out the long-range major problems that face the Museum and of suggesting a solution to them." He did so by reprinting a statement that he had prepared during the summer at the request of the Editor of the *Christian Science Monitor* in answer to the question, "What is the major problem of the art museum administrator in America today?" The opening paragraph and the two final ones contain the gist of his argument.

The major problem of the art museum administrator in America is a financial one. This is the fundamental and central concern. In the future the quality and extent of every aspect of museum performance will rest upon the solution of this problem. No amount of idealistic thought, imaginative planning, or specialized knowledge will quicken the future existence of our proud treasures of art unless there is also that tangible asset essential to the job — hard cash . . .

Industry and commerce created the vast private fortunes of the past which provided our museums. From the same ultimate source must come the support in the future. But one cannot hope for support in any way commensurate while our tax laws permit an exemption to industry of a mere 5 per cent. Great benefits to culture and education have derived from the adjustment in personal tax laws permitting exemptions of up to 30 per cent of annual income.

Industry under enlightened and humanistic control has already shown inspiring concern for its responsibility in advancing the cultural life of the United States. With the cooperation and encouragement of our lawmakers the corporate wealth of our country will, I believe, step into the breach and lead the American museum out of the financial crisis which confronts it and threatens the quality of its future existence.

Following this quotation from the *Christian Science Monitor* article, the Director continued: "The Museum of Fine Arts is perhaps in more serious need of corporate — and foundation — support than any other institution of its kind in the world. I am aware of no other great museum anywhere, with the possible exception of the Ny Carlsberg Museum in Copenhagen, which has been built and is maintained today without public subsidy of any kind whatsoever." The "possible exception" did not greatly weaken the argument, for everyone who drinks a bottle of Carlsberg beer, whether in Denmark or Boston, thereby contributes not only to the continued vitality of the Ny Carlsberg Glyptothek but to the advancement of learning in general, for the profits of that brewery not only go to the support of various Danish museums but to endow the investigations of scholars in many fields, among them the late Nils Bohr. Among the many engaging and unique aspects of Danish life, none is more sympathetic than this, which makes the drinking of admirable beer a contribution to the arts and sciences. Although Boston has never developed such an imaginative solution, it has long had able trustees, skilled in the management of investments, for the Director noted:

> It is obvious that we could not operate at present even as we do had our invested capital not appreciated to a very substantial degree thanks to the skillful management of our Finance Committee. We may congratulate ourselves that the operating income of the Museum was increased by 68% in the decade from 1948 to 1958 owing primarily to earnings on equities. Operating costs have increased in the same period by 56%. Thus it is gratifying to report that we have been able to reduce our annual deficit by 57%; but this must be paid out of unrestricted capital funds.

The Treasurer during this decade was Robert Baldwin, who had been elected in 1939 when William H. Claflin became treasurer of Harvard College. Claflin, however, continued to aid the museum by serving on the Finance Committee, in company with Richard C. Paine and Richard Cary Curtis. On the latter's death, the vacancy was filled by G. Peabody Gardner, the third generation of his family to serve on the museum board. He was joined in 1958 by his son and partner, John Lowell Gardner (Harvard A.B. 1945, M.B.A. 1948), who had been elected a trustee on 21 February 1957. The younger Gardner succeeded to the treasurership in 1960 upon the resignation of Robert Baldwin, who was then elected a Vice President. As Bob Baldwin soon after retired from his post at the State Street Bank and Trust Company, he began to spend considerable time at the museum, quietly and unobtrusively untangling administrative knots and making himself useful to everyone.

Perry Rathbone chose his words well when he wrote in the 1960 report of the retiring Treasurer: "No man has been more attentive to the obligations assumed, no man could have been more intelligent about the problems of this vast building, none could have been more sympathetic to the problems of the staff — and they were often of a personal nature; no one could have discharged the duties of the office and upon relinquishing it have so many friends at every level of the organization." Although Robert Baldwin resigned as trustee and Vice President in 1962, he continued his useful service as Administrative Counselor to the Director until the end of 1965. Another man who kept the gears of administration from grinding over an even longer period was Charles Edward Humphrey, long Assistant Treasurer and Comptroller, following whose death on 11 October 1968 his Harvard classmate Robert Baldwin wrote:

> Of his seventy-four years, forty-six were devoted to the Museum, a testimony to his loyalty, a quality rarely found in this present age of restlessness. He served under five presidents, four directors, and five treasurers — surely an impressive record in itself. In his Harvard College class report (1917) for his 50th Reunion he tersely wrote: "Set up Museum of Fine Arts accounts in 1922 and have handled the work for forty-six years — expect to continue as long as the old body holds out." That was his wish; alas, granted.

Since Perry Rathbone had become Director, four trustees of considerable seniority had died: W. G. Russell Allen (1955), Alvan T. Fuller (1958), T. Jefferson Coolidge (1959), and Paul J. Sachs (1965). Five besides Robert Baldwin had resigned: William T. Aldrich (1962), Samuel Cabot (1963), Mrs. Henry M. Bliss (1965), Henry Lee Shattuck (1965), and Richard C. Paine (1965). A change in by-laws had provided that every trustee elected after 1 January 1963 should hold office until his death, resignation, or the annual meeting following his seventy-fifth birthday, whichever came first. A customary "grandfather clause" exempting those elected earlier provided that any such who resigned after attaining the age of seventy-five should become a trustee emeritus. Although the venerable Edward W. Forbes was appointed a trustee emeritus in 1966 when past ninety, the other trustees who resigned when over seventy-five preferred to leave the board entirely.

Two vacancies had been filled by the previously noted elections of Nathaniel Saltonstall (1956) and John Lowell Gardner (1957). Christian A. Herter, Jr., elected in 1960, resigned the following year when he moved to New York. The architect Heyward Cutting was elected in 1961, while in 1962 two businessmen joined the board, Sidney R. Rabb, chairman of Stop and Shop, Inc., who was greatly involved in Jewish philanthropies, and John J. Wilson. Jeptha H. Wade, III (Harvard LL.B. 1950), a Boston lawyer, became a trustee in 1963. Mrs. Frank S. Christian and Mrs. Paul Bernat, who had earlier represented the Ladies' Committee on the board, were elected in their own right in 1965 and 1966 respectively, while Landon T. Clay and John Goelet, whose assistance to the Classical and Asiatic departments has been frequently noted in earlier chapters, were elected respectively in 1965 and 1966. In the latter year two more businessmen joined the board: Lewis Pickering Cabot (Harvard 1961), president of the Society of Arts and Crafts and a trustee of the Institute of Contemporary Art, and George C. Seybolt, head of the old food-packing firm of William Underwood and Company, who had accepted the chairmanship of the Centennial Development Fund campaign.

On the resignation of Francis Keppel, Harvard College appointed as a trustee of the museum in 1959 Charles L. Kuhn, Professor of

Fine Arts and Curator of the Busch-Reisinger Museum of Germanic Culture. The Massachusetts Institute of Technology appointed to the museum board in 1955 its provost (later Chancellor and President), Julius Adams Stratton, who served until 1966 when he left Boston to become chairman of the Ford Foundation. He was succeeded in 1967 by James R. Killian, Jr., chairman of the M.I.T. Corporation. On the death of Dean William Emerson, John Ely Burchard, Dean of Humanities, was an M.I.T. appointment from 1957 through 1960. Two of William Emerson's successors as dean of that School of Architecture have served as trustees: Pietro Belluschi 1959 to 1965, and Lawrence B. Anderson since 1966. M.I.T. also designated in 1961 William Appleton Coolidge (Harvard A.B. 1924, LL.B. 1936), a younger brother of T. Jefferson Coolidge, and a distinguished collector of paintings. As Chairman of the Visiting Committee of the Department of Paintings, and as a Vice President, William A. Coolidge has been an exceptionally useful and generous member of the museum board. The Boston Athenæum in 1957 designated its president, Carleton Rubira Richmond (Harvard A.B. 1909), a collector of American furniture as well as of horticultural books and the works of John Evelyn and Samuel Pepys, and Parkman Dexter Howe (Harvard A.B. 1911), a collector of American literature. In 1967, by Athenæum appointment, Parkman Howe was succeeded by William Bradford Osgood (Harvard A.B. 1949, M.B.A. 1954), a trust officer in the State Street Bank and Trust Company, who collects New England paintings, prints, and furniture of the past two centuries. In 1968 James Barr Ames (Harvard A.B. 1928, LL.B. 1936), a partner in the law firm of Ropes and Gray, succeeded Carleton Richmond both as president of the Boston Athenæum and as a trustee of the museum.

For a generation it has often been asserted by institutions that large benefactors are a vanishing race, and that a small number of them must inevitably be replaced by a vastly increased number of supporters on a more modest scale. The latter method has considerable disadvantage, because of the immense effort and expense involved in recruiting and maintaining the interest of great numbers of people. That the assertion, however sincere, cannot claim the status of an absolute truth is indicated by various instances within the past generation of generous and imaginative benefactions of single private individuals, of which the Paul Mellon Center for British Art and British Studies at Yale University is a conspicuous recent example. Earlier chapters of this book have indicated the considerable number of individuals who have enlarged and enhanced the collections of the Museum of Fine Arts in recent years by gifts that will bear comparison with any of the past.

Although Perry Rathbone's *Christian Science Monitor* article of 1958 suggested that mounting taxes had "driven the great patron from the scene," the Museum of Fine Arts was still to receive considerable posthumous support from devoted friends of earlier decades. The most generous instance occurred upon the death of Mrs. William R. Mercer (1872–1960) of Doylestown, Pennsylvania, for her will provided that the income from her residuary estate be divided equally among the Boston Symphony Orchestra, the Arnold Arboretum of Harvard University, and the Museum of Fine Arts. Although Martha Dana Mercer lived away from Boston for all but twenty years of her long life, she frequently returned to the city of her birth. Years before she had given the Boston Athenæum a fund that provided fresh flowers throughout the building, and on her death made a specific bequest to the library that understandingly directed that any portion not needed for flowers should be used for the improvement of staff salaries. Although in 1928 she had given the museum a vivid portrait of herself, painted by Anders Zorn in 1899, the extent of her bequest had hardly been anticipated. Her will established a trust, the income of which was to be distributed annually. The museum's share has each year been considerably in excess of $200,000. In 1960 the Mercer bequest was used to expand the pension plan and place it upon a more equitable and realistic basis. In succeeding years it has helped make up the operating deficit and offset the constant outlay for building repairs and improvement.

Although Mrs. Mercer's generosity entitles her to a unique place in the history of the museum, many other devoted friends have steadily added to capital. In 1965, for example, when the endowment funds were increased by over $3,000,000, three legacies were received — from Edward Jackson Holmes ($582,059), Maxim Karolik

MRS. WILLIAM R. MERCER.
Swedish, Anders Leonard Zorn,
signed and dated 1899. *Gift of
Mrs. William R. Mercer 28.513*

($447,896), and J. H. Payne ($388,673) — the income of which
is restricted to the purchase of works of art. There were also two
sizable bequests entirely without restriction: $474,663 from Eliza-
beth R. Vaughan and $636,356 from James Parker. It is difficult to
read a statement in the 1965 report — "almost the entire sum of the
Parker bequest was disbursed during the year for major repairs and
new equipment and for operating deficit" — without recalling the
verses of Ecclesiasticus xliv. 9–10: "And some there be which have
no memorial, who are perished as though they had never been, and
are become as though they had never been born . . . But these were
merciful men, whose righteousness hath not been forgotten."

Bequests like Martha Dana Mercer's, which provided the equivalent of more than 20,000 new $10 members without the slightest
demand for services and entertainment, were clearly intended to
stabilize the operations of the Museum of Fine Arts, and relieve it
from the harassing agitations of fundraising. Unfortunately, through
a constant expansion of activities, operating expenses always remained a lap ahead of increased income, for during the second half-

century of its life neither the trustees nor the staff of the Museum of Fine Arts sufficiently appreciated that a privately supported institution cannot be all things to all men. This is understandable enough, for American art museums of any size provided no exact standard for comparison.

The Museum of Fine Arts and the Metropolitan Museum of Art in New York were both incorporated in 1870, the former on 4 February, the latter on 13 April. Just as the City of Boston provided a site in the recently filled Back Bay for one institution, the New York Park Commissioners made available in 1872 to the other a portion of Central Park, running along Fifth Avenue between 79th and 84th streets. Both museums had archaeologically minded Civil War generals as their first directors, for while Charles Greely Loring guided the growth of the Museum of Fine Arts until 1902, Louis Palma di Cesnola was in charge of the Metropolitan Museum until his death in 1904. The museum in Copley Square opened on 4 July 1876; the one in Central Park on 30 March 1880. The resemblances stopped there, for the New York Legislature had on 5 April 1871 passed an act authorizing the City Commissioners of the Department of Public Parks "to construct, erect, and maintain . . . a suitable fireproof building for the purpose of establishing and maintaining therein a Museum and Gallery of Art by The Metropolitan Museum of Art." Once the Copley Square site was received, the Boston trustees were on their own; everything to do with the construction and maintenance of the building, as well as the assembly and care of the collections, had to be accomplished entirely from private funds.

At moments the Boston trustees thought enviously of their New York counterparts, as in 1897 when, faced with a deficit of $4,580 on an operating budget of $39,922, William Endicott, Jr., wrote: "It is understood that the Metropolitan Museum of New York has an annual grant of $90,000 from the city treasury for current expenses. It is to be remembered in this connection that our Museum has never received a dollar for any purpose from either city or State, excepting the land upon which the Museum stands." In 1908, in the midst of the construction of the Huntington Avenue building, Gardiner M. Lane reflected somewhat plaintively upon the assistance given mu-

seums by the cities of New York, Chicago, St. Louis, and Philadelphia. From 1909 through 1912, he attempted to secure municipal
support in Boston, but eventually gave it up as a bad job.

What never seems to have crossed the minds of Boston trustees
when hard pressed for funds was that a great part of any money
given by a city or state has to be expended for the coddling of voters.
Life was not all beer and skittles for General di Cesnola, who had
budgetary problems in spite of his municipal assistance. The Central
Park museum had no sooner opened than he found it to be suffering
from a severe shortage of guards at the very moment when crowds of
curiosity seekers were swarming in. He reported early in May 1880
that

> Visitors of the lowest class soon detected this and began throwing
> peanut shells and spitting on the floors everywhere; successful
> pickpockets were also reported. The barriers placed around the
> modern statuary, and especially those in the Picture Galleries, were
> disregarded; and people crossed them in order more closely to
> examine the paintings, and touch them with their hands. In the
> basement, it was with difficulty that men could be kept out of the
> ladies' closets, while those destined for men, became in a few hours,
> filthy beyond description.

Even when the initial curiosity of the hoodlums had been satisfied,
the Metropolitan Museum still had greater obligations to the tax-
payers who helped support it than did the Museum of Fine Arts,
which relied solely upon the generosity of private individuals.

Because of the uniqueness of support of the Museum of Fine Arts,
it is necessary to turn to historical libraries to understand the full
implications of the difference between private and public support.
In that field Yin and Yang are personified by the oldest in the country, the Massachusetts Historical Society, founded in 1791 and maintained ever since by the gifts of a rigidly limited semi-honorary
membership, and the State Historical Society of Wisconsin, char-
tered in 1853, which has from the beginning depended on legislative support. The former has assembled a manuscript collection
second only to that of the Library of Congress for American history,
which it makes freely accessible not only to scholars who come in

person, but, through an immense series of publications in letterpress, photostat, and microfilm, to everyone who has need of its materials. The State Historical Society of Wisconsin, in addition to maintaining a great library, has always energetically "sold history" to the people of the state. Its great superintendent, Reuben Gold Thwaites, commenting at the 1909 meeting of the American Historical Association on a paper by Worthington C. Ford, Editor of the Massachusetts Historical Society, pointed out the essential difference between the Eastern organizations and Western historical societies dependent upon state appropriations.

In order to secure political support it seems essential, at least in the earlier years of the society, to produce publications having a quasi popular character. When it is remembered that legislators and public officials seek these books for free distribution to constituents, and often regard their popularity as their only excuse for being, one may hardly blame the society management for desiring to make the volumes, or at least part of them, readable by men of average interest and intelligence. This is one quite sufficient reason why so much interest is paid in many States to the narrative side of history — for the story of the pioneers always appeals strongly to the "general reader."

After a society has become firmly established as a State institution, a necessary adjunct of the State's educational machinery, then it becomes possible to maintain publications of a more scientific character. For instance, if I may mention my own State, in Wisconsin we are at last able to devote our collections entirely to the presentation of documentary material, and our proceedings to the usual administrative reports, monographs, pioneer recollections, and such other matter as is presented at the annual meeting. This sharp difference, in which we follow quite closely the custom of Mr. Ford's own Massachusetts society, would not have been thought possible a dozen years ago [i.e. 1897].

That it probably costs six times as much to operate in Wisconsin as in Massachusetts is due to the great emphasis upon popularization that is essential in an organization relying upon legislative support. Privately supported and publicly aided institutions are different kinds of animals, as different as Pegasus was from a milch cow.

Ancient libraries, like those of the Massachusetts Historical Society and of the American Antiquarian Society (founded 1812) in Worcester, and newer ones, like those assembled and endowed by John Carter Brown, William L. Clements, J. Pierpont Morgan, and Henry E. Huntington, have continued to operate through private gifts solely because they have carefully limited their fields and refrained from missionary work on an immense scale. Such libraries have assembled and preserved outstanding collections of books and manuscripts, which they make freely available to readers who are qualified to use them; through publication of their unique holdings they provide resources for a wider audience. They are, in short, a kind of reservoir from which scholars and teachers in certain fields derive their materials, rather than a fountain at which all the thirsty are invited to drink. By limiting their holdings to noncompetitive areas in which each has a particular strength, they continue usefully upon their self-appointed courses. The Astor and Lenox libraries, however, chose in 1895 to join forces with the municipality in creating the New York Public Library, which has in recent years, through the very magnitude of its operations, been in a constant state of financial crisis that has hampered its usefulness both to scholars and to the public at large.

An ideal of completeness, in any library or museum, imposes ever-increasing obligations because of the extraordinary expense involved in the proper care and preservation of objects — whether books or works of art — once they have been acquired. An essential element in the ability of the libraries just mentioned to continue to operate on private funds has been the decision rigidly to limit their fields of acquisition and to build only upon existing specialized strengths. We have seen in previous chapters, however, how the Museum of Fine Arts has, decade by decade, increased rather than limited the scope of its collections, with corresponding increase in its obligations. We have further seen how, from purely altruistic motives rather than from any need to endear itself to the taxpayer, it has endeavored to bring those collections to the widest possible audience. In a publicly supported institution, the principle of "one man one vote" often justifies great attendance in the hope of maintaining or increasing appropriations; this by no means is always equally convincing when funds come by private gift. Crowds are expensive in any case, but in Boston in the early sixties they were becoming alarmingly so. Since the abolition of the admission charge in the highly emotional atmosphere of 1918, the trustees and staff of the Museum of Fine Arts had given more thought to the breadth of service that they might render than to the means of paying for it.

The docent service, which had begun modestly enough in 1906 with Benjamin Ives Gilman's suggestion that the trustees "consider the permanent appointment of one or more persons of intelligence and education who could act as intermediaries between Curators and the many who would be glad to avail themselves of trained instruction in our galleries" expanded decade by decade. By 1965 the activities of its grandchild, the Division of Education and Public Relations, consumed about 12 ½ percent of the total museum budget, for successive heads had followed the precept: "Go out into the highways and hedges, and compel them to come in, that my house may be filled." For two decades, until his retirement at the end of 1961, nearly every year for William Germain Dooley represented a new peak, with steady and notable expansion, save where limits of space inflexibly restricted growth. As an example, he reported in 1960:

> The Extension Study now has 318 exhibits travelling to 165 public and private schools and to 21 colleges. Fifty-three of these are new users of our material. The slide library reports a record of 62,260 slides borrowed. The gallery talks and lectures had an attendance of approximately 36,000, a new high, and the student attendance at all our classes is clocked at 37,500. An estimate would be that about one of every six persons entering the Museum was directly involved with an educational department activity.

The museum was then in its sixth year of television, with Dr. Brian O'Doherty, Fellow for Research in Education, conducting a weekly program over WGBH-TV entitled "Invitation to Art." This had evolved from "Open House," inaugurated in 1955 and subdivided in 1957 into "The Intent of Art" and "The Vision of Art." A half hour program for children, "Adventures in Art," begun in 1955 and subsequently folksified into "Mary Ellen's Adventures in Art," ran for four years, until Ture Bengetz and Peter Abate of the faculty of the Museum School began to offer instruction in drawing and sculpture. Truly, as William G. Dooley remarked in 1959, "the Division of Education does not wait for people to come to the Museum." It went out into the community not only with lectures to schools, but with ads in telephone books, on the backs of taxicabs, and even on an occasional billboard.

Diggory Venn, who succeeded Bill Dooley in 1962, pointed out the eight aspects in which his division's efforts stretched "almost from the cradle to the grave — from the primary grades who weekly storm the ramparts of the Children's Room to their grandparents, who, with more decorum but equal zeal, follow our Lecturers through the galleries." With lectures and gallery talks, members of the division staff made over 1,100 appearances to almost 36,000 listeners. In seven classrooms, tucked in cellars and attics of the museum, eighteen instructors conducted thirty-six day and evening classes for children and adults in drawing, painting, and sculpture. Over 2,000 were enrolled in these, and more could have been taken had there been room, for there was a waiting list of 200 children and 173 adults.

For eight seasons, Diggory Venn wrote, "the Museum has irrigated the wastelands of television with a superbly competent series of art programs." Thus "it was hardly a surprise, but certainly a satisfaction, when the long-awaited New York educational television station went on the air this Fall, and asked our home station, WGBH-TV, Channel 2, for three regular programs — two of which are produced by the Museum. With this new outlet for our programs," he continued

> it is hard to resist playing TV's own game of numbers. So let it be stated that through television, the Museum now reaches into a population area of 17½ million people. Our programs are carried not only in New York and Boston, but also in Schenectady, New York; Durham, New Hampshire; and Lewiston, Maine; through the Eastern Educational Network. Nor is this the end of our space conquests in 1962. For two and a half years, WNBC-TV, a New York commercial station, has been carrying repeats of Brian O'Doherty's *Invitation to Art*. In addition, 15 of these programs were nationally

distributed to educational stations, and another 18 were shown this summer on wjw-tv, a commercial station in Cleveland.

On Monday evenings in the first half of 1962, staff members and guests, introduced by the Director, presented a program called "Angles on Art"; in the second half of the year George Peters, a young New York teacher and painter, conducted "The Artist's View." On Friday nights, "Images," a program of slides and photographs, ranged over a wide variety of subjects from Van Gogh to outer space.

In Extension Study, a museum staff member gave 301 lectures in 41 schools to 16,000 children, while another stayed at home to "mind the store of 640 sets of display materials available for loan." Some 2,406 loans went to 435 borrowers that included 211 public schools, 58 private schools, 38 colleges, and 47 adult groups. In the Slide Library, rental fees for outside borrowers were increased from $2.00 to $4.00 per group of forty slides, out of deference to the budget; nevertheless, 71,000 slides were circulated, and 2,545 new ones added to the collection. "The job was done," Diggory Venn noted, "by a staff of two with a part-time volunteer assistant. The record is remarkable in comparison to other major museums: one circulates 99,000 slides with a staff of seven; another circulates twice as many slides with four times our staff."

The Leslie Lindsey Mason Collection of Musical Instruments continued to be the inspiration for a highly imaginative series of musical activities. When ousted from its gallery in the Decorative Arts Wing in 1960 in the course of the shifts described in the preceding chapter, it was moved to an inaccessible subterranean classroom of the Division of Education. The instruments' chief protagonist, Miss Narcissa Williamson, whose initial responsibility had been the editing of sets of display materials for Extension Study, was simultaneously given the formal title of Keeper of the Collection of Musical Instruments. The new location, though extremely inelegant in its approaches, was sufficiently far from crowds of visitors to permit the free and uninterrupted use of the instruments by the talented group of young musicians and instrument-makers that Miss Williamson attracted to it. With furniture fished out of the attic but disposed with taste, this basement area has, through the quality of its

THE LESLIE LINDSEY MASON COLLECTION OF MUSICAL INSTRUMENTS IN 1969.

occupants, become one of the most charming rooms in Boston. The Keeper and her Assistant, Miss Barbara Lambert, will be working at a refectory table; a quartet of young musicians may well be playing Praetorius in the center; while in a corner others may be at work repairing, restoring, or copying instruments taken from the cases that line the walls. And from this center spring the concerts of the Camerata of the Museum of Fine Arts and the Museum Friends of Early Music.

The seventh and eighth aspects of the division's work in 1962 were the Children's Room, attended by an average of a hundred small children each week, and the Press Department, which coped with press releases, the preparation of the monthly Calendar of Events, and the organization of the annual Overseas Art Tour for Museum Members. The following year an Educational Aides program was added, in which present and past members of the Ladies' Committee, marshaled by Mrs. William H. Claflin, 3rd, and trained by Mrs. Elinor Brown, volunteered to assist the Museum Lecturers in guiding groups of schoolchildren through the Classical and Egyptian departments. This effort proved so successful that in 1964 there were sixteen ladies trained as volunteer aides who gave 106 talks to 2,620 children. By 1968 there were more than forty such educational aides to escort fifth- and sixth-grade classes about the museum.

In 1966 when Diggory Venn became Administrative Assistant to the Director for Development and Special Projects, William Lillys, formerly Assistant Director of the Montclair Art Museum, became head of a renamed Department of Education, with the hitherto unfamiliar title of Dean. Matters of public relations and publicity were for the first time in years separated from the division; in November 1967 this area became the independent responsibility of David Pickman, who was the third generation of his family to have been closely associated with the museum. In the spring of 1966 the museum embarked on a new school effort through active participation with the Brookline Title III Arts Project, which is related to the Federal Government Education Act of 1965. Dean Lillys was on leave from September 1966 until the end of July 1967 to plan this project, in the anticipation that federal funds for three years of operation, with the museum participation, might be obtained. To help Miss Elma Lewis' Afro-American Center for the Arts in Roxbury organize exhibitions, the museum in June 1968 engaged John Wilson, a black artist and teacher at Boston University, for part-time work as Curatorial Aide. So programs have proliferated in the Department of Education, with only one notable retrenchment. In 1968, after more than a decade of continuous broadcasts, a year's moratorium was declared on television programs in order to reconsider the direction of the effort and to resolve problems involving the use of color. Miss Thalia W. Kennedy has been at work in this field.

Diggory Venn described the quarters of the Division of Education in 1962 in the Churchillian paraphrase, "Never have so many done so much in so small a space." No space had ever been contemplated for such activities in the planning of the building, and as everything snowballed, with paid staff members replacing outside volunteers (like the long-faithful Professor Henry L. Seaver), people roosted where they could: "in corridors (which retain their original function as passageways), stairways, basements, and even the old dog kennels (complete with barred windows)." Finally they spilled over into the first-floor temporary exhibition galleries that had replaced the

Renaissance Cast Court. As this happened coincidentally with the Centennial Development campaign, I have never known how education and fundraising divided the spoils, but only that five useful galleries are now filled with desks, filing cases, and typewriters, rather than with works of art. I have never penetrated them since their metamorphosis, for one can see the machinery of bureaucracy anywhere, while Chinese bronzes, Attic vases, and Blake drawings are not so easy to come by elsewhere. It had become clear by the mid-sixties that, if the Division of Education were to continue, it must have additional space somewhere.

The housing of the Museum School has in recent years created even more puzzling problems than the crowding of the Division of Education, for in 1960 it became apparent that the school's building at 230 The Fenway lay directly in the path of one of the proposed routes of a new Inner Belt. The future of the school thus came into jeopardy at the very moment when its enrollment had begun to improve. In 1955 Karl Zerbe and four other members of the faculty had resigned, while in 1956 Gardner Cox, who had been Acting-Head of the Painting Department for two years, asked to be relieved to give his full time to portrait commissions. The following September the young Belgian painter Jan Cox became head of the department. It had been felt for some time that in a world increasingly dominated by degrees, the Museum School was at a disadvantage in offering its graduates only a certificate indicating completion of the course. Since 1945, candidates for the degree of Bachelor of Science in Education at Tufts University had been able to fulfill part of their requirements by work at the Museum School. In 1956 this cooperative arrangement was extended to a new program by which students at the school might become candidates for a Tufts degree of Bachelor of Fine Arts, while in 1960 a graduate program toward the degree of Master of Fine Arts was instituted. These opportunities had a stimulating effect upon applications for admission, for the enrollment of full-time day students rose from 199 in 1955 to 310 in 1960. In the next few years there were normally another hundred, chosen with increasingly selective requirements. The Evening School, which had enrolled 177 in 1955, had increased in 1960 to 351, and in 1963 attained 767. In that year, with 405 day students, the total enrollment reached the record of 1,172.

The Museum School offered instruction in ceramics, commercial art and design, drawing and graphic arts, painting, jewelry and silversmithing, and sculpture. A first year basic course was required of all students. At the end of that year, candidates who chose to seek a four-year diploma would choose one of the six fields for major work, and another as a minor field of study. Candidates for the Tufts B.F.A. would take three years of the school's regular diploma course, spread through a four-year period, with additional required and elective courses offered by the university. Holders of this degree, or the B.S. in Education might continue to the degree of Master in Fine Arts. A limited number of students who had received either the diploma or the M.F.A. degree might be accepted for the Fifth Year Program at the Museum School, in which they would select individual problems and work on their own under direction of the head of their respective departments, without relation to courses.

Routing the Inner Belt through the Fenway was long and bitterly opposed by the Museum of Fine Arts, the Isabella Stewart Gardner Museum, Simmons College, and other institutions that would be adversely affected, until 1965, when the Department of Public Works gave assurance that it would recommend tunneling the entire route. Nevertheless, even this concession would involve demolition of the Museum School, then scheduled for 1967. (It is still in use in 1969, because of innumerable delays and controversies over the Inner Belt.) Even though air rights over the tunnel were promised to the museum, there was bound to be immense disruption and expense, for any damages that might be awarded would hardly begin to cover the cost of temporary quarters, followed by new construction after the completion of the tunnel. This prospect caused a number of trustees seriously to question the wisdom of continuing to operate the school as an adjunct of the museum. True it had been started in 1876, but simply in space that was then vacant in the Copley Square building, with the clear proviso that it had to stand upon its own feet. It had done so perfectly simply in Copley Square, but ever since the move to Huntington Avenue there had been increasing problems, usually connected with housing or deficits. As it was by no means clear to many of the trustees that there was any longer an obvious or necessary connection with the museum, it was suggested that the school might reasonably be handed over to a university, whether

Tufts or the neighboring Northeastern, with such restricted scholarship funds as the museum held on its behalf.

As other trustees were loath to do so without thorough investigations, an ad hoc Committee on the future of the Museum School was appointed. Its chairman was Heyward Cutting; the other members were Bartlett H. Hayes, Jr., Perry T. Rathbone, Nathaniel Saltonstall, and Charles L. Kuhn. At the instigation of Bartlett Hayes, a two-day seminar on The Art School and its Contribution to National Culture was held at Wingspread, Racine, Wisconsin, in June 1966. This nationwide conference, made possible with the help of the Johnson Foundation, was attended by thirty representatives of independent art schools, including Russell T. Smith, who had been head of the Museum School since 1940. The conclusion reached was that the continuation of this school was indeed desirable, for its independent status offered the possibilities of accomplishing various things that would be more difficult on a university campus or in a craft school.

Thus the ad hoc Committee reported affirmatively to the trustees in November 1966, pointing out the advantages of retaining the school, with the suggestion that these would be realized by an emphasis on professionalism and on instruction of the highest quality. Such excellence would be achieved by a small faculty of great distinction, a much smaller and more carefully selected student body, and a rigorous simplification of the curriculum. The committee pointed out that financial worries were largely a misconception, deriving from a terrifying figure of $5,438,750 that had been suggested as the cost of rebuilding and maintaining an even larger school than at present. As the committee saw no need of this, and believed that a little over one-tenth that sum would be adequate to construct the basic core of such a new school as they contemplated, the trustees accepted their recommendations, which included a closer administrative tie between the museum and the school. This involved giving the school departmental status similar to the present Division of Education and placing both under an elected trustees' Committee on Education that would be equated in responsibility with the Committee on the Museum.

With its continuation approved, the Museum School spent the year from September 1967 to June 1968 in a fruitful period of self-study, directed by George Nelson of the New York firm of designers, George Nelson Associates, during which a blueprint for the future was evolved. When Russell T. Smith, who was approaching retirement after nearly thirty years of service, became Secretary of the Museum in succession to David B. Little, who had resigned at the end of 1967 to become director of the Essex Institute in Salem, Joseph H. Hodgson, Dean of Freshmen, became Acting Dean. In June 1968 William A. Bagnall, an architect and product designer, strongly recommended by George Nelson, was appointed Dean of the School, while Hodgson became Dean of Students.

As a result of the self-study, the former first-, second-, third-, and fourth-year structure was replaced by a Lower and an Upper School, whose characters are thus defined in the temporary mimeographed substitute for a school catalogue that is the only document available to me at the time of writing.

LOWER SCHOOL: Technically and conceptually this is a foundation training period for the Upper School. The student is exposed to and trained in a variety of media, including metal, wood, painting, plastics, sculpture, light, color, photography, film, graphic arts, earth materials, as well as core courses in design, drawing, and art history.

UPPER SCHOOL: In the belief that a meaningful and valid education for professional work need not require that study be concentrated in a single discipline students in the Upper School construct their own curriculum on an open elective basis, in consultation with a faculty-student advisory group. Advanced courses are available in all media introduced in the Lower School. The only limitation on the elective system is the observation of prerequisites and required classes in drawing and history of art.

Throughout the School, team teaching takes place wherever possible to encourage cross-fertilization between the various media. A free communication among faculty, students and administration is encouraged at all times. Student-faculty advisory groups will meet periodically with small groups of students to evaluate progress and recommend adjustments in programs. Review Boards, with students and faculty represented, will assess each student's portfolio during the last three weeks of every twelve-week term. The student concerned participates in these assessments. A narrative evaluation is placed in his file for conversion to credits, or, where necessary for transcripts, to letter grades.

This is in the mood of the times. An article about the Museum School by Marc Metraux (Harvard 1971) in the Summer 1969 issue of the *Harvard Art Review* notes "the individual is the focus of the School, learning is his tool. The fifty-three faculty teach in their own ways and manners, but style is not taught, only technique." He further says that "while the individual is allowed to pursue his own interests, he is encouraged to experience art from every angle possible."

Mixed or multi-media is the orientation of the School. Within each field of the visual arts, the student is shown all the techniques which are relevant; in the area of the graphic arts, for instance, courses include, among others, etching, lithography, offset printing, engraving, book design, and silk-screen. The School tries to help the student realize the relevance and the relation of these specialities to one another. Thus, painting is not restricted to the canvas, paper, glass, or wood, but becomes stage sets and backdrops as well. These works have been used in productions of Elma Lewis's National Center of Afro-American Artists, or in multi-media productions at the School itself.

Finished works in Al Rubin's course "Fourth Dimensional Multi-Media" constitute some sort of dramatic presentation. Mr. Rubin tries to emphasize the relationships between life and art in a created environmental situation. Starting with concepts of two and three dimensional art, students begin to expand these concepts in order to create a "fourth dimensional" multi-media presentation. Elements may include, for instance, films, slides, painting, actors, sets, sound, dancing, etc. Presently, a group in Mr. Rubin's class is working on a project which includes live performers, film, slides, colors, shapes, sounds, and various objects. The center of the production is an actress who acts and reacts to the various parts of the show. She thinks about making love to one man, and gazes onto a film of her making love to another. There are slides of her making love to a man, and slides of the man she loves. She also reacts to two other actresses who change back and forth from film to reality. There are hundreds of balloons which start bursting. People in the audience start popping all the balloons. There are sounds of balloons exploding, doors opening, water dripping, airplanes, acid rock, Indian sitar, etc. Colors, and shapes are projected onto various screens around the room, and continual change cuts back and forth from the different parts of the room and the different elements which make up the presentation. Everything is ordered and planned to create a complete environment in which the relationships between ideas, objects, sounds, colors and forms are coordinated, and in which the audience is totally immersed.

Returning from this excursion into the fourth dimension to simpler matters of double-entry bookkeeping, it became apparent early in 1966 that the Museum of Fine Arts could no longer continue on its charted course without incurring a persistent operational deficit that would spiral even more violently than the current inflation. Consequently, in February 1966 the trustees voted to charge a general admission fee, beginning 5 July, to all nonmember visitors, at the rate of 50 cents for adults and 25 cents for children up to the age of eighteen. Children under six were admitted free if parents were so misguided as to bring them. Students presenting identification could purchase a year's pass allowing unlimited admissions ($5.00 for college and university; $2.50 for elementary and secondary schools).

The problem of the dearly beloved groups of schoolchildren resulted in a request to the Governor to submit a bill to the Legislature subsidizing the admission fee of schoolchildren who came in organized groups. Pending action upon this request, the admission charge on all such groups was withheld until the close of the then current school year in June 1967. Governor Volpe's bill to reimburse the museum for educational services to schoolchildren, in the amount of $100,000, died in committee early in 1967. In his report for that year, Perry Rathbone observed:

Then, backed by the strongest editorial support from newspapers throughout the state, by letters from concerned educators, and by our own direct mail approach to school authorities and members of the General Court, the bill was to have been submitted once again in December in the Governor's Supplementary Budget. But urgent business before the legislature gave rise to such protracted debate that the Supplementary Budget never was submitted in 1967. At the year's end, the Museum was continuing its efforts to obtain this reimbursement and the Governor had agreed to file an appropriation request both for fiscal 1968, ending June 30, 1968, and for the full fiscal year 1969, ending June 30, 1969.

In making the Museum's case to the General Court, our legislative leaders responded to invitations to luncheons at the Museum, tours of those collections in greatest demand as teaching aids to schools, and made the acquaintance of our educational staff and facilities.

In the end in April 1968 an annual subvention of $100,000 was voted to underwrite by the Commonwealth the free admission of children.

In view of the 1876–1918 experience, by which almost no one came on pay days, and everyone on Saturdays and Sundays, the re-imposed admission charge applied to all days when the museum was open. Boston seemed to take it in its stride, for the Director reported: "Attendance for 1966, a total of 779,768, surpassed the record figure of 1965 which was 766,354" — an increase of 13,414. "Except for the abnormally high attendance occasioned by the John F. Kennedy Library display of 1964, the figure for 1966 surpasses those of all the ninety-six years in the Museum's history." And the receipts during the six-month period from 5 July 1966 brought in $63,110. Attendance declined in 1967 by 13 percent to 680,197, but this was not surprising, for the experience of other institutions had led everyone to expect a drop in the first year of admission charges of at least 26 percent, and the $170,459 received was useful.

The financial problem remained, for in 1968 increased costs of operation, new posts for new services, and the mounting costs of building promised a projected deficit that would be insupportable.

To increase income, admissions were raised to 75 cents on 1 February 1968, restaurant prices were raised, and it was agreed to put the Research Laboratory and other technical services, so far as possible, on a self-supporting basis by accepting outside work. As retrenchment was mandatory, various projected new positions were eliminated, the publications and exhibition budgets were reduced, and, in an ill-chosen form of economy, it was attempted to reduce lighting, guarding, and cleaning by closing one-seventh to one-tenth of the museum galleries on each of the six open days. This, financially, was tantamount to closing the whole building one entire day, and in effect going on a five-day week. It was undoubtedly an economy, but an inappropriate and exasperating one, for no visitor ever knew what section would be temporarily denied to him when he came to the museum. It caused such general unhappiness that in June 1969 it was concluded that all galleries *must* be available the full six days of the week when the museum was open, and that economies would have to be in some other quarter. As there had been no loan exhibition comparable to *The Age of Rembrandt*, the 1968 attendance dropped to 503,346, with $142,305 received from admissions during the year. Effective 1 July 1969, the admission charge to nonmembers over sixteen was raised to $1.00. It was further agreed, as a means of making the collections available to nonmembers who could not readily pay a fee, to have an experimental period of free entrance on Tuesday evenings from 5:00 P.M. to 9:00 P.M. and of a reduced entrance fee of 50 cents on Sundays from 10:00 A.M. to 1:00 P.M., beginning 1 October 1969.

On several occasions during the past fourteen years it has proved necessary to advance the membership charges to keep the increased numbers a financial asset, rather than allowing them to become a liability. Very early in the experience of previews, it was found desirable to charge for drink provided. A family membership at $15.00 was introduced in 1959 to give husband and wife all the privileges of two single memberships. Hitherto these had been assumed after a single $10.00 payment. Single memberships were raised from $10.00 to $12.50 in 1963. During the crisis of 1966, when admission began to be charged, the rate for single memberships was increased from

$12.50 to $15.00, and for families from $18.00 to $25.00. And in 1968 the single payment for the category of Fellow for Life was raised from $1,000 to $5,000.

Such increases are, alas, one of the byproducts of an inflation that renders the dollar of dubious value. Within my memory two cents bought a newspaper, or sent a letter by train across the North American continent. Today the penny has no function more exalted than coping with the sales tax on small purchases, while the dollar, being composed of only one hundred present-day pennies, has fallen on hard times. An article in the 15 August 1969 issue of *Life* suggests that in "the new math of inflation" fifty thousand 1959 dollars, plus twenty-five thousand 1969 dollars, total not $75,000 but $50,515.

The value of money over a century is one of the insoluble dilemmas of a centennial history. It would be comforting to know, for example, how Harvey D. Parker's 1884 bequest of a capital sum of $100,000, which had such phenomenal usefulness in its time, rates in St. Peter's ledger with Mrs. Mercer's 1960 bequest of an annual income of more than double that sum. There seems to be no easy answer. At odd moments during the writing of this history I have importuned eminent Boston bankers and trustees for a rule of thumb that might intelligibly relate the dollar of 1870 with that of later periods. As such inquiries have never produced a clear answer, I cannot enlighten my readers beyond recording what various devoted friends of the museum have done, in their days, with money as they knew and had it.

To compound financial confusion, the aims and purposes of the Museum of Fine Arts have startlingly evolved in the course of a century. In the 11 March 1911 issue of the *Boston Evening Transcript* H. L. Kennedy, inspired by the new Huntington Avenue building, contributed a full-page spread entitled "The Life of Boston's Old Art Museum." It was a sober and reasonably accurate review of matters which any reader who has persevered to this chapter would already find familiar. But there was a section entitled: "A Museum of Reproductions: This Was the Original Idea — Why It Was so Projected and Why the Scheme Was Changed," which is worth rescuing from the impermanence of pulp newsprint. The argument as summarized was this:

A museum of original works of art was expensive, very partial and very limited. It would be better to have it unlimited and inexpensive so a museum not of originals but of reproductions was planned. It was to be mainly a museum of plaster casts. For a few thousand dollars, all the masterpieces of Greece, Rome, Egypt, modern times, etc., could be seen. The city of Boston, it was argued, could not afford not to have a museum which would be so valuable, so cheap and so educational. Moreover, a museum of this character could be housed in a series of cheap, inexpensive wooden buildings, and in case of accident, it would cost less to replace such casts than it would be to build a fire-proof building. Such a museum would not be like the Louvre, the British Museum or that of Berlin but of a different character, more unique, more cosmopolitan. It would also be better on the holidays for people from out of town to be in the shade in these wooden buildings than to sit on handkerchiefs on the Common.

If we had never risen above the ideal of plaster casts, the Museum of Fine Arts in its tenth decade would have had fewer financial problems, but it would have been a solvent, pedagogical dreariness of a low order. Happily the Doctors Bigelow, Weld, and Ross, Francis Bartlett, the Evanses, Spauldings, Holmeses, Karoliks, Harriet J. Bradbury and her brother, Theodora Wilbour, Martha Dana Mercer, Charles Bain Hoyt, Keith McLeod, Forsyth Wickes, Bullards, Paines, Friedmans, and dozens of other devoted friends by their generosity completely foiled such a logical prospect. It is only the defect of the museum's virtues, in having become the possessor of irreplaceable masterpieces, that has imposed the nagging necessity of constantly worrying about money.

CHAPTER XXIV

Centennial Development

By the middle of its ninth decade the Museum of Fine Arts was consistently living beyond its means, and in the course of doing so had become grievously overcrowded. The proposed solution was to give a vast birthday party and hope that the numerous guests would bring presents. Nearly forty years had gone by since the last substantial addition to the building, while, during the last ten, activities had snowballed. The courtship of the public, pursued with the ardor of an eager lover, had been all-too-successful. In 1955 Perry Rathbone had observed that "the museum, like the successful and popular host, has had to meet new obligations in providing for the pleasure and comfort of its guests." In 1965 he wrote: "Until space and funds are supplied, the Museum cannot function efficiently or even satisfactorily; and surely without space and money it cannot realize the almost unlimited opportunities for service to an expanding audience in its second century. To answer these critical needs the Trustees voted to establish the Centennial Development Fund."

In 1955 he had proposed an accelerated program of exhibitions and special events, the reinstallation of many galleries and displays, and "providing for visitors the ordinary creature-comforts more abundantly and attractively." The exhibitions held in the following decade had brilliantly and successfully drawn their thousands, but they had imposed steadily increasing demands upon the museum staff and upon the existing provisions for packing and shipping.

Visitors who see objects from all over the world hanging for a few weeks in exciting but unfamiliar surroundings seldom realize the immense labor, and risk, that has been involved in bringing them this temporary pleasure. To pack safely objects of great value and fragility requires not only knowledge and care, but room. The staff of the Museum of Fine Arts abundantly possessed the first two qualifications, but had become woefully lacking in the third. It will be recalled that the curator accompanying the Vienna treasures to Boston in 1951 had remarked that "he had never had in another museum as many men, as competent men, or as good equipment for installation as he found here." The men and equipment were as good in the sixties as they had been then, but as the pace and number of loan exhibitions increased, the Registrar, David B. Little, who was responsible for the receipt and accountability of other people's property, became increasingly alarmed about the inadequacy of the shipping room. During Harold Edgell's administration some of the shipping room had been "borrowed" to gain space for the burgeoning activities of the Division of Education, and had never been restored.

The Lecture Hall under the Tapestry Gallery, opened in 1915, was equally inadequate for the demands of a half-century later, as was the rather dreary Restaurant, located in the basement of the Asiatic Wing. The staff of the Division of Education, jammed like sardines into odd corners, preached the gospel wherever they could. Fifty exhibition galleries had been handsomely renewed, but in the exchanges of space involved the Department of Textiles had clearly become low man on the totem pole. It had gained nothing, and had lost two of its improvised galleries, with no hope of replacement short of new construction. On top of these long-standing problems, the terms of the gift of the Forsyth Wickes Collection imposed a new urgency for additional space, as the Director explained in his 1965 report.

Before his death, Mr. Wickes had expressed his desire that the collection be kept together as a unit; that it be installed in such a way as to recreate the atmosphere of Starbord House, indeed to preserve the arrangement of furniture, the combinations of pictures and objects insofar as would be practicable, for he was deeply convinced that a harmonious ensemble of compatible works in a domestic ambience was more enjoyable and ultimately more meaningful than a strictly scientific subdivision of objects into categories. Under his will a committee of heirs was charged with the responsibility of selecting a museum to receive the collection on a basis which would meet his wishes on the most satisfactory basis. We were pleased to have been able to work out an attractive plan for the installation of the collection for a period of twenty-five years which met with the approval of the committee and resolved some of the difficult problems inherent in moving it from a private home to a museum setting. As the Museum has no space that is not already overtaxed, our architects were instructed to draw up plans for an addition to the east end of the building bordering Forsyth Way as an extension to the Department of Decorative Arts and Sculpture. In this addition, approximately 3,200 square feet on the first floor will be assigned to the Wickes Collection.

Architecturally this addition amounted to the completion of the Decorative Arts Wing which, forty years before, had been only partially constructed, with a single line of galleries running from south to north along the east side of the interior garden court. The area proposed for the Wickes Collection would fill the space between these galleries and the street that bounded the museum's property on the east. The entrance to the Fenway from Huntington Avenue had, some years before, presciently been named Forsyth Way in honor of the neighboring Forsyth Dental Infirmary, now to be joined by the new home of the quite unrelated Forsyth Wickes Collection. Urgent as were all these needs for space, it was even more essential to obtain additional endowment that would not only balance the operating budget, but provide more adequate salaries for the able scholars of the museum's curatorial staff. Consequently, whether one liked it or not, there was no alternative in 1965 to a major public appeal for funds.

Since the public meeting held in the Music Hall on 3 February 1871 to solicit funds for the construction of the Copley Square building, the trustees of the Museum of Fine Arts had made no widespread popular appeal to the city at large. The later stages of construction in Copley Square and the entire effort in Huntington Avenue had been accomplished by quiet solicitation among friends. Now the shotgun was chosen in preference to the rifle. The first steps of the Centennial Development Fund campaign were taken in 1965. President Ralph Lowell appointed a Campaign Council that recommended the employment of Ketchum, Inc., as professional fundraising counsel. In August 1965 they established the Centennial Fund office in first-floor temporary exhibition galleries. Such a "drive" was so completely foreign to the practices and temperament of the Museum of Fine Arts over its previous ninety-five years that it was not easy to find among its existing trustees and long-time supporters anyone who was eager, or even willing and able, to assume the general chairmanship. Early in 1966 Perry Rathbone persuaded George C. Seybolt, who had become a member of the Visiting Committee of the Department of Decorative Arts and Sculpture only two years before, to do so. Being a man of great energy and resourcefulness, George Seybolt tackled the problem in the manner generally recommended by professional fundraisers who are aiding American institutions, whether they be colleges, hospitals, or museums (other than the MFA). As Perry Rathbone reported in 1966:

> Under his inspiring and efficient leadership the complex organization of the campaign began to move with alacrity. Chairmen of the four divisions were the first to be recruited by the General Chairman. Before the year was over some 800 volunteers had signed up as vice-chairmen, captains or workers of the rank and file. The names of some 4,500 prospective donors were marshaled and brought into workable sequence. Meanwhile the inescapable requirements of the Museum were studied and restudied. The Trustees recognized that the actual needs of the Museum could be provided only with a sum of upwards of $20,000,000. But it was also considered imperative that the campaign — the first ever undertaken by the Museum — should succeed. To establish a more realistic goal was therefore compelling. To this end the President appointed a Priorities Committee under the chairmanship of our Treasurer, John L. Gardner. After much study and far-reaching

deliberations this committee recommended to the Board the sum of $13,400,000 as the minimum amount needed to provide the most urgent improvements by 1970. It was further decided to establish an interim goal of $6,000,000 to be raised by March of 1967. The needs were now defined; the challenge spelled out.

In anticipation of this campaign, the trustees in November 1964 elected more than eighty persons, living and dead, to the newly established category of Benefactor, to recognize publicly the principal donors of money or works of art since the foundation of the museum in 1870. In today's terms, a Benefactor is one who gives or bequeaths the sum of $250,000 or works of art of an equivalent value, although the requirements for earlier decades were set at a lower level out of respect for the greater value of earlier dollars. In November 1965 a second category of Great Benefactor was created to honor those whose gifts had amounted to $1,500,000 or more. During the year the names of donors in both categories were placed in bronze letters on the walls at the foot of the main staircase at the Huntington Avenue entrance. Readers of this book will hardly be surprised to discover that the Great Benefactors commemorated are the following: Francis Bartlett, Dr. Charles Goddard Weld, Mr. and Mrs. Robert Dawson Evans, the brothers William S. and John T. Spaulding, George Robert White and his sister Harriet J. Bradbury, Dr. William Sturgis Bigelow, Dr. Denman W. Ross, Miss Theodora Wilbour, Charles Bain Hoyt, Keith McLeod, Mrs. William R. Mercer, Mr. and Mrs. Edward Jackson Holmes, Mr. and Mrs. Maxim Karolik, and Forsyth Wickes. Collecting and generosity clearly run in families, for of the nineteen names, six are husbands and wives, and four are brothers or sisters. Among the Benefactors are four couples: Mr. and Mrs. Richard Perkins, Mr. and Mrs. Martin Brimmer, Dr. and Mrs. Henry C. Angell, and Mr. and Mrs. Sigmund Katz. Mrs. Walter Scott Fitz, the mother of Edward J. Holmes, is there, as are four pairs of brothers and sisters: Francis and Katherine Eliot Bullard, Helen and Alice Colburn, Robert J. and Grace M. Edwards, Lee M. and Sophie Friedman.

The opening of the Centennial Development Fund Campaign was thus described in the Director's report for 1967:

On January 5, the Museum inaugurated its Centennial celebration by "kicking off" the first fund-raising drive in its history. This formal declaration of the Museum's needs and its intentions took place in the ballroom of the Sheraton-Boston hotel where nearly 2,000 special guests gathered at 5:15 P.M. The arrangements were made by a Special Events Committee under the Chairmanship of Mrs. Thomas B. Gannett. The theme and slogan adopted for the campaign, "The Challenge of Greatness," was the subject of brilliant slides with sonic background and running commentary by the Director. Revealed with drama and style were the principal treasures of the Museum from every age and culture, as well as the personalities who comprise the curatorial and technical leadership of the Museum today. It was followed by a sound film projection of Special Greetings to the Museum on its Centennial by Pablo Picasso and Henry Moore.

The meeting was then addressed by President Ralph Lowell, Honorary Chairman of the Centennial Development Fund, and General Chairman George Seybolt who announced the goal of $13,400,000 and that $3,385,000 had already been raised or pledged. The Honorable Edward M. Kennedy, United States Senator from Massachusetts, and the Honorable John F. Collins, Mayor of Boston, followed with special remarks; a congratulatory message from Governor John A. Volpe was read. It was then the Director's pleasure to introduce the principal speaker of the day, William S. Paley, Chairman of the Board, the Columbia Broadcasting System. His brilliant address not only recognized the challenge of greatness that museums deliver to us today, but also the challenge to American business in particular to share responsibility for museums in this generation and advance their meaning and influence in American society. His speech was published and proved a most helpful instrument in our further fund-raising.

The formal part of the program was followed by a cocktail reception at which Mr. and Mrs. Paley were our guests of honor. Ladies attending the event were given a pin — a reproduction of the obverse of the Museum's most famous and beautiful Greek coin: the Victory chariot of the Syracusan decadrachm of the fifth century.

In the campaign that ensued, some nine hundred volunteers were organized into four divisions for solicitation, with the following sub-chairmen: Initial Gifts, John L. Gardner, Jeptha H. Wade, Nelson W. Aldrich; Primary Gifts, Henry H. Meyer, Jr.; Special Gifts, John P. Chase; Major Gifts, Mrs. Roger H. Hallowell, Mrs. Paul Bernat, Mrs. Frank S. Christian. The names of 4,500 prospects were assigned to groups of volunteers at special meetings at the museum. Weekly report meetings were held until 30 March 1967, when, at a "victory party" in the Tapestry Gallery three months after the "kickoff," George Seybolt announced that a total of $6,726,433 had been raised or pledged, which surpassed the initial goal of $6,000,000. The volunteers worked to extraordinary purpose. The energetic members of the Ladies' Committee having achieved 176.5 percent of the goal assigned to them, moved on to assist other divisions in soliciting. At the end of the year, Perry Rathbone expressed warm thanks to all participants, and to the "most generous, indeed unexampled, cooperation" of the Boston press, radio, and television stations. The communications media had responded to the efforts of the Public Information Committee which, under the imaginative and knowledgeable leadership of Stacy Holmes of Filene's, secured "press coverage that by actual linage count exceeded that of any campaign in the city's history." The Director concluded his account of the effort:

> The campaign continued at a lower key throughout the year, so that by December 31, a total of $7,710,203 had been raised or pledged. The breakdown is as follows: Individuals: $5,147,000; Foundations: $1,950,000; Corporations: $407,700. Of the total sum, nearly one million dollars represent special gifts of works of art to be announced and shown for the first time in the Centennial Acquisitions Exhibition in 1970.
>
> Yet we cannot rest our oars. In spite of this prodigious accomplishment, we have only passed the halfway mark and many friends and potential donors, both private and corporate, have not yet been approached.

At the beginning of August 1967, the fund amounted to $7,200,-000, with contributions from 3,385 donors, of whom 9 (6 individuals and 3 foundations) had each given more than $100,000, and 2,732 less than $1,000. At that time 17 individuals, 4 corporations, and 11 foundations had made gifts of more than $25,000, but less than $100,000 each. With the conclusion of the intensive first phase of the campaign, additions have naturally come chiefly from substantial gifts, made for specific purposes. Between the beginning of the campaign and 1 July 1969, gifts of $50,000 or more were made by 18 individuals and 10 foundations. Of the personal gifts, 5 came from people who had become members of the museum since the intensive efforts of the Ladies' Committee began in 1955; the other 13 were made by friends of long standing, some of whom had been members for more than forty years. In the next lower category — more than $25,000 but less than $50,000 — individual gifts were equally divided, there being 12 each from the newer and older groups, while 6 gifts from corporations and 5 from foundations were of this magnitude.

In anticipation of the Centennial Development Fund's returns, ground was broken on 25 May 1966 for the completion of the Decorative Arts Wing. This addition, which was known in promotional parlance as Phase I, provided 12,000 square feet of space for the Department of Decorative Arts and Sculpture. Of this only the first floor, destined for the Forsyth Wickes Collection and a new gallery of English silver, was to be immediately completed and occupied. The second-floor space above was left unfinished, for future expansion of the department, while the area below, on the court floor, was destined for a new installation of the American period rooms at some future date when funds permitted. The opportunity was seized to continue to the second floor the staircase at the southeast end of the Decorative Arts Wing, which had hitherto only linked the court and first floors.

The exterior work on Phase I was completed in the course of 1967. By October 1968 the five rooms designed to house the Wickes Collection in manner reminiscent of Starbord House were finished, furnished, and opened to visitors. These attractive galleries are today the only air-conditioned display area in the museum; without rigidly copying the former owner's Newport rooms, they permit the grouping of objects in similar manner. A 110-page handbook, *The Forsyth Wickes Collection*, prepared by Perry T. Rathbone and illustrated with numerous color plates, which describes representative examples from the more than eight hundred items received, was published at

THE FORSYTH WICKES COLLECTION AS INSTALLED IN 1968.

the time of the opening. To the north of the Wickes galleries a handsome new room for English silver, so much of which had come through the Theodora Wilbour Fund, was also completed. The floors above and below are, however, still unfinished.

Phase II, which got under way in August 1967, comprised a three-story addition to the Decorative Arts Wing south of the Karolik galleries, as well as completely filling in the area between this and the Classical Wing on the court-floor level only. The latter space provided 3,700 square feet of basement work-storage to relieve the long congested study-storage and work area of the Egyptian and Classical departments. The adjacent three-story addition furnished 6,800 square feet for the Textile and Decorative Arts departments. The basement was assigned to textile storage, the first floor to long-needed exhibition galleries for that department, and the second floor to a new medieval gallery for the Department of Decorative Arts and Sculpture. The several storage areas are now completed and occu-

THE FORSYTH WICKES COLLECTION AS INSTALLED IN 1968.

THE GEORGE ROBERT WHITE WING

pied; the new exhibition galleries are scheduled to open in the spring of 1970.

Phase III is a five-story administrative and service structure, enclosing the main west court, to be known as the George Robert White Wing, in accordance with the hope expressed by his sister, Mrs. Frederick T. Bradbury, in 1930 when she bequeathed the museum one of its larger funds. In July 1968 ground was broken for this wing, which will provide 43,500 square feet of new space. The first floor will contain a new restaurant, and the second floor administrative offices. The Library will occupy the third floor, while the fourth floor will provide convenient new quarters for the Research Laboratory, painting restoration, and the editorial office. The Division of Education will occupy the court (or basement) floor, with a separate new entrance from the parking lot, by which groups of children can be brought directly from buses to the areas designed for them, with workable staff offices adjacent. To the south of the White Wing a loading platform leads directly to an adequate new shipping room, while adjacent quarters for the Registrar are being converted in the basement of the Asiatic Wing.

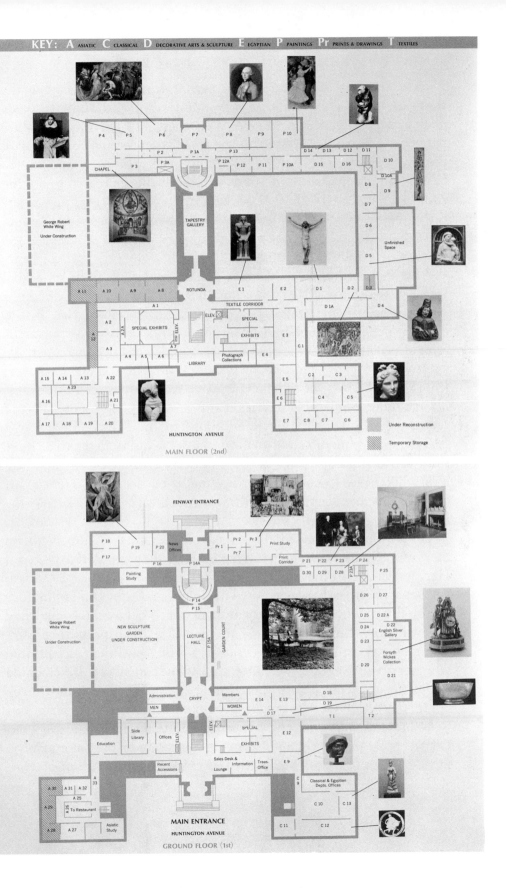

Phase III has been planned to permit further expansion to the west, in which, hopefully, a new auditorium and similar conveniences may some day be added. The plans also provide for future painting galleries on ground to the north that would connect with the Evans Wing. These additions are, however, still over the horizon, for the museum must find funds to absorb the increased operating costs of Phases I-III before embarking upon additional building. The earlier chapters of this book furnish sufficient instances of the problems that arise when new space is provided without commensurate increase in endowment funds.

Although building is the most visible aspect of the Centennial Development Fund, there was another less conspicuous but even more important goal: the improvement of curatorial salaries. Just as a university is made or broken by the quality of its faculty, so the reputation and usefulness of a great museum depend upon its curators, and as the Museum of Fine Arts must find its new curators from the same body of scholars in which universities seek professors, it must offer comparable salaries if it is to retain its present staff and recruit equally knowledgeable additions in the future. In the past decade, as innumerable new colleges have been founded and as huge state universities have by parthenogenesis created new campuses, able scholars are in competitive demand as never before. Hence part of John Goelet's Centennial gift was specifically earmarked to the betterment of curatorial salaries.

For a number of years before his death in January 1969, William Stevenson Smith, Curator of Egyptian Art, had regularly offered a Harvard course in that field. Although in the past decade the Classical Department, as has been noted in Chapter XIX, has had numerous personal ties with universities, most of the other curators had had too little opportunity to share their specialties with promising graduate students. This was to be regretted, for the continuity of learning, whether in universities or museums, is best achieved by catching promising students before their careers are crystallized and developing their interests in some specific direction. To alleviate this isolation, the museum undertook in 1967, with the aid of John Goelet's gift, an experimental plan for formal and systematic involvement of the curatorial staff with the Fine Arts curriculum of Harvard, Brandeis, and Boston universities and Wellesley College. This provided for two seminars each semester strictly limited in enrollment, to be announced in the catalogues of the universities as available for academic credit toward degrees, although held at the Museum of Fine Arts in order to have unlimited access to collections on exhibition and in storage. Given a full complement of fourteen curators and assistant curators, each would offer his half course only once every two years.

The program began in the fall term of 1967–68 with a seminar by Dr. Hanns Swarzenski on Romanesque and Gothic objects in the museum; in the spring term Harry H. Schnabel, Jr., gave one on the source of American design, and Dr. Edward L. B. Terrace another on the Middle Kingdom painting of Egypt. In the academic year 1968–69 the Department of Prints and Drawings offered an introductory course on the history of printmaking in Europe, as well as Miss Eleanor A. Sayre's graduate seminar on prints, while the Asiatic Department's survey of Buddhist art was given jointly by Dr. Jan Fontein and Dr. Pratapaditya Pal. At the time of his death in January 1969, William Stevenson Smith was within a few weeks of beginning an announced spring term seminar on Egyptian Old Kingdom sculpture. It is hoped that this cooperative effort may continue indefinitely.

In addition to the very necessary improvement of curatorial salaries, another goal of the Centennial Development Fund was to raise $2,000,000, the capital of which would be spent for the purchase of new works of art of the first rank. Objects purchased by this means, as well as a number of important gifts from private collectors, have remained unannounced against a spectacular exhibition of Centennial Acquisitions, scheduled to open on the one hundredth anniversary date, 4 February 1970, and continue on view through 12 April. As a special catalogue of these gifts and purchases will be published at the time, it need only be indicated here that they include the complete range of the departments. In the course of 1968, gifts of $940,409 were added to the Centennial Development Fund, bringing the total above $8,000,000. While in theory that left only $5,400,000 to be raised to reach the original goal, it was clear that, because of constantly increasing building costs and the inflationary spiral in every aspect of life, more would be needed even to stand still.

Centennial Development activities not only stretched but strained the energies of everyone connected with the museum. Even in 1966 Perry Rathbone noted the quickening of the pace. Recalling a hardly felicitous simile of Benjamin Ives Gilman, which likened the Museum of Fine Arts to a "great engine of culture," the Director observed that "in 1966 we continued to tune it up, and to all those involved it often seemed that we were racing the engine." There was little doubt that the bearings were getting overheated in the early months of 1967, when the intensive solicitation of prospects coincided with the mob scenes of *The Age of Rembrandt* exhibition. The ordinary work of the museum was disrupted; the nerves of the staff were worn to a frazzle, and, with continual coming and going of campaign workers, visitors found little of the peace and quiet that is essential for contemplation of works of art. It was clear that the level of general public enthusiasm that had been aroused during the intensive campaign could not be revived again in the immediate future. The remainder of the Centennial goal would have to be sought by other means, in a lower and more bearable key.

With the prospective disbanding of the large volunteer force of solicitors in the spring of 1967, George C. Seybolt was rightly con-

THE APPROACH TO THE 1967 AGE OF REMBRANDT EXHIBITION.

A CROWDED ROOM IN THE 1967 AGE OF REMBRANDT EXHIBITION.

cerned about the form that the next stage of the effort should take.
Having given nearly three-quarters of his working hours to the campaign during the preceding year, he freely expressed his disappointment that only a quarter of his fellow-trustees had taken a very active
part in the detailed mechanics of the effort. While many American
institutions have recruited the majority of their trustees largely because of personal solvency or ability in fundraising, the Museum of
Fine Arts had never worked on this theory. It had from the beginning
sought a balance between men knowledgeable in the arts who were
often distinguished collectors, those who represented learning in
general through their positions in universities and other educational
institutions, men highly respected in the public and financial life of
the region, architects, and a few men of substantial property who
were chiefly chosen in the hope of substantial contributions. Earlier
chapters have indicated the way in which the board sought during
its first eighty years to maintain such a balance by filling vacancies
with the nearest possible facsimiles of the individual trustees who had

just died. It was, after all, a private institution, unaccustomed to general public appeals. While those trustees who could, gave generously, some played their part by linking the museum with the other learned and educational efforts of the region. Although this was the tradition of an earlier and more civilized world, in 1967, when every institution in New England was engaged in a competitive scramble for money, it seemed to George Seybolt comparable to having executives of Filene's sitting in quantity on the board of directors of Jordan Marsh. He felt strongly that, if the museum's present courses of limitless expansion of collections and services were to continue, more trustees would have to give more constant and personal attention to fundraising and budget control for an indefinite future, and that the administrative management of the institution must be revised to bring it more into conformity with current business practices.

When I became a trustee in 1953, the meetings of the full board, held three times a year, were brief, for Ralph Lowell presided firmly and had no truck with longwindedness or irrelevance. In essence the board acted upon the recommendations of a smaller body which met monthly, the Committee on the Museum, of which the Director was Chairman, with the President and Treasurer serving *ex officiis*. This was a body of nine, for each year two trustees were elected to it for three-year terms, on the expiration of which they were not immediately re-elected. The Committee on the Museum approved purchases of objects recommended by curators, and loans, and generally served as the means of formulating policies and of official communication between the trustees and the director. A Finance Committee that advised the Treasurer and a Committee on the School were the only other standing committees. There were, however, the Visiting Committees to the seven departments, the Library, the Museum School, and the Research Laboratory, each with a trustee as chairman. Any matters of departmental or curatorial business that required action by the trustees reached them through the Director and the Committee on the Museum, always with a recommendation, which was usually promptly accepted or rejected, without lengthy debate. This was all in the Boston tradition that trustees should place the running of an institution in the hands of a responsible administrator, and let him attend to his business without interference.

This theory of administration was admirably expressed by Charles A. Coolidge, a trustee of the Museum of Fine Arts since 1946, in an essay that he wrote shortly before his retirement in 1965 after thirty years' service on the Harvard Corporation. After pointing out that the governing boards do at most 10 percent of the job of governing Harvard, he offered a few rules of conduct which he summarized "by a big 'don't' — *don't meddle.*" He suggested that "the job of a lay member of a governing board such as the Corporation boils down to this. Do your best to see that the organization is good, that it is well manned, and that it runs smoothly — but don't try to run it. Make your decisions on evidence furnished you by experts, and not on your own imperfect knowledge of academic matters." In the same vein, Major Henry Lee Higginson half a century before had pondered on the future of the Boston Symphony Orchestra, which he had founded in 1881. For thirty-seven years he had met the deficits, while scrupulously leaving all musical matters in the hands of its conductors. In 1918, a year before his death, he wrote a friend:

> Now, as to a committee to manage the Orchestra as in Chicago and Philadelphia: I do not know how it would work. Several times I have tried it here, and the good people always defer to me and ask what I want. Do you suppose a committee can be found that will sign yearly contracts, or longer, say for $400,000 a year, and who will hire the hall at a loss of $15,000 a year, and supply the music, and get and keep the confidence of the men, as well as find a great conductor, and take him for a period of years? The hardest of all is that they must keep their hands and tongues off the conduct of the art side, or they will make trouble.

The last sentence is the key to the matter.

The Trustees of the Museum of Fine Arts had engaged in 1955 a Director whose policies had greatly expanded the activities and services of the institution. These policies had also increased its income in certain directions, but never sufficiently to offset the increased outgo that inevitably accompanies all efforts to provide services to great numbers of people. As they had every intention of keeping "their hands and tongues off the conduct of the art side," it seemed to some trustees that the character of the board must be altered to attain a larger number of trustees who would give substantial sums themselves or assume close personal responsibility for continuing fundraising in relation to a permanent Development Department within the museum staff. In short, if the Director was to manage the "art side," the trustees must take a more active concern in the "money side."

In 1967, after the conclusion of the intensive phase of the Centennial Development Fund campaign, Ralph Lowell, who had passed his seventy-seventh birthday, indicated his wish to retire from the presidency at the next annual meeting. Thus in February 1968, when Lowell was appointed President Emeritus, George C. Seybolt succeeded to the presidency. At the same meeting Mrs. Frederick W. Hilles of New Haven, Connecticut, and Richard P. Chapman, Chairman of the Board of the New England Merchants National Bank, were elected trustees. Vacancies on the board had been secured by the resignations of Philip Hofer (elected in 1944) and Bartlett H. Hayes, Jr. (1951), who were then appointed as representatives of Harvard College, in lieu of Charles A. Coolidge and Charles L. Kuhn, who had served respectively since 1946 and 1959. William Appleton Coolidge, G. Peabody Gardner, and Mrs. Roger H. Hallowell were elected vice-presidents at the same time.

Almost immediately a series of administrative changes began to take place. The President proposed seeking legislative approval of a revision of the 1870 act of incorporation to permit the enlargement of the board of trustees. This request involved not only raising the limit of numbers, but reducing the appointed representatives of the three founding institutions from three to one. The governing bodies of Harvard and the Massachusetts Institute of Technology, who had less immediate concern with the museum than they had had ninety-eight years before, readily agreed; the Trustees of the Boston Athenæum, whose finest works of art had been lent to the museum for ninety-six years, pondered the matter at greater length before voting to interpose no objection to the proposal. The Legislature in 1969 passed the requested amendment to the act of incorporation, permitting the election of a certain number of new trustees at the annual meeting in September 1969.

With George C. Seybolt as President, meetings began to proliferate, and trustees were urged, through a multiplication of committees, to concern themselves more intimately with the detailed operations of the museum. By the sacrifice of the Primitive Art Gallery, an office was provided for the President and Trustees. Through the Visiting Committees and through old personal friendships, a number of museum trustees had close ties with departments and curators, but most of them, in normal Boston fashion, went out of their way to avoid seeming intrusive. Although such a system had worked naturally with earlier generations, there were doubtless a certain number of more recently elected trustees, who being less familiar with the ropes, actually knew somewhat less than was desirable of the collections and operations of the museum. George Seybolt's multiplication of standing committees was designed to involve all members of the board more intimately with the affairs of the museum, for no trustee escaped with membership in less than two. An Executive Committee, of which the President was chairman, and the Committee on the Collections, with the Director as its head, divided the former functions of the abolished Committee on the Museum. The former body dealt with general policies and matters of administration; the latter with recommendations for the purchase of works of art. Financial matters were subdivided among Investment, Operating Budget, Capital Budget, and Development committees. In addition there were Education, By-laws, and Nominating committees, as well as a new Men's counterpart of the Ladies' Committee. The Men's Committee was designed to strengthen support of the museum from hitherto unexplored segments of the business and professional community. As all these bodies met with some regularity, and minutes of their deliberations were circulated among the entire board, the trustees began to have more detailed current knowledge of many phases of operations and policy than in the past.

Ten years before (in 1958) the administrative staff had consisted of the Director, of David B. Little, Secretary and Registrar, and of Charles E. Humphrey, Assistant Treasurer and Comptroller, with three administrative assistants, Miss Betty L. Parks, Assistant to the Comptroller, Miss Elizabeth P. Riegel, Supervisor of Sales, and Carl F. Zahn, Designer for the Museum. After his retirement as Treasurer, Robert Baldwin for several years lent a much appreciated hand in coping with the phenomenal increase of problems that arose with accelerated activity. His final retirement, and David Little's resignation in December 1966, after thirty years in the museum, left voids that were nearly impossible to fill without major enlargements of the staff. Consequently, in the summer of 1968 a new post of Assistant Director for Administration was created, which was filled by Heyward Cutting, who thereupon both resigned as a trustee and gave up his architectural practice. As chairman of the Building Committee and of the committee considering the future of the Museum School, he had acquired great familiarity with the current administrative problems of the Museum. Walter C. Anderson also joined the staff in August 1968 as assistant and understudy to Charles F. Humphrey, upon whose unexpected death in October he succeeded as Assistant Treasurer and Comptroller. Diggory Venn, who had been concerned with the Centennial Development Fund, became Special Assistant to the Director to deal with special events and exhibitions, especially with the Centennial celebrations, while James W. Griswold joined the staff as Manager of Development. The latter post was created to establish in the museum a permanent development office, that, in close association with various trustees, would seek support for a variety of specific projects. The gift of $500,000, made in the summer of 1969 by the Frederick J. Kennedy Memorial Foundation of Boston for the specific purpose of returning to exhibition space ground-floor galleries that had been poached upon for fundraising, administrative, and educational offices, is a hopeful augury.

A President's report appeared at the beginning of *The Museum Year: 1968, The Ninety-Third Annual Report of the Museum of Fine Arts, Boston*; this was still another innovation, for the President had not been heard from in such a document since 1934. George Seybolt noted that, while the museum continues to expand and to improve its usefulness to the community,

> There is not, however, light without shadow. Funding the Museum's operations is a constant topic of Trustee discussion. In this, Boston is not unique. Almost without exception, major cultural institutions from coast to coast are experiencing financial difficulties. The Boston Museum is perhaps more vulnerable than other similar institutions, having been created and supported entirely by private contributions. Furthermore, all of us are increasingly in competition with the demand for the welfare and education dollar.

He cited the manner in which the institution had attempted to help itself by noting the following dramatic percentages of growth since 1954 in areas that were under museum control: increase in sales of publications and educational materials, 599 percent; in annual membership dues, 611 percent; in other funds (admission fees, contributions, and additions to endowment), 692 percent; in book value of investments, 98 percent. But, he continued:

> Encouraging and meritorious as these growth statistics may be, they do not offset the necessary cost increases for an institution which devotes over 60 per cent of its operating costs to wages, salaries, and employee benefits. As a result, the full range of Museum services cannot be totally exploited; vitally needed expansion programs must be curtailed. Fortunately there has been no diminution in the generosity of donors who continue to support the Museum with the enthusiasm that has been the basis of its greatness.

He defined "the overriding concern of the Trustees in reorganizing and directing their own efforts" as "this single goal: to establish a firm financial base for the Museum. From this base, the Trustees can then proceed to support and enlarge the educational mission of an organization whose human abilities and physical collections are already the envy of communities the world over."

There can be no disagreement about the wisdom or necessity of this goal. The year 1970 will doubtless be devoted to the celebration of the achievements of the museum's first century. But even before the celebration begins, there must be continued cerebration about the course to be followed in the second century, for the Museum of Fine Arts has acquired responsibilities not only to the Boston community but, through possession of unique collections, to the entire world of learning. The 1870 charter incorporated the founding trustees "for the purpose of erecting a Museum," which they have twice done, "for the *preservation* and exhibition of works of art, of making, maintaining, and exhibiting collections of such works, and of affording instruction in the Fine Arts." I have italicized one word in the charter to emphasize the primacy of its position. Many other desirable activities have been developed during the past hundred years that must stand or fall in the future in accordance with the support that they receive, whether from private or public sources. But the one inescapable obligation that must take precedence over all others is the *preservation* of the irreplaceable works of art that have been so lovingly assembled, by gift and purchase, over the past hundred years. This means the continuation, as the first priority upon funds, of the several curatorial departments, of the Research Laboratory, and of the other technical services that fulfill that obligation. And it further means that somehow, somewhere a very large sum of money has to be obtained to control the temperature and humidity of the building in which those works of art are kept. The time is already late.

A unique work of art that will first be exhibited with the Centennial acquisitions is an Egyptian black granite statue of a hawk, whose pedestal is inscribed with the name of Amenhotep III (1410–1372 B.C.) of the Eighteenth Dynasty, and of his temple of Soleb, just below the third cataract of the Nile, where it was originally placed. This remarkable sculpture, more than 5 feet high, which was unearthed in fragments in the winter of 1968 in the museum basement by Dows Dunham, Curator Emeritus of the Egyptian Department, exemplifies the observations of the previous paragraph. In the pantheon of Egypt the hawk was the sun god Horus, who was personified on earth by the ruling king, in this instance the luxury-loving Amenhotep, whose prenomen as King of Upper and Lower Egypt remains inscribed in one cartouche of hieroglyphics on the pedestal. A second cartouche, bearing his other name as Son of Ra, in which the name of the god Amon was included, has been scratched out. Amenhotep's son and successor, Akhenaten, a prototype hippie who, disliking father's religion, banned the cult of Amon, the state god, obliterated his name from innumerable monuments like this up and down the Nile Valley. Although Akhenaten encouraged the exclusive worship of the sun, his "monotheism" did not survive his seventeen-year reign. With his death, the cult of Amon returned, although his name remained obliterated on the pedestal of this hawk.

Some seven centuries after the hawk was carved, the Kushites, of what is now the Sudan, who had been conquered and thoroughly Egyptianized during the New Kingdom, rose against their conquerors. About 730 B.C. they took over all Egypt. The Kushite Taharqa (690–664 B.C.), the fifth king of the short Twenty-fifth Dynasty, who inherited a precarious kingdom that was threatened by Assyrians, Babylonians, and Persians, speeded up the adornment of a temple to Amon he was building at Gebel Barkal by appropriating some of the finest sculptures of the Eighteenth Dynasty from Amenhotep's temple at Soleb. By such theft the hawk migrated to Gebel Barkal, where George A. Reisner uncovered its fragments on 10 January 1919. In due course the granite hawk migrated a second time, coming to

BLACK GRANITE STATUE OF A HAWK. Egyptian, 18th Dynasty. Drawing by Suzanne E. Chapman to aid in its reassembly for exhibition.

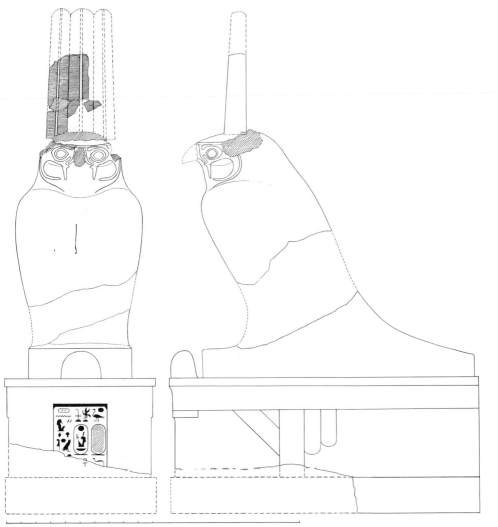

Boston, where it long remained in a museum storeroom, in the company of tons of other excavation finds, awaiting study. As we have seen in Chapter VIII, Reisner excavated so steadily that some of his reports are still only now, decades after his death in 1942, being prepared for the press by Dows Dunham. As Dunham was serving with the United States Army in France while Reisner was excavating the Temple of Amon at Gebel Barkal, he only became concerned with the monument half a century later, while continuing work on the publication of Reisner's Sudan campaign. When he went to the museum basement to locate and measure the hawk fragments, he discovered that here was something of remarkable importance. The original records of the excavation gave no hint of the statue's completeness, and people do not casually start rummaging among granite fragments weighing thousands of pounds that have been shipped from Egypt decades ago.

Dows Dunham's investigation then led him to the work of the German archaeologist Richard Lepsius, who had surveyed the Barkal site in 1844, and had carried to the Berlin Museum fragments of a similar black granite figure, consisting only of the pedestal and lower body of a hawk. Seemingly this, and the bird discovered by Reisner in 1919, had stood facing each other on either side of the main axis of the temple of Amon at Barkal. But the Boston figure, being far more complete, is unmatched in any museum. From drawings prepared by Dunham and Miss Suzanne E. Chapman, William J. Young is once again assembling in the Research Laboratory scattered fragments, and restoring the personification of Horus by Amenhotep to his original dignity of three and a half millennia ago. This kind of thing can happen in only a few institutions in the world.

Among the Centennial gifts that will be unveiled on 4 February 1970 is a fragile but magnificent Greek gold crown of oak leaves and acorns, given by Landon T. Clay. Although perhaps ultimately placed in a tomb, this exquisite ornament of the fourth century B.C. may have adorned a statue of Zeus, or the head of a victor in the games dedicated to the chief Olympian. When it first entered the museum a few weeks ago its authenticity was immediately confirmed, when William J. Young, with his battery of microscopes, detected on the solder by which the leaves, acorns, and tiny gold wires are linked

GOLD CROWN OF OAK LEAVES AND ACORNS. Greek, 4th century B.C.
Gift of Landon T. Clay, 1969.

together, formations of crystals, invisible to the naked eye, that could only have developed in the millennia between the fourth century B.C. and our own. So this crown may be considered as a symbolic collective tribute to the generous benefactors who have formed the collections of the Museum of Fine Arts, and to the scholars and scientists who have so lovingly cared for them in the century that has passed since the gallery of the Boston Athenæum became intolerably crowded.

Notes and References
Index

Notes and References

THE PRINCIPAL SOURCES OF THIS BOOK are the printed annual reports and the *Museum of Fine Arts Bulletin*. *Proceedings at the opening of the Museum of Fine Arts: with the reports for 1876, a list of donations, the act of incorporation, by-laws, etc.* (Boston, 1876) briefly covers the first six years. The regular series opens with *Trustees of the Museum of Fine Arts: First Annual Report, for the year ending Dec. 31, 1876.* The title changed to *Museum of Fine Arts, Boston* with the *Twenty-seventh Annual Report for the year 1902*, and continued for more than sixty years until the present style — 1965 — *The Museum Year: The Ninetieth Annual Report of the Museum of Fine Arts* was adopted. From the beginning until 1920 the annual reports contained lists of purchases, gifts, and loans of the year. From 1902 until 1919 they included reports of all departments. Prior to 1902 only the curators of the Print and the Classical departments regularly gave a detailed account of their work; from 1920 until 1935 departmental activities were very briefly summarized in the Director's report. These changes are discussed in the texts of Chapter XIII and Chapter XVIII.

The *Bulletin* first appeared in March 1903. From the June 1916 issue lists of accessions, accompanied by small illustrations of the more important objects, were regularly included. From 1921 on, such detailed information was omitted from the annual reports; through the summer issue of 1955 the *Bulletin* is the best published source for the study of additions to the collection. Since the autumn of 1955 it has had less value as a source for systematic reference, for its format has constantly changed. In recent years, it has contained longer references to fewer works of art; while it is often better reading than in the past, it no longer offers as complete a record of what has been given or purchased within a given period as it did from 1921 to 1955. From 1925 to the present the highlights of accessions are contained in the annual reports. Although the *Bulletin* has always been profusely illustrated, pictures only entered the annual report more recently. A frontispiece was first used in 1953; the following year extensive illustration began.

The annual report for 1901 included (pp. 13–23) "Twenty-five years of the Museum's growth" by General Charles G. Loring, the first Director. The *Handbook of the Museum of Fine Arts*, first published in 1906, contained not only floor plans and illustrations of the most important works of art in the several departments, but a brief concluding section of historical data. As the buildings changed and new objects were added, the *Handbook* was constantly revised, with no change in format, for more than fifty years. In the newly designed *Illustrated Handbook* of 1964, some of the historical statement was reprinted. To observe the first half-century, Benjamin Ives Gilman prepared a forty-page illustrated pamphlet, *Museum of Fine Arts, Boston, 1870–1920*, with a brief historical sketch and a chronology of creation of departments and staff appointments. Otherwise there has been little attempt at historical retrospection in the first century of the museum.

I have drawn considerable information from the many catalogues of permanent collections and temporary exhibitions that the museum has published. References to some of these appear in the chapters. For information about individuals not included in the *Dictionary of American Biography*, Harvard class reports have been a frequent source. Consequently I have often noted the Harvard classes of trustees, members of the staff, and donors, both as a means of indicating their relative ages at the time of mention and as a reference to the class reports, which are a remarkable source of biographical information. Old Boston city directories, *Blue Books*, and *Social Registers* have yielded a number of facts about dates and places of residence.

The views of the Boston Athenæum, the Peace Jubilee Coliseum, and the first section of the Copley Square museum that illustrate Chapter I are reproduced from the photograph collection of the Boston Athenæum. The Henri Matisse etching of Matthew S. Prichard in Chapter VI is reproduced by permission of the Isabella Stewart Gardner Museum. All other photographs were provided by the Museum of Fine Arts.

Chapter I. The Foundation

The chief published accounts of the Boston Athenæum are Josiah Quincy, *The History of the Boston Athenæum, with Biographical Notices of its Deceased Founders* (Cambridge, 1851); *The Athenæum Centenary: The Influence and History of the Boston Athenæum from 1807 to 1907 with a Record of its Officers and Benefactors and a Complete List of Proprietors* (Boston: Boston Athenæum, 1907); and Mabel Munson Swan, *The Athenæum Gallery, 1827–1873: The Boston Athenæum as an Early Patron of Art* (Boston: Boston Athenæum, 1940). I have supplemented the latter by reference to the unpublished records of the Athenæum's proprietors, trustees, and committees.

Edward Waldo Emerson, *The Early Years of the Saturday Club, 1855–1870* (Boston: Houghton Mifflin, 1918) contains valuable sketches of the lives of Thomas Gold Appleton, Charles Eliot Norton, James Elliot Cabot, Martin Brimmer, and William Morris Hunt. Its sequel, M. A. DeWolfe Howe, *Later Years of the Saturday Club, 1870–1920* (Boston: Houghton Mifflin, 1927), contains accounts of Charles Callahan Perkins, Edward Newton Perkins, William Barton Rogers, William Endicott, Jr., and Edward William Hooper. Neil Harris, "The Gilded Age Revisited: Boston and the Museum Movement," *American Quarterly*, XIV (1962), 545–566, is a good study of the backgrounds and purposes of the founders of the Museum of Fine Arts, which would have saved me some time had I encountered it before the earlier chapters of this book were completed. He published a letter of 1882 from Martin Brimmer to Charles Eliot Norton concerning the representation of many interests in the board of trustees.

The article "The Museum of Fine Arts, Boston," *The American Architect and Building News*, VIII (253, 30 October 1880), 205–215, gives not only the plans for the Copley Square museum, but contributions on its purposes by Martin Brimmer, Arthur Rotch, Charles C. Perkins, E. H. Greenleaf, J. T. Clarke, and F. D. Millett, and accounts of the School of Drawing and Painting, the School of Carving and Modelling, and the School of Pottery and Painting on Porcelain. For criticism of the building, see my "Boston Society of Architects, 1867–1967, A Centennial Sketch," in Marvin E. Goody and Robert P. Walsh, ed., *Boston Society of Architects: The First Hundred Years, 1867–1967* (Boston: Boston Society of Architects, 1967), pp. 15–70.

Chapter II. The First Decade

H. Winthrop Peirce, *History of the School of the Museum of Fine Arts, Boston, 1876–1930* (Boston, 1930), is an attractive but discursive account by an early student, written half a century later. Marian Lawrence Peabody, *To be young was very heaven* (Boston: Houghton Mifflin, 1967) includes extracts from her diaries while a student in the school.

The Museum of Fine Arts and its school ventured into the national numismatic arena for the first and last time in 1908 when Dr. William Sturgis Bigelow and Bela L. Pratt collaborated in the design for new $2.50 and $5 gold pieces. Unlike the $10 and $20 gold coins, which were modeled by Augustus Saint Gaudens in relief, the Bigelow-Pratt designs of an Indian head on the obverse and an eagle on the reverse, were incised in a manner inspired by Egyptian carvings. These designs were attacked by the numismatist Samuel Hudson Chapman in a letter of 7 December 1908 to

President Theodore Roosevelt. Chapman's letter, with Dr. Bigelow's rejoinder and Chapman's unconvinced rebuttal, are published in the American Numismatic Association, *Selections from The Numismatist* (Racine, Wisconsin: Whitman, 1960), 207–210. I owe my knowledge of this incident to Cornelius Vermeule.

CHAPTER III. THE LEAN YEARS

For the development of the Back Bay, see my *Boston: A Topographical History* (Cambridge: Belknap Press of Harvard University Press, 2nd ed., 1968), chapters VII–IX.

The recollection of S. R. Koehler's superlative profanity was given me, like many other details concerning the Print Department, by Henry P. Rossiter, who obtained it from a sometime head custodian named Faulkner, who knew Koehler well.

Professor Kenneth J. Conant told me of Denman W. Ross's practice of earmarking profits from The Ludlow for purchases of works of art. These would be placed for a time in his Cambridge house, and, as others were acquired, would be sent to the Museum of Fine Arts. Having come to Harvard as a freshman in 1911 and remained there as a professor in the Department of Fine Arts until his retirement, Kenneth Conant knew Dr. Ross well for nearly a quarter of a century, first as a student and then as a colleague. Mrs. Edward Cunningham (1873–1961), who once lived at The Ludlow told me of the consternation created by the spectacle of Henry James walking up Boylston Street, arm in arm with a police officer, who obviously was not arresting him. It was eventually discovered that, on an earlier visit to Boston, James while absentmindedly crossing a street, had almost been run down by a horse-drawn dray. The policeman, after hearing the gentleman's extended and involved thanks, rightly guessed that he had been listening to Mr. Henry James, whose style he had come to know through novels regularly lent him by one of the Ludlow residents. The officer expressed his admiration for *The Golden Bowl* so movingly that thereafter, whenever James was in Boston, he would seek out this admirer on his beat and have extended discussions with him on the art of fiction.

CHAPTER IV. THE JAPANESE COLLECTION

Dorothy G. Wayman, *Edward Sylvester Morse: A Biography* (Cambridge: Harvard University Press, 1942), and Lawrence W. Chisolm, *Fenollosa: The Far East and American Culture* (New Haven: Yale University Press, 1963), are the best sources for two of the protagonists of this chapter. Van

Wyck Brooks, *Fenollosa and His Circle* (New York: E. P. Dutton, 1962) admirably catches the spirit, but is not always to be trusted for accuracy of detail.

Dr. W. T. Councilman's sketch of William Sturgis Bigelow was published in *Later Years of the Saturday Club*, pp. 265–269. A letter of 26 October 1926 from John Ellerton Lodge, Curator of the Department of Chinese and Japanese Art, concerning the Buddhist robes in which Dr. Bigelow's body was clothed for burial, is published in *Proceedings of the Massachusetts Historical Society*, LXXV (1963), 108–109. The funeral was, nevertheless, conducted in Trinity Church by Bigelow's boyhood friend and Harvard classmate, the Right Reverend William Lawrence, Bishop of Massachusetts. The gift of his Buddhist diplomas to the Massachusetts Historical Society in 1920 was reported in *Proceedings*, LIII (1919–20), 66. There are various references to Bigelow in Worthington C. Ford, *The Letters of Henry Adams, 1858–1891* (Boston, 1930), and *Letters of Henry Adams, 1892–1918* (Boston, 1938); Harold Dean Cater, *Henry Adams and His Friends: A Collection of Unpublished Letters* (Boston, 1947); and Ward Thoron, *The Letters of Mrs. Henry Adams, 1865–1883* (Boston, 1936).

Dr. Charles Goddard Weld, the fourth significant figure of this chapter, has no biography beyond reticent references in Harvard class reports and the vital statistics recorded in my *Portraits of Shipmasters and Merchants in the Peabody Museum of Salem* (Salem, 1939), pp. 138–139. A posthumous portrait of him by Fred G. Quimby, given in 1918 by Mrs. Weld, hangs in Weld Hall at the Peabody Museum. His daughter, Mrs. Sumner Pingree, to whom I applied in the hope of finding journals or letters of his Japanese years, tells me that he was so reticent that she and her mother knew very little about his early travels or, indeed, of many details of his life. They were aware that he had helped many promising students through art and medical schools, but never knew who they were.

The late Carl Purington Rollins, sometime Printer to Yale University, who grew up in West Newbury, Massachusetts, often spoke to me with admiration of Arthur Wesley Dow's Japanese-inspired prints of Essex County subjects. Carl Feiss, F.A.I.A., A.I.P., of Washington, D.C., tells me how in the summer of 1937, while restoring the Heard house in Ipswich, Massachusetts, he was given as a birthday present various Japanese prints and other objects that had formerly belonged to Dow, who had been a native of Ipswich. Among these was a Japanese scroll with working drawings and text showing how to assemble the elements of a wooden Japanese pagoda of such importance that Carl Feiss gave it to the Avery Library, Columbia University, in memory of Dow.

John Gardner Coolidge, *Random Letters from Many Countries* (Boston, 1924), pp. 3–37, contains letters written to his parents during his voyage to Japan and residence there in 1887–88. The circumstances concerning J.

Randolph Coolidge's purchase of a painting for the Museum of Fine Arts were remembered by his youngest son (and my father-in-law), Julian Lowell Coolidge (1873–1954), who passed them on with some relish to my wife.

For Mrs. John Lowell Gardner the official biography is Morris Carter, *Isabella Stewart Gardner and Fenway Court* (Boston, 1925). There are some additional details in Louise Hall Tharp, *Mrs. Jack: A Biography of Isabella Stewart Gardner* (Boston, 1965), and in Morris Carter's whimsical reminiscence of old age entitled *Did You Know Mrs. Gardner? Morris Carter's Answer* (Boston: privately printed, 1964). Although Carter's pamphlet has provided some useful information for Chapter VI, it contains the odd suggestion that I was an acolyte at the Christmas Eve Mass in the chapel of Fenway Court in 1907 or 1908. As I was only three years old at the latter Christmas Eve, I set the record straight in "A Fable for Historical Editors," *The New England Quarterly*, XXXIX (1966), 513–515. Further details of the Gardner family are in Frank A. Gardner, *Gardner Memorial* (Salem, 1933), and in William Crowinshield Endicott, *Captain Joseph Peabody: East India Merchant of Salem* (Salem: Peabody Museum, 1962), to which I prefixed a sketch of Joseph Peabody's life.

Okakura-Kakuzo's books, *The Ideals of the East with Special Reference to the Art of Japan* (London, 1903), *The Awakening of Japan* (New York, 1904), and *The Book of Tea: A Japanese Harmony of Art, Culture, and the Simple Life* (New York, 1906), are timeless in their simplicity and beauty. For recollections of Okakura, and many other aspects of the Asiatic Department, I am indebted to Kojiro Tomita, who kindly lent me the partially edited transcripts of lectures that he gave on the history of his department in 1957.

CHAPTER V. THE CLASSICAL COLLECTION

Osbert Burdett and E. H. Goddard, *Edward Perry Warren: The Biography of a Connoisseur* (London, 1941), is the only life. Chapter XVI, "Warren as Collector," by Sir John Beazley is of particular interest in regard to the Boston Collection. I am grateful to Professor Bernard Ashmole of Oxford University for helpful letters, and for obtaining Sir John Beazley's permission to quote extracts from this work. Kevin Herbert, *Ancient Art in Bowdoin College* (Cambridge: Harvard University Press, 1964), describes E. P. Warren's interest in the Bowdoin Collection.

The correspondence between E. P. Warren and various officers of the Museum of Fine Arts, chiefly Martin Brimmer, Charles G. Loring, and Edward Robinson, which is in the Department of Classical Art, was only partially exploited in the Burdett and Goddard life. Cornelius C. Vermeule, III, made this available to me; from it I gained a clearer idea of the evolution of Warren's links with the Museum of Fine Arts. The photographs of Warren and

John Marshall were furnished by William J. Young, who came to Boston in 1929 to start the museum's Research Laboratory at Warren's instigation.

CHAPTER VI. THE BATTLE OF THE CASTS

Matthew Stewart Prichard, who figures largely in this chapter, had been to me only an unexplained and insubstantial figure in museum reports until July 1968, when, through a friendly act by James Bishop Peabody of Groton School, I fell into correspondence with the late Henry Maxwell Andrews of Ibstone House, near High Wycombe, Bucks. Mr. Andrews had sent me, at Jim Peabody's suggestion, a copy of the memoirs of Lewis Einstein, recently published by the Yale University Press. To reciprocate, I sent him a copy of my recent *Dumbarton Oaks: The History of a Georgetown House and Garden, 1800–1966*, because Lewis Einstein had given Mrs. Robert Woods Bliss a very beautiful piece of furniture for the Garden Library at Dumbarton Oaks. That book was dedicated to the memory of Royall Tyler (1884–1953), just as this one is dedicated in part to his son, William Royall Tyler.

In a letter of acknowledgment, Henry Andrews wrote that he had known Royall Tyler "in the interwar years and had heard of him first in Ruhleben Concentration Camp outside Berlin in the first war from M. S. Prichard who was a fellow prisoner." Having written at once to ask more about Prichard, I received several remarkable letters telling me of his brief career in Boston, of his friendship with Mrs. John L. Gardner and Okakura-Kakuzo, and of his later life as a student of Bergson and Byzantine art. Mr. Andrews told me, for example, how Okakura, on leaving a Paris private collection that they had visited, turned to Prichard in the street, making the little bow that was suitable to his Samurai robes, and inquired: "Why is it that every collector always shows you the object which he bought for 20 shillings?"

Mr. Andrews had long been fascinated by the "great row" in Boston more than sixty years before that had caused Prichard to return to England. He had heard a story from a reliable source of a gold necklace of supposed Greek origin that Mrs. J. Montgomery Sears had bought. Edward Robinson had thought it genuine, but as Mr. Sears felt that so substantial a purchase called for a second expert, Prichard was consulted, who seemingly proved that it was a forgery, made of tin. According to this story, relations between Robinson and Prichard soon became less than cordial. With these clues from England, I inquired at the Isabella Stewart Gardner Museum and learned that some 285 letters from Prichard to Mrs. Gardner, written between 1902 and her death in 1924, were indeed preserved there. I made an appointment to see them on 11 October 1968, but on the previous day landed in hospital. I soon heard that Henry Andrews had been taken equally suddenly to hospital in High Wycombe a few days earlier, where, alas, he died on 3 November.

Some weeks later I went to Fenway Court, where, through the kindness of the Director, George L. Stout, who gave me access to the Prichard letters, I found a rich vein of ore for this chapter. It saddened me that I could not share this discovery with Henry Andrews, who had led me to it. The extracts that are quoted here make it clear that there were more fundamental differences of opinion between Robinson and Prichard than the authenticity of a forged Greek necklace. The letters are quoted with the kind permission of the writer's great-nephew, Charles William Stewart, Esq., of Port Elizabeth, Republic of South Africa, and of the Trustees of the Isabella Stewart Gardner Museum.

The very rare portrait of Prichard, etched by his close friend Henri Matisse, that is reproduced here by permission of the Isabella Stewart Gardner Museum, is thus described in a letter of 26 June 1914 from Strassburg to Mrs. Gardner. "Matisse made a little etching of me the other day when I happened to be in his studio and he has now offered to put at my disposal eleven or twelve of the copies which have been made from his plate. The prints are only to be 15 in number. It is a simple drawing of very few lines. I have accepted his kindness and have mentioned you as one of my friends to whom I intend to offer an example. You will receive this little gift on my return to Paris . . . which will not take place until later in the year." Nearly six years were to pass before the etching reached Fenway Court, for Prichard went on to Germany, where he was caught by the outbreak of war. Having been imprisoned in Ruhleben, he spent nearly four years instructing his fellow inmates in philosophy and related subjects. It was 1918 before he returned to England, and February 1920 before he was able to send Mrs. Gardner, by means of Thomas Whittemore, "the little outline which Matisse made of me just before plunging into the German cauldron." On 10 April 1920 he wrote her: "It was very gratifying to know that you found something in the little Matisse etching. It was made in June 1914, what a time it has taken to reach the shelter which it desired during those years! As it stayed in Paris it must have heard many explosions of bombs and shell bursts from German guns."

Frederick Jackson Turner's perceptive comment on *The Education of Henry Adams*, which applies so aptly to Matthew S. Prichard's vigorous analysis of the Museum of Fine Arts, comes from Wilbur R. Jacobs, *The Historical World of Frederick Jackson Turner, with Selections from His Correspondence* (New Haven: Yale University Press, 1968), p. 54.

CHAPTER VII. THE HUNTINGTON AVENUE MUSEUM

Matthew S. Prichard's description of the "great slice of 'architecture'" comes from the correspondence with Mrs. John L. Gardner, acknowledged in the preceding chapter.

CHAPTER VIII. THE EGYPTIAN DEPARTMENT

Dows Dunham, *The Egyptian Department and Its Excavations* (Boston: Museum of Fine Arts, 1958), a model of departmental history, is the only record of its kind achieved by any of the departments of the museum. Alexander Agassiz's remark about the effect of Martin Brimmer's *Egypt: Three Essays* upon Theodore M. Davis is from George R. Agassiz, *Letters and Recollections of Alexander Agassiz* (Boston, 1913), pp. 435–436. Joseph Lindon Smith, *Tombs, Temples and Ancient Art* (Norman: University of Oklahoma Press, 1956), and Corinna Lindon Smith, *Interesting People: Eighty Years with the Great and Near-Great* (Norman: University of Oklahoma Press, 1962), are lively and pertinent. George R. Agassiz's memoir of Gardiner Martin Lane is in *Later Years of the Saturday Club*, pp. 399–403. Herbert E. Winlock's tribute to George A. Reisner was published in the American Philosophical Society *Year Book* (Philadelphia, 1942), pp. 369–374. I owe much to the continued friendship of Dows Dunham.

CHAPTER IX. THE DECENT DOCENT

I owe the title of this chapter, and permission to reprint the quatrain "History of Education," to my dear friend David McCord. After I first heard him recite the verse at a very good dinner of the Colonial Society of Massachusetts, I passed a restless night trying to remember how it went. When it appeared in his anthology *What Cheer* (New York, 1945), p. 372, my troubles were at an end.

Benjamin Ives Gilman printed "Thoughts for Saint Sylvester's Day" in *The Art Bulletin*, II (1919–20), 148–159. I stumbled onto this text recently by mere accident. As I reread the piece almost fifty years later, it still seemed awfully good.

The William Morris Hunt Memorial Gallery, opened in 1914, fell victim thirty years later to chronic overcrowding of the museum. For some years it has housed the Morse Collection of Japanese Pottery and the overflow book stacks from the Library. When the completion of the George Robert White Wing begins to relieve this kind of congestion, I hope that the gallery can be restored for the study-storage of Hunt's paintings.

CHAPTER X. THE EVANS WING AND PAINTINGS

The account of Robert Dawson Evans comes from *The National Cyclopedia of American Biography*, XIV, supplement 1, 452–453. A catalogue was published in 1918 entitled *Quincy Adams Shaw Collection: Italian Renaissance Sculpture, Paintings, and Pastels by Jean François Millet* for the exhibition that opened on 18 April 1918. Alexander Agassiz's remarks come from his

Letters and Recollections (cited in Chapter VIII), chapter IV, and p. 382. The six articles "Boston Painters and Paintings" by William Howe Downes that appeared in *The Atlantic Monthly*, LXII (July – December 1888), 89–98, 258–266, 382–394, 500–510, 646–656, 777–786, provide a systematic consideration of the subject. The July and August installments dealt with the Colonial period, with Copley, Trumbull, Stuart, and Allston. In September "Old Galleries and New Lights" described the Athenæum and other early galleries. October was devoted to French works in the museum of Fine Arts; November to other schools there, and December to private collections. The quotation from Mrs. Harold Peabody comes from *To be young was very heaven* (cited in Chapter II). Another evidence of Boston interest in French painting is Lilla Cabot [Mrs. Thomas Sergeant] Perry, "Reminiscences of Claude Monet from 1889 to 1909," *The American Magazine of Art*, XVIII (March 1927), 119–125. She and her husband had gone to Giverny in the summer of 1889 with a letter of introduction to the painter and for some seasons rented the house and garden next to his. As Monet's pictures were not yet fully appreciated, Mrs. Perry, like a good New Englander, wrote several friends and relatives pointing out that they could be bought from his studio at Giverny for $500. "Only one person responded, and for him I bought a picture of Etretat . . . When I brought it home that autumn of 1889 (I think it was the first Monet ever seen in Boston), to my great astonishment hardly any one liked it, the one exception being John La Farge." Perry T. Rathbone's Lowell Lecture, "The Department of Paintings, A Contemporary Judgement," given on 8 December 1964, has unfortunately not been printed; I appreciate his having given me a xerox copy, which proved useful in drafting this and other chapters concerning paintings.

Gérôme's diatribe against the acceptance by the French Government of paintings from the Caillebotte collection comes from James Laver, *French Painting and the Nineteenth Century* (London, 1937), p. 112. The paintings that aroused his wrath are now in the Louvre.

As a footnote to the museum's 1923 purchase of El Greco's *St. Dominic Kneeling Before a Crucifix*, which had belonged to Jean François Millet and to Edgar Degas, David McCord suggests the inclusion of a poem by Richard Wilbur, published in *Ceremony and other poems* (New York: Harcourt, Brace, 1950), which is reprinted by permission of the author.

I am grateful to David McKibbin for much information about the Sargent decorations, as well as for telling me that the eminent art critic, who pronounced them "very ladylike," was Bernard Berenson.

CHAPTER XI. THE WAR AND THE YEARS FOLLOWING

S. Durai Raja Singam, of Kuantan, Malaya, edited *Homage to Ananda Coomaraswamy* in two parts: *A 70th Birthday Volume*, published in 1947, and *A Memorial Volume*, that appeared in 1951. Many eminent friends throughout the world joined in these remarkable tributes of affection. Eric Schroeder's "Memories of the Person," from which I have quoted, was published in *A Memorial Volume*, pp. 65–80. Dr. Coomaraswamy's *Why Exhibit Works of Art?* was reprinted in 1956 in paperback by Dover Publications, under the new title *Christian and Oriental Philosophy of Art*. As should happen more frequently when missionary work is needed, the reprint was not copyrighted and there was a statement that quotations long or short might be made without express permission.

The reminiscences of Edward Jackson Holmes come chiefly from Kojiro Tomita's recollections. Miss Florence Virginia Paull, who came to the museum as General Loring's secretary in 1895, married Henri Léon Berger in 1918 and thereafter became General Curator of the Wadsworth Athenaeum in Hartford, Connecticut. When she became Curator Emeritus in 1950 at the age of seventy-eight, she began jotting down some of her recollections of fifty-five years of museum work in Boston and Hartford. In 1964 she sent her notebook to Perry T. Rathbone, who passed it on to me. The photographs of General Loring at his desk and of Matthew S. Prichard come from Mrs. Berger's notebook. I am grateful to Joseph A. Coletti for his thoughts about the "Mino da Fiesole" tomb.

CHAPTER XII. THE DECORATIVE ARTS WING AND THE DEPRESSION

Dr. Hanns Swarzenski unearthed in the files of the Department of Decorative Arts and Sculpture the solemn minute book concerning the installation of the new wing. The portentousness of the deliberations greatly amused us both.

I am grateful to R. H. Ives Gammell for many conversations about the Museum School within the years of his memory, and about the state of painting in Boston, as well as for his kindness in having allowed me to read two of his unpublished essays.

My old friend Daniel Varney Thompson, who was a professor at the University of London at the time, made the arrangement for Denman W. Ross's funeral in England. He told me of the T'ang jar provided by Yamanaka's staff for the ashes, as well as many other things about Dr. Ross in life.

CHAPTER XIII. THE SEVENTH DECADE AND WORLD WAR II

I was delighted to find early in 1969 that, through the methodical record-keeping of the Department of Paintings, William R. Tyler's verses of 1940 were safely filed in the folder relating to Poussin's *Mars and Venus*. I sent a xerox copy of them to him at The Hague. When he told me of an amendment that he had made in line 6, substituting *un tantinet* for *un petit peu* of the typewritten text, Miss Laura C. Luckey promptly allowed me to insert a note thereof in the folder.

Everything concerning the attempt to buy the Albertina Collection has come from the chief protagonist, Henry P. Rossiter, who very kindly lent me a loose-leaf volume containing correspondence, newspaper clippings, and notes, as well as the genial photographs of the Hotel Bristol luncheon table that are reproduced in this chapter. This is only one of many instances in which I am indebted to Mr. Rossiter, whose vivid recollections and acute comments cheered me throughout the writing of the last dozen chapters of this book. Had he not been in England during the early months of 1969, I feel sure that he would have been equally encouraging while the first twelve were being drafted.

Maxim Karolik's letter of 7 December 1938 was published in Edwin J. Hipkiss, *Eighteenth-Century American Arts: The M. and M. Karolik Collection . . .* (Boston, 1941), pp. 343–346.

Although I used to carry home free samples of Cuticura products from my earliest trustees' meetings, I only heard of the miraculous improvement of the Yuba Consolidated Gold Fields stock through conversation with Robert Baldwin.

CHAPTER XIV.

THE SPAULDING AND KAROLIK COLLECTIONS OF PAINTINGS

Frank Lloyd Wright, *An Autobiography* (New York, 1943), pp. 524–527, gives an extended account of his activity collecting prints in Japan for the Spauldings. In earlier visits to Japan, Wright had assembled a considerable number of actor prints, 100 of which he sold to William S. Spaulding in Chicago for $10,000. As he was about to return to Japan, the Spauldings telegraphed him, asking him to come to Boston for a conference. During dinner at 99 Beacon Street with Mr. and Mrs. William and with John Spaulding, he was asked if he would act as agent for them in Japan. Wright proposed taking whatever sum they wished to give him, spending it, and dividing the purchases. When John Spaulding suggested that that was hardly a business proposition, the architect replied that he was not a businessman. The next morning at breakfast the brothers agreed to the proposition, telling Wright that he would find $20,000 to his credit in the Yokohama Specie Bank when he arrived in Tokyo. Not a line was put on paper.

Wright arrived in Japan, spent the money, cabled for more and more, until in five months he had spent about 125,000 Spaulding dollars for what he considered about a million dollars' worth of prints. Although he kept some for himself, anything unique or superior was set aside for the Spauldings. When he returned to Massachusetts, he spent three days with the brothers at Prides Crossing going over the haul. The Spauldings were completely delighted, but told Wright that obviously he could not have kept much for himself in view of what he had turned over to them. Although he assured them that he had enough, they pressed a check for $25,000 upon him, and gave him an exquisite slightly toned copy of Utamaro's *Ryogoku Fireworks*. They had bought this from Baron Sumitomo, but as Wright had brought them an even finer copy, they wanted him to have what they considered the second-best copy in the world. As they were driving after lunch in a Stearns-Knight touring car with the top down, Wright, sitting on the back seat between the brothers, stood up, caught a baseball that had been batted from schoolgrounds, and threw it back into the game. That instantaneous reaction made clear to William Spaulding how Frank Lloyd Wright had got the prints that he had.

Charles Hovey Pepper's recollections, "John T. Spaulding as a Collector," were published in a catalogue, *The Collections of John Taylor Spaulding, 1870–1948, with Japanese Prints and Sword-mounts from the William S. and John T. Spaulding Collections*, prepared for the May – November 1948 exhibition.

Maxim Karolik's second letter to the Director was published in *M. and M. Karolik Collection of American Paintings 1815 to 1865* (Boston, 1949), pp. ix–xiv.

CHAPTER XV.

THE SECOND GOLDEN AGE OF THE ASIATIC DEPARTMENT

Many details of this chapter have come from the personal recollections of Kojiro Tomita. In 1966 the museum published a fully illustrated catalogue, *The Arts of India and Nepal: The Nasli and Alice Heeramaneck Collection*.

CHAPTER XVI. THE VARIETIES OF ARTISTIC EXPERIENCE

Richard B. K. McLanathan, *Ship Models*, a Museum of Fine Arts Picture Book published in 1957, illustrated many of J. Templeman Coolidge's gifts. Another in the series, Kathryn C. Buhler, *Paul Revere, Goldsmith*, issued in 1956, reproduced the Liberty Bowl and other examples of Revere's craftsmanship from the museum's collections.

CHAPTER XVII. RESEARCH, CROWDS, AND DOCENTRY

Chiang Yee's "Looking at the family portraits," published in *The Silent Traveller in Boston* (New York: W. W. Norton, 1959), p. 10, is reproduced from the original drawing, now owned by the Boston Athenæum. His "Kuan Yin slips out of the Boston Museum for meditation," published on page 60, also owned by the Athenæum, suggests what is likely to happen to the Chinese sculpture if crowds continue to afflict the institution. It would be sad to have all the Immortals slip away in disgust, if only for short periods of meditation.

Miss Annette B. Cottrell's *Dragons*, a picture book of 1962, appeals quite as much to adults as to children. It is one of the most attractive of a pleasant series.

Chapters VII and VIII of Edward A. Weeks, *The Lowells and Their Institute* (Boston: Atlantic-Little, Brown, 1966), are devoted to Ralph Lowell and WRUL.

David B. Little, "The Misguided Mission: A Disenchanted View of Art Museums Today," *Curator*, X (1967), 221–225 is a spirited attack upon the proliferation of traveling exhibitions, based upon twenty-one years of experience as Registrar of the Museum of Fine Arts.

CHAPTER XVIII. THE NEW DEAL

The Sargent charcoal sketches of William Sturgis Bigelow and Denman W. Ross are reproduced in Chapter IV. The latter's remark about his portrait was recalled by Daniel V. Thompson.

CHAPTER XIX. THE RENAISSANCE OF THE CLASSICAL DEPARTMENT

Among the numerous publications by Cornelius C. Vermeule of museum material in learned journals are "Greek, Etruscan, Roman, and Early Christian Marble and Bronze Sculpture in the Museum of Fine Arts, Boston," *The Classical Journal*, LXI (April 1966), 289–310; "Small Sculptures in the Museum of Fine Arts, Boston" in the same periodical, LXII (December 1966), 97–113; and "Vases and Terracottas in Boston: Recent Acquisitions," LXIV (November 1968), 49–67. The Warren Gift Collection of 1908 is published by Professor Emily T. Vermeule, "Some Erotica in Boston," *Antike Kunst*, XII, 1 (1969), 9–15. *Bodrum, 1963* was privately printed at The Stinehour Press, Lunenburg, Vermont, for distribution among friends of the expedition.

CHAPTER XX. THE EXPANSION OF EUROPEAN SCULPTURE

The Edward P. Warren statements come from letters in the files of the Department of Classical Art, cited in Chapter IV.

Chapter XXI. Four Aspects of Curatorship

Maxim Karolik's third letter of transmittal was published in *M. and M. Karolik Collection of American Water Colors and Drawings, 1800–1875* (Boston, 1962), I, 15–18. Karolik's views on togetherness and coddling the public come from *Maxim Karolik, 1893–1964* (Boston: Museum of Fine Arts, 1963), which is a reprint from the 1962 winter issue of *Art in America* of Brian O'Doherty's retort. This charming little volume, prepared by the museum as a memorial to Karolik, lacks pagination.

Chapter XXII. A Decade of Facelifting

Henry P. Rossiter tells me that, to the best of his knowledge, Harvey D. Parker, with whose bequest the Henry F. Sewall Collection of prints was purchased, never set foot inside the Museum of Fine Arts. In this respect his name may be linked with those of Theodora Wilbour and Forsyth Wickes, as evidence that generosity makes strange companions.

Chapter XXIII. Financial Crises

Winifred E. Howe, *A History of the Metropolitan Museum of Art* (New York, 1913–1946), 2 volumes, contains little that is as useful as General de Cesnola's remarks on the "misbehaving public," which I owe to the kindness of Wendell D. Garrett in sending me a copy of his forthcoming article "Museum Manners on My Mind: An Early Footnote to the History of the *Metropolitan* Museum of Art," that is to appear in *The Walpole Society Note Book, 1969*. The lugubrious respectability of Miss Howe's literary style, combined with her excessive respect for great and good trustees and patrons, makes her work one to be approached only in desperation. Calvin Tomkins' forthcoming history has all the qualities that its predecessor lacked, to judge from the few chapters that he was kind enough to let me read in manuscript.

The question of privately supported institutions is discussed at length in my *Independent Historical Societies: An Enquiry into their Research and Publication Functions and their Financial Future* (Boston: Boston Athenæum, 1962), which is the report of a study that I conducted in 1959–60 for the Council on Library Resources. It goes somewhat beyond historical societies into problems of museums and historic preservation.

CHAPTER XXIV. CENTENNIAL DEVELOPMENT

George C. Seybolt's views upon the composition and obligations of the board of trustees are derived from various conversations with him, and from copies that he kindly lent me of some of his personal correspondence with other trustees of the museum.

Index

This index is more concerned with people than with subjects, although references are given that should facilitate following specific subjects through the chapters. The principal relation of the Museum of Fine Arts to many of the persons listed is indicated by the following symbols: C, curator of a department; D, donor to the museum in cash or kind; DI, director; MS, member of the staff of the School of the Museum of Fine Arts; P, president of the board of trustees; S, member of the museum staff (other than honorary); T, trustee, whether elected or appointed. Artists mentioned in the history are indexed only when there is more than a passing reference to their work, when there is an illustration, or when they are cited on two or more occasions. No subjects of works of art are indexed.